UNDERSTANDING THE SOCIAL SECURITY ACT

Understanding the Social Security Act

The Foundation of Social Welfare for America in the Twenty-First Century

Andrew W. Dobelstein

OXFORD

UNIVERSITY PRESS

2009

OXFORD
UNIVERSITY PRESS

Oxford University Press, Inc., publishes works that further
Oxford University's objective of excellence
in research, scholarship, and education.

Oxford   New York
Auckland   Cape Town   Dar es Salaam   Hong Kong   Karachi
Kuala Lumpur   Madrid   Melbourne   Mexico City   Nairobi
New Delhi   Shanghai   Taipei   Toronto

With offices in
Argentina   Austria   Brazil   Chile   Czech Republic   France   Greece
Guatemala   Hungary   Italy   Japan   Poland   Portugal   Singapore
South Korea   Switzerland   Thailand   Turkey   Ukraine   Vietnam

Copyright © 2009 by Oxford University Press, Inc.

Published by Oxford University Press, Inc.
198 Madison Avenue, New York, New York 10016

www.oup.com

Oxford is a registered trademark of Oxford University Press

Library of Congress Cataloging-in-Publication Data

Dobelstein, Andrew W.
Understanding the Social Security Act : the foundation of social welfare for America in the
Twenty-first century / Andrew W. Dobelstein.
p.   cm.
Includes bibliographical references and index.
ISBN 978-0-19-536689-1
1. Social security—Law and legislation—United States.
2. United States. Social Security Act.   I. Title.
KF3649.D63 2008
344.7302′3—dc22
2008031013

9   8   7   6   5   4   3   2   1

Printed in the United States of America
on acid-free paper

Preface

America stumbles into the twenty-first century without the euphoria of its gay 1990s; its optimism has been replaced by a gruesome, costly war of modern imperialism, a deepening economic depression fueled by excessive individual and corporate borrowing, a devaluation of the American dollar against all major foreign currencies, rising joblessness, and foreclosures on individual homes, all of which recall the early days of the Great Depression of 1929–1934. Even the Chairman of the Federal Reserve, Ben S. Bernanke, who replaced Alan Greenspan, warns, "Those who doubt that there is much connection between the economy of the 1930s and the supercharged information-age economy of the twenty-first century are invited to look at the current economic headlines—about high unemployment, failing banks, volatile financial markets, currency crises and even deflation."[a] Bernanke himself has presided over lowering the federal interest rates, the lowest in the past fifty years, and he has advocated for and participated in the largest government "bail-out" of failing private investment houses.

This is just not a good time for America, and, for some, it may seem dubious to be writing about America's social welfare programs and policies. Yet, somewhat in contrast to a wide range of government-driven economic policies, which have proved inadequate to keep America's economy vibrant, America's social welfare architecture has put in place a solid foundation able to protect individual Americans from the kind of personal economic disaster similar to that which they experienced more than seventy years ago. Over the past seventy-four years, the Social Security Act of 1935 has developed as America's premier social welfare policy document, providing the legislative authority for the administration of over one hundred social welfare programs in America, and dispensing over 60 percent of the federal budget to fund them. But in spite of its public policy significance, and in spite of the crucial assistance it provides to many Americans, the Social Security Act is shrouded in darkness and misunderstanding. Perhaps it is precisely America's present economic malaise that affords a unique opportunity to examine how America meets its social welfare

---

[a] Ben S. Bernanke, *Essays on the Great Depression* (Princeton, NJ: Princeton University Press, 2000), vii.

obligations to its people. Perhaps now is, indeed, a very good time to discuss America's Social Security Act.

For the past forty years, I have taught about America's social welfare obligations and how they are met through the Social Security Act. Unfortunately, the following episode has repeated itself in different iterations too many times:

One afternoon, a student came into my office shortly after I finished teaching the Introduction to Social Welfare class. She flopped down in a chair, and in an aggravated voice exclaimed.

"Dr. Dobelstein, why do I have to take this course? I plan to be a therapist and help children and their parents. What good does learning about this Social Security Act stuff do?"

I tried to explain that even the most capable therapist needed to know which programs were most helpful to children and their parents, and anyone trying to help children and their parents needed to know what limits formal organizations placed on the kinds of help they could provide, even if only to explain to those helpers how they were going to get paid. Her eyes glazed over as I talked.

As the student left, I knew my explanation failed, a revelation confirmed as the semester progressed and the student struggled with class discussions, assignments, and examinations. Only a few students showed interest in the social programs and policies provided by the Social Security Act, but even those students wanted to learn about "policy analysis," not about the public policies and social programs provided under the Social Security Act.

A few years later, a young woman came up to me at a professional meeting and introduced herself as a former student. "I was a student in your Introduction to Social Welfare class several years ago and I was terribly impatient because I had to learn about the Social Security Act," she recounted.

"Yes, I remember," I told her.

"Well, I want you to know that was one of the most important classes I ever took. I'm a supervisor with a lot of administrative responsibility," she told me. "Without the background of the Social Security Act I would never have risen to this job, and if I did I wouldn't know what to do once I got it. I didn't remember all the details, but I remembered how the programs were organized under Social Security Act, and it was easy, then, to get the specific information I needed to do my job."

Of course, the problem might be the way I try to explain the Social Security Act and its programs; yet when I tell friends and colleagues of my professional interest in the Social Security Act, their eyes, too, seem to glaze over and they begin to discuss a different subject. Sometimes, when I mention the Social Security Act, people ask whether it's true that Social Security is running out of money. (It's not.) Young people seem resigned to the rumor that there will be no Social Security for them when they reach retirement. (There will be.) Business people in particular tell me that Social Security cannot be "fixed" as long as there are so many cheaters on the welfare rolls. (Social Security is not welfare.) Legislators and their staffs, too, frequently fail to discriminate among the different ways the Social Security Act attempts to meet America's social welfare obligations. In my efforts to help implement the 1996 welfare reform in North Carolina, I constantly confronted legislators, their staffs, and administrative officials who failed to understand that this most recent welfare reform effort was limited to a very small part of those government efforts under the Social Security Act to ensure adequate income for economically dependent children, and at least one presumably well-informed congressional staff member proclaimed the 1996 welfare reform "the law that reshaped American social policy."[b] Misunderstanding abounds about America's social welfare commitments and the Social Security Act that responds to those commitments.

"Why would I want to read your book?" my friends and family have asked repeatedly when I told them about this latest writing project. Students might have to read this book as a course requirement, but they might not *want* to read it. Friends might read it to show sympathy or as a favor, but the question of who will read this book and why, continues to nag me. In the final analysis, this book is about things Americans prefer not to think about. This book is about needy, dependent people, not about national heroes. This book is about our obligations to our fellow Americans, people we seldom think of as part of us, except perhaps at Thanksgiving or Christmas. This book discusses the responsibilities we have undertaken to help others when most of us have all we can to take care of ourselves. This book is also about spending large amounts of money on people we think ought to be taking care of themselves. This book is about things we probably do not want to think about, let alone spend time and energy reading about. Few people will *want* to read this book, but they should.

After many years of active teaching, consultation, and "grass roots" work with the rich and poor, I remain constantly dismayed by the shortage of social welfare information and the erroneous social welfare messages spread by an otherwise informed public. Clearly, some express their distaste for forms of public social welfare through deliberately distorted messages, but many who are willing to accept the idea of public responsibility for social welfare struggle to find a base of authority from which to draw a broader understanding of America's social welfare obligations. This book seeks to serve that latter need. This book is an effort to begin an informed discussion about the social welfare contract we have made with our fellow Americans and how a singular public policy document, the Social Security Act, functions to carry out that contract. This book is an effort to replace America's sound-bite social welfare education with a substantive foundation.

I have mentioned "social obligation," and I will refer to America's social welfare obligation throughout this book. The idea of a social welfare obligation alone might be enough for some to avoid reading any further. No one likes to

---

[b] See Ron Haskins, *Work Over Welfare: The Inside Story of the 1996 Welfare Reform Law* (Washington, DC: The Brookings Institution, 2006), 364.

be obligated, but I believe social obligation is the foundation of the modern civilized state, and a major purpose of effective governance is to transform that social obligation into a useful product that will help all citizens of the state contribute to the welfare of the state and to enjoy its benefits. Americans' infatuation with the myths of "rugged individualism" and the "self-made man" has made it difficult for us to accept the contrasting idea of social obligation. Often referred to as a "reluctant welfare state," America was forced to accept its welfare responsibility by the Great Depression (circa 1929–1934), and today America is dragged, kicking and screaming, into its twenty-first-century welfare obligations. It is precisely the social and economic demands of twenty-first-century America, framed by a reluctance to embrace social obligation, that call for a discussion of the Social Security Act that will lead to an improved use of our public resources.

This book is provided primarily for students in academic programs, but it will also appeal to a wider audience of people who presently occupy policy-making positions and those who have responsibility for shaping social welfare policy and programs in the future. For people in academic programs, the book is designed to provide foundational knowledge for students in social work and public health programs as well as for students in public policy study programs with major interest in social welfare policy development and analysis. The book also addresses the needs of those people who presently hold social welfare policy development positions, both in and out of government. Many people with policy development responsibilities understand one set of social welfare programs in great depth, but they may be less knowledgeable about the complementarity of programs and how they do or do not interact with one another under the broad authority of the Social Security Act. Moreover, as the social welfare programs under the Social Security Act cry out for review in twenty-first-century America, it behooves policy makers to consider the whole of America's social welfare commitments before proposing any further incremental program changes to individual programs.

Finally, I am bold enough to suggest that an interested American public will find this book useful. Not only will concerned people gain a theoretical understanding of American social welfare—what we do, why we do it, and how it is done—but also they will expand their knowledge of the specific social welfare programs they hear about and employ in their daily lives. Social Security retirement, day care for children and elderly adults, health insurance for the aged, adoption services, weekly unemployment payments, and many other services all are among the many programs provided under the authority of the Social Security Act that Americans are likely to encounter in their daily lives. I believe that well prepared professionals combined with a well informed public will lead to the adjustments America must make to its social welfare commitments as we move into America's twenty-first century.

Andrew W. Dobelstein
Chapel Hill, NC
November, 2008

Acknowledgments

The development and final production of any book really depends on the work of many contributors. From the editorial staff and production department of Oxford University Press, particularly Mallory Jensen, who took careful steps to find reviewers who could help hone this book's many complexities, to the several reviewers who read and commented on manuscript draft materials, to friends and colleagues who offered comments and continued to urge me on, to my family, particularly my wife Carol, who listened patiently to my ideas and offered helpful comments, so many people have been involved in this endeavor that it seems unfair that only one person is acknowledged as author. For example, Edward Berkowitz was extremely generous in sharing his vast knowledge of social welfare history, going well beyond a usual commentary on draft material in order to contribute his well-respected insights. Alfred Field, my colleague at the University of North Carolina, provided thoughtful comments on Unemployment Insurance and labor issues, discussed in Chapter 4, while other colleagues provided feedback on other sections of the book. There are others, too, who unknowingly have had an influence on this book, in particular the students who sat patiently through my classes for over thirty years. They constantly asked questions, challenged my answers, and remained unsparing when my comments seemed unclear, confused, or "muddle-headed." I am sure that many of these students, now in policy-making positions or as teachers themselves, may still find my explanations far from clear, but they forced me to try. Thank you all for your help and inspiration. Yet, in spite of all this help, those who read this book will find disagreements, statements that may still confuse, and discussion of materials that seems too brief. For all these and other shortcomings, and for any errors of fact, as author, I remain solely responsible.

Contents

PART I

OVERVIEW OF THE SOCIAL SECURITY ACT

Introduction

Prelude

Sometimes a most unexpected American persists in a most unusual mission that flames into a startling public policy debate. Dorothea Dix was one of those people. Her social mission was to improve the care for the mentally ill, and her efforts cumulated in a social welfare policy that continues to stir debate over social welfare to the present day. Dix's mission: federal government support for hospitals for the mentally ill. President Franklin Pierce's decision: "no."

Dorothea Dix seemed an unlikely social welfare advocate. Born in 1802, in Hampton, Maine, her mother was emotionally unstable and her father was an alcoholic, abusive itinerant Methodist preacher; Dix was raised by her grandmother in Worcester, Massachusetts. Dix aspired to be a school teacher, and an acquaintance, Edward Bangs, an attorney several years her senior who later became her suitor, helped her establish a private school for girls. At the age of 39, Dix the school teacher was asked to teach a Sunday School class for women in the local prison, and what she found there completely shocked her senses and sent her on her mission. Mentally ill women, many naked, most dirty and in tattered clothing, and some chained to the walls to restrain their violent behavior, presented a level of inhumanity Dix had never before seen.

With the help of Bangs, a local court order was issued that required the jail to improve its treatment, but Dix was not satisfied. She visited the local jails throughout Massachusetts, collecting detailed information on how the mentally ill were treated, and she presented this information, called a testimony, to the state legislature. She asked the state to provide funds so that the mentally ill could be placed in a hospital, and the legislature agreed. But Dix was still not satisfied. She visited jails and almshouses in all the neighboring states, compiling information and giving testimony to state legislatures asking that they create hospitals for the mentally ill, and most states complied.

But still, Dix was not satisfied. She took her petitions to the U.S. Congress and asked it to provide grants of federal land to states for the construction of mental hospitals. Congress enthusiastically agreed. But when the Dix legislation got to President Franklin Pierce in 1854, he vetoed the "Act making a grant of public lands to the several States for the benefit of indigent insane persons ...," in spite of Congress's enthusiastic response to Dix's pleas. The hopes of Dix and other social reformers across the country were dashed. Dix had traveled successfully more than 60,000 miles and had visited personally over 9,000 "insane," "epileptic," and "idiotic" persons throughout the country. She had received a wide and warm reception from the nation's politicians and had convinced several states to develop hospitals for the mentally ill so they could receive humane treatment, far removed from squalid jails and almshouses.

Dix only wanted the Federal Government to give federal lands to the states so that the states could continue to build and maintain hospitals for the mentally ill. After all, federal lands had been given to states to establish agricultural colleges, so Dix's request did not set a new federal policy, only asking that it be extended to provide care for the mentally ill; Congress readily agreed. But President Pierce saw the Dix legislation differently. Acknowledging his own sympathy for Dix and lauding her humanitarian efforts, Pierce proclaimed a policy that continues to befuddle the development of social welfare policy in America; in summary, Pierce said welfare is not the responsibility of the federal government.

> I can not find any authority in the Constitution for making the Federal Government the great almoner of public charity throughout the United States. To do so would, in my judgment, be contrary to the letter and spirit of the Constitution and subversive of the whole theory upon which the Union of these States is founded.

Pierce continued.

> [I]f the several States, many of which have already laid the foundation of munificent establishments of local beneficence, and nearly all of which are proceeding to establish them, shall be led to suppose, as, should this bill become a law, that Congress is to make provision for such objects, the fountains of charity will be dried up at home, and the several States, instead of bestowing their own means on the social wants of their own people, may themselves, through the strong temptation, which appeals to the states as to individuals, become humble suppliants for the bounty of the Federal Government, reversing their true relations to this Union.[1]

Congress might have overridden the veto, but instead it let stand a public policy that frustrated social reformers who continued to chip away at the nonintervention welfare position of the Federal Government. Those social reformers who followed in Dix's footsteps continued to press toward greater Federal Government social welfare responsiveness. They were active in President Theodore Roosevelt's presidential campaigns and convinced him to set in motion the first White House Conference on Children held in 1910, which led to the creation of the Children's Bureau in 1912. In 1920, as it looked certain that women would be granted the right to vote in federal elections, President Harding, no advocate for social welfare reform, succumbed to social welfare activists and somewhat suddenly reversed himself and supported the "Maternity Bill," a program to provide federal money grants to states to support a wide range of maternal and child health programs.[2]

The crowning achievement of social welfare advocates was the creation of the Social Security Act, signed into law in 1935, by President Franklin Roosevelt. Roosevelt's wide-ranging emergency social welfare Depression programs, often called "alphabet soup" programs, were ending, and Roosevelt, no great advocate for social welfare, agreed with his cabinet members that a federal architecture for further economic recovery should be laid down that would provide for personal economic security, opportunities for employment, and security against the "hazards and vicissitudes of life."[3] Roosevelt's welfare philosophy was not too distant from that of President Pierce. Speaking when signing the Emergency Relief Act, he made his welfare ideas clear.

> The principle I have on many occasions explained is that the first obligation is on the locality; if it is absolutely clear that the locality has done its utmost but that more must be done, then the State must do its utmost. Only then can the federal Government add its contributions to those of the locality and the state.[4]

But the early 1930s were a time of severe personal economic misfortune in America, and Frances Perkins, President Roosevelt's Secretary of Labor and a social activist who served in FDR's administration when he was Governor of New York (along with Harry Hopkins, also a social welfare advocate who served as the President's Minister of Relief), became the nucleus of those in the administration who combined to push the Federal Government to a new level of welfare commitment. But even then caution about the proper role of the Federal Government limited the scope of America's first effort to develop a nationwide social welfare initiative.

In 1935, the President's Committee on Economic Security drafted, Congress created, and the President signed into law the nation's first comprehensive social welfare policy document. The Social Security Act provided a policy framework for administering retirement and unemployment insurance as well as providing welfare payments to aged adults, the disabled blind, and children. (Health care was also proposed for the original Social Security Act but given only modest attention for political reasons.) Ambitious as they were for their day, the original limited programs in the unique Social Security Act of 1935 soon gave way to continued unwavering pressure from social welfare advocates and persons who administered the Act for expanded, more comprehensive social programs. In spite of assuming a measure of responsibility for social welfare, the Social Security Act did not settle the controversy raised by the Pierce veto. Instead, as the Social Security Act matured, those who sought greater Federal Government social welfare responsibility sought that authority under the shelter of the Social Security Act; to this day, the Act resembles its original form, but its programs have expanded beyond anything envisioned by its 1935 developers.

The Federal Government and Social Welfare Policy

The debate over the proper role of the Federal Government continues to influence social welfare development in America. Subsequent incremental expansion of the Social Security Act has been buffeted by sharp differences over the proper role of government. Whether or not the social welfare commitment of the Federal Government should be limited, as advocated by President Pierce and alluded to by President Roosevelt and other Presidents who followed, or whether it should be expanded, as argued by social welfare advocates and political leaders sympathetic to their views, remains a nagging question about the appropriate responsibility of American governance. A strong case has been made for both positions, and the Social Security Act is caught in the middle of vigorous opposing views. For the most part, advocates for expanded Federal Government social welfare responsibility, often led by politically able federal administrators, have dominated social welfare policy by influencing the expansion of the Social Security Act through amendments to its original programs. But more recently, particularly with increases in Federal Government spending, less social welfare friendly political advocates, too, have succeeded in amending parts of the Social Security Act designed to reduce the federal responsibility for social welfare. Often vitriolic, contemporary welfare debates and the changes they have fostered in the Social Security Act have eroded a public commitment to the Act's objectives and diminished its capacity to provide necessary social welfare products to Americans.

Like a Phoenix rising from the ashes, the Social Security Act emerged from the chaos of the Great Depression, overcoming the longstanding aversion to a federal social welfare role. It is a remarkable story: the Social Security Act of 1935 has become the majestic social welfare policy document that has survived for over seventy years, responding to constantly changing calls for government to ensure a level of economic security for all Americans. Yet, for all of its majesty, the Social Security Act falls short of providing an adequate measure of social welfare for American today. Many of its programs are being called into question amid rising public cries to eliminate the Act's most significant elements. The purpose of this book is to provide some perspective to the ongoing social welfare debates, for as the Social Security Act has been expanded, it has become closer to the vortex envisioned by President Pierce. This book is about the Social Security Act as it has developed into the centerpiece of American social welfare policy. Chapter by chapter the book explains the programs administered by the Act, both as they were created in 1935 and how those program operate today. This book lends insight into how federal responsibility for America's social welfare obligation has been able to expand within a political environment that questions its legitimacy. Absent the economic meltdown of the 1930s, today's political challenges to the Social Security Act's programs revive elements of President Pierce's 1854 challenge to the social welfare responsibility of the Federal Government.

America's Welfare Myth

America's greatest welfare myth envisions a comprehensive leviathan gnawing away at the roots of American capitalism, recklessly doling out money and services to welfare cheaters, and eroding the very foundation of America's most cherished values. But, praised by political liberals, and damned by political conservatives, America's effort to provide for the social welfare of its citizens falls far short of any coherent package of public social programs, lacks the energy of generally accepted public goals, and, in spite of its widespread programs, suffers from what Gilbert Steiner once called tireless tinkering. In spite of the fact that about two-thirds of the nation's federal budget is involved in social spending,[a] America has none of the characteristics that might confer the title of "welfare state" on America's response to those suffering social and economic hardship. As important as they are for many Americans in need, the present-day haphazard-looking social programs convey a confusing social purpose and lack structural unity. Most disheartening of all, perhaps, American welfare efforts have had little effect on some of the nation's longstanding pressing social problems, and by many measures, in spite of heavy expenditures, according to antiwelfare critics, America's social problems seem to be increasing.[5]

At the center of this American social welfare enigma stands the Social Security Act. Perhaps America's greatest social welfare achievement, the Social Security Act has become the vehicle for ever expanding social welfare initiatives, an enlargement within a policy environment conflicted over the steps that should be taken to protect the welfare of Americans, how such protection should take place, and who should provide it. The majesty of the Social Security Act lies in its value as America's foundational social welfare policy document, the statutory source for as much as 90 percent of all social welfare spending; the Act's splendor, however, reveals "two-handed" complexity. On the one hand, the established stability of the Social Security Act makes it an attractive source for the advancement of a wide variety of social welfare objectives. On the other hand, the Act's stability attracts politically expedient amendments to its basic programs, greatly straining the established purposes for those programs and creating a public policy document quite different from the original. In its singular importance, the Social Security Act today has evolved from an aimless social welfare policy drift. Its 21 parts (major titles) contain a bewildering array of programs, one piled on top of another, with an ever decreasing connection to America's social welfare concerns. The size of social welfare spending does not define a "welfare state" any more than an expensive automobile defines the character of the driver.

---

[a] Disagreement exists over items counted as federal social welfare expenditures. Table PI.1 and Figure PI.1 list expenditures by functional categories, leaving some to conclude that the above estimates are too large and others to conclude that they are too small.

Table PI.1. Federal Expenditures, 2007

Item	Amount ($)	Percent (%)
Defense	466,035,000,000.00	17.26
International Affairs	32,498,000,000.00	1.20
Science & Technology	25,037,000,000.00	0.93
Energy	1,081,000,000.00	0.04
Environment	33,084,000.00	1.23
Agriculture	27,030,000.00	1.00
Housing/Commerce	9,622,000.00	0.36
Transportation	76,935,000.00	2.85
Community Development	2,677,000.00	0.99
Education/Social Security	89,921,000.00	3.33
Health	276,393,000.00	10.23
Medicare	394,515,000.00	14.61
Income Security	367,029,000.00	13.59
Social Security	586,051,000.00	21.70
Veterans	72,558,000.00	2.69
Law & Justice	43,483,000.00	1.61
General Government	20,092,000.00	0.74
Interest on Debt	243,713,000.00	9.02
Off-setting receipts	(91,171,000.00)	−3.38
Total Expenditures	**2,799,676,000,000.00**	**100.00**

Source: Budget of the United States. The White House, 2006.

The sobering evidence of the magnitude of the Social Security Act is found in Table PI.1 and Figure PI.1. In 2007, for example, the Federal Government expects to spend approximately $1,822,858,000,000 for social welfare purposes, or *about 65 percent of the whole federal budget*.[b] About $1,713,909,000,000 of the whole federal budget, or over 92 percent of all social welfare spending, takes place under the authority of the Social Security Act.[c] Social welfare spending under the Social Security Act overshadows federal spending in all other budget areas including national defense.

The magnitude of government social welfare spending is multiplied when state and local revenues are added. And when the private sector social welfare spending is added, the amount of social welfare spending defies a good estimation. All in all, social welfare spending in America constitutes a large and significant amount of public and private money. But even with this huge outlay of public funds, social welfare spending fails to satisfy criticisms that America's social welfare commitments fall short of solving the deeply layered social problems facing America today. Poverty rates, presently 12.3 percent, have hovered 13 percent for all persons, over 20 percent for all children under age 5, over

---

[b] Housing/Commerce, Community Development, Education/Social Services, Health, Medicare, Income Security, Social Security, Veterans.

[c] Education/Social Services, Health, Medicare, Income Security, Social Security.

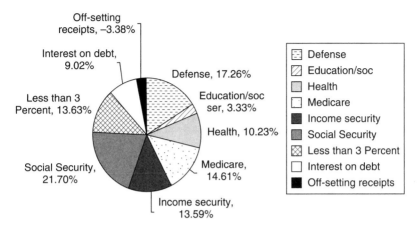

Figure PI.1. Federal Government Expenditures, 2007.[d]
Source: U.S. Bureau of the Budget, 2006.

24 percent for all African Americans, and almost 40 percent for African American children under age five years. Substandard housing persists in urban centers and in rural America. Access to health care, although improved somewhat for the very poor, remains expensive and elusive for too many Americans. The educational levels of Americans remain persistently low, particularly in inner-city schools. None of the social indicators have shown any sign of remarkable improvement regardless of social welfare spending over the past twenty years, with the notable exception of poverty among the elderly, a reduction due entirely to the Social Security Act's Title II Social Security.

Some might argue that America has to spend more just to keep social conditions from becoming worse. Others might argue that changes in American demographics contribute to the lack of America's forward social welfare progress. While these and other analyses of American social welfare spending and its impact on America's social problems all have merit, it is also true that America is trying to deal with social problems of the twenty-first century using the same policy instruments created to deal with twentieth-century problems. The foundational social welfare policy document remains the Social Security Act: expanded but structurally unchanged. While it is important to point out that every day millions of Americans are assisted by programs funded and administered under the Social Security Act, this commitment of abundant social welfare resources is directed at the consequences of America's social problems, rather than at their causes, and often the provision of these resources has proven highly ineffective even for those who must make use of them.

---

[d] "Less than 3 percent" of spending referred to in Figure PI.1 is a combination of all those budget items in Table PI.1 that constitute less than 3 percent of federal spending. Added together, they constitute 13 percent of all projected 2007 federal spending.

In many ways, the Social Security Act was created to satisfy the residual symptoms of the Great Depression. Much of the underlying philosophy supporting the Act's creation reflected a public commitment to create a social welfare architecture that could protect against personal economic disaster. Alleviating financial dependency, attributed largely to the economic meltdown of the Great Depression, became the clearest objective for mitigating a small but important set of the social problems evident in the 1930s. Over the years that followed, however, other objectives, such as health care, protecting children from abuse, supporting the disabled, and even promoting families, for example, appealed for social welfare programs that went well beyond the original objectives of the Act. The original Social Security Act might have adequately met its original objectives, but over the past years, the Act has become thinly stretched in its ability to support new social welfare initiatives through incremental changes without needed adjustments to the basic structure of the Act itself. Recipients of social welfare rightly applauded improved benefits while political actors in Congress and various administrations welcomed the praise and political support they received from their efforts. But taken together, such changes have severely weakened the original social welfare architecture of the Act, leading to a growing recognition that the Social Security Act is limited in its ability to make the United States into any kind of "welfare state."

Viewed from twenty-first-century America, the Social Security Act established a limited social welfare architecture designed to address a limited set of American social welfare concerns. The Social Security Act never proposed to address the full range of American social issues during the late 1930s, nor in its development has a social welfare structure been created sufficient to address the full range of Americans' social welfare problems today. America has always responded reluctantly to its social welfare needs and were it not for the Great Depression, the Social Security Act might not exist today; but were it not for the Social Security Act, the economic welfare of Americans past and present would be considerably more dismal than reflected in Table PI.2. Yet, for all its present-day importance, the Social Security Act has developed within the confines of the Pierce doctrine, rather than invalidating it.

Assumptions about the Social Security Act

A clamor to tear down the Social Security Act arises from two sources: a deep-seated ambivalence about all welfare activities, whether public or private, and a reluctance to understand the Social Security Act and the role it plays in America's welfare commitments. This book is designed to confront directly deficient Social Security Act knowledge. Although its initial reach was modest, the Act integrated a complex mix of social objectives, which have become more difficult to harmonize as changes to the Act have been made over the past seventy years. The following chapters carefully lay out the different policies and the social welfare programs they now support. Although many social

Table PI.2. Selected Poverty Characteristics, by All Persons, Children, the Elderly, and Race

	All Persons			Persons in Families		
	All Incomes	Below Poverty	% Below Poverty	All Incomes	Below Poverty	% Below Poverty
All Races[1]	296,450	36,460	12.3	245,199	25,915	10.6
Under Age 5	20,415	4,220	20.3	20,237	4,119	20.4
65 and older	36,035	3,394	9.4	24,202	1,346	5.6
Males	145,486	16,000	11.1	120,331	11,411	9.5
Under Age 5	10,429	2,146	20.6	10,339	2,097	20.3
65 and older	15,443	1,020	6.6	12,017	577	4.8
Females	150,964	20,460	20.6	124,867	14,504	11.6
Under Age 5	9,987	2,073	20.8	9,898	2,022	20.4
65 and older	23,773	2,670	11.3	12,389	752	6.1
White (Alone)[2]	237,916	24,416	10.3	196,061	16,444	8.5
Under Age 5	15,528	2,662	12.9	15,390	2,590	16.8
65 and older	31,270	2,473	7.9	20,995	940	4.5
Black (Alone)[3]	37,306	9,048	24.3	30,621	7,072	23.1
Under Age 5	3,073	1,225	39.9	3,054	1,215	39.8
65 and older	3,085	701	22.7	1,880	279	14.9

Source: U.S. Bureau of the Census, 2007 (http//pubdb3.census.gov/macro/032007/pov/new01_100_01-03).
[1] in thousands. (296,450 = 296,450,000).
[2] "White Alone" means only white, not mixed races.
[3] "Black Alone" means only identifiable African American, not mixed or other races.

welfare experts are well versed in one or another parts of the Act, the development of social welfare policy over the years has created a social welfare mosaic that requires an understanding of the whole before the parts can be properly addressed for potential changes. Enhancing public and professional understanding of the entire Social Security Act also provides a window for examining the public ambivalence toward public social welfare, particularly those social welfare commitments that continue to stir deep-seated public resentments.

The discussion of the Social Security Act in the following chapters rests on several assumptions. First, the far-reaching nature of its programs of social insurance, assistance to the needy, access to health care and provision of social services, establishes the foundation for an impressive array of social welfare commitments designed to satisfy the social welfare expectations of Americans. Thus, the Social Security Act holds a singular place in American social welfare policy because of its comprehensiveness. Its programs, in total, touch the lives of more Americans than any other federal social welfare undertaking. Second, the Social Security Act authorizes a complex mix of social welfare programs, each with a specific propose, yet all of the programs interact with one another, working as the scaffolding, arches, and beams of America's social welfare architecture. This social welfare architecture that represents America's most ambitious social welfare undertakings lends a coherence to America's social welfare commitments. A change to one of the programs ripples through the entire Social Security Act. The various pieces of this social welfare program lack a unity, but together the programs define America's social welfare enterprise. Third, the Social Security Act provides welfare linkage with other public policy instruments that have been created outside the authority of the Social Security Act, but clearly express social welfare objectives. Some of these instruments are identified and discussed in Chapter 10. While not created as specifically social welfare instruments, these public policies achieve an enhanced effectiveness with America's social welfare objectives through their connectivity with other programs authorized under the Social Security Act. The influence of these assumptions becomes clear as each part of the Social Security Act is discussed in the following chapters.

Conclusion

Given the social, economic, and political environment in which the Social Security Act was created, there was no way such a landmark legislation could have achieved social welfare policy comprehensiveness. As the following chapters demonstrate, some early administrators of the Act had a social welfare vision, but to realize their vision required incremental program development, and thus American social welfare policy emerged as patch-work policy, capable of addressing the economic problems of the 1930s but incapable of addressing today's social welfare problems. Thus, in spite of the high standard of living enjoyed across our nation, far too many Americans suffer from having too little. Too many Americans live in squalid housing in despicable neighborhoods. Too many children in America attend inadequate schools, dressed in ragged clothing, and struggle to learn while living on inadequate diets. Too many children and adults are deprived of basic medical care. Too many older people are trapped in near poverty for lack of retirement resources. Too many Americans work long hours at menial jobs and find themselves without enough money to pay their bills each month. For these Americans, some would say it is their own problem. But others would say that America has a contract with her people to promote the general welfare and preserve the blessings of liberty for all. For those of this latter sensibility, the Social Security Act has been the framework under which they can attempt to achieve those goals, even in the present skeptical political environment. Because of its position as America's foundational social welfare policy document, the Social Security Act will continue as a source for achieving those goals only if it recreates itself to meet the political challenges and social welfare expectations of America's twenty-first century.

This book is about the Social Security Act, not just about one or another part of this omnibus social welfare policy document. Studying and evaluating only one part of the Social Security Act as separate from its other parts risks continuing the path of incremental social welfare adjustments and a further erosion of America's commitment to the whole of its social welfare obligations. The following chapters provide useful information for future social welfare policy debates by raising for careful examination each part of the Social Security Act, separately and with reference to the other parts of the Act, in order to clarify how the Act might more effectively satisfy America's social welfare expectations. As they read the following chapters, social welfare policy students and the general public will understand better America's social welfare enterprise and the resources committed to it through various parts of the Social Security Act. America will continue to spend a large share of its wealth on social welfare, and the greatest share of this spending will take place under the authority of the Social Security Act. The following chapters provide a foundation for further discussion about how the Social Security Act can meet America's twenty-first-century social welfare objectives.

NOTES

1. *Congressional Globe* (33rd Congress, 1st Session, May 3, 1854), 1063 ff.
2. Joseph B. Chepaitis, "Federal Social Welfare Progressivism in the 1920s," *Social Service Review* 46, no. 2 (June 1972): 213–229.
3. H.R document No. 397, 73rd Congress, 2nd Session, 1934.
4. Quoted in Richard H. Leach and Andrew Dobelstein, "The Federal Role in Public Assistance Programs," *Forensic Quarterly* 47 (May 1978): 73–74.
5. Charles Murray, *Losing Ground. American Social Policy 1950–1980* (New York: Basic Books, 1994).

1

The Social Security Act in Perspective

Introduction

The Social Security Act is an imposing policy document; it contains 21 titles, or major parts. The public statutes that have created and changed its various parts stretch out for more than 1,000 pages; the codification of these statutes spans another 500 pages in the United States Code. The federal regulations that translate the statutes into workable social welfare programs are scattered throughout several volumes of the Code of Federal Regulations, and the various parts of the Act are administered by the largest administrative agency in the U.S. government, with spending authority over four times greater than the Department of Defense. See Figure 1.1 for the development of the Act since 1935. In addition to the statutes and the Federal Regulations that form the basis for administrating today's Social Security Act, there are decisions by the U.S. Supreme Court that have required legislative and administrative changes, and there are numerous presidential executive orders—some later turned into statute law, others changed by different presidents—that also form the framework of this extensive social welfare policy document. Finally, the Act establishes an intimidating number of social programs, discussed below and in subsequent chapters.

To help reduce the broad scope and the complexity of the Social Security Act to a manageable and understandable form, this chapter provides an overview of the Act's major program and policy features. The chapters that follow describe the Act's specific programs and policies that constitute America's most far-reaching set of social welfare commitments. These general program and policy features of the Social Security Act are important to discuss at the outset since the various program titles of the Act rest on these features; they function as the Act's uniform themes, and they provide a foundation for an integration of the Act's sweeping social programs. It is these policy and program features that make it difficult to change one major part of the Act without also profoundly impacting on another part of the Act, and a related effect on the whole of America's social welfare commitments. Studied carefully, these general program and policy features of the Social Security Act provide a theoretical framework for understanding and further development of American social welfare policy.

The General Structure of the Social Security Act

The structure of the Social Security Act consists of both programs and policies: policies determine the character of specific programs and policies guide the implementation of those programs. In some ways, policies can be thought of as goals; the programs can be thought of as the ways to realize those goals, and the products of those programs are provided to the people through specific activities. For example, an organization may say that its policy is to treat everyone with respect, and to achieve this goal, the organization may initiate a public relations program. To carry out or implement the public relations program, the organization might have employees attend weekly sensitivity training sessions. Or, for example, adequate prenatal health care may be a social welfare goal, followed by programs of medical screening, counseling on dietary and health matters, and economic support to ensure a healthy diet. The programs may be carried out in a number of different ways. Medical screening may be done by doctors or nurses. Counseling might be carried out in a doctor's office or in classes at a community college, and so forth. The Social Security Act has a program structure that defines its social welfare commitments. It also has a policy structure that defines what the programs should accomplish and how they should be implemented.

Today's public environment has become increasingly antagonistic and pessimistic to forms of social welfare, and doubts exist as to whether a comprehensive social welfare document such as the Social Security Act could be re-created in the first decade of twenty-first-century America. Part of this public anxiety over America's welfare commitments, in general, and the Social Security Act in particular, may arise from a confusion over the goals sought by the Social Security Act, whether its programs meet those goals, and finally whether the way the programs are implemented coincide with both the goals and the programs. Sometimes the programs become so important that the policies that guide those programs become lost, or sometimes the way the programs are carried out become more important than the programs themselves. While subsequent chapters discuss the details of the parts of the Social Security Act, as they exist today, this chapter presents the broad structural program and policy themes that support America's social welfare undertakings. This overview provides a foundation for considering how various parts of the Social Security Act do, and do not, fit into America's social welfare commitments as it slowly moves into the twenty-first century. Neither this chapter nor those that follow proposes to establish what those commitments should be; rather the discussions in this and following chapters examine the present sufficiency of the programs and policies of the Social Security Act for meeting present and future social welfare goals.[a]

I: THE PROGRAM AND POLICY STRUCTURE OF THE SOCIAL SECURITY ACT

The Program Structure of the Act

Figure 1.1 summarizes the wide sweep of social welfare activities nested under the Social Security Act. The continuous development of the Social Security Act over the past seventy-five years gives some indication of America's growing social welfare undertakings and their complexity. The original Act contained 13 titles, or major parts. Seven of those titles spelled out social programs, while the remaining titles of the Act were directions for administering various features of the Act. Beginning with seven program titles in 1935, the Act has been expanded to provide 18 major programs under eight program titles. In its present form, the Social Security Act today touches all age groups and reaches from income maintenance to health and basic social services. The development of the Social Security Act's programs provides a picture of how the program titles have changed over its seventy-year history; some original programs have been changed, some combined, some eliminated, and some new program titles have been added.

It should be noted that the name "Social Security" has been used loosely, contributing to considerable public confusion. The Social Security Act really contains three types of "Social Security" programs: social insurance, assistance programs, and health insurance and assistance programs. The *social insurance* programs are really made up of three programs: the Social Security retirement/disability program, most often referred to as "Social Security" (Title II), social insurance for unemployed workers (Unemployment Insurance, Title III), and the health insurance program, Medicare (Title XVIII), added to the Social Security Act in 1965.

Moreover, there are three major parts to the Social Security program administered under Title II: old-age insurance, survivors' insurance, and disability insurance. There are four major program parts to medical insurance, Medicare: Part A, insurance for care in a hospital; Part B, supplemental insurance for various outpatient medical services; Part C, explained in Chapter 6; and Part D, prescription drug benefit created in 2004 and only recently fully implemented. All the insurance programs are in white background in Figure 1.1.

---

[a] Policies are more than an articulation of goals. As social constructs, public policies are also efforts to solve problems, legitimize social goals, and create a context for resolving social conflicts, among their other functions. The relationship between programs and the policies that shape them begins with articulated social goals, the creation of programs that meet those goals, the implementation of programs consistent with the goals, and evaluation of the results. The paradigm proposes that policy decisions take place at all stations in this process. See Andrew Dobelstein, *Social Welfare Policy and Analysis*, 3e (Pacific Grove, CA: Brooks-Cole, 2003), chap. 1.

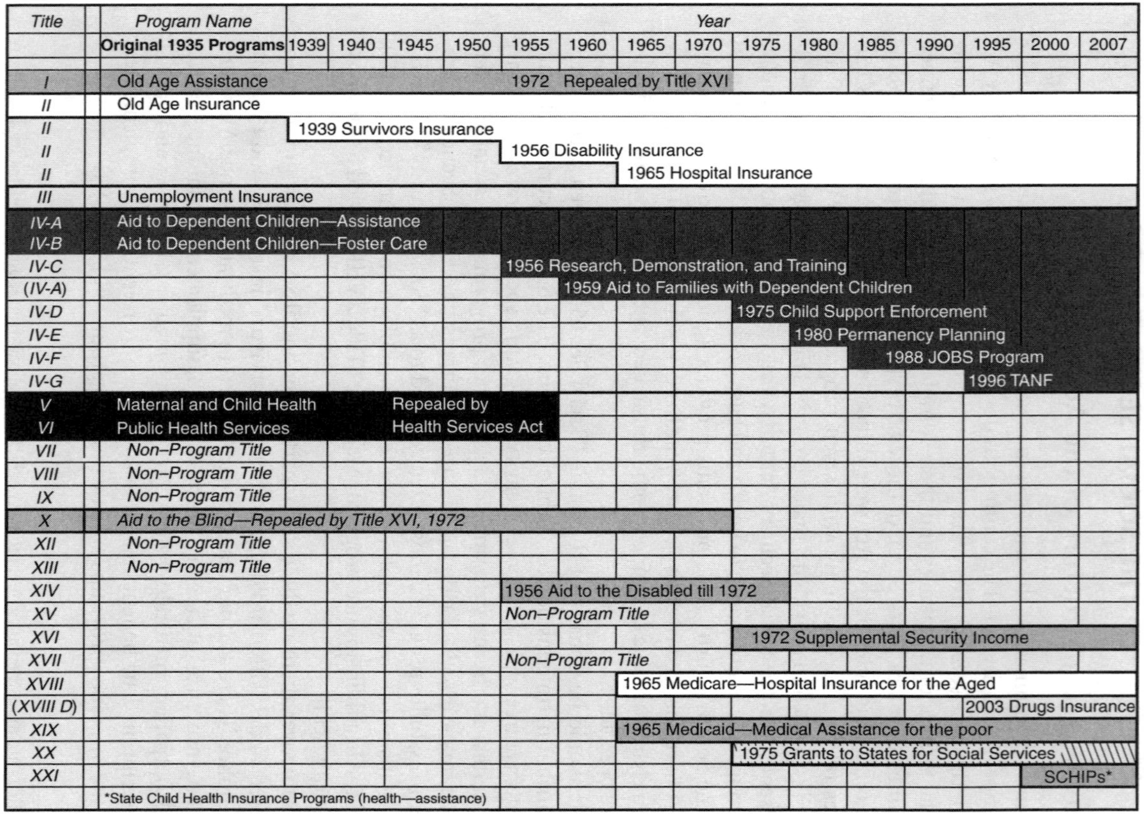

Title	Program Name	Year
	Original 1935 Programs	1939 · 1940 · 1945 · 1950 · 1955 · 1960 · 1965 · 1970 · 1975 · 1980 · 1985 · 1990 · 1995 · 2000 · 2007
I	Old Age Assistance	1972 Repealed by Title XVI
II	Old Age Insurance	
II		1939 Survivors Insurance
II		1956 Disability Insurance
II		1965 Hospital Insurance
III	Unemployment Insurance	
IV-A	Aid to Dependent Children—Assistance	
IV-B	Aid to Dependent Children—Foster Care	
IV-C		1956 Research, Demonstration, and Training
(IV-A)		1959 Aid to Families with Dependent Children
IV-D		1975 Child Support Enforcement
IV-E		1980 Permanency Planning
IV-F		1988 JOBS Program
IV-G		1996 TANF
V	Maternal and Child Health	
VI	Public Health Services	Repealed by Health Services Act
VII	Non–Program Title	
VIII	Non–Program Title	
IX	Non–Program Title	
X	Aid to the Blind—Repealed by Title XVI, 1972	
XII	Non–Program Title	
XIII	Non–Program Title	
XIV		1956 Aid to the Disabled till 1972
XV	Non–Program Title	
XVI		1972 Supplemental Security Income
XVII	Non–Program Title	
XVIII		1965 Medicare—Hospital Insurance for the Aged
(XVIII D)		2003 Drugs Insurance
XIX		1965 Medicaid—Medical Assistance for the poor
XX		1975 Grants to States for Social Services
XXI		SCHIPs*

*State Child Health Insurance Programs (health—assistance)

Figure 1.1. The Development of the Social Security Act—1935–2007.

The Social Security Act also contains a form of "Social Security" for persons without sufficient income, otherwise known as *financial assistance* programs. Originally, in 1935, there were three assistance programs: Title I, Old Age Assistance; Title IV, Aid to Dependent Children; and Title X, Aid to the Blind. A fourth assistance title was added in 1950 (H.R. 6000), as Title XIV, Aid to the Permanently and Totally Disabled. In 1972, Titles I, X, and XIV were combined into a single program, Supplemental Security Income, under Title XVI, but the long-standing controversies over Title IV, Aid to (Families with) Dependent Children, left it standing alone. In 1965, Medicaid, medical assistance for the poor, was added as Title XIX.[b] The assistance programs are in light gray in Figure 1.1, with the exception of Title IV, which itself has gone through many changes and is dark gray in the figure.

A comprehensive health care plan was considered for the original Social Security Act, but it was dropped because of political pressures to do so. However, the original Social Security Act did contain two health programs: Title V, Maternal and Child Health, and Title VI, Public Health Services. Title V revived the Sheppard Towner Maternal and Child Health program that died from lack of funding before the Depression (see Introduction and Chapter 6). Title VI was a modest title that provided money to states for public health work. The administrative authority for both these programs was removed from the Social Security Act and placed in a Health Services Act in 1956, although the legislative authority for Title V remains in the Social Security Act. In 1965, when Congress created Medicare, a program of *medical insurance* for those receiving Social Security benefits (Title II beneficiaries), Congress also created a companion program, Medicaid, a *medical assistance* program of grants to states to help states pay for medical care for poor people. In 2000, Congress created the State Child Health Insurance Program, Title XXI. This program has both insurance and assistance features, but it is clearly a program to ensure a level of health care for all children. The health programs are in a black background in Figure 1.1.

Finally, the Social Security Act contains provisions that help states pay for social services (Title XX), as determined by the states. This social service provision was added to the Act in 1974. Social Services are in stripes in Figure 1.1.

The development of the Social Security Act depicted in Figure 1.1 attests to the incremental development of America's social welfare programs. As discussed in detail below, the social insurances (Title II and Title III) broke new social welfare ground. The other program parts of the original Act were established based on the then existing state assistance programs and two modest health initiatives. The program structure of the Social Security Act reflected in Figure 1.1 established an original limited public social welfare

---

[b] For this discussion, Medicare is treated as a social insurance program and Medicaid and SCHIP (State Child Health Insurance Program) are treated as assistance programs, even though all three provide resources to assist individuals obtain health services. The reason for this categorization is explained in the appropriate chapters that follow.

reach and modest social spending under the Act. However, as the programs expanded over the years, the Act's social welfare undertakings increased, and spending increased as well. The programs authorized under the Act have expanded considerably, creating a social welfare enterprise that has become difficult to control.

The Policy Structure of the Act

The policy structure of the Social Security Act emerges from two sources: **program policies** and **implementation policies.** The fundamental program policy of the Social Security Act is to provide **financial security** against the economic "hazards and vicissitudes of life,"[1] The implementation policies determine the way the Act's various **financial security** programs are carried out. The Act's programs were created as activities that would ensure financial security for the aged, the unemployed, children, and persons in ill health.[2] The Act's programs are implemented through four distinct ***implementation policies***: (1) **entitlement** policies, (2) **benefit** policies, (3) **administrative** policies, and (4) **program** policies.

Program Policies

Originally, a straightforward set of five programs satisfied the commitment to financial security: Title II for aged retired persons, Title III for the unemployed, and Titles I, IV, and X to help states provide funds for the needy aged, children, and blind respectively. But as the Social Security Act developed over the years, new program components have been added to satisfy demands for program changes. For example, when the Social Security Act was created, the specific objective for the Title II Social Security retirement program was to ensure a measure of income for retired workers. The Title II program, however, has been expanded by demands to provide income support for survivors of retired workers—widows, children, the disabled, and others. The detailed examination of the programs in the following chapters discusses whether the foundation program policy of the Social Security Act, financial security, continues to be met by today's programs as summarized in Figure 1.2, whether the Act's programs no longer reflect the original policy objectives of the Act, and whether the objectives of the Act have changed over the years, giving rise to new or changed programs.

To the extent that programs are the tools of public policy, and operate to achieve defined objectives, it is not unusual that over time as programs change they become disconnected from their objectives. For example, often athletic programs at educational institutions begin as programs that help educate students, but over time they become programs that no longer connect with educational objectives. When programs become displaced from their original goals, they lose their original authority, and in order to remain effective, they must develop a new authority or be recast in a way that will give them authority

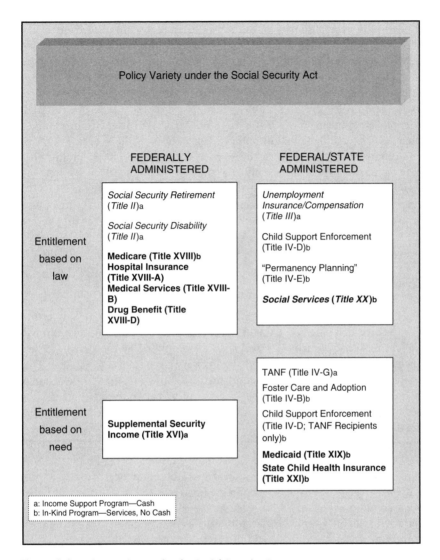

Figure 1.2. Policy Variety under the Social Security Act.

apart from their original objectives. Subsequent chapters will discuss the extent to which changes to the Social Security Act and its programs represent a displacement of objectives and the extent to which changes to the Act lack the authority of the original objectives for those programs.

Implementation policies

Although it is not always apparent, programs of the Social Security Act also depend on choices over how to implement them. The different programs funded under the authority of the Social Security Act are implemented in a variety of ways and for different reasons, constituting a complex interaction between what the programs are supposed to accomplish and the choices about how programs are to be provided. The variety of implementation options is often overlooked in a discussion of America's welfare architecture, but it is these varied options for program implementation that constitute one of the most complex issues facing any effort to improve America's social welfare commitments. Policy implementation options determine how the specific programs are accomplished; they underlie the execution of all of the Act's programs. They may or may not apply specifically to a single program or title in the Act, and they criss-cross in the implementation of the Act's various elements. Four distinct policy implementation options comprise the choices for carrying out the Act's far-reaching social programs: (1) entitlement policies, (2) benefit policies, (3) administrative policies, and (4) program policies. These implementation policies and their interrelatedness with the specific program titles of the Act are pictured in Figure 1.2. Each of these implementation policy strategies is discussed below.

(1) **Entitlement Policies:** Programs may be guaranteed based on law or they may be provided based on a test of need. This policy distinction runs through the entire Social Security Act and is best exemplified by the striking differences between the insurance and the assistance programs. Eligibility to the *social insurance* programs is an entitlement to those people (and their family members) who contributed to the program as defined in the law, regardless of economic need. Eligibility to the *assistance* programs is extended to those who are defined as needy, and who must prove their financial need. *Assistance* programs based on need are the most contentious forms of social welfare because of the difficulty of defining what constitutes economic need. Federal statutes provide some general definitions, and state statutes and local ordinances provide broad guidelines for determining who is in need of welfare and under what conditions. Persons who meet statutory conditions are usually eligible for assistance, but even with statutory clarification, eligibility for assistance is compromised by the difficulty in determining what constitutes economic or medical need and this area retains considerable discretionary ambiguity.

Assistance programs satisfy "residual" social welfare issues by providing money for those who are unable to maintain sufficient income or gain access to necessary services using their own financial resources. Residual welfare is the oldest of all welfare ideas. Sometimes called "charity," residual welfare provides resources when individuals have no other options at their disposal. Because people are expected to take care of themselves or the family or friends are expected to help out in times of need, when these options are not available, then welfare is given in the form of *assistance*, "residual welfare." Residual welfare programs provided under the Social Security Act are administered through the grant-in-aid system and are in light gray and dark gray in Figure 1.1 and are in gray and in bold italics in Figure 1.2.

Insurance programs are quite different from assistance programs. Although well known in Europe, and in spite of social insurance programs in a few of the states, social insurance programs on a national scale were a new idea in 1935, and they continue to attract debate over how to classify them. The American social insurance programs are designed to protect income and, presently, to provide access to health care for the aged, disabled, and unemployed, but eligible persons must have worked and contributed to the programs through the taxes they paid in order to receive these benefits. Insurance programs are called "institutional" welfare programs by Wilensky and Lebeaux because they promote a particular public good and become more or less "permanent" or "institutionalized" social welfare activities.[3] Eligibility for insurance benefits is not based on economic need.

The word "entitlement" has been used loosely in such a way so as to create a lot of confusion when it is applied to the welfare programs under the Social Security Act. There are at least three ways to think about entitlement and the provision of social welfare in America. First, it is important to recognize that there is actually nothing in the Social Security Act that entitles an individual to social welfare benefits as a response to the human condition. Although one might argue that everyone has a right to medical care, or that everyone has a right to basic subsistence, there is nothing in the Social Security Act that recognizes that form of entitlement. Second, another kind of entitlement to social welfare is ensured when persons meet basic social obligations as spelled out in law. Specifically, when persons work, and allow some of the proceeds from their work to be set aside for their future economic or medical well-being, a contract becomes established that entitles those persons to the benefits accruing from those proceeds. This second form of entitlement, a contractual entitlement, is essential to understanding the policy objectives, which drive the development of the social insurance programs. Finally, there is a third form of social entitlement that places a burden on society to care for its citizens. This form of entitlement is a social obligation rather than a contract between individuals and government. In this view, those who need assistance cannot claim it as a right, but rather must depend on the benevolence of society to satisfy this need.

(2) **Benefit Policies:** Providing benefits in cash or in kind constitute a second set of social welfare policy implementation options. Some programs administered by the Social Security Act are designed to provide cash, while others are designed to provide specific products. Providing benefits in cash enhances personal autonomy in as much as the recipients can make their own choices about how the resources can be used. Cash benefits are often preferred forms of welfare in America since money plays such an important part in everyone's life. The provision of specific products, however, acts to target resources to specific problems. Various forms of foster care and adoption, child care, medical services, and social services constitute an important source of in-kind social welfare benefits, focused on a specific problem, provided under the Social Security Act. Some may argue that the use of in-kind benefits is more effective

because they deal with a specific concern, although cash benefits may be more efficient because they allow the recipient to obtain exactly what he or she feels is needed.

(3) **Administrative Policies:** Administration of the programs authorized under the Social Security Act may be by the Federal Government alone or administration may be shared with the states. This policy option is discussed below both as a feature of the grant-in-aid and in the context of the historic responsibility for welfare which rested with the states. As Figure 1.2 indicates, both some insurance (entitlement based on law) and all assistance (entitlement based on need) programs are administered both by the Federal Government and in a federal–state administrative relationship. In the federal–state relationship, states may have considerable administrative flexibility, as in the Temporary Assistance to Needy Families (TANF) program (Title IV–G, see Chapter 6), or more limited administrative latitude as in the Medicaid program (Title XIX, see Chapter 7). Developing the rules that determine how programs must be administered becomes a complex policy process under the federal–state administrative structure.

(4) **Program Policies:** A wide variety of programs exist under the various titles of the Social Security Act. Although a clear distinction can be made between program policies, generally thought of as goals, and social programs, generally thought of as ways to achieve goals, decisions over whether to have many or few programs to reach a goal are one of the implementation strategies exercised under the Act. For example, Title II of the Act, the Old Age, Survivors, and Disability Insurance program, provides benefits to at least six major beneficiary groups, all under a single program. Somewhat by contrast, the greatest variety of programs, including cash assistance payments, child day care, adoption and foster care, and efforts to reunite families and promote marriage, for examples, are found in the wide-ranging Title IV (Chapter 6) of the Act. A single program with multiple beneficiaries may offer opportunity for administrative efficiency, but it also tends to limit the range of alternative ways to achieve a desired objective. A variety of subprograms may enhance the likelihood of achieving desired goals, but greater program variety often leads to program overlaps, conflicting program elements, and programs that become separated from their fundamental goals, as the case of the 1996 welfare reform discussed in Chapter 6 illustrates.

The development of numerous programs under any one of the major program titles of the Social Security Act may also be explained by an expanded number and growing effectiveness of social welfare advocacy groups that influence the development of the Social Security Act. The growing effectiveness of advocacy groups is discussed below, but it is important to note that politically it is easier to attach a new program to an established title in the Act than it is to bring about a change in the whole program title. The interests of many social welfare advocacy groups are narrow enough that new programs can be amended to major titles of the Act with less political conflict than if the same groups were advocating for major program title changes.

Summary of Programs and Policies

The Social Security Act has a program structure and a policy structure. The program structure is most obvious and has been subject to numerous changes over the past seventy years. The program structure is subject to most of the public debates that question how the programs under the Act might be changed to make them more effective. But underlying the program structure of the Social Security Act is its complex policy structure. The policy structure gives the programs their meaning, both in the ways the programs are constructed and in the ways they are carried out. The Act's programs have been developed from a fundamental commitment to financial security, and the policies that implement these programs have had a profound impact on the way the programs of the Act are carried out in order to meet its fundamental policy commitments.

The Dilemma of Insurance and Assistance Implementation Policies

The policy implementation options discussed above present a number of difficulties and create inconsistencies in the administration of the Social Security Act's programs. In other words, implementing one program from a particular policy approach, for example providing health insurance, may not be compatible with providing cash to persons to pay for their own health expenses or funding government health centers with free access to health care. Although the program policy (providing health care) may be the same, each way of providing that health care in this example is implemented by a different policy. In some cases, implementation policies may result in efforts to use a program created for one purpose to realize a different policy objective. For example, the use of health insurance as the implementation policy to provide health care may result in promoting insurance rather than obtaining health care. Providing cash may encourage people to buy the health care they want, rather than the health care they may need, and so on. Implementation policies may also overlap one another and thus obscure underlying policy objectives. For example, the implementation of Supplemental Security Income (Title XVI) as a need-based assistance program overlaps the Title II Social Security program and obscures the primary purpose of Social Security, as discussed in the next chapter. Some of the policy implementation problems can be traced to original "design issues" brought about by the Act's initial political compromises, and as the Act has matured, several conflicting implementation policy agendas for the same program have been developed and the programs themselves have become less focused.

Perhaps the most profound dilemma for the Social Security Act and its programs grows out of the riddle caused by dual insurance and assistance program implementation. It is of more than historical interest that President Roosevelt recommended and Congress approved mixing into the Social Security Act insurance and assistance, two different ways of implementing programs designed to provide financial security for individuals. The basic differences between insurance and assistance are explained above. Using both approaches as the way to implement financial security objectives has become one of the most compromising features of the entire Social Security Act. In fact, most of the displeasure with all of the programs authorized under the Social Security Act orginated with efforts to meld insurance and assistance into a single Federal Government social welfare initiative.

Pragmatically, because the original social insurance programs would take some time before workers would "contribute" enough to their Social Security accounts to be able to draw benefits, or for state Unemployment Insurance Funds to become solvent, at the outset there were many unemployed, many retired workers, and many children and spouses of retired workers who were all without income. Roosevelt preferred work-related forms of economic relief, as reflected in his emergency programs, and he disliked what he called "the dole" (the assistance programs). Yet, in the face of continuing inability of states to meet financial assistance needs, the social reformers who had already convinced the Federal Government to establish the first Children's Bureau in 1912 continued to advocate for a federal assistance program for children. Older people, too, were vigorously pushing Congress for some form of immediate assistance.[4] Impatient to get on with an economic recovery package, Congress was already drafting a variety of assistance and social insurance legislation when Roosevelt decided to put together his comprehensive Economic Security package.

The assistance programs, therefore, proposed a temporary Federal Government bridge until people obtained social insurance coverage, either through the retirement program, through unemployment insurance, or, later, through a familial relationship with someone who had established eligibility for either program. In this early view, the assistance programs would diminish in significance as the insurance programs matured, and whatever need for assistance remained would be absorbed by the states. The Committee on Economic Security that was charged with developing the Social Security Act (originally called the Economic Security Act) was quite clear that any form of assistance was the responsibility of the states. "Public funds should be devoted to providing work rather than to introduce a relief element into what should be strictly an insurance program."[5] The Committee conceded, however, that assistance to children, the aged, and the blind was necessary and that under the circumstances the Federal Government had little choice but to help the states. Called "residual relief" by the Committee, assistance was to remain the responsibility of the states and local governments, just as it was before the economic crisis of the Great Depression.

To justify their support of state assistance programs, Committee members argued that as more and more workers gained income protection from the social insurances, fewer and fewer would need assistance. In subsequent years it became possible to capitalize further on this rhetoric and argue that by actually expanding social insurance coverage, the need for assistance programs would decrease even faster. The power of this argument was quickly rewarded by the first expansion of the Social Security retirement program in 1939. Four years after the insurance program was initiated for retired workers, Congress agreed to extend Social Security coverage to survivors of workers.

The argument that social insurance and assistance worked together promoted the belief that both forms of implementation were truly part of the same program policy goal. In reality, however, these two different forms of implementation were rooted in different ideologies, constituted different goals, and became two different program forms; they were not simply a matter of doing the same thing in different ways. As discussed in the subsequent chapters, additional beneficiary groups were added to the basic insurance programs, while the need for assistance required the Federal Government to expand its assistance commitments to the states as well. Although evidence supports the idea of an inverse relationship between social insurance and assistance, particularly as Title II Social Security has expanded, and as the need for assistance among the aged has decreased, in reality two very different policy approaches became mixed into one financial security package, leading to the incremental expansion of both insurance and assistance.

The Committee and the Congress were also committed to keeping the authority for assistance programs, or welfare, in the hands of states. Part of this motivation involved respecting the traditional role of the states in providing welfare to the needy. Part of this motivation, however, also grew from the highly charged question of whether the states or the Federal Government would decide who was eligible to receive welfare assistance. Of particular concern was whether an assistance program administered by the Federal Government would force Southern states to provide welfare to African Americans (Negroes), persons these states had not otherwise chosen to support. According to Edwin Witte, who directed the Committee's work and kept copious notes on the process of developing the Social Security Act, Virginia Senator Harry Byrd was supported by nearly all the Southern members in Congress who feared that Old Age Assistance might serve as an entering wedge for federal interference with "the negro question" in the South, and did not want to give authority to anyone in Washington to deny federal funds to any state because it discriminated against Negroes.[6] In his testimony in support of the Social Security Act, Dr. Frank Porter Graham, Chairman of the Advisory Committee on Economic Security, attempted to smooth over the issue by assuring the Senator that "you have to trust the administrators [of the Act] to do the right thing."[7]

While the centerpiece of the Social Security Act was the social insurances, which were also supposed to enhance the value of work, the need for assistance did not evaporate, but instead grew with continuing public pressure for the Federal Government to assume fiscal and administrative responsibility for both insurance and assistance. As a result, each time the insurance features of the Social Security Act were amended to create new beneficiary groups, a parallel program of assistance was also created. For example, in 1950, under pressure to create a federal program to assist the disabled who had worked but became unable to work, Congress created an assistance program, Aid to the Disabled under Title XIV, to forestall an expansion of Title II Social Security. But as pressure to provide social insurance for disabled workers continued, Congress also agreed to include disabled workers under Title II, as discussed in Chapter 5. When Congress created medical insurance (Medicare) for the elderly (and others who qualified under Title II) in 1965, it also created Medicaid, formalizing the practice of reimbursing states for vendor payments to help states defray the costs of medical care for the poor (see Chapter 8).

In an effort to reduce assistance costs, and as the Social Security trust funds continued to grow, beneficiary groups were added to the insurance provisions of the Act. For example, in 1950, social insurance benefit provisions were liberalized, extending benefits to almost 10 million new workers, most of whom were self-employed, leading the way to expanding Title II Social Security six years later. In 1961, provision was made to extend a reduced benefit for men who chose to retire at age 62. In 1964, benefits for disabled persons were liberalized, and in 1972, all Social Security eligible persons aged 72 and older were granted a minimum Social Security benefit, if otherwise they had insufficient Social Security income. Congress also "indexed" Social Security payments to rises in cost of living so that each January Social Security benefits are adjusted upward at the same percentage as the cost of living increased in the previous year. These and other changes were driven by administrative efforts to transfer as many as possible from assistance to social insurance coverage.

Expanding Social Security so as to gradually replace public assistance programs was clearly an ideal of the early administrators of the Social Security Act. For example, early in 1940, the Social Security Board reviewed a proposal submitted by the administrator whereby each elderly, retired person would receive a base amount from the Federal Government, and Social Security would pick up the difference between this amount and whatever retirement benefits the person might be eligible for, based on the person's wage contributions to Social Security. This idea, called the "double-decker," was supported by the Federal Security Administrator but strongly opposed by Arthur Altmeyer, who objected to any proposal to distribute "unearned benefits" from the Social Security Trust Fund. Altmeyer urged President Roosevelt to oppose any plan that would turn Social Security into anything that could not be justified as strictly an insurance program.[8]

In 1972, Congress transferred fiscal and administrative responsibility for the Aid for the Aged (Title I of the original Act), Aid for the Blind (Title X of the original Act), and Aid for the Disabled (Title XIV created in 1950) to the Federal Government by creating a new program, Supplemental Security Income (Title XVI). However, in the vitriolic struggle over this significant policy change, Congress left Aid to Families with Dependent Children (AFDC) and the whole of Title IV stand alone as a federal–state assistance program.[9] Now, the Social Security Act has the responsibility to provide assistance for the elderly and disabled and the responsibility to provide social insurance to the same group of people, bringing assistance and social insurance into a tighter program bond, but creating an overlap of two different policy objectives. The "backup" for the original limited assistance role of the Federal Government remains social insurance. Thus a form of the "double-decker" found life in the 1972 changes to the assistance programs, as discussed in Chapter 5.

In summary, the Social Security Act developed with two different ways to implement its programs, and each way of implementation was based on a different policy objective. A contractual relationship between those who worked and were taxed to ensure economic benefits for themselves and their dependents formed the basis for the social insurances. Economic support for the needy aged, children, and disabled, who were not expected to work, established federal financial support for assistance programs that were administered by the states but monitored by the Federal Government. Throughout the history of administering the assistance programs, the Federal Government and the states often conflicted over setting standards for beneficiary eligibility and level of benefit payments. Thus, in spite of the fact that the Federal Government provided upwards of two-thirds of state-related assistance costs, states asserted their prerogatives to use these monies in ways consistent with state customs and traditions.

Benefits entitled by work (the social insurances) avoided the contentious issues that surround the provision of welfare. The existence of previously operating state welfare structures allowed the Federal Government to provide financial support to state assistance programs without actually administering them. As long as the Federal Government left assistance administration to the discretion of the states, the philosophies underlying the different programs did not surface, and in fact this limited state support for assistance provided some justification for the expansion of the insurance programs. But once the Federal Government began to tighten standards over how states used their assistance money, or in the case of Supplemental Security Income (SSI) when the Federal Government assumed most of the financial and administrative responsibility for the assistance programs, policy differences between social insurance and assistance became more obvious, challenging the policy foundation of both. While a change in administrative responsibility has been the most obvious manifestation emerging from the creation of Title XVI, combining assistance and social insurance blurs the distinction between the two. Chapter 5 deals with the policy problems caused by combining these two programs.

II: THE SOCIAL SECURITY ACT IN THE AMERICAN POLITICAL AND IDEOLOGICAL CONTEXT

That the Social Security Act can occupy such a central place in American social welfare policy and yet at the same time lack the characteristics of welfare comprehensiveness in spite of the incremental expansion of its programs is one of the paradoxes of American government. The structure of American governance limits its social welfare capacity, and to label America as a "welfare state" greatly exaggerates America's social welfare commitments. Some of the answers to this American riddle are found in the U.S. Constitution, some in the nature of divided governmental power, both among the branches of government and among the states, and some in the traditional approach America has taken toward its welfare responsibilities.

Constitutional ambiguity, as discussed in the Introduction, limits the reach of federal authority for social welfare. The U.S. Constitution was crafted by delegates from the original 13 states that were reluctant to give up power to a centralized authority. (Not all of the original "states" were present at the Constitutional Convention, nor did all of the states ratify the final document that has become today's Constitution.) The American Constitution, even with its 23 amendments attached to it over its 217-year history, sets a prescribed and thus limited role for the Federal Government and provides a carefully constructed set of rules for what the Federal Government can do. In other words, Federal Government activities must stay within the powers given to it in the Constitution. Powers not explicitly given to the Federal Government are reserved "to the states and to the people."

The constitutional authority for a federal role in social welfare is found in two brief phrases, one in the Preamble, the other in Article I Section 8, in the grant of power to the Congress to "provide for the general welfare." Until the Social Security Act was passed in 1935, welfare responsibility rested clearly with the states. Not only did states all have their own constitutional provisions defining their welfare obligations, and extensive state statutes to implement those obligations, but President Franklin Pierce's veto had drawn a sharp line in America's social welfare policy sand by affirming insufficient constitutional authority for federal "public charity." Pressures to improve America's social welfare responses became concentrated in various forms of public and private welfare activities at the local and state levels. As a result, by 1935, all states had forms of social programs that eventually formed the basis for the original Social Security Act.[10]

But the Great Depression (circa 1929–1935) strongly influenced the political climate affecting the Federal Government's "hands off" social welfare policy. A report in 1929 by the newly established Bureau of Social Statistics showed that over 70 percent of all welfare aid in the major cities was provided from local or state public funds and the remaining welfare aid was provided by private efforts, mostly through churches. The Bureau declared that these funds were just not sufficient to meet the growing social welfare need.[11] As the Great Depression deepened, out of a labor force of approximately 39 million people, 15 million were unemployed by the spring of 1933, constituting over one-third of the labor force, and calls for federal welfare support only intensified as resources shrank under the weight of the unemployed.[12]

The constitutional ambiguity over federal authority to provide welfare, particularly in light of the Pierce veto, caused considerable concern for the

Committee on Economic Security that President Roosevelt had formed and charged to develop legislation to protect the economic security of Americans into the future. Frances Perkins, chair of the Committee and President Roosevelt's Secretary of Labor, reported that the Committee struggled with the constitutional issues inherent in the social insurance provisions of the proposed act. The Committee finally decided to create separate taxes to support the retirement and unemployment insurance provisions of the proposed act on the advice that the constitutional power to tax (under the 13th Amendment) provided stronger authority than those inherent constitutional powers to provide welfare under Article I Section 8.[13]

The Social Security Act was discussed by the Supreme Court in 1937. The constitutional question turned on the narrow consideration of whether taxing and spending for Old Age Insurance and Unemployment Insurance constituted taxing and spending for the general welfare, as allowed under Article 1 Section 8 of the Constitution, or whether such taxing and spending constituted a specific form of welfare and thus not constitutionally permissible. Writing for the Court, Benjamin Cardozo confirmed the constitutionality of the Act, recognizing that "the spending power advocated by Hamilton . . . has prevailed over that of Madison", yet recognizing that "the line still must be drawn between one welfare and another, between general and particular."

> Where this [line] shall be placed can not be known in advance of the event. There is a middle ground or certainly a penumbra in which discretion is large. This discretion, however, is not confined to the courts. The discretion belongs to Congress, unless the choice is clearly wrong, a display of arbitrarily power, not an excess of judgment.[14]

Although other provisions of the Social Security Act have been litigated over the years, there has been no challenge to the decision in *Helvering v. Davis*.[15] Taxing is constitutional, and Congress decides whether spending satisfies the general welfare provision of Article I Section 8. Therefore, congressional politics, not constitutional authority, drives the direction for America's social welfare policy.

The division of governmental power is the chief characteristic of the American system of governance. Horizontally, power is divided by assigning limited authority to the "branches" of government. Functionally, no single governmental unit can develop or carry out social welfare policy. All the "branches" must concur, as litigation over the original Social Security Act demonstrates. Vertically, power is divided between the Federal Government and the states, who in turn share power with localities. Structurally, the 10th Amendment of the U.S. Constitution states, in part, that "all powers not herein defined are reserved to the states and to the people." Since federal power to provide welfare is ambiguous, most welfare prerogatives are therefore reserved to the states. Since many states have their own constitutional provisions to provide welfare, and since states have developed wide-reaching networks of social welfare legislation, states retain the authority for most welfare development.

The validity of this conclusion becomes evident both in the wide variety of social welfare programs states offer and in the administration of state social welfare programs, even those funded with federal money. For example, there are over 100 program variations in the 1996 federally funded TANF, one of the most recently discussed social welfare programs. States determine what constitutes abusive treatment of children. When parents are no longer able to care for their children, and in cases of divorce, children come under the protection of the state, not the Federal Government, and states determine the conditions of custody for children under state protection. These and other welfare programs are administered by states, under authority developed by the states, and with state personnel, not by the Federal Government.

The themes of consistency that run throughout American social welfare programs are a product of the ubiquitous grant-in-aid. Because of the uncertain nature of constitutional authority for social welfare, the Committee on Economic Security sought a safe method of spending federal money on the assistance programs. The Committee risked a constitutional confrontation by its use of the payroll tax to finance the social insurance programs. But funding the assistance programs required a different fiscal strategy. The Committee finally settled on the method Dorothea Dix had proposed years earlier and which was vetoed by President Pierce—a grant in federal aid. By 1935, the use of federal grants-in-aid to states had achieved legitimacy through the expanded use of land grants for educational purposes under the Morrill Act of 1852. Under this Act, Congress agreed to give a portion of its public lands to each state, permitting the state to use or to sell these lands and use the proceeds to establish colleges dedicated to teaching agriculture and mechanical arts. The act was amended in 1890 and in 1907, expanding the gifts of land and adding federal monies to the grants. In 1920, Congress created the Maternal and Child Health Act (Sheppard-Towner) and funded it using cash grants to states for maternal and child health work, without serious objection, and the constitutionality of the Maternal and Child Health Act was upheld in a legal action filed by Massachusetts.[16] Thus, these early uses of the grant-in-aid not only propelled the Federal Government into matters not specifically assigned to it by the U.S. Constitution, but also established the grant-in-aid as the most creative mechanism for the distribution of federal funds, including federal funding for programs that exist outside the Social Security Act.

Intergovernmental relationships are the secret of American social welfare consistency, and the grant-in-aid has become the most ingenious mechanism of American governance. The grant-in-aid permits the Federal Government to set national priorities and policies without violating state sovereignty or moving beyond the limitations of the U.S. Constitution. Essentially, the Federal Government offers a grant to states if states will use the money (or the land in the 1800s) for the purposes specified by the grant. States are free to refuse the grant should they choose not to undertake the purpose of the grant. In this arrangement, the Federal Government is not administering any programs, leaving that to the states. Under the grant-in-aid, the Federal Government's role is to "explain," sometimes "interpret," and to monitor the specific terms of the grant, so as to award the funds within the framework set forth by the grant and to ensure that federal funds are spent consistently with their purposes.

The grant-in-aid and its cousin the block grant are the carrot and stick of American social welfare policy. It is extremely unlikely that states will refuse to accept a federal grant, particularly if the grant provides funds for purposes the state is undertaking anyway. However, accepting the grant means the state must make sure that the way the grant's purposes are carried out are consistent with the terms of the grant, and usually this means making some changes in the way the state would normally administer its social program. The grant-in-aid thus not only makes large sums of federal money available to states, but also provides a way for all levels of governance to have some role in the development and implementation of social welfare programs, thus providing some harmony for a system of welfare that otherwise would have components singing very different songs. The grant-in-aid brings together, in a patchwork fashion, the social welfare objectives of the Federal Government, which it is not able to implement on its own, with the social welfare objectives of the states, which have sufficient governmental authority to implement social welfare objectives.

Experience with the grant-in-aid over the past seventy years of welfare administration has revealed its disruptive influences on efforts to develop coherent social welfare objectives. Grants-in-aid for welfare purposes have expanded well beyond their modest use in 1935. Today, Congress creates numerous grant-in-aid programs to satisfy narrow-range constituent interests, catering to social welfare interest groups seeking special legislative treatment. Congress has created a grant-in-aid program here, another there, until today there are over 300 federal grant-in-aid welfare programs, including those under the authority of the Social Security Act. Thus, a network of poorly connected, sometimes overlapping, programs has proliferated as federal public welfare initiatives, and the special interest groups the programs serve are loath to permit combining or refocusing programs. And since legislators are usually identified with the creation of the program sought by advocates, the legislator has developed a solid constituent base. Whereas the grant-in-aid and its block grant cousin are the least controversial mechanisms for the Federal Government to fund domestic social programs, politically they have contributed considerably to the fragmentation and inefficiency of the nation's social welfare enterprise. Nor are these special programs always focused on the nation's most pressing social problems. To the extent that these various social welfare grant-in-aid programs need a policy home, they have been patched into the Social Security Act's numerous already existing programs.

The policy significance of providing federal grants is two sided. On the one side, both grants-in-aid and block grants pass considerable policy-making authority from the Federal Government to the states and to localities. On the other side, this devolution greatly fragments social welfare policy and its products. For example, when the AFDC program was reformed into TANF in 1996, broad welfare flexibility was given to the states over the use of welfare money.

While the Federal Government set the framework for TANF programs, states and localities now have considerable authority to develop social welfare policy that fills in and makes the broad policy conditions operational. In particular, under TANF, states and localities determine who will get welfare benefits and what levels of financial support they will provide. In other words, there is no uniform standard for providing welfare (under TANF) in the United States.

From the federal perspective, the creation of grant-in-aid programs raises questions over how individual programs will be overseen. In other words, each grant-in-aid program must have a statutory home and an administrative authority, and since the Social Security Act covers the broad range of social welfare concerns, new grant-in-aid programs have been amended to this Act in the form of new titles, amendments or attachments to existing titles, or as changes within existing titles themselves. As subsequent chapters show, every part of the Social Security Act has received a large share of add-ons or changed programs. Title IV, the title dealing with providing for the welfare of children, now has seven subparts, or seven distinct program elements, some of which conflict with other parts of Title IV, and some that reflect implementation options that conflict with a commitment to enhance and protect the welfare of the nation's children. The specter of these wide-ranging policies and programs for children is thoroughly discussed in Chapter 6.

The disruptive influence of the grant-in-aid and the need to place new policy initiatives under the Social Security Act contributes further to the fragmentation of America's social welfare efforts. Since no overall philosophy driving the Social Security Act exists, grant-in-aid add-ons not only produce confusions within specific program groups, such as child welfare, but also constantly changing programs compromise the other program parts within the Social Security Act itself. For example, as mentioned above, when the welfare programs supporting aged and disabled persons were changed from a grant-in-aid to states to a federally administered program (Title XVI, Supplemental Security Income), it linked Title II social insurance with welfare assistance under the new SSI so that changes to Title II Social Security benefits impacted Title XVI benefits, and vice versa. While Social Security benefits were usually counted as resources by states in determining state-administered welfare benefits, the overlap between Social Security and SSI means that federal earned social insurance benefits offset federal welfare assistance benefits. The further implication of these changes is discussed in Chapter 3.

The prevalence of grant-in-aid social welfare program development often places additional fiscal burdens on states, and thus Congress created the Unfunded Mandate Reform Act (UMRA) in 1995 in order to monitor the fiscal burden such grants put on states. If the administrative burden is estimated to be over the allowable fiscal limit, then additional funds must also be provided to implement the program. The Congressional Budget Office reviews proposed programs to determine whether or not they impose a significant fiscal burden on the states, as shown in Box 1.1.

Box 1.1 An Example of How the Grant-in-Aid Works

H.R. 5403, introduced in the U.S. House of Representatives on May 17, 2006, would amend the Social Security Act to require states that receive foster care payments under the federal IV-E program of the Social Security Act to meet certain requirements when placing children in adoptive or foster homes in other states. The bill would require states receiving requests from other states to assess the suitability of placing a child in a home to complete such studies within sixty days. States may be granted up to seventy five days, under certain circumstances.

The bill would authorize appropriations of $10 million in each of the fiscal years from 2007 through 2010 to provide incentive payments to states that complete home studies within thirty days. For each home study completed within the thirty-day period, a state would receive a payment of up to $1,500. The amount could be reduced on a pro rata basis if the appropriation is insufficient to cover the number of eligible placements. Assuming appropriation of the authorized amounts, enacting H.R. 5403 would result in increased outlays of up to $40 million over the 2007–2011 period. Those costs would fall within budget function 600 (Income Security).

Completion of studies for appropriate homes within sixty days would be an intergovernmental mandate as defined in the Unfunded Mandates Reform Act (UMRA). States would have to devote more personnel to shortening the length of time it takes to complete home studies, or they would have to contract with private entities to carry out the home studies within the sixty-day deadline. In either case, they would need to spend additional resources. The costs of the mandate would not exceed the threshold established in UMRA ($64 million in 2006, adjusted annually for inflation).

Source: Summarized from U.S. Congressional Budget Office, *Cost Estimate, H.R. 5403, Safe and Timely Interstate Placement of Foster Children Act of 2006.* Washington, DC, May 19, 2006.

Monitoring and supervising grant-in-aid programs adds other complexities to social welfare program development. Bureaucracy needs to expand in order to monitor so many different and sometimes very complex programs, and grant-in-aid program funding also puts administrators in positions of policy making. The federal administering agency must develop guidelines for how funds will be obtained and how they must be spent. Whether the statute creating the program is broadly or narrowly drawn determines the extent of policy-making discretion that rests with the administrative agency. Such policy discretion may easily direct the implementation of a particular program in a way quite different from the intent of Congress when it crafted the legislation creating the program. Thus, not only is the amount of bureaucracy increased, but the increased role of the administering bureaucracy has the capacity to alter, significantly, the products of the program from those objectives intended by the

Congress. A good example is found in the creation of the public social service amendments to the Social Security Act, discussed in Chapter 9.

In many respects, it has been the use of administrative policy making, rather than political discourse, that has shaped the development of the Social Security Act. In his carefully researched biography of Wilbur Cohen, Edward Berkowitz shows clearly how Edwin Witte, Arthur Altmeyer, and Wilbur Cohen successfully engineered the development of the Social Security program (Title II of the Act) to meet their own ideological goals for American social welfare. Not only was the Social Security program complex and required special knowledge, and not only were the Social Security funds in a protected trust fund, but both Altmeyer and Cohen used the discretion provided in the law to shape Social Security as they thought would best serve the American people.[17]

In conclusion, vertical power sharing with the states, often examined as a feature of American Federalism, has become the most expedient way to expand a federal social welfare presence within the limits set by the Constitution, and a well-established state social welfare authority. While the grant-in-aid has been refined sufficiently so as to provide federal monies to states for welfare, it also subtly undermines efforts to develop social welfare comprehensiveness. Not only are there abundant social welfare special interest groups lobbying for policy consideration, but every state has its own special way of dealing with the terms of the grant-in-aid, or, in other words, adapting the federal initiative to its own exigencies. Additionally, as the grant-in-aid has become a political tool for special social welfare interest groups, the internal comprehensiveness of the Social Security Act, sparse as it is, has also been compromised, further fragmenting American social welfare.

Public attitudes about welfare have not been an inconsequential contributing factor to America's fragmented social welfare efforts. American social welfare has developed in the shadow of two compelling American ideas: "rugged individualism" and the "work ethic." Both of these welfare-shaping ideas are products of traditional liberal thought so richly ingrained in the development of American institutions. Rugged individualism has acted as a limitation on government activity, while the work ethic has become the standard solution for welfare need. "Help yourself by working" summarizes the impact of these two ideas on welfare development. The myth of rugged individualism depends on a geographically limitless country and a social environment where the action of one person does not compromise the activities of another. The myth of the work ethic depends on both an intrinsic and an economic value of work. Work must have a larger purpose beyond making money, but at the same time generate enough income to live in economic security. Neither limitless social nor physical geography exist, nor are workers usually fairly rewarded for the economic or intrinsic value of the work they do.

Because of their shortcomings, neither rugged individualism nor the work ethic provides any ideological energy for the creation of a less fragmented, more comprehensive welfare system. American social welfare policy finds some ideological support when welfare programs are limited to providing assistance for those who cannot work. This form of welfare, taking care of those who cannot care for themselves, has been discussed earlier as "residual" welfare. American social welfare policy as it exists under the Social Security Act certainly satisfies the expectations of residual social welfare, although as discussed above there is little support for residual relief to be provided by the Federal Government. Moving beyond residual relief, however, ideological support for welfare weakens considerably. Social welfare that promotes social goods, like day care for children of working mothers (who may or may not be economically disadvantaged), or social welfare policies designed to develop healthy families, all count as forms of comprehensive social welfare policy so clearly lacking in American social welfare. Such undertakings, however, lack an ideological foundation in this country. In fact, even support for residual social welfare is complicated by decisions over when persons lack individual capacity to work or when people work but still do not have adequate income.[18]

Both rugged individualism and the work ethic are well represented in residual programs of the Social Security Act, often referred to as "a safety net," but the Act has been stretched to provide programs well beyond safety net initiatives. Title II Social Security, for example, was never designed as a residual welfare programs, but rather as programs that would protect the income of workers when they retired. Although from the beginning, social insurance benefits depended on a formula that provided more generous benefits to low-wage workers, over time this formula has changed to expand Title II's redistributive elements to favor low-income earners. These residual elements of social welfare are discussed in Chapter 3. A similar example of efforts to gain ideological support for welfare programs might be found in the confusing ideological objectives woven through the many policy changes reflected in efforts to provide support and care for children under Title IV. As discussed in Chapter 6, the Title IV programs offer residual welfare in the form of public aid, while at the same time attempting to promote the welfare of children with programs designed to create socially healthy families. Tinkering with existing programs in order to satisfy strongly held ideological viewpoints has greatly fragmented their overall effectiveness.

Roosevelt and his committee were quite aware of the ideological strength of both rugged individualism and the work ethic. Roosevelt's emphasis on programs that put people to work is often overlooked in analyses of Roosevelt's social welfare efforts to bring the country out of the Depression. Most of Roosevelt's emergency programs were designed to put people to work, rather than providing forms of cash assistance. The retirement benefits of Social Security (Title II) were strongly attached to a work ethic ideology. In their original form, Social Security taxes were created as a "contribution" made by each worker and from the worker's employer. People who did not work, therefore, paid no Social Security tax and thus did not develop Social Security eligibility. Workers with larger incomes from work accumulated larger

accounts and thus received greater retirement benefits than those who contributed less. In other words, the value of retirement benefits was closely related
to the economic value of the work. Chapter 3 discusses the Social Security
program changes that have gradually unraveled the tie between work and
future benefits, but at the outset, Roosevelt strongly believed workers were
contributing to their own retirement, and he and the Committee on Economic Security sold the program to Congress and the public based on this
belief.

An ideological aversion to welfare existed long before there were state public welfare laws. American ideology supported private welfare activities, mostly
through efforts of the churches. Almshouses and "County Homes" substituted
for cash assistance. For African Americans, particularly during the period of
slavery, the church was their only form of welfare, independent of the needs of
the plantation owners. Today, there is probably no church in America that does
not have some social welfare effort as part of its religious mission. Such efforts
are visible collectively in forms such as Jewish Family Services, Lutheran Family
Services, Catholic Charities, and others. The Church of Latter-Day Saints has
one of the most comprehensive social welfare systems in the nation. Moreover,
the tradition of private forms of welfare is vividly expressed in times of personal and national disasters, such as fires and hurricanes, and each fall during
United Appeal campaigns, which take place in every community in America.
The recent efforts to "privatize" Social Security (Title II) reflect such strongly
held beliefs, even as evidence shows that America's social obligations are much
greater than the capacity of private efforts to meet them.

Attitudes opposing public welfare activities have a long history in the helping professions as well. When public monies began to be generated for welfare
purposes in the late 1800s and early 1900s, Mary Richmond, best known
for founding modern social work, urged that public funds be turned over to
private agencies, the Charity Organization Societies, to distribute along with
their private contributions. Richmond's concerns, shared with devout social
activists of her day, were based on the belief that the provision of public
relief would be used as forms of political patronage, destroy the motivation
to work, and lead to permanent welfare dependency.[19] Today, most public
welfare agencies administering funds provided under the Social Security Act
contract with private social agencies to carry out at least some of their programs. More recently, the Social Security Act has been amended to provide
funds to churches to carry out welfare activities through programs called
"Charitable Choice." These and other private welfare activities are consistent
with America's welfare ideals and certainly provide valuable assistance to those
in need. But the vast expanse of private welfare activities presents a confusing array of programs that compete with public activities both for funds
and for public support, thus increasing the degree of welfare fragmentation
in America. In summary, the American idea that good government is less
government collides with the idea that good government promotes a healthy
society.

Conclusion: Shifting Politics and the Social Security Act

Lacking clear policy guidance for future generations, the Social Security Act began as a pragmatic document, driven by the ideals of its administrators, while the subsequent development of the Social Security Act has been driven by the growing influence of diverse advocacy groups. The ideals of the original administrators sought to satisfy several pressures for a form of financial security consistent with their own visions, and they were successful at creating programs that stretched to meet those visions. They enjoyed immunity from the policy conflicts that developed later from those program expansions and the public policy debates that arose over promoting their own interests. Their purposeful pursuit of programs but limited policy development have been well documented by Martha Derthick in her highly acclaimed study of the Act's Title II program's development.

> [The Social Security executives] wanted to achieve a certain kind of program, designated by the name of social insurance, and to extend its coverage broadly over the population and over different types of risk, including retirement from work in old age, disability and poor health. They were very successful in this. . . . Had goals been defined in terms that stipulated ultimate social outcomes with some precision, success would surely have been much harder to achieve.[20]

Facing the immediate concerns of the severe economic Depression, early administrators had their own design for the social welfare programs they created, and they were able to work to advance those programs as the political opportunities arose. These administrators believed their goals were indeed shared goals and promoted their own visions to an almost arrogant degree. A revealing exchange between Arthur Altmeyer, who was director of the Social Security Administration at the time, and Senator Robert A. Taft of Ohio, early into the blinding strength of ideals held by the early administrators of the Social Security Act. Senator Taft questioned the wisdom of extending benefits to retiring workers without increasing the contributions from workers. In a lengthy exchange with Arthur Altmeyer, Taft pointed out that the additional benefits would not be equal to the taxes workers would have to pay. "Is that not right?" Taft asked. Altmeyer responded. "[T]he formula is weighted to give the lower wage earners a larger benefit in proportion to their wages . . . than the higher wage earners."

> Senator Taft: That is not an insurance principle, of course, that is a social-welfare principle.
> Mr. Altmeyer: That is a very sound social-insurance principle.
> Senator Taft: It is a social-welfare principle. It has no relation to insurance.[21]

But the administrators' strong ideals found difficulty maturing as the Act became the centerpiece of American social welfare undertakings. Whereas the early administrators of the Social Security Act believed that social insurances would not only replace the need for welfare but also provide a level of economic security for all Americans, today's social welfare beliefs are driven by the partisan political ideologies of social welfare advocacy groups these administrators help to create. The early administrators had a strong commitment to a statutory right to social insurance benefits based on the value of work and held strong humanitarian views about those who could not work or could work but did not earn enough to ensure their economic security. The Social Security Act today is devoid of a consistent social welfare theory and has been used as a political wedge to exploit public responsibility for America's social welfare obligations. Given the views of the early administrators, it is hard to criticize the heavy hand they used to shape America's early welfare architecture. As economic prosperity began to return to the nation, it was easy for these administrators to realize their social welfare objectives, and indeed, the ease by which this early expansion was accomplished suggested to the administrators that their goals were mirrored by the rest of the country. Even Roosevelt himself eventually abandoned his earlier unwavering commitment to a Social Security program "actuarially sound . . . in perpetuity," and agreed to freeze Social Security taxes for macroeconomic reasons beginning in 1943.[22] Today, America's social welfare enterprise remains locked by the ideas of its 1935 creators while trying to find its way through America's twenty-first-century social welfare challenges.

Four individuals, in particular, dominated the expansion of welfare commitments under the Social Security Act: Edwin Witte, Arthur Altmeyer, Robert Ball, and Wilbur Cohen. All four were involved in the development of the Social Security Act from the beginning. Witte became the staff director of the Committee on Economic Security in 1934, and although he returned to a teaching post in Wisconsin, he remained an advisor as the Social Security Act developed. Arthur Altmeyer rose from assistant secretary of labor in the first Roosevelt administration to the chair of the Technical Advisory Committee of the Committee on Economic Security, second Chairman of the Social Security Board, and later he became the first Commissioner of the Social Security Administration. Wilbur Cohen was hired fresh out of college by Edwin Witte in 1934 and remained a principal player in the development of the Act, eventually becoming Secretary of Health Education and Welfare in 1968. One administrator followed another with a similar welfare ideology, creating a social welfare dynasty that existed until Richard Nixon became president. The influence of these four people over the direction of the Social Security Act is difficult to overestimate, but it is a legacy that has outlived its time.[23]

Clearly, as the programs administered under the Act expanded, the Act's ideological inadequacy gave way to its political transparency. President John Kennedy emphasized rehabilitation as a welfare goal, and President Lyndon Johnson felt forced to create his Great Society programs outside the authority of the Social Security Act, yet the foundation of the Social Security Act barely budged from its earlier roots. Administration of the Act was no longer directed by people with ideologically favored social welfare persuasions. When President Richard Nixon replaced social welfare program specialists with cost accounting budget specialists, the Act's ambiguity of purpose provided a rich opportunity for a new cohort of administrators to reform programs as seemed best to them. Social Security retirement, the cornerstone program in the Social Security Act, was not the only program that suffered significantly from its historic origins. The assistance titles, particularly Title IV dealing with the welfare of children, has suffered from administrative tinkering, as have Titles XVIII (medical insurance), Title XIX (medical assistance), Title XX (social services), and Title XXI (child health insurance). The changes in these programs, reflected in Figure 1.1, all attest to an administrative capacity to create new program initiatives under the Act without a reformed welfare vision capable of responding to America's social welfare obligations in a completely new political environment for welfare policy development.

The development of the Social Security Act reveals the limitations faced by social welfare without a vision or a social welfare theory. Left to strictly political processes, both the limited constitutional authority to provide welfare and the division of power between the states and the Federal Government create an environment in which partisanship, rather than social commitment, sets the framework for social welfare policy development. The political influence of the early generations of Social Security Act administrators who effectively built the social insurances into a comprehensive social welfare policy instrument has been replaced by the influence of competing social advocacy groups that see the Social Security Act as a source for achieving narrow interest group goals, or, more seriously, a gradual deconstruction of the foundation document for America's social welfare commitments. Political influence, rather than social welfare concerns, sets the agenda for social welfare policy, and partisan politics, rather than social welfare objectives, has now increasingly molded the social welfare programs and policies administered under the Social Security Act.

It is true that the work ethic has always been the economic foundation for social welfare development. Benefits are guaranteed for those who have worked and who have paid for their social welfare benefits, and those who do not work continue to be left to the generosity of federal, state, local, or private benevolence. Work, therefore, determines welfare eligibility for both social insurance and assistance. Needy persons are expected to work, even if their wages are less than the amount of assistance payments. Assistance payments might supplement income from wages, but they will not substitute for wages. Whether either work or the benefits of work pays a living amount offers little support for developing welfare policy. This minimalist social welfare foundation fails to account for the problems that work raises for issues of financial security in America today, and falls far short of a foundation capable of supporting twenty-first-century American social welfare.

Unfortunately, America has never articulated a strong ideological commitment to social welfare. Personal self-sufficiency, independence, "rugged individualism," and other American self-ascribed virtues dwarf values of social and political obligation. The Social Security Act's effective and necessary provision of social welfare benefits has done little to change Americans' ideas about social welfare, nor has the efficient administration of those programs, particularly the administration of social insurances under Title II, done anything to change the minds of Americans about the proper role of government-administered social welfare. Americans' historic view of government, that good government is limited government, stands in stark contrast with contemporary public demands for government activities well beyond those authorized under the Social Security Act. Only a synthesis of public attitudes about government and social welfare will suggest a new paradigm for welfare policy development.

The political, economic, and social contexts of America in 2009 raise fundamental questions about the purpose and substance of social welfare policy and its programs as they are presently provided. In 1935, America was slowly emerging from a serious economic Depression, during which time almost one-third of the labor force was unemployed and many thousands had lost their homes and their savings, and their way of life. There was no economic "safety net." The Social Security Act that was presented to Congress in 1935 sought to develop a system to protect income for the aged and the unemployed and succeeded to do so through the insurance provisions of the Act. The legislation also sought to help the states provide economic support to people who would not be covered by the new insurance programs. In spite of the initial clarity of purpose, later political compromises led to program and policy design flaws, which when put in the context of the limited federal social welfare authority, opened the way for incremental program and policy changes that the original structure of the Act has difficulty supporting.

Social welfare policy today is caught in a much different position. On the one hand, the Social Security Act continues to serve as the nation's fundamental social welfare policy document, but through its many changes it has become a complex, multi-layered policy document with conflicting, overlapping programs that are provided with increasing confusion over their policy objectives and criticism as to their effectiveness. At the same time, today's political pressures and ideological conflicts lack a sense of unity that existed in 1935, when Social Security was created. Addressing present program dissatisfactions, fragmentation, and ineffectiveness through additional changes chips away at the most effective parts of the Act, while proposing significant changes risks losing the entire social welfare architecture embedded in the Act itself. This dilemma will become more clear as the major parts of the Social Security Act are discussed in the following chapters.

While the Social Security Act is not the only source of social welfare policy in America, other public policy documents exist with much more limited social welfare scope. Social welfare policy is found in the Food Stamp program, administered by the Department of Agriculture. Social welfare policy is found in the Earned Income Tax Credit program, administered by the Treasury Department, a program increasing in importance. Social welfare policy plays a small but important part of the Housing Act through Public Housing and Rental Housing (Title II and Section 8) assistance programs, and social welfare policy elements are found in public policy documents and programs such as the School Lunch program, immunization program, and other legislative sources. However, it is the Social Security Act that establishes a unique foundation and serves not only to provide most of the social welfare spending, but binds together social welfare initiatives in related policy documents. Perhaps a more thorough understanding of the Social Security Act will begin to unlock an understanding about how social welfare policy in America can be stabilized and promoted in these first decades of the twenty-first century.

NOTES

1. Franklin Roosevelt, Message to Congress, June 8, H.R Document No. 1 397, 73rd Congress, 2nd session, 1934.
2. "This Social Security measure gives at least some protection to thirty millions of our citizens who will reap direct benefits through unemployment compensation, through old-age pensions and through increased services for the protection of children and the prevention of ill health. We can never insure 100% of the population against one hundred percent of the hazards and vicissitudes of life, but we have tried to frame a law which will give some measure of protection to the average citizen and to his family against the loss of a job and against poverty-ridden old age." Franklin Roosevelt, "Statement on Signing the Social Security Act, August 24, 1935." Messages of the President, 1935.
3. Harold Wilensky and Charles Lebeaux, *Industrial Society and Social Welfare* (New York: Free Press, 1965), 138–147.
4. Abraham Holtzman, *The Townsend Movement* (New York: Harper and Row, 1963). Holtzman provided a vivid discussion of the importance of the aged as a political force in the development of the Social Security Act.
5. Report to the President of the Committee on Economic Security (Washington, DC: Government Printing Office, 1935), 4.
6. Edwin E. Witte, *The Development of the Social Security Act* (Madison: University of Wisconsin Press, 1963), 144–145.
7. U.S. Congress, Senate Committee on Finance, *Hearings on S. 1130, the Economic Security Act* (Washington, DC: U.S. Government Printing Office, 1835), 309, ff.
8. Arthur Altmeyer, *The Formative Years of Social Security* (Milwaukee: University of Wisconsin Press, 1966), 125–127.
9. See Joseph F. Zimmerman, *Interstate Disputes: The Supreme Court's Original Jurisdiction* (Albany: State University of New York, 2006) for a discussion of pre-Constitutional conditions placed on the states and carried into the U.S. Constitution as ratified in 1789.
10. Andrew Dobelstein discusses six political and economic necessary pre-Social Security Act conditions. See Andrew Dobelstein, *Moral Authority, Ideology, and the Future of American Social Welfare* (Boulder, CO: Westview Press, 1999), 92–102.
11. See Josephine C. Brown, *Public Relief, 1929–1939* (New York: Henry Holt, 1940), 55–56.
12. Dobelstein, *Moral Authority*, 88.

13. Frances Perkins, *The Roots of Social Security* (Washington, DC: U.S. Government Printing Office, 1963), particularly 34. Material.

14. *Helvering v. Davis.* U.S. 633 at 640.

15. The silence of the U.S. Supreme Court in social welfare matters may be due to "the intimidating nature of the welfare structure" and the fact that Section 1983 of the United States Code required administrative fair hearing procedures that could be substituted for judicial review of federal and state laws until *Brown v. Board of Education* challenged the provision. [See "Individual Rights and Emerging Social Welfare Issues," *Yale Law Journal,* 74 (1965), 90.] Several challenges to the *assistance titles* were brought by individuals following *Brown v. Board of Education* [see Andrew Dobelstein, *Politics, Economics, and Public Welfare* (Englewood Cliffs, NJ: Prentice Hall, 1980), 61, ff], and later other challenges were brought against the *insurance titles* (see Chapter 3 below), but the whole of the act has never been litigated.

16. The U.S. Supreme Court ruled. "We have reached the conclusion that the cases [brought against the legality of the use of the grant-in-aid] must be disposed of for want of jurisdiction, without considering the merits of the constitutional questions." *Massachusetts v. Mellon,* 262 U.S. 477, 478 (1923)

17. Edward D. Berkowitz, *Mr. Social Security. The Life of Wilbur J. Cohen* (Lawrence Kansas: University of Kansas Press, 1995). See Chapter 5 in particular.

18. Dobelstein, *Moral Authority,* 175–181.

19. "[Public relief] is administered by politicians and becomes a source of political corruption. Moreover, public relief comes from what is regarded as a practically inexhaustable source, and people who once receive it are likely to regard it as a right, implying no obligation on their part." Mary Richmond, *Friendly Visiting Among the Poor* (New York: Macmillan, 1899, 151). See also June Axinn and Mark J. Stern. *Social Welfare. A History of the American Response to Need (6e)* (Boston: Allyn and Bacon, 2005), particularly 149 and 169.

20. Martha Derthick, *Policy Making for Social Security* (Washington, DC: Brookings Institution, 1979), 22.

21. Quoted in *Dobelstein. Moral Authority,* 126.

22. F. J. Crowley, "Financing the Social Security Program—Then and Now." *Studies in Public Welfare, vol. 18* (Washington, DC: U.S. Government Printing Office, 1974), particularly 25–28.

23. In addition to Martha Derthick's analysis of the development of Social Security, Edward Berkowitz's biography of Wilbur Cohen (*op.cit.*) makes the influence of these three persons abundantly clear.

PART II

THE SOCIAL INSURANCES

Introduction

The social insurances were the centerpiece of Roosevelt's Social Security Act and remain so today. The social insurances provide a minimum level of income support for more than 51 million American beneficiaries, slightly over 17 percent of the American population. Social Security benefits for retired workers, spouses and family members, and the permanently and totally disabled provided under Title II of the Social Security Act, and unemployment insurance benefits provided under the authority of Title III of the Act anchor America's efforts to establish a base of economic security for her people. Far reaching in 1935, the social insurance programs have expanded providing more comprehensive social insurance coverage than the Committee on Economic Security ever visualized. Today, social insurance for the aged retiree has become the largest social welfare initiative in America, both in terms of the amount of money it distributes and the number of persons who receive its benefits. Moreover, the Title II social insurances have had an important impact on reducing poverty among the aged. Yet, in spite of the established social welfare value of the social insurances, the Title II program raises some of most profound questions about America's social welfare undertakings.

Chapter 1 identified three social insurance program titles of the Social Security Act: Title II, most frequently called Social Security, Title III known as Unemployment Insurance, and Title XVIII, health insurance for Title II beneficiaries called Medicare. Medicare is a special form of social insurance that provides access to health care and is discussed in Chapter 7. Titles II and III are discussed in the next three chapters.

Although some states had rudimentary retirement and unemployment insurance programs in place in 1935, and some major employers provided retirement benefits for their workers, developing a program of national social insurances sailed uncharted waters. The idea for social insurances was borrowed from Europe, where successful social insurance programs had been established, and the European social insurance framework took on new urgency during the economic chaos of the Great Depression. Political pressures during the Depression from Francis Townsend and his estimated 25 million supporters, one among several advocacy voices for federal pensions, paved the way for America's new social welfare adventure, in spite of the continued uncertainties over the welfare role of the Federal Government. The Committee on Economic Security sought wide-ranging advice from European and American economists and insurance experts, and finally settled on the present form of social insurance, even though the form raised questions over its legitimacy and usefulness in 1935, and continues to raise similar questions today.

The Committee designed two kinds of social insurance to protect the income for America's workers: one for aged retirees (Title II of the original Social Security Act) and one for people who became unemployed due to economic circumstances not of their own making (Title III of the Social Security Act). Later, in 1965, Congress added a third form of social insurance, medical insurance for Social Security recipients, which is called Medicare. Because of the size and complexity of Title II, the next two chapters examine both the programs and the policy issues that have developed as the Title II Social Security program has now grown to its present form. Chapter 2 describes the program characteristics of Title II, while Chapter 3 discusses Social Security's policy issues. Chapter 4 discusses the insurance program created for persons who become unemployed, Title III of the Social Security Act. One of the original parts of the Social Security Act, Unemployment Insurance, also called Unemployment Compensation, has also gone through many changes from its original form. By providing payments to persons who lose their jobs, Unemployment Insurance is an important social welfare program, but because it is administered by the U.S. Department of Labor, in partnership with the states, Unemployment Insurance is usually not discussed as part of America's social welfare architecture in spite of its important welfare functions. Finally, Medicare, Title XVIII of the Social Security Act created in 1965, is a medical insurance program for persons who receive Social Security.

There is little doubt from the work of Martha Derthick and others that the members of the Committee on Economic Security and their supporters both in and out of government sought a comprehensive economic safety net for all Americans through the insurance programs. The 1929–1934 collapse of the American economic system offered empirical support for government programs that would protect everyone's economic security. The early social insurance administrators formed a tightly knit group that guided the development of social insurance and pushed for the expansion of the programs when the opportunities were right. They promoted Social Security, in particular, because it seemed the right thing to do at the time. Today's world of private enterprise has been promoted as a better way to insure economic security than yesterday's world of government insurances. Both views merit consideration, but John Kenneth Galbraith's view of government as the balancing point between private interests and public obligations continues to provide justification for the efforts of these early social visionaries and for the existence of the many social insurance programs today.

Although the social insurances are well-established social welfare programs, and to some extent they are taken for granted, they continue to represent a unique set of welfare activities with still unresolved issues. Not only do the social insurances put the Federal Government in the uncertain role of directly providing welfare, but, ideologically, the insurance programs also raise

challenges of interfacing government activities with America's private enterprise system, particularly as the social insurances have grown to become the
largest form of federal public expenditure. Political conservatives argue that the
social insurances constitute a tax on the working population to pay benefits to
a nonworking population, rather than a form of unemployment or retirement
investment. Thus, they argue, building one's personal unemployment or retirement resources is best left to the private sector. Political liberals, on the other
hand, argue that both Social Security and unemployment taxes constitute an
acceptable employee expense and constitute a means for government to make
sure workers have "saved for a rainy day." Whether these social insurance programs constitute a right to future benefits or whether they are secured only by
political promises also complicates an understanding of these programs. A further examination of the Title II and Title III social insurance programs will
provide a foundation for the specific programs that follow.

2

Title II: The Program Structure of Old Age, Survivors, and Disability Insurance

Introduction

Once again, names are important. *Social Security* is used in the following two chapters to designate the program of benefits paid under Title II of the Social Security Act. Title II of the Social Security Act began modestly as a program to ensure income to persons who reached retirement age and were no longer able or expected to work. However, the program structure of Social Security is much more complex today, as shown in Figure 2.1. In 1935, only retired workers received Title II Social Security. Today, there are five major categories of beneficiaries: retired workers, their survivors, spouses, children, and the disabled. Although the number of Title II Social Security recipients has increased by 24 percent between 1990 and 2008, the number of beneficiaries as a percentage of the national population has remained rather constant at slightly over 16 percent. Today, retired workers constitute only about 62 percent of the total number of Social Security beneficiaries, a percentage that has also remained rather constant over the past decades even though other beneficiary groups

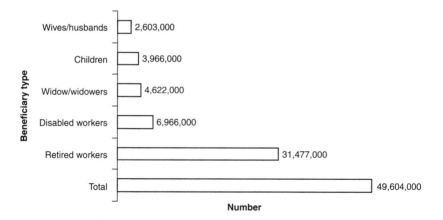

Figure 2.1. Program Structure of Title II Social Security (2008).

Table 2.1. Benefits by Type of Beneficiary, 1990 and 2007

Type of Beneficiary	Number 1990	Percent 1990	Number 2002	Percent 2002	Number 2007	Percent 2007
Retired Workers	24,838,000	62.4	29,190,000	62.8	31,477,000	63.4
Disabled Workers	3,011,000	7.6	5,544,000	11.9	6,966,000	14.0
Wives and Husbands	3,367,000	8.4	2,833,000	6.2	2,603,000	5.2
Children	3,187,000	8.0	3,910,000	8.4	3,966,000	8.0
Widows/ Widowers	5,415,000	13.6	4,965,000	20.7	4,622,000	9.4
Others	13,000	—	2,000	—	—	—
Total	39,832,000	100	46,444,000	100	49,604,000	100
Total U.S. Population	**248,710,000**	**Social Security 16.0%**	**288,368,000**	**Social Security 16.1%**	**330,022,000**	**Social Security 16.4%**

Source: Statistical Abstracts of the United States, 2008, Table 533.

have increased. Table 2.1 also shows that the percentage of disabled workers has increased significantly, while the percentages of wives and husbands and widowers have shown decreases due to the fact that more husbands and wives have their own Social Security based on their own work histories. The growth in the number of Social Security beneficiaries along with increases in benefits has also caused increases in spending. It is important to note that more children receive social insurance benefits under Title II than children who receive cash welfare benefits under Title IV.

The Social Security Program Structure

The basic idea underlying Title II Social Security becomes an important starting place to understand the entire range of benefit programs now authorized under Title II. The whole structure of the Social Security insurance program is based on the principles of a *defined benefit* insurance plan. A *defined benefit* insurance plan usually promises participants a specified (*or defined*) monthly benefit (or a defined lump sum) at retirement or disability. Whether in the private or public sectors, *defined benefit* insurance plans work the same way. *Defined benefit* types of retirement (or disability) plans link retirement (or disability) benefits to a worker's earnings over the worker's earning years or some part thereof. Workers pay into these plans with the assurance that they will receive retirement or disability benefits in some proportion to their average wages. The plan might state this promised benefit as an exact dollar amount, or, more commonly, it may calculate a benefit through a plan formula that considers such factors as overall earnings and length of employment. For example, a benefit formula might specify a benefit of 2 percent of average salary for the last ten years of employment for every year of service with the employer, adjusted by other factors such as age. Benefits can be paid from these plans because the funds for all the workers in the plan—from those who have just come into the plan to those ready to collect their benefits from the plan—are pooled into one fund. Benefits are usually based on life expectancy. Those who live longer than expected receive more total benefits than those who do not live as long. *Defined benefit* plans are characteristic of most state employee retirement plans, as well as a diminishing number of plans in the private sector. *Defined benefit* plans became the model for the development of Social Security.

Somewhat in contrast, *defined contribution retirement (or disability) plans* have become the basis for a growing number of private retirement plans today. In *defined contribution* plans, an employee and often his or her employer place an agreed-upon amount of money into a fund for the worker. The benefit to the worker at the time of retirement or disability depends upon the actual amounts put into the fund and how well the investments in the fund increase in value over time. The contributions of the employer, if any, are determined by some sort of employment agreement, so that after a period of time, the worker may have access to part or all of the funds in his or her account. No specific benefit is guaranteed in *defined contribution* plans. The value of the individual's account will fluctuate due to changes in the value of investments. *Defined contribution* plans have become a more popular private sector preference for employer-sponsored retirement plans, since the risks associated with inflation, financial return on the investment, and/or prolonged worker illness or job loss, for example, are borne by the individual rather than by the pension provider. By contrast, in the case of Social Security, a *defined benefit plan,* the financial risks are borne by the government.

The fact that Social Security has been enlarged to include people other than the specific retiree does not change the basic principles of a *defined benefit* plan upon which Social Security is constructed. As discussed in detail below, all the beneficiaries covered under Social Security must have some legal relationship to the primary insured worker. The benefits to the legally defined beneficiary have been guaranteed by the worker's financial participation in the plan.

Beneficiaries

Eligibility for benefits under Title II has become complex as Congress has redefined the beneficiary pool over the years. Because all Title II benefits are guaranteed by law, those people who meet the legal criteria are entitled to receive the specified benefits and thus possess a legal entitlement to the benefits.[a] Since workers have also been told that their taxes are contributing to their own retirement, Title II benefits constitute a political entitlement as well. The conditions for eligibility have been changed over the years both as a means

---

[a] As noted in the introduction to this chapter, the legal status of beneficiary rights under Title II is ambiguous. In 1960, the U.S. Supreme Court ruled that employees have a "noncontractual" interest in Title II Social Security that is "earned" but that it is not an "accrued property right." See *Flemming v. Nestor* 363 U.S. 603 (1960). This concern is discussed further in Chapter 10.

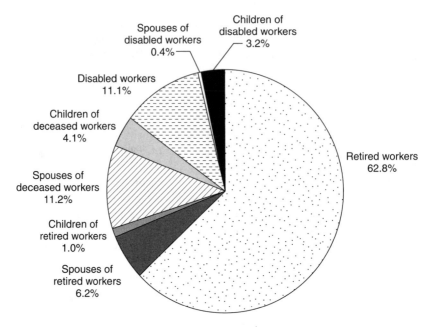

Figure 2.2. Distribution of Social Security Beneficiaries, by Type of Benefit Received.
Source: Social Security Administration, *Annual Statistical Supplement, 2001* (draft), Table 5.A1 (available at www.ssa.gov/statistics/Supplement/2001/index.html).

to include more beneficiaries, at some times, and at other times, as a means to reduce overall Social Security spending. A summary of the major changes affecting the beneficiary pool is provided in Figure 2.2 and also is discussed below. The most up-to-date eligibility criteria, as well as more details than those summarized below, are available from the Social Security Administration (SSA) website.[b]

Retired workers are the primary beneficiary group of Title II Social Security. The criteria for benefits for **retired workers** under Title II are relatively straightforward compared with eligibility criteria for other beneficiary groups. A worker must have worked in employment covered by Social Security and paid into the program for a specific number of quarters, some of which in the later work years must be consecutive. Presently, the retirement age to receive full benefits depends on the worker's year of birth. For people born before 1938, the retirement age is 65. For those born after 1938, the retirement age increases by two months per birth year, reaching age 66 for people born in 1943. The retirement age begins at age 66 for workers born between 1944 and 1954, again increasing in two-month increments until reaching age 67 for workers born in 1960 or later. In general, covered retired workers can take reduced benefits beginning at age 62.

---

[b] www.ssa.gov/work/index

Wives and husbands of eligible beneficiaries who are at retirement age have the option of taking her or his own retirement benefit, or if one spouse has a benefit less than an amount equal to one-half of the other spouse's retirement benefit, that benefit is brought up to one-half of the benefit of the higher-benefit spouse depending on whichever is greater.

Disabled workers with Title II coverage may receive a portion of their retirement benefits before retirement age if they are medically and vocationally certified to be permanently and totally disabled and are thus unable to work. This feature of Title II, disability insurance, was created in 1956 as shown in Figure 1.1 (Chapter 1). To qualify for disability benefits, a worker who attains age 31 or older must have earned at least 20 consecutive quarters during the 40 calendar quarters ending with the quarter in which the disability began. In general, workers disabled at ages 24 through 30 must have earned consecutive quarters in one-half of the calendar quarters between age 21 and the calendar quarter in which the disability began. Workers under the age of 24 need six consecutive quarters in the 12-quarter period ending with the quarter of disability onset.

Widows and widowers: Figure 1.1 reflects the changes Congress made in 1939 extending Social Security benefits to survivors of covered workers, thus greatly expanding the beneficiary pool. Survivors of covered beneficiaries, either **widows or widowers,** or **children** are eligible beneficiaries under Title II. The amount of the survivor's benefit today is based on a percentage of the deceased's basic Social Security benefit, as follows: **Widow or widowers** who have reached full retirement age receive 100 percent of the deceased's benefit. The benefit for widow or widowers age 60–64 ranges from about 71 to 94 percent of the deceased's benefit, depending on the survivor's age. In addition, a disabled widow or widower may receive benefits as early as age 50 based on a percentage of the deceased's benefit. A widow or widower at any age may receive up to 75 percent of the insured's benefits if he or she takes care of the deceased's child under age 16.

Unmarried children: Children up to age 19 may receive benefits, based on the eligibility of the parent beneficiary, if they are attending elementary or secondary school full time. A child of an otherwise eligible beneficiary can receive benefits at any age if he or she was disabled before age 22 and remains disabled. Under certain circumstances, benefits can also be paid to stepchildren, grandchildren, or adopted children. Benefits for eligible children and widow or widowers cannot be combined.

Other beneficiary categories also exist: A number of other beneficiary categories exist and are not broken out in Figure 2.1 or Table 2.1. For example, a divorced spouse can receive benefits under the same circumstances as a widow or a widower if the marriage lasted ten years or more. It is important to stress that all the different beneficiary groups require some relationship to a worker who has or had sufficient Social Security Title II coverage. Unlike the assistance programs, the Social Security benefits are not determined by financial need. Rather, in a general sense, the benefits are determined by the worker's contribution (taxes paid based on earnings record) to his or her own personal Social Security account.

While Social Security was designed to provide income support for retired workers, both age and medical condition also define the basic eligibility criteria for each program. Thus, it is possible to be working, with earnings, and still be eligible for retirement or disability benefits. Under the retirement program, if an individual has not reached full retirement age, but is receiving Social Security, the person is penalized $1.00 for every $2.00 of earnings above $12,480. If the person has not reached the full retirement age, the individual is penalized $1.00 for every $3.00 earned above $33,240 until reaching age 70. A fully covered person may be eligible for disability benefits if the person is determined medically disabled although still working and earning less than $860.00 per month and $900.00 for the blind. Other detailed criteria apply to disability benefits, but in general these earnings amounts are relevant for 2007 and are subject to change in subsequent years.

Social Security beneficiaries are taxed, and benefits are counted as taxable income.

Benefits

Not only is defining the beneficiaries complex, but computing the actual benefit is complicated as well. Like most *defined benefit* plans, Social Security Title II benefits are computed by a complex three-step formula.

Step one: The first step in the process of benefit determination requires determining whether the person qualifies for benefits. To qualify for Social Security benefits, everyone born in 1929 or later needs 40 Social Security credits to be eligible for full retirement benefits. Credits are earned at the rate of up to four credits per year, based on average earning levels for that year. In 2005, one credit was earned for each $920 of earnings per quarter, up to the maximum of four credits per year, or a total earnings of $3,680 for the entire year. For 2006, one credit is earned for each $950 of earnings. The required amount of earnings for credits increases each year.

Step two: Once it is determined a person is eligible for benefits, based on earnings and/or age (or disability for the disability part of the program), the amount of earnings of each primary beneficiary during the thirty-five years of greatest covered earnings is averaged and then adjusted or "indexed" to account for changes in average wages since the year the earnings were received. This calculation provides an Average Indexed Monthly Earnings (AIME).

Step three: Finally, a formula is then applied to the AIME to determine the basic benefit, or Primary Insurance Amount (PIA). The formula used to compute the PIA from AIME is weighted to provide a higher PIA-to-AIME ratio for workers with comparatively low earnings. The formula applies declining percentage conversion rates at three AIME brackets. For most retired or disabled workers, the following formula is used to determine the PIA: 90 percent of the first $680 of AIME, plus, 32 percent of the next $4,100 of AIME,

**Table 2.2. Estimated Average Monthly Social Security Benefits
Payable in January 2006, After 2006 4.1% COLA**

All Retired Workers	$1,002
Aged Couple, Both Receiving Benefits	$1,648
Widowed Mother and Two Children	$2,074
Aged Widow(er) Living Alone	$967
Disabled Worker, Spouse, and One or More Children	$1,571
All Disabled Workers	$939

Source: Social Security Administration, Annual Statistical Supplement, 2007.

plus, 15 percent of AIME over $4,100.[c] Because the AIME is computed on the amount of individual earnings up to the earnings ceiling (covered earnings) which is set at a yearly maximum, the formula to achieve the PIA eventually reaches a maximum amount which can be paid in a monthly benefit. For 2006, the maximum benefit payment for retirees born in 1940 reaching full retirement age of 65 and 8 months old is $2053.00 per month. The PIA or benefit is increased each year based on the rise in the Consumer Price Index (CPI). The benefit levels in Table 2.2 below will change each year depending on each year's CPI computation.

Even though the formula weighs benefit payments in favor of lower earning workers, the method of determining the monthly benefit, however, maintains a relationship to the amount of earnings each worker put into the fund during working years. The formulas for determining beneficiary eligibility have become a web of complexity since they change almost every year, as do the formulas for computing benefits. An example of this complexity is shown in the abstract of one example of beneficiary determination summarized in Box 2.1 from rules provided by the Social Security Administration.

Not all employment is covered by Social Security. For example, members of the clergy are automatically covered unless they choose not to be, and those who work in state and local governments, if covered by a state retirement plan, may, as a group, be exempt from Title II Social Security at the state option. Self-employed are required to participate in Social Security. Even with these and other exemptions, about 96 percent of all full-time workers in the American economy are covered by Title II Social Security. Each applicant for benefits is evaluated individually against the many definitions of the present rules. In other words, these standard rules for determining eligibility are applied individually and fail to establish any uniform benefit amount. Each person must have his or her eligibility and benefit determined individually.

---

[c] PIE computation used for 2007.

Box 2.1 An Example of Eligibility and Benefit Determination

The full retirement age (FRA) is the earliest age at which an unreduced retirement benefit is payable (sometimes referred to as the *normal retirement age*). The age for full retirement benefits is scheduled to rise gradually from age 65 to age 67, with the first incremental increase affecting workers who reached age 62 in the year 2000. Workers over the age of 62 who retire before FRA can receive reduced benefits. The monthly rate of reduction from the full retirement benefit (that is, the PIA) is 5/9 of 1 percent a month for the first thirty six months immediately preceding FRA. The reduction rate is 5/12 of 1 percent a month for any additional months. The maximum overall reduction for early retirement will have risen from 20 percent to 30 percent for those workers who reach age 62 in 2022, when age 67 becomes the full retirement age.

If a disabled worker receives a reduced retirement benefit for months before disability entitlement, the disability benefit is reduced by the number of months for which he or she received the reduced benefit.

For workers who postpone their retirement beyond the full retirement age, benefits are increased for each month of nonpayment beyond that age up to age 70. This increase is called a *delayed retirement credit* and is potentially available for any or all months following attainment of the full retirement age (maximum of sixty months for persons who attained age 65 before 2003). The annual rate of increase for delayed retirement credits is 7 percent for workers who reach age 62 in 2002, 7½ percent for workers who reach age 62 in 2003 and 2004, and 8 percent for workers reaching age 62 in 2005 or later.

Source: Social Security Administration, *Handbook of Social Security*, 2008.

Financing Social Security

The payroll tax: Chapter 1 summarized the Committee on Economic Security's deliberations over the payroll tax as the method for financing the Title II program. Social Security is financed by a federal tax on wages, as distinct from a federal tax on income. The Social Security tax burden is equally split between employee and employer. The tax schedule is based on a percentage of pay levied only on the first portion of the pay, creating a form of a payroll or tax cap. The payroll cap is now designed to increase at determined intervals. Both the percentage of the tax and the cap on taxable payroll have increased sufficiently over the years, as shown in Table 2.3, to keep enough money in the trust fund to pay benefits. In the past, as greater funds were needed for Title II Social Security, Congress changed both the rate of tax and raised the cap on taxable income. The changes in the tax rates reflected in Table 2.3 have been made by Congress

Table 2.3. Tax Rate for Employees and Employers in Selected Years

Calendar Year	OASDI	HI	Total
1937–40	1.000	—	1.000
1950–53	1.500	—	1.500
1954–56	2.000	—	2.000
1957–59	2.250	—	2.250
1960–61	3.000	—	3.000
1962	3.125	—	3.125
1963–65	3.625	—	3.625
1966	3.850	0.350	4.200
1967	3.900	0.500	4.400
1968	3.800	0.600	4.400
1969–70	4.200	0.600	4.800
1971–72	4.600	0.600	5.200
1973–77	4.850	1.000	5.850
1978	5.050	1.000	6.050
1979–80	5.080	1.050	6.130
1981	5.350	1.300	6.650
1982–83	5.400	1.300	6.700
1984	5.700	1.300	7.000
1985	5.700	1.350	7.050
1986–87	5.700	1.450	7.150
1988–89	6.060	1.450	7.510
1990	6.200	1.450	7.650
2006	6.200	1.450	7.650

Source: Social Security Administration, 2008.

when actuarial forecasts called for more funds to keep the program solvent.[d] In 2007, the cap on taxable Social Security income was $97,500 per year.

Roosevelt was strongly committed to the idea that all workers would build their own retirement funds based on the taxes they paid and those paid by their employers. Like any *defined benefit* retirement program, the Social Security monies would be "earmarked" for that person's retirement based on the formula for determining the amount of the benefit. The Social Security Act was amended to create the Social Security Trust Fund to receive the special Social Security payroll taxes.

The Social Security Trust Funds: All the Social Security taxes that are collected are committed to trust funds. The 1939 Social Security amendments created only one trust fund that functioned to hold the money for the retirement part of the Social Security program. When Social Security for the disabled (disability insurance) was created in 1956, a separate Disability Trust Fund was also established, and when medical insurance (Medicare) was created in 1965,

---

[d] The issue of Trust Fund "solvency" is discussed in Chapter 3.

a Hospital Insurance Trust Fund was created as well. As Table 2.3 indicates, the total Social Security tax is really a combination of taxes to fund all three parts of the program, and the collected taxes are allocated to each of the designated trust funds. Even though all three taxes are collected as a unit, the Social Security taxes (Old Age and Survivors Disability Insurance (OASDI) in Table 2.3) are under the administrative authority of the SSA, while the Hospital Insurance Trust Fund Monies are under the administrative control of the Centers for Medicare and Medicaid. Chapter 7 provides further discussion about the Health Insurance Trust Fund.

Title II Trust Fund: Federal trust funds with tax monies set aside for restricted purposes are not unusual. For example, gasoline taxes are set aside in the Highway Trust Fund for highway construction and maintenance, and taxes on airline tickets and fuel are set aside for airport improvements. Title II Social Security is funded by monies placed into two trust funds: one for the retired, their survivors, and their otherwise eligible beneficiaries, and the other for the disabled. The Title II Social Security trust funds stand out as one of Social Security's most debated, least agreed upon element of all its program features.

There is a mystique about Title II trust funds that seems to defy a single explanation for their existence and conceals the part they play in securing the financial foundation for Title II Social Security, as well as the relationship of these funds to larger American economic policy. The mechanics of the trust funds are relatively straightforward: Money is collected from employees and employers. The monies (taxes) are deposited in the various trust funds, like putting money in special savings accounts. The monies are held in trust, and can only be used to pay Social Security benefits. Each person who works under Social Security coverage has an individual account of the amount of personal (Social Security eligible) earnings, and the earnings record provides the basis for later benefit calculation and benefit payment to that individual. The monies to pay the individual benefits are drawn from the trust funds. The idea is simple "cookie jar" accounting. Put enough money in the cookie jar to pay today's bills and a little extra for a rainy day. In reality, unfortunately, the trust funds are not simple "cookie jar" accounting.

The reason for creating trust fund financing raises the first set of questions. In retrospect, it seems that Roosevelt and his advisors established this form of Title II financing for at least three reasons: First, as pointed out in Chapter 1, considering the kind of program the Committee on Economic Security was creating this method of financing held the best chance passing a test of constitutionality. Second, it seemed an economically sound and prudent way to protect Social Security revenues from being used for general-purpose government. These funds were for Social Security and could not be used for other purposes. Finally, "earmarked" taxes, as Social Security taxes began to be called, satisfied an important political objective. One paid the taxes believing that the money was being set aside for one's own retirement, with the Federal Government acting as the trustee over the funds.

Presently, the trust funds secure the fiscal foundation of the Title II programs. With one minor exception,[e] they are the only source of funding Title II Social Security. The monies in the two Title II trust funds (retirement and disability insurance) can be used only for the purpose of paying benefits provided by those programs. In other words, monies collected for Title II Social Security cannot be used for other government purposes, nor can money collected for the retirement or disability program be used to pay for hospital insurance (HI) benefits, although "inter-fund borrowing" has occasionally taken place under specific limited legislation. Proposals to use Social Security surpluses to pay down the national debt, promoted a few years ago when surpluses in the Social Security retirement fund began to rise, were not possible to implement without borrowing from those funds and thus running up higher deficits in the trust fund accounts.

Although the Social Security Trust Fund monies cannot be spent for purposes other than Social Security, the Federal Government borrows monies from the trust funds, just as the government borrows from financial markets, private individuals, and other countries. Social Security Trust Fund borrowing is restricted to purchase of bonds only by the government, not by the general public. The interest paid on the borrowed funds fluctuates moderately in short term value and, in 2007, earned about 5 percent interest. Government borrowing from private individuals or markets may cost the Federal Government more, so, in effect, reserves in the Social Security Trust Fund have saved federal dollars. In any event, all funds borrowed from the trust funds, plus interest, constitute a fiscal obligation to Title II Social Security. At present, the general-purpose Federal Government owes the Social Security retirement trust fund approximately $1.3 to $1.5 trillion, including interest. At the end of 2005, the total value of the Social Security Trust fund (including government IOUs.) was $1,858,660,000,000.[1] Significant changes to the Social Security retirement program, such as allowing workers to use some of their Social Security retirement obligations to buy private annuities, would have to take into account both losses to the trust fund by diverting payroll taxes to private accounts, and how previously borrowed funds would be returned to the two trust funds so that they remain stable enough to pay benefits.

Title II Trust fund viability: Some of the important policy issues regarding the use of Title II trust funds are discussed in the next chapter. However, considerable discussion revolves around whether the trust funds truly fund Title II Social Security or whether they are some sort of unnecessary funding artifact. Although the trust funds sustain Title II programs, arguably, the reasons for the trust funds are decidedly political in today's world. In other words, from a strictly economic viewpoint, since the Federal Government guarantees Title II Social Security benefits, the two Title II trust funds have limited economic

---

[e] A small infusion of federal general purpose funding is provided to make up a shortfall in funding for low-income Title II beneficiaries.

value for the implementation of Title II Social Security. Benefits could just as easily be paid from general revenue taxes, rather than Social Security taxes. While there are bookkeeping advantages to keeping trust funds, and trust fund surpluses may help keep Title II taxes under control, particularly in periods of fluctuations in the larger economy, there is limited Title II economic need to secure Title II benefits through the trust funds. However, the trust funds do affect the larger economy, although these effects are difficult to establish with undisputed authority. Some have always argued that an accumulation of government assets tend to "freeze" funds that otherwise might be available for private use, while others argue that trust fund assets offer an accounting artifact offsetting general-purpose government indebtedness. Although not discussing Title II trust funds directly, the economic issues of government asset accumulation were recently addressed by Alan Greenspan, when he testified before Congress in 2001.

> I have noted in the past, that the federal government should eschew private asset accumulation because it would be exceptionally difficult to insulate the government's investment decisions from political pressures. Thus, over time, having the federal government hold significant amounts of private assets would risk sub-optimal performance by our capital markets, diminish economic efficiency, and lower overall standards of living than would be achieved otherwise.[2]

Thus, while the necessity of trust funds may be of limited economic value for securing Title II programs, the Title II trust funds may have important policy considerations for the economy at large, and for how Title II social insurance programs will be secured in the future. A further discussion of the policy considerations surrounding Title II trust funds continues in Chapter 3.

According to Eric Patashnik, the trust funds secure Title II Social Security for three reasons: First, the Social Security Trust Funds create financial autonomy for the programs, insulating them from routine government spending decisions. Second, the trust funds are controlled by trustees who depend on elaborate actuarial forecasts, thus removing taxing and spending decisions from a considerable amount of general budgetary pressure and political chicanery. Finally, Patashnik points out, the trust funds act to cement a bond between present workers and future benefits, thus establishing a strong political foundation for the programs.[3] In other words, trust funds secure Title II programs by insulating program decisions from the usual political social welfare debates rather than from any inherent economic value the trust funds might hold.

Preserving the integrity of the trust funds as the requirement for Title II social insurance funding requires the expert knowledge of program administrators and persons well versed in taxing matters. Program decisions made by "experts" provide a degree of insulation from political debates. Particularly in the case of Title II Social Security, expert decisions about the size of the trust funds often determined program decisions. In particular, growing surpluses in the Title II Retirement Trust Fund allowed administrators to pursue program and benefit expansions in order to keep trust fund balances under control. Under these circumstances, it is reasonable to conclude that financing Title II benefit through trust funds account in large measure for the ability of the early Social Security administrators to pursue their program objectives as concluded by Martha Derthick. The program development distinctions between Title II trust fund funding and Title IV general purpose funding, the former based on expert knowledge and the latter based on political discord, present striking contrasts for the study of social welfare politics.

Initial ambivalence about Title II trust funds: Undoubtedly, initial ambiguity about the use of trust funds to fund Title II Social Security has led to the uncertainty about this method of financing today. Roosevelt's views and those of his advisors about Title II financing lend further mystery to original economic intent of the Title II trust fund. Roosevelt expected that Title II Social Security should be actuarially sound,[4] but the meaning of an actuarially sound program was not exactly clear. Originally, Title II trust funds were projected to be adequate until 1965, and after that time they would begin to run a deficit. When Roosevelt learned about this apparent shortfall in revenues, apparently from Treasury Secretary Morgenthau the day before Roosevelt was to present the Economic Security Act to Congress,[5] Roosevelt ordered the Committee on Economic Security to revise their tables to guarantee actuarial soundness forever. However, Morgenthau abandoned his initial view of actuarial soundness in 1939.

> Four years of experience have shown that the benefits of the act will be so widely diffused that supplemental funds from general tax revenues may be substituted—without substantial inequity—for a considerable proportion of the expected interest earnings from the large reserve contemplated by present law. Therefore, it becomes apparent that the argument for a large reserve does not have the validity which 4 years ago it seemed to possess.[6]

Following the lead of his Treasury Secretary, Roosevelt, too, reversed his earlier view of actuarial soundness and recommended to Congress that the 1940 scheduled tax increases not be implemented. Altmeyer reported, "The [Congressional] committee also decided to eliminate the increase in the contribution rate which was scheduled to take place January 1, 1940, from 1 percent . . . suggested by Secretary of the Treasury Morgenthau. . . . This, of course, represented a complete reversal of [Morganthau's] attitude in 1935."[7] According to Roosevelt,

> those [Social Security] taxes were never a problem of economics. They are politics all the way through. We put those payroll contributions there so as to give the contributors a legal, moral and political right to collect their pensions and their unemployment benefits. With those taxes in there, no damn politician can ever scrap my Social Security program.[8]

Spending Social Security Funds

Whatever the reasons for trust fund financing, there are ample funds in the Title II accounts to secure Title II benefit obligations. The current payroll taxes are paid into the trust funds and are used to pay benefits. The difference between what is paid in and what is paid out in benefits accrues to the trust funds. In 2006, for example, $229,000,000,000 was paid into the trust funds; $143,600,000,000 was paid out in benefits leaving a surplus of $85,000,000,000 that stayed in the trust funds, swelling them to their present size. At the present time, the Social Security retirement trust fund has enough money to pay all beneficiary obligations until approximately 2041, assuming that Social Security benefits and income from taxes remain constant. After approximately 2041, taxes and/or benefits would have to be adjusted in order to keep the Social Security program financially solvent. In other words, if income and benefits remain constant, beginning in 2041, there would not be enough money in income or in trust fund reserves to pay the present level of benefits. The next chapter discusses the policy issues of Social Security trust fund financing in more detail. See Box 2.2.

As a result of decisions made by Roosevelt and his advisors, Social Security revenues collected in the present are spent on present-day benefit commitments. In other words, today's payroll taxes pay today's Social Security recipients. The idea that present-day workers were building their own retirement "nest egg" with their monthly "contributions" never had a basis in economic reality. The policy problems connected with this kind of "pay-as-you-go" Social Security or with "inter-generational transfer payments" are discussed in Chapter 3, but it is important to note that the same kinds of problems exist with nongovernmental *defined benefit* forms of retirement insurance. The reality of today's Social Security spending is: what comes in goes out. The reality of Social Security pay-as-you-go spending has raised fears, particularly by the younger working-age population that when they reach retirement age there will be no money left for them. However, as long as the statutory authority for Social Security remains in its present form benefits will have to be paid, regardless of the size of the trust fund or the ratio of workers who pay Social Security taxes to the beneficiaries who receive payments.

A Board of Trustees was established under the Social Security Act to oversee the financial operations of the Old Age and Survivors Insurance (OASI) and Disability Insurance (DI) Trust Funds. The Board is composed of six members. Four members serve by virtue of their positions in the Federal Government: the Secretary of the Treasury, who is the Managing Trustee; the Secretary of Labor; the Secretary of Health and Human Services; and the Commissioner of Social Security. The other two members are appointed by the President. The Deputy Commissioner of the SSA is designated as Secretary of the Board. The Social Security Act requires that the Trustees report annually to the Congress on the financial and actuarial status of the OASI and DI Trust Funds.

**Box 2.2 Concluding Summary of the 2006 Annual Report
of the Trustees of the Social Security Trust Fund**

Annual [benefit] cost will begin to exceed tax income in 2017 for the combined OASDI Trust Funds, which are projected to become exhausted and thus unable to pay scheduled benefits in full on a timely basis in 2040 under the long-range intermediate assumptions. For the trust funds to remain solvent throughout the seventy-five-year projection period, the combined payroll tax rate could be increased during the period in a manner equivalent to an immediate and permanent increase of 2.02 percentage points, benefits could be reduced during the period in a manner equivalent to an immediate and permanent reduction of 13.3 percent, general revenue transfers equivalent to $4.6 trillion (in present value) could be made during the period, or some combination of approaches could be adopted. Significantly larger changes would be required to maintain solvency beyond seventy-five years.

The projected trust fund deficits should be addressed in a timely way to allow for a gradual phasing in of the necessary changes and to provide advance notice to workers. The sooner adjustments are made the smaller and less abrupt they will have to be. Social Security plays a critical role in the lives of this year's 49 million beneficiaries, and 162 million covered workers and their families. With informed discussion, creative thinking, and timely legislative action, we will ensure that Social Security continues to protect future generations.

Note: The 2008 report concluded that "timely benefits" could be paid until 2041.
Source: Social Security Administration, *Annual Report of the Trustees of the Federal Old Age and Survivors Trust Funds*. Washington, DC: U.S Government printing Office, 20.

Although the Board of Trustees must project Social Security income and expenditures seventy-five years into the future, there is no requirement that the trust fund must hold all the money to meet obligations that far into the future. Both actuary projections and the management of the trust funds created problems almost immediately. "Static" actuary forecasting assumed both a lineal growth in population and stable economic conditions. Only years later did the trust fund actuaries adopt a form of "dynamic" forecasting. Thus demographic and economic fluctuations, particularly during World War II, created trust fund instability. Trust fund management also created problems. At the beginning of the Social Security program, large sums were flowing into the fund but almost no benefits were being paid because workers had not yet "earned" enough credits to qualify for them. Together, both conditions created the threat of large surpluses as World War II ended.

Although the Title II trust funds more likely serve political objectives, there are larger economic issues associated with this kind of social insurance financing. Keeping enough revenue in the trust funds to preserve the political integrity of Title II Social Security, but striking a balance between what is needed to keep Title II Social Security actuarially sound without burdening the economy, seems to pit Title II politics against Title II economics. As the social insurances operate today, the size of the Title II trust funds is determined by both income and expenditures, and both depend on demographic estimates, employment estimates, payroll estimates, and other factors. For example, in times of high wages and economic growth, the funds become quite full, but during periods of high unemployment and low wages, the fund may become quite small. Future total benefit payments are equally uncertain. The number of beneficiaries who will need to draw on the fund depends on demographic factors such as longevity and on national economic conditions as well such as the size and composition of the labor force. In many ways, however, the trust funds using long range estimates of these factors help smooth out revenue unevenness that these factors could precipitate. It is safe to assume, however, that fluctuations such as those in Social Security retirement and disability are not unusual in *defined benefit* type retirement plans. Perhaps, the most important summary statement about Title II Social Security financing lies in the fact that there are enough Title II funds, both in reserves and in current incomes, to fully fund Title II until approximately 2041 for retirees and their related beneficiaries, and perhaps for as long for the disabled,[f] based on the best, although conservative, estimates of the Trustees of the Social Security Trust Funds.

Administering Social Security

Social Security under Title II is administered solely by the Federal Government; state governments are not involved. However, state governments are responsible for making medical decisions regarding the eligibility criteria for the disabled. When the Social Security Act was created in 1935, the Title II program was administered by a separate Social Security Board, but in 1939, when President Roosevelt created the Federal Security Agency, the Social Security Board became a federal agency within this larger sub-cabinet-level agency. In 1946, the Social Security Board was decommissioned, and the Social Security Administration was established to administer Title II Social Security and was later reorganized into the Department of Health Education and Welfare in 1953. When the Department of Health, Education, and Welfare was reorganized again in 1980 into the Department of Health and Human Services (DHHS), the SSA remained an agency in the new Department, but in 1994, at the urging of President Clinton, Congress upgraded the SSA to an independent agency in the executive branch of government.

While an agency in the Department of Health and Human Services, the SSA's activities concentrated on providing those programs of Title II described above, although from its inception it always acted independently as its history shows. The parent department DHHS, however, maintained policy-making

---

[f] The expected beneficiary period for the disabled is slightly less optimistic with respect to resources in the Disability Trust Fund.

authority for the programs administered by the SSA. Given its authority now as an independent agency, however, the SSA holds a position at an equal level with the DHHS, raising speculation that its decisions for Title II Social Security and Title XVI Supplemental Security Income may become less well integrated with social welfare policy decisions exercised under other sections of the Social Security Act.[g] Time will tell how much these changes will influence the program structure of Title II Social Security.

The central administration of the SSA is now headed by a commissioner. A separate Social Security Advisory Board of seven members provides nonbinding recommendations to the SSA. SSA employs more than 60,000 persons in its central Baltimore office, its 10 regional offices, and its 1,300 field offices. SSA also includes a Chief Actuary who has responsibility for developing forecasts of the programs' needs. The field organization is decentralized to provide service at the local level, and the 1,300 field offices provide eligibility and beneficiary services to Title II Social Security beneficiaries. The Social Security retirement system is highly efficient. Over 49 million beneficiaries are receiving monthly payments, including approximately 1 million new beneficiaries each year. The Title II programs had a 99.9 percent accuracy of payments in 2004, and the costs for administering the program are 0.9 percent of the total benefits paid.

Related Retirement Instruments

In addition to the programs provided by Title II Social Security under the authority of the Social Security Act, other related retirement (and disability) instruments exist in the public and private sectors that have important connections to Social Security. In one of his early discussions of Social Security President Roosevelt expected Social Security to contribute only a part of retirement benefits. He explained that he anticipated that about a third of retirement income should come from Social Security, a third from personal saving, and the other third from private pensions. Thus, the overall effectiveness of Title II Social Security, by design, is linked with private pension instruments. Figure 2.3, below, shows the steady growth of private pension plans over the past decades. These private pension plans continue to increase in importance as they intersect with Social Security to provide retirement and survivor benefits to a growing number of Americans. Figure 2.3 also shows the decline of *defined benefit* plans in favor of *defined contribution* plans.

Private sector pension programs consist mostly of employee–employer plans established under a wide range of employment contracts. In general, such plans include contributions from both employees and employers and include the use of government-legislated retirement instruments, such as Individual Retirement Accounts (IRA) and Internal Revenue Code Section 401-Ks, which

---

[g] The Social Security Administration, however, is not a cabinet level administrative agency.

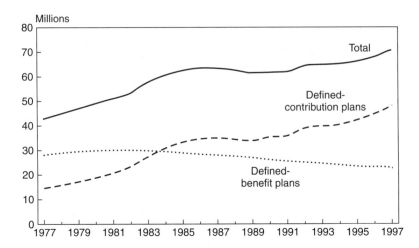

Figure 2.3. Private Pension Plans.
Source: Congressional Budget Office, *A Primer on Social Security.* Washington, DC, 2004.

provide a tax deferment for a portion of income invested in forms of private securities under these plans. Both *defined benefit* and *defined contribution* plans are found among these private pension programs.

In 1974, Congress created The Employee Retirement Income Security Act (ERISA) to protect the assets placed in federally approved retirement plans. ERISA specifies when employees must be allowed to become participants in a plan administered by a private employer, how long employees have to work before they have a nonforfeitable interest in their pension, how long participants can be away from their job before it might affect their benefit, and whether their spouse has a right to part of their pension in the event of their death. ERISA does not require any employer to establish a pension plan. It only requires that those who establish plans meet certain minimum standards. Nor does the law specify how much money a participant must be paid as a benefit.

Although approved pension plans must be established with the intention of being continued indefinitely, employers may terminate plans. If a plan terminates or becomes insolvent, ERISA provides participants some protection. If it is a tax-qualified plan, where the employer receives a tax credit for the plan, a participant's accrued benefit must become 100 percent vested immediately upon plan termination, to the extent that the specific plan is funded.

The Pension Benefit Guarantee Corporation (PBGC) was also created by the ERISA of 1974 to encourage the growth of *defined benefit* pension plans and to provide timely and uninterrupted payment of pension benefits if private plans fail. PBGC collects insurance premiums from employers who sponsor tax-qualified pension plans and earns money from the premiums and investments it receives from funds from pension plans it takes over. In the case of a failed private pension plan, in 2007, PBGC paid monthly retirement benefits, up to a guaranteed maximum, to about 459,000 retirees in 3,287 pension plans that ended since 1975. PBGC holds supervisory responsibility for the current and future pensions of about 934,000 people, and as many as 40 million persons are enrolled in tax-qualified pensions programs that are supervised by PBGC.

An employer offering a tax-qualified plan can voluntarily ask to close its single-employer pension plan in either a standard or a distress termination. In a standard termination, the plan must have enough money to pay all benefits, whether vested or not, before the plan can end. After workers receive promised benefits, in the form of a lump sum payment or an insurance company annuity, PBGC guarantee ends. In a distress termination, where the plan does not have enough money to pay all benefits (underfunded plans), the employer must prove severe financial distress—for instance, the likelihood that continuing the plan would force the company to shut down. Under those circumstances, PBGC will pay guaranteed benefits, usually covering a large part of total earned benefits, and make strong efforts to recover funds from the employer. In addition, PBGC may seek to close a single employer pension plan without the employer's consent to protect the interests of workers. In any event, PBGC must act to terminate a plan that cannot pay current benefits.

Not unlike characteristics of all *defined benefit* plans, the maximum pension benefit guaranteed by PBGC is set by law and amended yearly. For plans ended in 2004, workers who retire at age 65 can receive up to $3,698.86 a month (depending on the employer–employee agreement) in the event that the employer plan is taken over by PBGC. The guarantee is lower for those who retire early or when there is a benefit for a survivor. The guarantee, of course, is based on years worked and amount of contribution to the plan and may be increased for those who retire after age 65.

Employers of tax-qualified pension plans pay PBGC yearly insurance premiums: $2.60 per worker or retiree in multiemployer plans; $19 per worker or retiree plus $9 for each $1,000 of unfunded vested benefits in single employer plans in 2007. Premium rates increase only if Congress approves.

In 2004, President Bush reported that the large number of employer underfunded *defined benefit* retirement programs that have been terminated has created a record deficit of more than $23 billion by PBGC. Bush also called for and received new legislation to correct both underfunding by companies and increasing company payments to PBGC for tax-qualified plans to insure the vitality of these plans. Subsequently, Congress passed, and the president signed into law, the Private Pension Protection Act of 2006 designed to shore up the assets of PBGC by adjusting the formulas for insurance payments. This legislation also contained provisions to encourage the development of *defined contribution* plans. While the legislation broke little new ground, it did contain policy elements that will encourage the parallel development of private retirement instruments and Social Security. Some of the policy implications of this most recent pension protection legislation are discussed in the next chapter.

The Treasury Department's Internal Revenue Service is responsible for ensuring compliance with the Internal Revenue Code, which establishes the rules for operating a tax-qualified pension plan, including pension plan funding and vesting requirements. A pension plan that is tax qualified can offer special tax benefits to the employer sponsoring the plan by offsetting part of the Social Security taxes the employer would normally be required to pay. Clearly, the growing value of private pension plans has important consequences for the integrity of Title II programs. The Federal Government has undertaken efforts to protect the integrity of these plans, since if plans fail, at least part of the burden of protecting retirement income falls to Title II.

From a program standpoint, proposals for strengthening Social Security Title II by blending Social Security and private investment instruments would require the development of new benefit structures for Social Security, as well as improvement in the management of investment options in the private sector. If the Federal Government were responsible for the investment, rather than the individual worker, additional regulation of the investment instruments would also have to be considered.

Conclusion

Title II of the Social Security Act, often referred to as the Social Security program, extends itself well beyond providing benefits to retired persons. Social Security has expanded over the years of its existence from a program to provide benefits to previously retired workers to a comprehensive income maintenance program, perhaps similar to that envisioned by the early Social Security administrators. But the incremental expansion of program elements and the range of beneficiary payments has produced a fragmented Social Security program, rather than a well designed and carefully thought out approach to the economic needs of the retired, the disabled, and those who are dependent on them for their financial security.

Under Title II, social welfare development in America has been accomplished by extending original Social Security Act programs into forms that attempt to respond to the nation's present-day social welfare needs, and Title II social insurance offers a vivid case example of program development through incremental beneficiary changes. Title II program development through beneficiary expansion has extended the social insurance initiatives of the Federal Government without clear political support for what have become separate Title II social insurance programs. An income security floor has been successfully established for American workers, but it is built on an old foundation that strains to support it.

Title II Social Security programs project a simplicity that belies their underlying complexity. Every program subcategory, such as those identified in Table 2.1 contains many program subcategories. Two examples are provided in Box 2.3 below. For example, Box 2.3 identifies a program called the Government Offset Pension that creates a subprogram category for spouses, widows, and widowers who receive a government/civil service pension. These people are treated differently from spouses who may receive a private pension but who did not establish their own Title II Social Security benefit either. Another

example reflected in Box 2.3 modifies benefits to children of eligible beneficiaries. A maximum family benefit limits a child's benefit to a maximum
determined by the number of dependents in the family. While the value of
the primary beneficiary is not reduced, the maximum family benefit establishes a subprogram for children within the larger program category. That is,
dependent children are eligible for half of the benefit of a Title II beneficiary
unless that child lives in a large family. This gradual atomization of Title II
programs has become characteristic of the entire Title II program, and while
not unexpected in a program forced to develop cautiously, it seriously weakens
the comprehensiveness of the social welfare obligation assumed under Title II
social insurance. At the very least, the present-day Title II Social Security program constitutes patchwork of social welfare commitments that work relatively
well under the circumstances, but labor under the weight of their fragmented
commitments.

Box 2.3 Two Examples of Social Security Sub-Program Beneficiary Categories

Spousal Benefits: If a person receives a pension from a government job
in which they did not pay Social Security taxes, some or all of that persons' Social Security spouse's, widow's or widower's benefit may be offset
due to receipt of that pension. This offset is referred to as the Government Pension Offset. The offset will reduce the amount of spouse's, widow's
or widower's Social Security benefits by two-thirds of the amount of the
government pension. Thus, persons who receive a monthly civil service
pension of $600, two-thirds of that, or $400, must be used to offset spouse's,
widow's or widower's Social Security benefits. Thus, persons eligible for
a $500 spouse's benefit, will receive $100 per month from Social Security
($500 − $400 = $100).

Generally, however, spousal benefits will not be reduced if the person is
receiving a government pension that is not based on their earnings (or a
private pension), the person is a state or local employee whose government
pension is based on a job where the person was paying Social Security taxes,
and the last day of employment was before July 1, 2004, or received or were
eligible to receive a government pension before December 1982 and meet
all the requirements for Social Security spouse's benefits in effect in January
1977, or received or were eligible to receive a federal, state or local government pension before July 1, 1983, and were receiving one-half support from
the person's spouse.

Children's Benefits: When someone qualifies for Social Security retirement benefits, their children may also qualify to receive benefits based on
the person's Social Security record. An eligible child can be a biological
child, adopted child or stepchild, and a dependent grandchild may also

continued

Box 2.3 continued

qualify. To receive benefits, the child must be unmarried and be under age 18, or be 18–19 years old and a full-time student (no higher than grade 12), or be 18 or older and disabled from a disability that started before age 22.

Normally, benefits stop when children reach age 18 unless they are disabled. However, if the child is still a full-time student at a secondary (or elementary) school at age 18, benefits will continue until the child graduates or until two months after the child becomes age 19, whichever is first.

Within a family, each qualified child may receive a monthly payment up to one-half of the primary beneficiary's full retirement benefit amount, but there is a limit to the amount that can be paid to the family as a whole. This total depends on the amount of the beneficiary's benefit and the number of family members who also qualify on the beneficiary's record. The total varies, but it is generally equal to about 150–180 percent of the beneficiary's retirement benefit. Each family member entitled to a monthly benefit will receive one. The total benefits received by the family, however, cannot exceed the family maximum amount. That amount is divided among all entitled dependents. The more dependents who receive benefits on the worker's Social Security record, the lower the benefit amount will be for each dependent. However, the family maximum does not affect the wage earner's benefit.

Source: Abstracted from the Social Security Administration, 2008. Obtuse language is in the original.

Title II funding also raises issues for future Social Security program development. The political value of the Title II trust funds may be diminishing under the weight of its economic burdens. Earmarked Social Security taxes are completely dependent on earnings to continue to fund benefits, and as these tax rates rise, they become more intolerable as burdens on earnings. Although the tax cap is expanding, the pool of payroll taxes, by design, is regressive since the current benefit structure is tied to earnings. Trust funds protect necessary-to-fund benefits resources, and they flatten out larger economic fluctuations assuring reserves necessary to provide a steady stream of benefits. However, earnings as the base for generating the almost exclusive source of revenue for Title II trust funds may be reaching their maximum. The Social Security Trustees do take changing employment trends into their estimates, but labor markets have changed significantly in the past seventy years and will continue to do so in the future. The shrinking ratio of workers to beneficiaries raises a legitimate concern as long as Title II financing is dependent on payroll taxes rather than were Title II funding supported by other revenue sources.

There are other reasons for concern about the future of Title II Social Security that are examined as policy issues in the next chapter. The complex, somewhat disjointed program development, coupled with funding issues raise specific program problems that have eroded the overall success of Title II social insurance, in spite of the essential value these programs ensure to the individuals who benefit from them.

The payroll tax, the trust fund reserves, and the projected needs of Social Security fail to establish a clear picture of the fiscal issues raised by Social Security and how these issues will be addressed beyond incremental marginal program changes. For example, future funding for Social Security can be maintained by exercising different tax policies, changing benefit formulas, modifying beneficiary categories, expanding coverage to include more tax paying workers, or any number of other options. But excluding consideration of options allow Title II Social Security to drift from one "crisis" to the next. Without a clear social welfare objective for Title II Social Security, combined with a political will to implement such an objective, the future of Title II Social Security appears at the limit of the present form of benefit expansion and stands in danger of unraveling a key element in America's social welfare enterprise. In this regard, perhaps the future of Social Security programs will depend on substituting economic soundness in exchange for political safety. These and other difficult policy issues will be addressed in the next chapter.

NOTES

1. The 2006 Annual Report of the board of Trustees of the Federal Old Age and Survivors Insurance and Federal Disability Insurance Trust Funds, 14.
2. Testimony of Chairman Alan Greenspan Before the Committee on the Budget, U.S. Senate, *Outlook for the Federal Budget and Implications for Fiscal Policy.* January 25, 2001.
3. Eric Patashnik, *Putting Trust in the US Budget. Federal Trust Funds and the Politics of Commitment* (Cambridge, UK: Cambridge University Press, 2000). See page 69 and as follows.
4. Edwin Witte, *The Development of the Social/Security Act* (Madison: University of Wisconsin Press, 1953), 74.
5. See Arthur Altmeyer, *The Formative Years of Social Security* (Madison: University of Wisconsin, 1968), 29. And Frances Perkins, *The Roots of Social Security* (Washington, DC: U.S. Government Printing Office, 1963), 30.
6. F.J. Crowley, "Financing Social Security Program—Then and Now," U.S. Congress, Joint Economic Committee, *Studies in Public Welfare* (Washington, DC: U.S. Government Printing Office, 1974), 28.
7. Altmeyer, *The Formative Years of Social Security*, 103.
8. Quoted in William E. Leuchtenburg, *Franklin D. Roosevelt and the New Deal* (New York: Harper and Row, 1963), 133.

3

Title II: The Policy Structure of Old Age, Survivors, and Disability Insurance

Introduction

Viewed from the perspective of the major policy varieties that exist under the Social Security Act (see Chapter 1), Title II Social Security maintains considerable clarity with respect to entitlement and administration of policy structure. Eligibility for Social Security retirement, survivors, and disability insurances is established based on law, and all of Title II Social Security is administered exclusively by the Federal Government, except for determining medical eligibility for disability insurance, a responsibility which rests with the states. Social Security is a cash program. However, Social Security's web of different, sometimes overlapping program elements, discussed in Chapter 2, creates economic and political vulnerabilities and seriously erodes its policy clarity; its cascading list of beneficiaries diverts its policy focus and detracts from its social welfare legitimacy as an entitlement program.

The Policy of Back Door Program Development

The policy issues that provided the environment for the creation of Title II Social Security in 1935 continue to influence the policy issues that confront Title II Social Security today. The bravado of those who framed the original Title II Social Security program was tempered by their reluctance to seek the comprehensive form of cradle-to-the-grave social insurance that they envisioned. The way Title II Social Security developed may have been the only course that could have been followed to realize the vision, but this path, "back door" program development, destabilized the basic idea of a government-guaranteed pension for retired workers. In other words, no one on the Committee on Economic Security or their advisors argued that Title II, as it was proposed to Congress, was a first step in a more comprehensive social insurance scheme, in spite of the dreams they held. Instead, the comprehensive structure of Title II Social Security today was built on the back of a more modest ideological and political commitment to the welfare of America's aged retirees who built their own retirement fund based on a portion of their wages.

Title II Social Security developed by gradually expanding its beneficiary base. Social Security's early program administrators, particularly Arthur Altmeyer and his protégée Wilbur Cohen,[1] had clear, if not fully articulated, designs for Social Security. Rather than proposing and promoting new social insurance programs, the early administrators proposed and supported the creation of new beneficiary groups within the existing Social Security structure. For example, instead of proposing a separate social insurance program, which would provide income for survivors of workers, the early Title II administrators proposed extending existing benefit eligibility to this group. In reality, this "back door" Title II Social Security expansion created new programs to fit the policy objectives of the early administrators without attracting significant political discourse over the direction of social insurance. Only fiscal questions, rather than political questions, were raised over an expansion of beneficiaries. "Can we afford it?" rather than "should we do it?" framed Social Security debates, and, because the Title II Social Security Trust Fund was always full, the answer was always "yes." The Social Security programs for survivors, widows and widowers, children, and formula adjustments to add value to the Social Security benefits for low-income workers were all created by an expansion of eligible beneficiaries. The major Title II beneficiary groups are summarized in Figure 2.1.

The effort to extend Title II Social Security to the disabled, finally established in 1956, broke with the practice of program development by expanding beneficiary groups. As discussed later in this chapter, the creation of Aid to the Totally and Permanently Disabled under the authority of Title II established a separate, distinct program category as a part of Title II social insurance, and as such it was fraught with political controversy during its development, which took over six years.

Expanding Social Security by enlarging the beneficiary pool has been a subtle form of program development, implemented under the social welfare political radar and without a clear policy base for that particular expansion. The new programs created by enlarging Social Security's beneficiary base lack some of the established policy commitments of the original Social Security program designed to insure income for retired workers. A result of incremental program expansion by adding eligible beneficiaries shifts the whole of Title II away from its original social insurance principle. For example, spouses are now entitled to a proportional Social Security benefit based on the benefit paid to the primary beneficiary, without a reduction in the benefit to the primary beneficiary. While this kind of program development may find support within a framework of defined benefit type retirement programs, it was easily attacked for its resemblance to welfare rather than social insurance. In other words, Social Security's spousal beneficiary element, like others that were created over the years, was established without the need to justify it as new social welfare initiatives undertaken by the Federal Government. Instead, beneficiary extensions were justified as expansions of a basic social insurance commitment that, in turn, would reduce the need for welfare assistance.

The heated exchange between Arthur Altmeyer and Senator Taft in 1950, reported at the conclusion of Chapter 1, reflects the depth of administrative struggles to avoid attaching a welfare stigma to social insurance. The formula designed to give low-income earners proportionally higher benefits than their higher-earning peers was not a welfare principle, Altmeyer indignantly stated, but "a sound social insurance principle." Social insurance was earned, through work, and thus was an entitlement. Welfare was not earned but a charitable act that Americans accepted with disdain. Social insurance epitomized personal independence. Workers were setting part of their earnings aside for their later use in retirement. Welfare epitomized dependency. No American is elevated by a "handout" from the government, or even from a neighbor. Respect comes with self-sufficiency in America. Social Security's "back door" program development conferred a statutory legitimacy on expanded federal social welfare commitments without engaging political debate over their appropriateness. While these original administrators tried to draw a sharp line between social insurance and welfare, the program expansions they achieved, indeed, resembled welfare more than social insurance.[a]

Changing public attitudes about the elderly and new expectations about retirement needs and social insurances only encouraged back door Social Security program development. For example, in 1946, survivors of war veterans were provided with benefits not as a separate program but by including them in the Social Security beneficiary pool. In 1956, partial benefits were extended to women who retired at age 62, and in 1961, the provision was extended to men as a social accommodation, creating another beneficiary group within Social Security. In 1960, benefits became payable to the disabled at any age. In 1972, all persons aged 72 and older were granted a minimum Social Security benefit. Automatic yearly benefit increases which replaced sporadic increases by Congress were motivated by objectives designed to keep Social Security free of politics while insuring that benefits would keep pace with costs of living. These and other changes created new beneficiary groups and expanded benefits to existing beneficiaries.

The Disability Insurance, created in 1956, represents a clear contrast to the back door approach to program development under the original Title II program. Instead of expanding the beneficiary pool to include disabled persons, disability insurance was created as a separate program entity; it was funded by a separate payroll tax, paid by the worker and his employer, and the income from the payroll tax was earmarked to a separate trust fund.

---

[a] Edward Berkowitz notes. "But of course there was debate in 1939 over this question, within an advisory council and within Congress, just not much political opposition from Democrats or Republicans because of the political and fiscal situations at that particular moment." Comments to author.

Even with its own funding mechanism in place, disability insurance was subject to considerable political examination and initially failed to win President Eisenhower's approval because of its potential to create a new "welfare" program, Eisenhower argued, which had little connection to retirement and would simply expand the reach of the Federal Government. Medicare presents an even more forceful contrast to "back door" program development. A form of medical insurance was proposed for the original Social Security Act in 1934, and various proposals frequently were put forward for a form of government-supported medical insurance. States were given funds under the assistance programs to pay some costs of medical care for the poor, but political opposition to health insurance persisted until 1965, when a form of medical insurance for Title II beneficiaries finally emerged.[2] Although a new title, Title XVIII, was created to administer medical insurance for the elderly, the program was still financed through Social Security's original Title II. The political compromises that were required to create Medicare are discussed in Chapter 7; however, both disability insurance and Medicare provide some perspective on the political obstacles inherent in creating new forms of social insurance that back door program development did not have to confront.

The overlooked story of Social Security development through the back door of beneficiary expansion depended on several conditions. First, in order to preserve the legitimacy of social insurance any new benefit or beneficiary had to have a legal relationship to the primary Social Security beneficiary, and any expansion of benefits had to continue a relationship to original beneficiary earnings. A greater public appetite for expanded benefits particularly after World War II lent legitimacy to beneficiary expansion. Second, there had to be enough money to support new program entitlements, and a willingness to spend it on new and existing program participants. Social Security's unique financing framework and skilled, respected, Social Security administrators, who had a vision for social insurance, smoothed program expansion. Third, there had to be support from a sufficiently strong political constituency that would endorse program expansion and marginalize unwanted challenges such as those exhibited by Senator Taft and others. The development of a Social Security policy monopoly buttressed proposals to expand programs. The first condition proved to be a reasonable expansion of insurance coverage, not unlike private sector insurance. But meeting the second and third conditions was much less obvious and has become a major source of Social Security's most difficult policy issues.

This chapter explores the policy issues facing Social Security arising from its back door program development. Both the complex programs and the ever troubling concerns for Social Security's financial and political stability are imbedded in the way Social Security has become more of a comprehensive social welfare commitment since its beginning. Although the original anxieties about how to secure Social Security focused on Constitutional issues, as Social Security's programs gradually expanded both political support and Social Security financing emerged as much larger problems that touched the

center of American economic life. Interestingly enough, the economically conservative approach to financing Social Security by setting aside large financial
reserves, strongly advocated by President Roosevelt, his economic advisors,
and the early administrators laid the foundation for program expansion while
threatening Social Security's long-term financial stability at the same time. That
economic considerations became an unlikely vehicle for back door program
expansion constitutes a paradox, which has given rise to some of the most
discussed policy issues confronting Social Security today. In a curious way,
financing Social Security aligned administrators, who sought program expansion, with economists who opposed the idea of large Social Security reserves,
and politicians who sought a greater federal governmental role in America's
social welfare development.

Financing Title II Social Security in Its Larger Economic Context

In the introduction to her comprehensive *Policy Making for Social Security*,
Martha Derthick says, "Decisions about Social Security were generally made in
isolation from decisions about other government activities, both structurally
and financially."[3] Derthick's conclusion, however, fails to take into consideration larger issues of American fiscal policy, and its narrower consequences
of tax policy, which have always played a decisive part in Social Security
development. Title II Social Security programs and taxes are inexorably tied
together, placing Social Security policy in the center of American economic
activity. In spite of the ambitions of presidents, from Franklin Roosevelt to
George W. Bush, and regardless of the ideological objectives sought by various Social Security administrators, Congress has been singularly responsible
for the complex development of Social Security largely through the tax writing
authority of the Ways and Means Committee in the House of Representatives.
The authority of the Ways and Means Committee has dominated decisions over
the source of Social Security revenues and how they would be spent to render
more salience to Social Security's economic decisions more than any political
discourse over the development of the Social Security programs themselves has
done. Most back door Social Security program changes effortlessly passed the
scrutiny of the most powerful committee in Congress largely because the tax
consequences of Social Security development always have been at the heart of
that Committee's debate. The decision of the Committee on Economic Security
to nest Social Security within the tax system, and the Supreme Court's affirmation of congressional spending power affirm the tightly woven relationship
between Social Security development and national economic concerns.

Throughout most of Social Security's early development, there had been
an unprecedented consensus between the administrators of Social Security
and the legislators on the Ways and Means Committee about two of its
basic economic foundations: Social Security financing should remain independent of general revenue spending in spite of some contrary opinions in

the 1940s, and Social Security should be "actuarially sound." For the Social Security administrators, protecting Social Security from general revenue financing avoided the welfare stigma. For Congressmen, particularly Wilbur Mills, protecting Social Security from general revenue financing meant maintaining political control over this politically important and very expensive program. For both administrators and Congressmen, actuarial soundness meant insuring long-term control over Social Security's development, even though there was no objective consensus as to what constituted actuarial soundness. Over the years, the substance of these two considerations has been debated within and outside the governmental policy-making process, and with few exceptions actuarial soundness[b] and specific ("earmarked") payroll taxes to achieve this soundness have most frequently directed the development of Social Security. Today, they remain at the center of some of the most important Title II Social Security policy debates.

Social Security Financing and American Fiscal Policy

Context

The implementation of American fiscal policy, and its resulting tax policy, particularly as developed after World War II, created the framework for Social Security financing and its subsequent program development. The consensus that Social Security should remain free of general revenue financing[c] and that it should remain actuarially sound was achieved by a Social Security policy monopoly consisting of administrators, economists, and politicians who shaped the Social Security program into its present form. It is difficult to understand the dilemma raised by Social Security financing without seeing Social Security financing in the larger context of American economic planning, usually called fiscal policy.

American Fiscal Policy

While popular views of the American economy see a freely operating market system, where economic development is fueled by independent, autonomous, personal economic choices, the reality of the American economic system has become quite different. The American economic system, often called "market capitalism," is manipulated by the capacity of the Federal Government to affect economic choices through its power to tax and to spend, a power which took on economic policy significance after World War II. Today, the Federal Government uses its authority to engage in a variety of "macroeconomic"

---

[b] The exact meaning of "actuarial soundness" was never made clear, even by economists. In general, it appears that Title II Social Security advocates want to be sure there would be enough money in the trust funds to pay benefits, without resorting to infusions of general revenue funding. How this form of "soundness" would be achieved became a contentious in the issue of the early days of Social Security just as it is today.

[c] Even though Arthur Altmeyer once proposed it.

activities that have become an acceptable part of the American economy. Deficit financing, monetary policy that establishes interest and controls the size of the money supply in order to influence personal spending, and "tax breaks" (tax expenditures) to individuals and corporations to encourage various forms of personal and corporate investments,[d] are all government activities, which, arguably, contribute to America's economic prosperity. And, of course, individual and corporate tax rates are also changed and applied variously in order to affect economic growth as well as funding government activity.[e]

At the end of World War II, American institutions were tumultuous. The wartime powers given to the president had created new government agencies, reorganized others, and took direct control over the activities of many others. The war had ended successfully; now, America needed to return to a peacetime society and put government back into its traditional place in American life. The emergency wartime powers assumed by the Federal Government had to be redistributed to states and the private sector, and the first Hoover Commission met in 1947 to begin reorganization of the Federal Government.[f] In addition to the need for government reorganization, the nation faced a massive influx of labor from men returning from active military service, many seeking to return to their old jobs. Furthermore, the Great Depression continued to loom in the minds of many who feared another economic depression as the potential for massive unemployment rose and as military spending was curtailed. But while traditional economists believed that the American economy was self-regulating and would adjust itself to these new challenges, a new school of economics fueled by the theories of John Maynard Keynes took a different approach to post-war economic recovery. Keynesian economics established government economic planning in America and was partly responsible for the expansion of Title II Social Security.

Keynesian Economics

An economist, journalist, and financier, John Keynes (1883–1946) was born in Cambridge, England; he was educated at Eton and Cambridge, where he studied under Alfred Marshall, the leading Cambridge economist. After leaving Cambridge, he served in a number of government posts, including economic adviser at the Treaty of Versailles (1919), where he wrote a scathing tract against excessive reparation requirements from Germany after World War I. In his

---

[d] Chapter 10 provides a discussion of tax expenditures and social welfare commitments.

[e] For example, President George W. Bush and Congress combined to provide massive emergency tax cuts in 2008 as an economic stimulus to the American economy, which was showing signs of a serious economic recession.

[f] Called the Commission on Organization of the Executive Branch of the Government, the Hoover Commission was appointed by President Harry Truman in 1947 to recommend administrative changes in the Federal Government. The Commission was named for the former president Herbert Hoover, whom President Truman appointed to head it. The Hoover Commission concluded its work in 1949 producing over 20 reports containing more than 200 recommendations, most of which were implemented and continue to frame the structure of the Federal Government today.

General Theory of Employment, Interest and Money (1936), Keynes departed from classic economic theories. He put forth ideas about government responsibility and its commitment to maintaining high employment, arguing that a fully employed population created a robust economic system and the government was responsible to act to achieve full employment.[8] The economic recovery from the Great Depression provided some empirical evidence of the positive results of government-regulated economic activity, and by the end of World War II, most Western democracies affirmed their commitment to Keynesian economic philosophy. Keynesian economics were endorsed more slowly in the United States, where they collided with traditional "free market" economic theories. Yet, a wave of new economic thought began working its way into government policy decisions that called for post-World War II job growth.

Keynes' economic theory was built on the simple observation that spending spurred economic productivity and economic growth. Thus, a strong economy was one that encouraged spending by keeping the population fully employed. The employed in turn would spend, spurring more employment. Employment and spending were keys to the Keynesian formula. Keynes also observed that governments like individuals could also save and spend, and thus government had great economic power to supplement its political power. If the economy was not at full capacity, when government spent then employment increased and the economy grew. If the economy was at full capacity, portending inflation, if government saved, economic growth contracted. In its ability to tax and spend, government therefore possessed the ability to force individuals to save and spend as well. Thus, the Keynesian economists concluded, government had the capacity to manage economic development directly through its own spending and indirectly through its taxing, which affected individual spending. When government taxed people more heavily, they had less money to spend, thus slowing economic growth, and conversely lower taxes left individuals with more money to spend, thus encouraging economic growth.

The Employment Act of 1946

Keynesian economics, as well as the necessity to return the United States to a post-war, prosperous, economy, accounts in large measure for the creation of the Employment Act in 1946.[4] While traditional economists argued that unemployment and recessions were part of a self-correcting economic cycle, the Keynesians argued that government had the capacity and obligation to adjust economic cycles so as to promote balanced economic growth. Since the need to reemploy returning service men and women was both a social priority as well as an economic one, the Employment Act first introduced in 1945, guaranteed a right to employment, and a Federal Government obligation to provide sufficient resources to assure "continuing full employment."[5] But business interests,

---

[8] Of course, no one defined "full employment." See the discussion of Unemployment Insurance in Chapter 4.

in particular, feared the rising strength of labor unions, and when the bill was reintroduced and eventually signed into law in 1946, the provisions that guaranteed jobs for Americans had been removed from the bill. Yet the Act gave the Federal Government limited authority to manage the American economy, an ironic twist in a nation that was fighting government regulated "socialist" economies at the same time.

The Employment Act created three governmental structures. First, the legislation created the Council of Economic Advisors that was required to prepare yearly reports for the president about current economic conditions and what measures would be needed to achieve the objectives of the Act. Second, the Act required the president to issue a yearly report to Congress based on the advice of the Council of Economic Advisors as to what legislative or administrative activities he or she would promote to achieve the objectives. Third, the Employment Act created the Joint Economic Committee in Congress and charged it to gather information necessary for Congress to act in such a way so as to achieve the purposes of the Act. America's tax structure in the macroeconomic world of Keynesian economics provided an essential foundation for the development of Social Security.

Keynesian Economics and Financing Social Security

In his meticulously researched book on Wilbur Mills and Mills' influence on Social Security, Julian Zelizer states:

> Although government officials of earlier historical periods were aware that taxation affected matters such as capital investment and regional industry, they did not deliberately manipulate taxation to help manage the national economy. The postwar period was different. Income-tax policy was used as a macroeconomic tool through which expert officials could stimulate national economic growth or restrain excessive expansion.[6]

Social Security was shaped in this vortex of taxing and spending.

While initially Roosevelt had argued forcefully for a large Social Security trust fund to keep it actuarially sound, as early as 1937 "Keynesian economists warned that the [Social Security] surpluses and the [Social Security] taxes themselves would drain consumer purchasing power."[7] National economic growth depended on government spending and large Title II Social Security reserves anticipated by Roosevelt's original thinking would slow economic growth, even if the Federal Government borrowed from those reserves, as it eventually did. Even borrowing Social Security funds reduced the value of private capital markets, and the Social Security taxes on earnings often took money out of the economy at inopportune times. Economists disliked the payroll taxes, while Title II supporters argued for their necessity.

Martha Derthick reports that as early as 1937, with Social Security reserves projected to reach $47 billion by 1980, Republican Senator Arthur Vandenberg expressed opposition "against the accumulation of a large reserve fund which conservatives feared would encourage government profligacy and

undermine private investment opportunities."[8] Senator Vandenberg introduced an amendment to the Social Security Act that called for the use of general
revenues to pay Social Security benefits whenever reserves reached a certain
size, an amendment that remained in force, although never implemented, until
it was counteracted by later Social Security amendments. These early advocates of limited Social Security reserves argued that general revenues would be
a more economically sound way to finance Social Security, rather than taking
large sums of money out of the economy and holding them for later use. Thus,
concerns over large Social Security surpluses from the program's beginning created a tension between advocates for a "fully funded" program and those who
argued for a "pay as you go" program. Each protagonist's argument proclaimed
its position best protected the actuarial soundness of Social Security. Thus, the
2001 testimony of Alan Greenspan during his last days as Chairman of the
Council of Economic Advisors (quoted in Chapter 2) was part of a consistent
economic message about government revenues and Social Security financing.

Growing Social Security reserves convinced Roosevelt's trusted Secretary of
the Treasury Henry Morgenthau to abandon his earlier commitment to a fully
funded program, and Roosevelt reluctantly accepted Morgenthau's reversal.
According to Eric Patashnik

> ... Keynesians achieved their greatest influence over Social Security finance
> in the controversy over Morgenthau's original plan to accumulate a vast
> reserve. Keynesians argued that a large reserve would drain money out of
> the economy, making it harder for the nation to overcome a recession.
> In passing the 1939 Amendments [to Title II of the Social Security Act],
> Congress responded to this criticism by reducing the size of the projected
> fund buildup by roughly half. This was accomplished *through an expan-*
> *sion of benefit payments* and the cancellation of a scheduled payroll tax
> increase—policy moves that Keynesians strongly approved of.[9]

By 1942, as the Social Security trust fund continued to accumulate large
reserves, Roosevelt accepted a freeze on scheduled Social Security tax increases
as an economic anti-inflationary measure rather than as a Social Security
financing issue.[10]

To the constant concern of Keynesian economists, the Social Security trust
fund continued to grow due largely to economic growth generally and to the
favorable ratio of workers to beneficiaries. Political conservatives joined the
otherwise economic liberal Keynesians who basically supported welfare programs but objected to large trust fund surpluses. Keynesian economists argued
that large trust fund surpluses would slow economic growth, and political
conservatives argued that large surpluses would tempt Social Security advocates and their political supporters to expand benefits.[11] The fiscal politics of
Social Security became even more transparent in 1969 when Congress adopted
a unified executive budget following the longstanding urging of Keynesian
economists. As part of the unified budget, the macroeconomic consequences
of Social Security's trust fund surpluses became more obvious. For example,

if general-purpose government accumulated debt, Social Security surpluses would be counted as government reserves and thus offset any federal deficit. Conversely, in times of general economic prosperity, when general-purpose government accumulated surpluses, either general revenue or projected Social Security taxes could be reduced, and/or Social Security could be expanded, which also functioned to reduce government surpluses.

The Social Security "Policy Monopoly"

Managing the nation's economy through the tax structure added consider-able economic power to the U.S. Congress' House of Representatives' Ways and Means Committee, requiring expertise which Congress had not previously developed. Robert ("Mulley Bob") Doughton of Sparta, North Carolina, was elected to Congress in 1911 and became Chairman of the House Ways and Means Committee in 1933, a position he held for all but two years until he resigned from Congress in 1953. Doughton, not particularly well schooled in the new Keynesian economics, was forced to rely heavily on the Social Security administrative experts who had taken responsibility for putting the original Social Security program together. In particular, Arthur Altmeyer and Edwin Witte provided the foundational economic calculations about Social Secu-rity, along with Wilbur Cohen who, as a new graduate of the University of Wisconsin, was hired to work on the Economic Security Act in 1934 by his teacher and mentor, Edwin Witte. The Social Security tax challenges faced by the Ways and Means Committee under Doughton's chairmanship required the expertise of these early administrators. When Witte and Altmeyer, and later Cohen, assured the Ways and Means Committee that there were sufficient Social Security funds to expand benefits while still keeping the program actuar-ially sound, they were not only promoting their own ideological social welfare objectives; their desire to expand Social Security fit only too well with economic views which had begun to question the economic wisdom of large government Title II Trust Fund reserves. Zelizer also notes that post-World War II govern-ment spending was easily accepted by Congress as an economic stimulus. Thus, the expansion of Social Security benefits and beneficiaries not only kept Social Security reserves at a minimum, but also allowed Social Security taxes to be pumped back into the economy through payments to beneficiaries.

Wilbur Mills assumed a larger profile in shaping Social Security than Bob Doughton. Mills was elected to Congress in 1938 at age 29, the second youngest member of the House of Representatives at that time. In 1942, Mills was appointed to the Ways and Means Committee by Sam Rayburn. He became Chairman and served in this position until 1974, when a sex scandal forced his resignation as chairman and his decision not to seek office again in the 1976 elections. Mills' thirty-eight years on the Ways and Means committee, twenty-four years as its chairman, equaled that of Doughton, and Mills, more than any other single Congressperson, oversaw the expansion of Social Security and its evolution into its present form. During his highly influential legislative years on

Ways and Means, Mills not only commanded the most far-reaching changes to the American tax structure, he also oversaw the greatest program expansion to Social Security in American history.

The growing complexity of tax policy, linked as it was to macroeconomic objectives well established after the Employment Act of 1942 was created, demanded a whole new congressional intelligence. Only those who had sufficient knowledge could guide the country through the labyrinth of taxing and spending decisions necessary to ensure economic development generally, and the development of Social Security, in particular. Those who held this knowledge secured a policy monopoly over Social Security. Wilbur Cohen was an established Social Security expert. Mills became an unprecedented tax expert. Cohen had become an undisputed leader of Social Security advocates both inside and outside of government, including Altmeyer, Robert Ball, Elizabeth Wickenden, and Nelson Cruikshank, of the American Federation of Labor; Mills learned his economics from influential academic economists and Social Security experts until he became an undisputed expert in his own right. Throughout his tenure on the Ways and Means Committee, Wilbur Cohen became Mills' closest advisor on Social Security taxes.[12] Although Mills did not always agree with Cohen, between the two of them Social Security evolved from its original form described in the previous chapter to the structure we know today. Wilbur Cohen became known as "Mr. Social Security." Wilbur Mills became known as "the tax man."[13]

Mills also relied heavily on the advice of Robert Myers who was Social Security's chief actuary, the person who oversaw the program's solvency. Myers favored "fully funded" Social Security reserves, but Mills was more persuaded by Cohen's more politically attractive Keynesian pay-as-you-go alternatives to keep the trust funds at lower levels. According to Cohen, Social Security revenues could always be increased, if necessary, by covering more workers, increasing the tax rates, and increasing the ceiling on Social Security taxes, all of which were done during the development of Social Security. Of course, such revenue changes were accompanied by program changes as well. Mills tightened his proprietary hold on Social Security taxes by insisting on a closed rule when Social Security taxes were presented to the full Congress, arguing that their complexity needed to be protected from changes by members who had insufficient Social Security tax knowledge. By the same logic, he continued to support the "earmarked" payroll tax to protect it from incremental tampering by other members of Congress, and he supported the payroll tax, specifically, as a form of political insurance for continuing the Social Security program. Thus, this most adroit legislator balanced actuarial soundness and the payroll tax with the expansionist objectives of Cohen and his predecessors, creating what Zelizer called a Social Security policy monopoly.[h]

---

[h] Contrary to Derthick's analysis, this account suggests that the expansion of Title II Social Security was not a product of strictly the expansion objectives of the early administrators, but was aided and abetted by the political ambitions and will of Wilbur Mills and robustly supported by leading economists of the day.

Social Security's Financing Policy Issues

The previous discussion helps provide a context for some of the most contentious policy issues concerning Social Security financing. The historic significance of the above financing issues has become magnified in today's Title II Social Security environment, and it provides the political atmosphere that structures the repeated, erroneous claims that Title II Social Security is running out of money.

The Payroll Tax

While Social Security's problems are usually described as coming down to increased beneficiaries due to an aging population and program expansion, placing Social Security within a context of macroeconomic policy suggests a different set of policy issues. First, since Social Security revenues are indeed a tax on earnings, regardless of what they are called, the payroll tax, compared with the income tax reflects important policy issues for funding Title II Social Security. The present payroll tax is regressive; it is capped to protect higher earners, and even though it is shared equally by employees and employers, the full tax burden usually falls on the individual earner.[i] Second, payroll taxes are "earmarked" for their specific purposes. Greater efficiency in program funding might be achieved, some argue, if payroll tax revenues were not designated specifically to fund Social Security. Payroll taxes lock the funds into exclusive use for Title II Social Security. Third, Social Security income is held in three separate trust funds: Social Security, disability insurance, and hospital insurance. While these funds are protected from political decisions over their use, the existence of Social Security reserves has public and private economic consequences. Publically, the reserves raise a question as to how large these trust funds need to be to assure short and long range program liquidity. Some argue that individual investing would produce more adequate retirement benefits for individual workers.

Social Security's fiscal structure was created in the context of the great economic depression of 1929–1935. Lacking previous experience with Federal Government spending for social programs, Social Security funding took a conservative approach to financing social insurance. The Federal Government had limited fiscal capacity based on personal income taxes, and the payroll taxes covered a smaller percentage of the labor force than it does today. The payroll tax not only made the overall tax burden seem much lighter, but it also was quite modest because the needs were so much less. Today, however, the economy has become more forceful in the long run and has grown considerably. In 1935, social insurance was an important social welfare innovation, and politically the payroll tax was an important distinguishing feature between social insurance and assistance, or welfare programs. But as Social Security

---

[i] In most situations, employers are able to recoup their payroll tax burdens by raising the price of their products. Employees, on the other hand, have no easy way to pass their employment costs on to the public.

programs have expanded and taken on more "welfare" characteristics in today's social insurance environment, and as Title II Social Security programs have become more pay-as-you-go, the payroll tax no longer provides as clear a distinction between social insurance and welfare. The redistributive features of Social Security, even though quite modest, challenge the fairness of a payroll tax as well. When Social Security was created, large Social Security trust fund reserves seemed the only way to preserve the liquidity of the program. But today, macroeconomic issues detract from the value of large government reserves, which, in some people's view, amount to little more than "paper IOUs." Furthermore, it is difficult to speculate how general-purpose government would be able to pay back $1.5 trillion to the Title II trust funds, the estimated amount general-purpose government "owes" the trust funds. These Trust Fund issues are a legacy of original Title II financing decisions. The policy issues facing Social Security today, therefore, need to be discussed in terms of the social and economic environment of the first decade of the twenty-first century, rather than the economic context of 1935.

Long-Term Financing Issues

Issues facing present and future funding for Social Security depend on the payroll tax, "earmarked" for the Social Security trust fund, and the integrity of the trust fund itself. The payroll tax survived economically due to the influence of the policy monopoly discussed above, and the payroll tax has survived politically because it continues to appeal to the American ideal of self-sufficiency; today's workers are contributing to their future retirement or possible disability by paying a Social Security tax. The larger economic issues of Social Security financing that has made it a pay-as-you-go program, or as some would say an inter-generational transfer program, do not detract from Social Security's fundamental ideal wrapped up in the payroll tax. In addition, by preserving the idea of prospective financing, the payroll tax insures that Social Security retains the ideal of protecting income earned today for use in retirement tomorrow, even if the dollars taken by the tax today are actually used to pay for today's benefits. Self-sufficiency, which is Social Security's defining element, sets it apart from its welfare cousins discussed in subsequent chapters. By virtue of the payroll tax, Social Security constitutes a statutory right to receive retirement benefits from the Federal Government. Prudent policy discussions, therefore, have always avoided considering either a substitute for or a supplement of general revenue taxes to the payroll tax, in spite of the many economic issues involved in the present method of financing Social Security.

Even if the political supporters of the payroll tax overshadow its economic usefulness, the payroll tax could be made more adequate and equitable. For examples, the payroll tax would not have to be evenly divided between employer and employee; it could be made more progressive without losing its relationship to earnings by such modifications as removing the earnings ceiling; it could be more closely integrated with other tax programs such as the income tax and the earned income tax credit provided to low-income employees.

The Social Security Trust Fund(s)[j]

Assuming the payroll tax continues as the means to finance Title II Social Security, the actuarial soundness of Social Security remains an important issue. Maintaining the fiscal integrity of Social Security depends upon policy choices affecting the Social Security trust fund(s) and the reserves necessary to pay benefits. Current calculations, such as those of the Congressional Budget Office reflected in Figure 3.1 below, show that there are sufficient funds to pay benefits

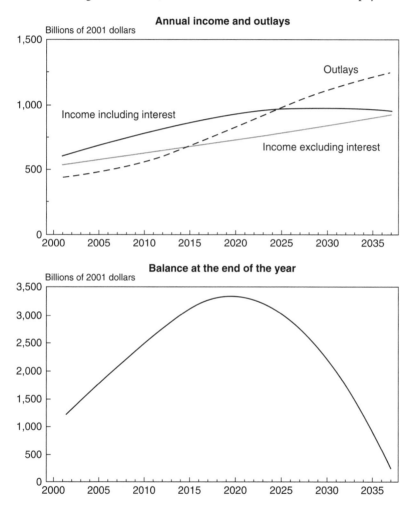

Figure 3.1. Income, Outlays, and Balances of the Social Security Trust Funds, 2001–2037.

Source: Social Security Administration, *The 2001 Annual Report of the Board of Trustees of the Federal Old-Age and Survivors Insurance and Disability Insurance Trust Fund*. Reprinted in *A Primer on Social Security*, Congressional Budget Office. Washington, DC, 2004.

---

[j] As noted earlier, there are two Title II Social Security trust funds, one for retirees and their survivors and one for the eligible disabled.

Table 3.1. Historical Operations of the Combined OASI and DI Trust Funds Selected Calendar Years 1957–2007 [Amounts in billions]

Year	Income				Expenditures				Net Increase During Year	Assets	
	Total	Net Contributions	Taxation from Benefits	Net Interest	Total	Benefit Payments	Administrative Costs	Interest		Amount at End of Year	Trust Fund Ratio*
1957	$8.10	$7.50	—	$0.60	$7.60	$7.40	$0.20	—	$0.50	$23.00	298
1959	9.5	8.9	—	0.6	10.8	10.3	0.2	0.3	-1.3	22	215
1960	12.4	11.9	—	0.6	11.8	11.2	0.2	0.3	0.6	22.6	186
1965	17.9	17.2	—	0.7	19.2	18.3	0.4	0.5	-1.3	19.8	110
1970	37	34.7	—	1.8	33.1	31.9	0.6	0.6	3.9	38.1	103
1975	67.6	64.3	—	2.9	69.2	67	1.2	1	-1.5	44.3	66
1980	119.7	116.7	—	2.3	123.6	120.6	1.5	1.4	-3.8	26.5	25
1982	147.9	145.7	—	1.4	160.1	156.2	2.1	1.8	0.2	24.8	15
1984	186.6	180.1	$3.00	3.4	180.4	175.7	2.3	2.4	6.2	31.1	21
1985	203.5	194.1	3.4	2.7	190.6	186.1	2.2	2.4		42.2	24
1987	231	222.4	3.2	5.3	209.1	204.1	2.4	2.6	21.9	68.8	31
1989	289.4	274.2	2.5	12.7	236.2	230.9	2.4	2.9	53.2	163	57

1990	315.4	296.1	5	17.2	253.1	247.8	2.3	3	62.3	225.3	75
1991	329.7	301.7	6.1	21.9	274.2	268.2	2.6	3.5	55.5	280.7	82
1992	342.6	311.1	6.1	25.4	291.9	286	2.7	3.2	50.7	331.5	96
1993	355.6	322.1	5.6	27.9	308.8	302.4	3	3.4	46.8	378.3	107
1994	381.1	344.7	5.3	31.1	323	316.8	2.7	3.5	58.1	436.4	117
1995	399.5	359	5.8	35	339.8	332.6	3.1	4.1	59.7	496.1	128
1996	424.5	378.9	6.8	38.7	353.6	347.1	3	3.6	70.9	567	140
1997	457.7	406	7.9	43.8	369.1	362	3.4	3.7	88.6	655.5	154
1998	489.2	430.2	9.7	49.3	382.3	375	3.5	3.8	107	762.5	171
1999	526.6	459.6	11.6	55.5	392.9	385.8	3.3	3.8	133.7	896.1	194
2000	568.4	492.5	12.3	64.5	415.1	407.6	3.8	3.7	153.3	1,049.40	216
2001	602	516.4	12.7	72.9	438.9	431.9	3.7	3.3	163.1	1,212.50	239
2002	627.1	532.5	13.8	80.4	461.7	453.8	4.2	3.6	165.4	1,378.00	263
2003	631.9	533.5	13.4	84.9	479.1	470.8	4.6	3.7	152.8	1,530.80	288
2004	657.7	553	15.7	89	501.6	493.3	4.5	3.8	156.1	1,686.80	305
2005	701.8	592.9	14.9	94.3	529.9	520.7	5.3	3.9	171.8	1,858.70	318
2006	744.9	625.6	16.9	102.4	555.4	546.2	5.3	3.8	189.5	2,048.10	335
2007	784.9	656.1	18.6	110.2	594.5	584.9	5.5	4	190.4	2,238.50	345

*Ratio = Year end assets/total expenditures.
Source: 2008 OASDI Trustees Report.

at existing levels beyond 2035, and perhaps as far into the future as 2042. The "breakeven" point, of approximately year 2018 shown in the Congressional Budget's graphic, is the point where income and outlays were expected to be in balance, based on projections made in 2001.

The farther the future projections are stretched, the less certain the fiscal soundness of the fund(s). The National Commission on Social Security Reform, chaired by Alan Greenspan, was created in 1982 during one of the many financing crises. Facing problems of increased concern over the potential adequately to fund future Social Security beneficiaries, the Commission issued its report in 1983 with recommendations designed to shore up Social Security for the next seventy-five years. Included in these recommendations were gradual increases in Social Security taxes, gradual increases in the Social Security tax ceiling, and a gradual increase in the full retirement age. These and other modifications were made by the Congress. But in 2001, less than eighteen years after the report was received and the recommended changes implemented, alarms were sounded again about financing future Social Security benefits, raising questions about any Commission's ability to make predictions about factors affecting Social Security so far out in the future. More recently in 1998, the trustees estimated that the Social Security trust fund would be depleted in 2032, but five years later, the trustees estimated that the retirement Trust Fund would not be depleted until 2042, making the projections too conservative even in a modestly performing economy.

The trustees of the Social Security Trust Fund clarified the Trust Fund's present fiscal issues in its 2004 annual report.

> The OASI and DI Trust Funds, individually and combined, are adequately financed over the next 10 years under the intermediate assumptions [of dynamic forecasting]. Combined assets were projected in last year's report to rise to 309 percent of annual expenditures at the beginning of 2004, and 461 percent at the beginning of 2013. . . . Under the intermediate assumptions the combined OASI and DI Trust Funds are projected to become exhausted in 2042. . . . Annual cost will exceed tax income starting in 2018 at which time the annual gap will be covered with cash from redeeming special obligations of the Treasury, until these assets are exhausted in 2042.[14]

Under current assumptions, projections, and present tax rates, if the Title II Trust Funds did become exhausted in 2042, workers paying into the system in 2042 would still provide enough money to fund about 75–80 percent of the benefits at the level those benefits are guaranteed for 2042. In the near future, therefore, the present income stream is sufficient to maintain an actuarially sound Social Security program.

Actuarial Soundness

While there is considerable disagreement about the character of the Social Security trust funds—whether they are a mere accounting artifact, or whether the trust funds are a real Social Security "bank account"—the size of the Trust Fund does not reflect the soundness of Social Security. The Social Security Trust Fund is not fully funded, and reserves are subject to ongoing economic pressures. There are no economic guidelines that might suggest the optimal size of the trust fund. At minimum, there should be sufficient income plus reserves in the fund to pay present obligations. In general, the trustees of the Social Security Trust Fund have tried to keep a five-year reserve in the fund. This means that there should be enough money in the fund to pay benefits for five years if Social Security income suddenly stops. At least 14 times over the past sixty-five years projected benefits exceeded projected income requiring Social Security to draw down reserves in order to pay benefits. The largest revenue shortfall took place in 1978. During the 1980s, the Social Security retirement trust fund had to borrow from the disability trust fund in order to meet obligations, while during parts of the Clinton Administration, the Social Security trust fund was running record surpluses. The size of the trust fund, therefore, will vary widely depending on economic and demographic conditions and on decisions over how much to pre-fund future liabilities as the estimates presently do.

As discussed above, Social Security was never "fully funded," and the size of the trust fund has fluctuated widely over its history with no apparent damage to Title II Social Security. In fact, as stated above, there have been deliberate efforts to keep the trust fund from becoming too large. Table 3.1 shows the fluctuations in Social Security trust fund reserves over the years, raising continued debate about the size of the Social Security reserves. Because Social Security is basically a pay-as-you-go program, it is financially sound as long as there is enough income today to pay today's benefits. But economic fluctuations require some "cushion" in order to insure that payments can be made without the use of general revenues. Thus, the Trustees of the Social Security Trust Fund have relied on a five-year reserve.

Projecting Future Social Security Needs

Relying on "earmarked" payroll taxes requires economic forecasting much more challenging than revenue projections for general-purpose government. There are two major considerations the Social Security actuaries must evaluate to make sure there is enough money to pay benefits now and seventy-five years into the future: the future ratio of workers to retirees and future economic performance. First, the ratio of present workers to retirees establishes a base to project necessary Social Security reserves. For example, in 1940, there were approximately 159 workers for every retiree (159:1). This ratio has been decreasing over the years as the Title II program matures and more people begin to receive their benefits. For example, in 1960, the ratio had become 5:1, 3.7:1 in 1970, 3.2:1 in 1980, 3.4:1 in 1990, and 3.3:1 in 2003 (Social Security Administration, 2004). As the ratio between workers and retirees becomes smaller, workers must pay more to keep Trust Fund reserves sufficient. This means that the trustees of the Fund have to estimate both the number of persons who will be working and how many people will be drawing benefits in order to determine whether the rate is sufficient to pay benefits. But such projections are informed assumptions. For example, the Social Security actuaries expect that the rapid immigration of labor (legal and illegal—most illegal workers still pay Social Security taxes) will become static over the next three years, while others suggest that labor immigration will continue to increase steadily. Since the present concern about the expanding beneficiary pool is due to the "baby boom," a significantly larger workforce brought about by worker immigration may result in an increase in worker–retiree ratios, rather than a continued decrease.

Second, although the Social Security actuaries are quite good at projecting the amount of income from taxes when the future economy is expected to act as past experience suggests (static forecasting), no one has a good understanding of unanticipated future events (dynamic forecasting) Since the Social Security reserves are extremely sensitive to macroeconomic activity, the actuaries do suggest different scenarios for estimating revenues, but, of necessity, such forecasts are conservative. If the economy performs above expectations as it did during the 1990s, large unwanted surpluses result. If the economy performs less well than anticipated, as it did during the late 1970s and early 1980s, then the Social Security trustees are forced to issue pessimistic reports that stimulate dire projections about the future of Social Security.

Because Social Security forecasting rests on little more than educated hypotheses, and because it is economically desirable to keep reserves at a minimum, it would be more prudent to adjust payroll taxes at smaller intervals, depending on the short range reserve needs, rather than setting tax increases far into the future as is presently done. For example, tax rates could be set for five-year intervals depending on both the beneficiary–worker ratio and current economic conditions. While such a policy may lead to uncertainties in tax rates, it might present a more realistic foundation for insuring an adequate financial base for Social Security, as long as the method of financing retains trust funds and earmarked taxes. After all, income tax rates change depending on both spending commitments and economic performance, and although such changes do not take place at regular intervals, the public, though perhaps reluctantly, accept such tax fluctuations.

Financing Summary

Economics, much more so than politics, explains today's Social Security's financing dilemmas. The development of American fiscal policy following World War II has brought into focus an incompatibility between the objectives of keeping Social Security actuarially sound and promoting a macroeconomic agenda of growth. Clearly, large trust fund reserves necessary for Social Security solvency "in perpetuity" would undermine America's capitalistic ideals. The danger for protecting and advancing Title II Social Security does not lie so much in a loss of political support for the idea of social insurance, or even in a lack of financial resources to meet present and future commitments. Rather, the macroeconomic desirability of keeping small Social Security reserves will continue to force repeated "crises" in long-term Social Security stability, thus undermining Social Security's previously established policy objectives. It is noteworthy that while the general-purpose Federal Governments' budget was running record deficits in 2008–2009, the Social Security Trust Fund had a surplus. Establishing social insurance required a long-term government financial commitment that quickly began to conflict with ideals of American capitalism. Thus, the economic undesirability of amassing large government financial reserves fit only too nicely with the desires of the early administrators to develop a comprehensive social insurance system that provided for the economic security of all Americans.

Managing Social Security financing from one "crisis" to the next is unnecessary and undermines its integrity. While the Social Security Trust fund is not a fiction, it is also true that the whole of Title II Social Security has lost most of its meaningful relationship to its historic means of financing. The payroll tax as presently administered is a regressive tax, and pay-as-you-go financing has detached its economic relationship to Title II Social Security's varied beneficiaries and benefit structure. In other words, the political commitments reflected by the payroll tax and the trust funds keep Title II Social Security alive today rather than any long-term financial solvency secured by any reserves the trust funds might hold. Unfortunately, advocates for a smaller role for the Federal Government are often cheered by large deficits as an excuse to restrict social welfare spending.[15] Maintaining Title II Social Security's present financing structure is bound to foster an increased number of private insurance alternatives that will eventually challenge Title II social welfare commitments. A public commitment to Social Security's policy objectives as a basic program of social insurance does not depend on the present complex and outdated system of Social Security financing.[16]

Policy Issues Confronting Social Security Programs

The expansion of the Title II Social Security program from its modest beginning in response to the economic needs of retired workers provides one of the most significant case studies of incremental program development. While Arthur Altmeyer, Edwin Witte, Robert Ball, Wilbur Cohen, and other administrators may not have had a plan for Social Security development, they had a large vision for social insurance. Had they put forth a plan to realize that vision, both Social Security and the vision would have been abandoned before its benefits ever began to be realized. Instead, these administrators (Wilbur Cohen, in particular) sought political opportunities to realize a vision of comprehensive social insurance whenever opportunities arose to expand Title II programs. Their efforts constituted more than bureaucratic politics or efforts to secure a form of personal gain. Rather, their successful expansion of Social Security programs evolved from a deep commitment to improve the lives of Americans within an existing economic context that demonstrated little care for America's welfare needs.

Title II's incremental program development, however, has produced a multitude of variations within a single program structure, as discussed in the previous chapter. Back door program development of Social Security required funds to pay for new beneficiaries and a willingness to raise benefits, thus making commitments well into the future. For example, with the exception of Aid to the Totally and Permanently Disabled, a separate social insurance program for children of beneficiaries with an independent money stream does not exist. Rather, children's benefits are provided as an extension of the basic Title II retirement program. Thus, while Social Security has matured into a much more comprehensive social insurance program, it has done so at the expense of separating out and providing a policy framework for each of the Title II beneficiary groups as reported in Table 2.1. This form of program development fails to provide adequate policy and program authority necessary to administer the Title II program to these beneficiaries in an equitable and efficient manner on their own terms.

Benefits and Beneficiary Program Concerns

Equity Issues

Generally speaking, equity issues can be thought of both as fair treatment and as equal treatment and the development of Title II Social Security has raised questions about both fairness and equality of treatment. The benefit formula adjusted to provide greater proportional benefits to low-income workers does not treat Social Security beneficiaries equally. Workers with low-wage jobs, who as a result had smaller contributions to Social Security, receive greater benefit for their contributions than those who worked in higher paying jobs. While adjusting the benefit formulas may result in fair treatment, particularly for low-income workers, the policy violates a principle of equal treatment and attaches elements of welfare to a program that has drawn its political strength on the basis of self-sufficiency.

Table 3.2 below provides some perspective on how the expansion of the beneficiary pool has affected the equality of benefit payments. Between 1940 and 2004, benefits to all retired workers increased by 97.63 percent; benefits to retired men increased by 97.84 percent, and benefits to retired women increased by 97.77 percent. In 1940, all wives received benefits amounted to 46.32 percent out of the amount of benefits paid to all workers, but in 2004, benefits paid to wives amounted to 49.63 percent out of the amount of benefits paid to all workers. In 1940, all wives of covered workers entitled to Social

Table 3.2. Average Monthly Benefits by Type of Benefit and Sex, December 1940 and 2004 (in dollars)

Year	Retired Workers Average Benefit Payment ($)			Wife Average Benefit Payment ($)			Husband Average Benefit Payment ($)		Children Average Benefit Payment ($)			
	All	Men	Women	All	Entitled by Age	Entitled by Children			All	Under 18 years	Disabled Children	Students
	A	**B**	**C**	**D**	**E**	**F**	**G**	**H**	**I**	**J**	**K**	**L**
1 1940	22.60	23.17	18.37	12.13	12.13	—	—	—	—	—	—	—
2 2004	954.90	1,076.10	826.10	480.90	482.60	394.00	272.00	—	465.00	437.70	500.50	518.50
Percentage Increase	4,125.00	4,544.00	3,947.00	3,865.00	3,433.00	—	—	—	3,705.00	3,481.00	—	—

1940	Wives entitled by age benefits—as a percentage of benefits to all workers	(Cells 1D/1A)	53.67%
2004	Wives entitled by age benefits—as a percentage of benefits to all workers	(Cells 2D/3A)	50.53%
1940	Retired women's benefits as a percentage of retired men's benefits	(Cells 1C/1B)	79.28%
2004	Retired women's benefits as a percentage of retired men's benefits	(Cells 2C/2B)	76.76%
2004	Children under age 18 as a percentage of benefits paid to all workers	(Cells 2J/2A)	48.96%
2004	Students' benefits as a percentage paid to all workers	(Cells 2L/2A)	54.29%

Source: Statistical Abstracts of the United States. Dates and Tables vary.

Security payments because of age (there was no entitlement to wives because of children) received a benefit equal to approximately 53.67 percent of the average benefit paid to all retired workers. But by 2004, however, the number of wives entitled because of age had dropped to approximately 50.53 percent of the benefits provided to all retired workers. In 1940, retired women received benefits equal to 79.28 percent of the benefits paid to men, but by 2004, women received 76.76 percent of the benefits paid to men.

Children under age 18 received no benefits in 1940, but in 2004, they received an average of $437.70, or equal to approximately 46 percent of benefits paid to all retired workers. Moreover, children under age 18 received an average of 10 percent more than wives who were entitled because of children. Eligible students received benefits equal to approximately 48.69 percent of that provided to all retired workers in 2004, an average amount greater than that received by all wives in 2004 (cell 4,E). Table 3.2 represents a summary of only a few of the equity issues that have challenged Title II Social Security.

While Social Security benefits are predicated on the presumption that benefits are determined by the earnings in each person's Social Security account, it is not reasonable to expect that every person as a member of a beneficiary group would receive an equal benefit. However, equality of treatment would expect that the method of arriving at the benefit amount be the same for all individuals in all groups. The percentage changes reflected in Table 3.2 are certainly small, but they show how changing demographic factors, increases in benefits through changes in formulas for calculating benefits, and the addition of new beneficiary groups tend to affect equal treatment of beneficiaries in the Title II Social Security program when these subprogram clusters do not have their own program base.

Issues of fairness also have crept into Social Security programs. African Americans and women, in particular, suffer from unfair Social Security treatment because they had low earnings. Married women, in particular, receive no earnings credits when they stay home to rear children or maintain a household, and if they do work, their earnings are usually less than men's largely due to labor market inequities. Such fairness issues are a product of the design of Social Security that ties benefit levels to earning levels, as discussed in the previous chapter. While these fairness issues are certainly a consequence of unfair treatment in the labor market, incremental back door program development simply has magnified original design issues into important equity policy problems for today' efforts to provide fair social insurance. In today's world, unfair earnings lead to unfair Title II benefits, or in other words, Title II Social Security perpetuates unfair earnings.

Efforts to reform Social Security run up against a conundrum. Providing equal benefits, for example by developing a standard formula to establish benefit levels, results in treating beneficiaries unfairly because of labor market inequities. On the other hand, efforts to provide fair treatment results in benefit inequality. Social Security has tried to strike a balance between equality and fairness by adjusting the benefit formula to advantage low-income workers, but further changes to the benefit structure may make a balance between equality and fairness impossible to achieve without serious changes to the basic structure of Title II Social Security. Chapter 10 discusses some possible approaches to this challenge.

The Social Security tax structure raises another equity issue. On the one hand, tax equity would argue for a system that treated all tax payers equally. If equality means that everyone should pay the same amount, a "flat tax" based on a set percentage would find strong support as exists in the present payroll tax. If on the other hand, tax equity means that those who have more should be expected to pay a larger share of the Social Security burden a progressive tax structure would be more appropriate. Since the original design of Social Security linked future benefits with an individual's "contributions" or payments into the system, the less progressive Social Security tax in its present form seemed appropriate at the time. But, as Social Security has been expanded to meet social insurance purposes other than providing for retirement income for a previously employed worker, the present Social Security tax system places a greater relative burden on lower earners, although, perhaps easing the burden for low earners with higher benefits in retirement. Perhaps a careful study of Social Security's program policy options would suggest separating the beneficiary groups, such as benefits for wives, children, and other dependents, and providing them with their own policy and program base, with corresponding worker payments adjusted accordingly. Equity issues also seem to suggest an importance to find an alternative way to fund Title II beneficiates without such a heavy reliance on the payroll tax and the Trust Funds.

Adequacy Issues

Social Security adequacy can be explored from its value as postretirement income, and from its value as replacement for preretirement income. While Social Security benefits were never intended to be the major source of income for retired persons, the question of their adequacy has always been an issue. Roosevelt himself believed that Social Security income would contribute one-third of the total retirement income, with savings and private pensions making up the remainder. Today, Social Security accounts for approximately 39 percent of the postretirement income for persons age 65 and older, as shown below in Figure 3.2. This Social Security share of retirement income, on the average, has remained rather constant for some time.

However, aged retirees are an economically diverse group. The 2006 median income for household units age 65 or older was $20,481, but there are wide income differences. Eighteen percent of persons age 65 and older have an income of under $10,000, while 17 percent have an income of $50,000 or more. As a result of such income differences, Social Security income plays a much more important part as postretirement income for low-income households. In the lowest income group, (lowest income quintile with an income ceiling of $10,400 per year) Social Security benefits provide about 83 percent of total

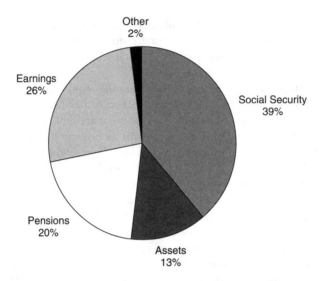

Figure 3.2. Source of Income for Persons Age 65 and Older, 2004.

income (about $719.00 per month) while another 8.4 percent (approximately $73.00 per month) of their income comes from public assistance, mostly from Supplemental Security Income (see Chapter 5). For this lowest income quintile, therefore, over 90 percent of their retirement income comes from a federal source. By contrast, the highest income group (income quintile range above $44,130 per year) receives only 19 percent of its income from Social Security (up to the maximum benefit payment of approximately $1,825 per month) and 40 percent of its income comes from earnings. Because Social Security plays such an important role in postretirement income support for low earners, the formula for determining benefits was adjusted so as to provide a higher benefit for lower workers in relation to their tax contributions, as discussed above.

The poverty threshold for 2006 for a single person aged 65 and older was $10,210, and for a couple aged 65 and older couple it was $13,690. Thus, most of the elderly in the lowest income quintile are likely to live below the poverty threshold even with their Social Security payment. While Social Security was never intended to carry the full burden of postretirement income, it does so for this group of persons, and as such it is very inadequate at meeting their postretirement income needs. On the other hand, Social Security provides only a modest addition to the income of the highest economic quintile of persons aged 65 and older. Supplemental Security Income (see Chapter 5) has been created to provide an income floor and bolster income for low-income earners and other aged retirees, but this assistance program has not succeeded in bringing the income of aged retirees up to livable levels.

From the public policy perspective, it seems terribly unfair that a worker who contributed to Social Security, even though the contribution based on this worker's wages was quite low, should be heavily dependent on Social Security only to find that Social Security does not provide a benefit adequate to keep this prior worker out of poverty. The relatively higher benefits provided to lower-income workers as an effort to address this adequacy issue have raised serious policy questions by those who argue that Supplemental Security Income has made Social Security less dependent on contributions and thus more like a welfare program. However, if Social Security benefits were not increased for low-income workers, more older retirees would be in poverty,[17] and more older people in poverty would likely increase the welfare burden carried by Supplemental Security Income, raising further question over the overlaps between Title II Social Security and Title XVI Supplemental Security Income. See Figure 3.3.

Social Security income adequacy can also be discussed as a measure of the amount of preretirement income it replaces. Such an examination also raises important adequacy issues. Figure 3.4 below shows the amount of total preretirement income Social Security replaces for high, medium, and low earning men and women. The Social Security value of both pre- and post-retirement income again point to a high dependency on Social Security for persons who were low wage earners during their working years.

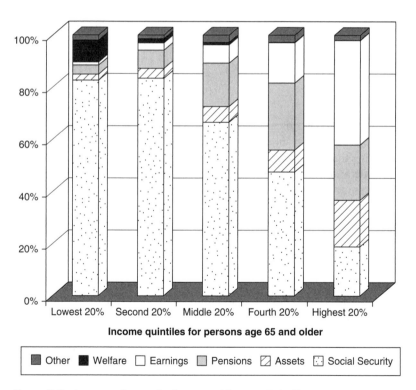

Figure 3.3. Aggregate Income by Source and Income Quintile.

Source: U.S. Department of Commerce, Statistical Abstracts of the United States, 2007. Tables vary.

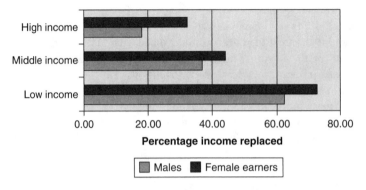

Figure 3.4. Preretirement Income Replaced by Social Security.

Incremental program developments based on funding principles established by macroeconomic policies have left Social Security programs in an
incomprehensible state as they are administered today. Even the most obvious
programs, outlined in the previous chapter leave students and policy makers
grasping for general principles which would lend some organization to this
complexity. Perhaps the foremost policy objective for Social Security should
be to review its multiple programs and consolidate them in a way so as to
insure a clear understanding of what Social Security provides to Americans
today.

Conclusion

Social Security today raises several serious fiscal and program policy issues.
Fiscally, Social Security financing is caught between larger macroeconomic
policy issues that seek limited government reserves on the one hand, and political considerations that require actuarially soundness on the other. Practically
speaking, some opponents of Social Security would eliminate the Trust Fund
reserves, while other opponents proclaim that the program is running out of
money. The payroll tax, as important as it is for Social Security's political stability, has become a regressive tax that will continue to face public objections as
current tax rates on earnings continue to increase. Actuarial soundness under
the present system of Trust Fund financing has become a major funding issue
facing Social Security as the nation looks forward to the social insurance needs
of the population in the twenty-first century. A forward-thinking examination
of Title II social insurance will also require consideration of a changing labor
force in addition to the traditional issues of population changes and economic
growth as factors important to developing projections of resources necessary
to support Title II commitments.

Title II's Social Security program issues are highlighted by the lack of a
coherent twenty-first-century social welfare policy foundation for the many
beneficiary elements of today's Social Security program. The historic Title II

policy objectives were reached largely by years of back door program development, and in the process, Title II Social Security has developed a complex array of beneficiary groups and even more complex set of benefits, leading to serious problems in the equity of benefits provided and their adequacy. The important distinction between social insurance and welfare assistance in the original Title II Social Security program has become less distinguishable, particularly with the creations of SSI discussed in Chapter 5. While Title II Social Security continues to provide benefits in an efficient and timely manner, the complexity of the program detracts seriously from Social Security's ability to maintain its crucial role in meeting America's social welfare obligations.

Without a doubt, Social Security as provided under Title II of the Social Security Act has become America's most important welfare commitment. It is also America's least understood welfare commitment, largely because of the complex way it has developed over the past seventy-five years. Social Security's piecemeal development can be traced partly to America's commitment to macroeconomic planning, the vision of its early administrators and their dogged efforts to achieve a comprehensive social insurance vision, and the confusing political and economic effects of Title II's program characteristics as they have developed. While the discussion of Social Security's programs and policy problems suggests areas where policy changes are seriously needed, perhaps a more prudent approach to reforming Social Security would involve a complete study of Social Security in its entirety as it exists today, with recognition of the nation's need for social insurance.

Social Security will continue to raise challenging questions because it is a dynamic effort to ensure economic security to Americans, and both the need for economic security and the best ways to provide it are in a constant state of change, just as American social and economic life, too, is in constant change. By incremental, opportunistic program development, Social Security has been seen as a static program that only needed fine tuning. Even during its initial planning in 1934, the complete idea of an American social insurance program was never fully envisioned, and as the program developed efforts to analyze Social Security were lost in the politics of program development and the economics of program funding. Without a thorough review and analysis of Social Security, it will remain a poorly understood program under constant attack. Chapter 10 offers some perspective on changes that will improve this most important social welfare undertaking.

NOTES

1. Wilbur Cohen, in particular, built a strong coalition of influential persons from labor, the social welfare community, and even the insurance industry, and Arthur Altmeyer remained his constant mentor. Cohen was not known as Mr. Social Security without good reason. His well-known views for a comprehensive social

insurance enterprise formed the base for his loyal political support. Berkowitz provides a compelling view of the scope of Cohen's vision and his vast influential network. See Edward D. Berkowitz, *Mr. Social Security. The Life of Wilbur J. Cohen* (Lawrence, KS: University of Kansas Press, 1995), particularly Chapter 4.

2. See James L. Sundquist, *Politics and Policy* (Washington, DC: The Brookings Institution, 1968), chap. VII.

3. Martha Derthick, *Policymaking for Social Security* (Washington, DC: The Brookings Institution, 1979), 7.

4. Steven Kemp Bailey, *Congress Makes a Law. The Story Behind the Employment Act of 1946* (New York: Columbia University Press, 1950). The Employment Act followed a tortured political course to its enactment, mostly pitting advocates for an active government policy against those who advocated for limited government intervention into the American economic system.

5. See *Full employment in a Free Competitive Economy*. U.S. Congress, Committee on Banking and Currency. (79th Congress 1st Session, 1945).

6. Julian E. Zelizer, *Taxing America. Wilbur D. Mill, Congress, and the State, 1945–1975* (New York: Cambridge University Press, 1998), 15.

7. Zelizer, *Taxing America*, 61.

8. Derthick, *Policy Making for Social Security*, 91.

9. Eric M. Patashnik, *Putting Trust in the US Budget* (New York: Cambridge University Press, 2000), 72.

10. See, for example, F. J. Crowley, "Financing the Social Security Program—Then and Now" in U.S. Congress, Joint Economic Committee, *Studies in Public Welfare, vol. 18.* (Washington, D.C.: Government Printing Office, 1974), particularly 25–28. One of the most comprehensive efforts to review America's social welfare enterprise authorized under the Social Security Act was undertaken between 1972 and 1974 by the U.S. Congress Joint Economic committee, sub-committee on Public Welfare chaired by Martha Griffiths. The Committee issued 20 reports (volumes) containing over 50 studies and recommendations. A summary of these reports can be found in Andrew Dobelstein, *Examining Poverty* (Greensboro, North Carolina: North Carolina Poverty Project, 1987), 39.

11. See for example, Carolyn Weaver, *The Crisis in Social Security* (Durham, North Carolina: Duke University Press, 1982), 110–111.

12. Zelizer, *Taxing America*.

13. Edward D. Berkowitz, *Mr. Social Security. The Life of Wilbur J. Cohen* (Lawrence, KS: University of Kansas Press, 1995).

14. Social Security Administration, Office of the Chief Actuary, *Report of the Trustees of the Social Security Trust Fund*, 2004.

15. See John L. Palmer and Isabel Sawhill, eds., *The Reagan Record: An Assessment of America's Changing Domestic Policies* (Washington, DC: The Urban Institute Press, 1982).

16. Of course this critique of Title II funding issues is hardly new. For years, the Brookings Institution has kept up a constant flow of studies documenting the economic vagaries of Title II funding and recommendations for reforms. See the latest statement by Brookings: Peter A. Diamond and Peter R. Orszag, *Saving Social Security* (Washington, D.C.: The Brookings Institution Press, 2005).

17. Social Security Administration, Supplemental Security Record, and the Department of Health and Human Services, 100 percent data, 2004. Appendix 3.1.

4

Title III: Unemployment Insurance

Introduction

Along with Title II Social Security, Unemployment Insurance, which is Title III of the Social Security Act, formed the second of two social insurances authorized under the Act (see Chapter 1). But Unemployment Insurance/ Compensation[a] differed significantly from Title II Social Security, both in 1935 when it was created and as it operates today. Unemployment Insurance has become one of America's most frequently used income security social welfare program, second only to Social Security with respect to the number of persons covered and the amount of spending. For example, in the second quarter of 2006, over 2.5 million persons applied for unemployment benefits, constituting an average payment of $2,796 to eligible beneficiaries. The Unemployment Insurance program collected $36.3 billion in 2006.[1]

Unemployment Insurance was designed to provide a temporary stream of income to workers who lost their jobs through no fault of their own and were searching for employment.[b] Interestingly enough, Unemployment Insurance receives very little attention as a social welfare program, probably because it is administered by the states under the supervision of the U.S. Department of Labor, and thus for the most part, Unemployment Insurance is seen as a labor program rather than as a social insurance program. The effectiveness of Unemployment Insurance has become compromised by co-mingling its income protection objectives of social insurances under the Social Security Act with Department of Labor objectives that emphasize putting people back to work.

In spite of the fact that Unemployment Insurance is a well-known, heavily used, social welfare program (see Table 4.1), it leaves many recipients confused about the benefits they receive and the processes they have to go through to receive those benefits. The idea of Unemployment Insurance appears simple. If you are out of work, you apply to the Economic Security Commission, and get a check from the government to keep you going until you are employed again.

---

[a] Unemployment Insurance is the name of the program. The product is Unemployment Compensation. The terms "insurance" and "compensation" are frequently used interchangeably.

[b] A second purpose for Unemployment Insurance was to help stabilize the economy during recessions.

Table 4.1. State Unemployment Insurance—Summary: 1970–2005

Item	Unit	1970	1980	1985	1990	1995	2000	2005
Insured Unemployment, Average Weekly	1,000	1,805	3,356	2,617	2,522	2,572	2,110	2,662
Percent of Covered Employment[1]	Percent	3.4	3.9	2.9	2.4	2.3	1.7	2.1
Percent of Civilian unemployed	Percent	44.1	43.9	31.5	35.8	34.7	37.6	35.7
Unemployment Benefits, Average Weekly	Dollars	50	100	128	161	187	221	267
Percent of Weekly Wage	Percent	35.6	36.6	35.3	36.0	35.5	32.9	35.5
Weeks Compensated	Million	78.9	149.0	119.3	116.2	118.3	96.0	121.1
Beneficiaries, First Payments	1,000	6,402	9,992	8,372	8,629	8,035	7,033	7,922
Average Duration of Benefits[2]	Weeks	12.3	14.9	14.2	13.4	14.7	13.7	15.3
Claimants Exhausting Benefits	1,000	1,295	3,072	2,572	2,323	2,662	2,144	2,856
Percent of First Payment[3]	Percent	24.4	33.2	31.2	29.4	34.3	31.8	35.9
Contributions Collected[4]	Billion dollars	2.5	11.4	19.3	15.2	22.0	19.9	34.8
Benefits Paid	Billion dollars	3.8	14.2	14.7	18.1	21.2	20.5	31.2
Funds Available for Benefits[5]	Billion dollars	11.9	6.6	10.1	37.9	35.4	53.4	28.6
Average Employer contribution Rate[6]	Percent	1.30	2.37	3.13	1.95	2.44	1.75	2.92

Source: U.S. Employment and Training Administration, *Unemployment Insurance Financial Data Handbook.*
http://www.workforcesecurity.doleta.gov/unemploy/finance.asp

[1,805 **represents 1,805,000.** Includes unemployment compensation for state and local government employees who were covered by state law].
[1] Insured unemployment as percent of average covered employment in preceeding year.
[2] Weeks compensated divided by first payment.
[3] Based on first payments for 12-month period ending June 30.
[4] Contributions from employers; also employees in states which tax workers.
[5] End of year. Sum of balances in all UI accounts.
[6] As percent of taxable wages.

But the way the program works is considerably more complex. This chapter is designed to provide a basic understanding of the program structure of Unemployment Insurance, and the many complex policy issues plaguing Unemployment Insurance that have contributed to that complexity. But in order to properly understand both the program structure of Unemployment Insurance and its excessive policy problems, a discussion of the context in which Unemployment Insurance was created in 1935 previews the present complex ways Unemployment Insurance currently provides economic assistance to unemployed persons. Of all the programs that comprise America's social welfare enterprise, the legacy of Unemployment Insurance's development has left what is probably today's most handicapped social welfare program, and the most in need of serious revision in order to meet the needs of today's unemployed.

The Political, Economic, and Social Context for the Creation of Title III Unemployment Insurance

Social, economic, and political confusions intensified as the Great Depression of 1929 grew steadily worse. Roosevelt's emergency programs began to get people working and rewarded them with a weekly paycheck, but raking leaves, repairing roads, and even constructing public buildings did not re-create a pre-Depression economy. Jobs in the Works Progress Administration were not the same as jobs in the steel mills, the coal mines, the railroads, and other vital industrial and commercial venues, and unemployment in the American economy persisted in spite of the emergency work programs. With perhaps as many as one-third of the labor force out of work, Congress was flooded with proposals to increase employment, setting off a scramble for new initiatives that could get people back to work. In this environment, the Wagner–Lewis Unemployment Bill (Senator Robert Wagner (NY) and Representative David Lewis (MD)) was working its way favorably through Congress when President Roosevelt withdrew his support for the bill and instead asked Congress for the authority to create the Committee on Economic Security in order to provide Congress with a comprehensive social welfare proposal that finally became the Social Security Act.

The debate over the Wagner–Lewis Unemployment Bill exposed some of the issues that later defined Title III, Unemployment Insurance. First, debates over unemployment insurance framed it as a labor issue. States had been experimenting with various forms of compensation for unemployed laborers, including in New York where minimum wage issues, worker safety, and unemployment concerns were part of the responsibility of Frances Perkins when she was New York's Chairwoman, New York State Industrial Commission. The University of Wisconsin had developed a renowned program in labor economics, and as pointed out in earlier chapters, the "brain trust" of the Committee on Economic Security was heavily weighted with University of Wisconsin labor economists. Under the influence of the Wisconsin labor economists, and with first-hand experience of Wisconsin's unemployment insurance law, the nation's first, as the reference point for these economists, unemployment insurance was discussed as a labor issue rather than as an income security issue in the Committee on Economic Security.

Additionally, particularly in early arguments over the Wagner–Lewis Bills, unemployment was considered an employer issue, not an employee issue. It might seem strange today, but particularly in the early days of the Great Depression, many employers believed that they had a responsibility to provide steady employment for their workers. This paternalistic attitude was not shared among all employers, by any means, but the employers who felt a responsibility to keep their workers employed believed they should not have to share the burden of unemployment insurance payments made necessary by employers who did not protect their labor force from unemployment. This "good business" view was sufficiently widespread, however, that when Wisconsin passed its unemployment insurance law, it stated in part that employers had employee obligations and thus should not hire or import workers and then leave them to be supported by the public dollars whenever employers no longer needed their services. Seasonal employers, in particular, were likely to employ persons on an intermittent basis. Employers, therefore, argued that they should not have to bear unemployment costs for employers who failed to provide steady employment for their workers.[2] Support for the Wagner–Lewis Unemployment Bills reflected the Wisconsin experiences and the success of its unemployment program.

Financing and administrative concerns were similar to those constitutional issues the Committee on Economic Security faced in the development of Title II Social Security, but they overshadowed Title II Social Security debates in their intensity. A state-administered program was clearly preferred, although some on the Committee on Economic Security, Harry Hopkins in particular, argued that only a federal program could provide sufficient worker protection; Roosevelt and Perkins supported the state-administered program.[c]

There were several forms Unemployment Insurance could take. It could be administered exclusively by the Federal Government similar to Social Security; it could be administered by the states with grants from the Federal Government, as was proposed for the assistance programs; it could be administered through a federal–state partnership. The first alternative was rejected on the grounds that unemployment characteristics varied from state to state, as did wages, and that it would be difficult to develop and administer a national Unemployment Insurance program. Moreover, a national Unemployment Insurance program might encourage labor independence and mobility, thereby

---

[c] According to Edward Berkowitz, Roosevelt remarked to Secretary Perkins. "We've got to keep a lot of responsibility . . . in the states. Just think what it would be like to have all the power in the federal government if Huey Long should become President." Edward Berkowitz, *America's Welfare Stater From Roosevelt to Reagan*, 32–33.

further enhancing the power of organized labor.[d] The second alternative was rejected because the grant-in-aid to states not only resembled the welfare type assistance programs, but since the characteristics of unemployment differed from state to state, the Committee on Economic Security believed that it would be essential for each state to take control of its own unemployment problems. The third alternative was similar to the Wagner–Lewis proposals, and as a preference of President Roosevelt and Frances Perkins this alternative was adopted after much of the contentious Committee debate had subsided.

The Wagner–Lewis type of federal–state partnership also appeared to have better potential to pass a constitutional challenge than Title II Social Security. The U.S. Supreme Court had upheld the Federal Excise Tax Act that allowed an offset of taxes owed to the Federal Government of inheritance taxes paid under state tax laws.[3] Supreme Court Chief Justice Louis Brandeis had suggested this method of financing the Wagner–Lewis bill, and the Florida case was cited as precedence avoiding a constitutional challenge to Unemployment Insurance.[e] The Unemployment Insurance program's taxes would be collected under the authority of Title IX of the Social Security Act, and the program of Unemployment Insurance would be administered under Title III of the Act by the Bureau of Unemployment Compensation (BUC) of the Social Security Board. The complexity of this arrangement provided no guidance to how the program would actually be administered once it became law.

Berkowitz reports that there were important ideological differences among members of the Committee on Economic Security over the kind of Unemployment Insurance that should be included in the Social Security Act. The Wisconsin model proposed that each industry would be responsible for its own unemployment problems; employers would make contributions the employer's separate fund, making financing the sole responsibility of the employer. Opponents to the Wisconsin model preferred a pooled fund with standard rates of payments for all employers to trust funds from which benefits would be paid. Opponents of the Wisconsin model argued that employer incentives to stabilize employment in a time of large-scale unemployment had little basis in reality. Labor also preferred a pooled fund model since the Wisconsin model gave employers more control over labor at a time when labor was struggling to develop a recognized and respectable place in labor–employer relationships.

---

[d] The Wagner Act passed Congress and was signed into law in July 1935, a month before the Social Security Act became law. The Wagner Act, without any Unemployment Insurance provisions, "granted labor the greatest power it had ever possessed in U.S. History." See David Milton, *The Politics of U.S. Labor From the Great Depression to the New Deal* (New York: Monthly Review Press, 1982), 74. The president's support of the Wagner Act marked an important shift in relations between labor and the Federal Government.

[e] Justice Brandeis's daughter, Lois, had been a student in the labor economics program at the University of Wisconsin along with her husband Paul Raushenbush, and they reportedly passed the Justice's observation on to the Committee on Economic Security. See Edward Berkowitz, *America's Welfare State From Roosevelt to Nixon* and http://www.ssa.gov/history/eliot/html.

The financing arrangement for Title III Unemployment Insurance had important consequences for the program's development. The offset tax principle established by *Florida v. Mellon* allowed the financing of Title III Unemployment Insurance by a federal tax levied against an employer, but the tax the employer paid became a credit against the business taxes the employer owed the Federal Government, less a small administrative fee. This arrangement meant that, in real terms, the Federal Government, not the employer, shouldered the financial burden for Title III Unemployment Insurance. Thus, contrary to the intent of the Wisconsin model, the method of financing Title III Unemployment Insurance removed much of the employer's responsibility for unemployment and shifted this responsibility to the Federal Government. This financing structure is discussed in more detail below.

Witte and Perkins urged Roosevelt to accept the modified Wisconsin model which he easily did since he had already supported the earlier Wagner–Lewis bill and because of his preference for a state-administered program. Under pressure to get money to the states for assistance payments, and faced with the uncertainties of Title II Social Security, Congress accepted the Committee's recommendations without much consideration of the program's more substantive issues. Yet, as Berkowitz points out, there was much more substance to the different approaches than simply Wisconsin pride. The Wisconsin model represented a "form of deferred wage, similar to sick leave . . . that the company owed the employee." Pooled funds, in contrast, "amounted to a form of charity: a subsidy from efficient to inefficient employers." In Berkowitz's words "[The Wisconsin model] represented benefits that an employee had earned by working: [pooled funds] guaranteed benefits to all who were not working."[4] Berkowitz's analysis shows that the Wisconsin approach, like Title II Social Security, conferred eligibility for unemployment compensation by earnings through working. It would be an "earned benefit," and therefore entitlement as a statutory right, but different in that the individual worker would not contribute to any unemployment fund.[f]

Summary of the Development of Title III Unemployment Insurance

Title III Unemployment Insurance began with a complex structure. Taxes were collected from individual employers by the Federal Government and deposited into separate federal trust fund accounts designated for each state. The states then would draw on these state designated funds to pay unemployment claims, according to the eligibility criteria set by each state. The unemployment taxes

---

[f] At first Secretary of the Treasury Henry Morgenthau refused to sign off on the proposals for Unemployment Insurance because they did not provide a provision for worker contribution to the program, but he later backed off his position and signed the report that went to President Roosevelt. See Arthur Altmeyer, *The Formative Years of Social Security* (Madison: University of Wisconsin Press, 1966), 14–17.

that were collected were used to "offset" the business excise taxes employers owed to the Federal Government. In other words, in its simplest form, business taxes were reduced based on the amount of unemployment tax paid by the business and based on the amount of unemployment the business experienced—later called unemployment "experience ratings." The Federal Government paid the administrative costs of the program from a small portion of the taxes it collected.

States were free to set their own criteria for Unemployment Insurance eligibility as long as they complied with the general purposes set forth by Title III: persons had to have worked in employment covered by Unemployment Insurance and have gained eligibility coverage; persons had to become unemployed through no fault of their own; unemployed persons had to be willing and able to accept a job. The details of these requirements were left to the states to work out for themselves. Some businesses were exempted from mandatory coverage in state plans. Title III of the Social Security Act authorized payment to each state, from each state's unemployment trust fund, as long as the state had an approved unemployment insurance law. The amount available to each state from each state's fund was based on the population of the state, an estimate of the number of persons covered by the state unemployment insurance law, and an estimate of the cost of proper and efficient program administration. The amount of the insurance payment to the unemployed person was calculated by the states, based on a minimum federal calculation.

The length of time a person could collect insurance benefits was limited. Later in the program, the number of weeks a person could collect Unemployment Insurance was lengthened using both offset funds from employers and federal funds, and later benefit limitations were extended further through emergency federal legislative provisions. These benefit extensions have not only added to the complexity of the program, but they suggest the income maintenance limitations characteristic of this program from its very beginning. Even with the extensions, time-limited benefits continue to exist to this day.

Thus, the original complexity of establishing Unemployment Insurance and the variation of benefits from state to state have made Unemployment Insurance a very difficult program to administer. Moreover, from the beginning, Unemployment Insurance differed from the social insurance principles established under the Title II Social Security (retirement) program. No workers contributed to Unemployment Insurance. Instead, on the surface, the employer bore the cost of the program, but in reality the Federal Government financed the program costs because the excise tax paid by the employer offset federal taxes the employer would have otherwise been required to pay. As a result, entitlement to Unemployment Insurance was not as fundamental as the entitlement to retirement benefits under Social Security. Unemployment Insurance had a statutory guarantee to persons who worked in "covered employment," but the terms of the guarantee were set by the states.

The work-related conditions placed on Unemployment Insurance made it a modest program of income support, clearly designed to get workers back to work. Ironically enough, those who were unemployed before the program became law in 1935, the persons who needed Unemployment Insurance most, were not eligible for Title III benefits since they had not worked in "covered employment" for the required period of time. In many ways, therefore, Unemployment Insurance ended up resembling an employee benefit program rather than a social insurance program. Unemployment Insurance developed as a mixed social insurance hybrid of both an emphasis on returning to work and an interim income support during a short period of unemployment, causing both program and policy problems as discussed below.

Although the original Title III program was administered by the Social Security Board, and later by the Federal Security Agency, administrative responsibility for Unemployment Insurance was transferred to the Department of Labor in 1949 on recommendation of the Hoover Commission. President Truman advocated strongly for this transfer in order to bring Unemployment Insurance into closer harmony with expectations of the Employment Act of 1946 (see Chapter 3). The 1949 reorganization, however, created a bifurcated system where the authority for the program, including raising the money to fund Unemployment Insurance rested in the Social Security Act and the Federal Security Agency, while the administrative responsibility for the program was given to the Department of Labor. This program separation has led to a certain amount of ambivalence about the program by both the federal agencies.

Unemployed and Unemployment Characteristics

The historic context of Unemployment Insurance provides part of the explanation for its complexity. The characteristics of unemployment explain another facet of Unemployment Insurance's complexity. Unemployment is more complex than a first glance might suggest. Unemployment for Unemployment Insurance purposes is more complex than being without a job. The present, official, definition of unemployment is based on a definition of the labor force. Once the labor force is defined, unemployment is someone in the labor force who is not employed. The civilian labor force in America today comprises about 66 percent of the civilian population over the age of 16 years. Retired persons and women are the largest populations not counted as part of the labor force, nor are persons who have become discouraged at finding work and who have not worked during the previous year counted in the labor force. Employment for those in the labor force is defined as those who have least 1 hour of a paid employment per week, and the unemployed are those who had no employment, as defined above, but who are available for work. It is important to clarify that people not in the labor force are therefore not considered unemployed. Some of the most important definitions that apply to unemployment are found below in Box 4.1.

Box 4.1 Official Definitions from the U.S. Department of Labor

Employed persons are those in civilian non-institutional population who worked at least 1 hour as a paid employee and those who were not working but had jobs they were away from temporarily for various personal or work reasons. Employed persons are counted only once even if they hold more than one job. Persons who work without pay are not considered employed.

Unemployed persons are those who had no employment, were available for work, and had made specific efforts to find employment sometime during the previous four weeks. Persons waiting to be recalled to their jobs need not have to be looking for work to be classified as unemployed.

Full-time workers are persons who worked 35 hours or more per week.

Discouraged workers are persons who are not in the labor force but want a job and have looked for work during the past year or since they lost their job, but are not currently looking for work because they believe there are no jobs for them.

Displaced workers are persons who lost jobs because their company closed or moved and there was not sufficient work for them.

Multiple jobholders are persons who had two or more jobs for pay, were self-employed or worked as an unpaid family worker and also held a paid job.

Marginally attached workers are persons not in the labor force but who want a job, have looked for jobs in the previous year, but were not counted as unemployed because they had not searched for work in the previous month. Discouraged workers are included in the group of marginally attached workers.

Source: Based on Definitions used by United States Census, Census of Population Surveys.

Figure 4.1 provides a graphic view of the relationship of unemployment to the adult population and labor force. At the height of the Great Depression, when unemployment reached over 30 percent of the working population, little attention was paid to the characteristics of unemployment and the unemployed population. Today, however, an apparently modest unemployment rate masks some important unemployment characteristics that complicate Title III Unemployment Insurance. Unemployment for August 2007, for example, was reported as a modest 4.5 percent. However, as Figure 4.2 shows, the unemployment rate has fluctuated from approximately 3.5 percent in 2002 and over 6.5 percent in 2003. While the percentage range may seem minute when compared with unemployment in the early 1930s, a 1 percent increase in unemployment amounts to unemployment for 1.5 million workers, based on the average 2007 labor force civilian participation rate. Moreover, Figure 4.2 shows wide percentage fluctuations within the 3.5–6.5 percentage range, both from year to year and within years. In other words, unemployment is a dynamic variable, not only in workers' lives, but as a macroeconomic concern as well. A 3 percent

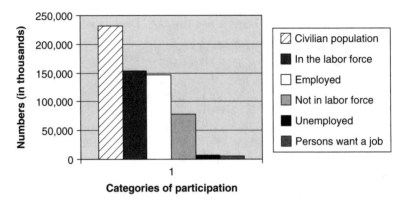

Figure 4.1. Labor Force Characteristics, Persons Age 20 and Older.

variation in unemployment over the past decade, sometimes called "frictional unemployment,"[g] may well reflect "balanced" economic growth, but even these modest unemployment swings produce economic problems for many individual laborers. Title III Unemployment Insurance has tried to address the problem of fluctuations in unemployment by providing federal extended benefits, but the efforts are sluggish and have become politically controversial. These benefits are discussed below.

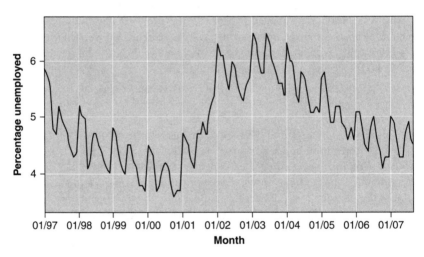

Figure 4.2. Percent Unemployed, January 1979–August 2007. All persons age 16 and older.

Source: United States Department of Labor, Bureau of Labor Statistics, 2007. Series number LNU04000000.

---

[g] "Frictional unemployment" is the term generally used to describe the percentage of the labor force that may be unemployed, but reflects that part of the labor force likely to be changing jobs or between jobs.

Table 4.2. Employment Status of the Civilian Population by Sex and Age

	August 2007	August 2006
TOTAL, 16 Years and Over	(Numbers in Thousands)	
Civilian Noninstitutional Population	232,201	229,167
Civilian Labor Force	153,493	151,734
Participation Rate	66.1	66.2
Employed	146,406	144,618
Employment-Population Ratio	63.0	63.1
Unemployed	7,088	7,116
Unemployment Rate	4.6	4.7
Not in Labor Force	78,717	77,433
Persons Who Currently Want a Job	4,965	4,887
Men, 16 Years and Over		
Civilian Noninstitutional Population	112,354	110,792
Civilian Labor Force	82,541	81,309
Participation Rate	73.5	73.4
Employed	78,972	77,482
Employment-Population Ratio	70.3	69.9
Unemployed	3,569	3,827
Unemployment Rate	4.3	4.7
Not in Labor Force	29,813	29,482
Women, 16 Years and Over		
Civilian Noninstitutional Population	119,856	118,376
Civilian Labor Force	70,952	70,425
Participation Rate	59.2	59.5
Employed	67,433	67,136
Employment-Population Ratio	56.3	56.7
Unemployed	3,519	3,289
Unemployment Rate	5.0	4.7
Not in Labor Force	48,904	47,951

Source: Table A-1. Employment status of the civilian population by sex and age. U.S. Department of Labor, 2006.

Not only does unemployment fluctuate from month to month, but it also fluctuates widely by labor sector, as shown in Figure 4.3. In 2007, unemployment in government and financial employment averaged 2.3 and 2.4 percent respectively, and unemployment in agriculture and construction averaged 10 and 8.9 percent. Such fluctuations in overall unemployment and among different labor sectors suggest the dynamic nature of unemployment and the difficulty of efforts to provide income protection for the unemployed. Figure 4.3 shows the differential unemployment risks among major employers, reflecting the Wisconsin concern that not all places of employment are equally responsible for the overall unemployment burden. The fact of unemployment, however, is an equal burden for individual workers regardless of their place of employment.

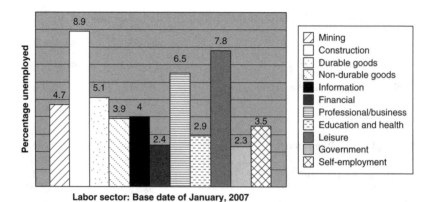

Labor sector: Base date of January, 2007

Figure 4.3. Unemployment by Labor Sector.
Source: U.S. Department of Labor, Bureau of Labor Statistics, 2007.

Unemployment Insurance Program Framework

One of the most important characteristics of Title III Unemployment Insurance is that it is a Federal Government social insurance program administered by the states. Yet, it is not a grant-in-aid program like the Title IV programs. Each state sets the specific rules for beneficiary eligibility and beneficiary benefits. Thus, in spite of its status as a Federal Government social insurance program, most administrative rules are set by the individual states with little federal supervision. The following discussion provides a general picture of the Unemployment Insurance program structure, highlighting these strikingly different characteristics.

Beneficiaries

The beneficiaries of Unemployment Insurance are workers who are covered by the program, have lost jobs due to no fault of their own, and are actively looking for work. Many of these workers are members of families, and as a result children, wives, husbands, and unrelated persons who might be living in the household of the unemployed worker may benefit indirectly from the program. However, benefits are not adjusted for family size or composition. A person is not obligated to accept work if the position offered is vacant due to a strike or labor problem.

Coverage

In order to receive Unemployment Insurance benefits, the unemployed person must first *(1) have worked for an employer covered by the state's plan, (2) have worked for a specified period of time, (3) have earned a certain amount of wages,* and *(4) have an ability and willingness to work.*

State Plan Coverage

While there is considerable state-to-state variation, beneficiaries must have worked for an employer who was required to participate in the state's Unemployment Insurance plan. In general, the minimum federal requirements for an approved state program must provide worker coverage when, first, workers worked full time in employment where they were paid at least $1,500 during any calendar quarter or, second, persons who worked for employers who employed workers full time in at least 1 day of each of 20 weeks in the current or prior year. Unemployment Insurance is available to agricultural workers who worked for employers who paid cash wages of at least $20,000 for agricultural labor in any calendar quarter or who employed 10 or more workers in at least 1 day in each of 20 different weeks in the current or prior year.

Unemployment Insurance is also available to domestic service workers from employers who paid cash wages of $1,000 or more for domestic service during any calendar quarter in the current or prior year. The requirements for coverage are slightly different in states for employees of nonprofit organization, state-local governments, certain agricultural labor, and certain domestic service workers. Full-time employment is considered at least 35 hours per week. Thus, Unemployment Insurance does not cover part-time workers.

Period of Time and Earnings

Eligibility for benefits depends on a combination of the amount of time a person worked and the amount of personal earnings. States vary in the length of time a person worked in covered employment and the amount of worker earnings, but generally a worker must have worked for two quarters and earned at least $1,770 to qualify for a minimum weekly benefit; to qualify for a maximum weekly benefit, the earnings could be as high as $30,888 in Colorado. The range of qualifying earnings benefit eligibility varies widely from state to state as shown in Table 4.2. Most states accept the two quarter employment period. See Table 4.3.

Demonstrated ability and willingness to seek and accept suitable employment: Perhaps the key component of Title III Unemployment Insurance that differentiates it from Title II social insurance is the emphasis placed on work rather than on income support. In addition to the requirement that persons must become unemployed "through no fault of their own," they must be willing and able to work at suitable employment. Most state laws list certain criteria defining "suitability" of work as work that does not include a degree of risk to the person's safety, morals, physical fitness, and must be consistent with prior training, experience, and earnings. A person is not obligated to accept work if the position offered is vacant due to a strike, or labor dispute, if the wages, hours, or other conditions of the work are substantially less favorable to the individual than those prevailing for similar work, or if the individual would be required to join a union or to resign from joining any bona fide labor organization. These provisions clearly exclude striking workers.

Benefits

Benefit Amounts

All the benefits of Unemployment Insurance are cash payments made directly to the unemployed worker. The states set weekly benefit amounts based on some fraction of the state's average weekly wage. In general, the state-determined weekly benefit amounts replaces between 50 and 70 percent of the individual's average weekly pretax wage up to some state-determined maximum. As the individuals' average weekly wages rise, the replacement ratios become smaller reflecting a slight redistributive bias in favor of lower wage

Table 4.3. Monetary and Quarter Qualification Requirements for Minimum and Maximum Weekly Benefit Amounts

STATE	Minimum	Maximum	Total Max.	Quarters
Alabama		$2,136	$9,096	$14,818	2Q
Alaska		1,000	26,750	26,750	2Q
Arizona		1,500	7,000	15,990	2Q
Arkansas		1,539	15,667	25,038	2Q
California		1,125	9,487	11,958	
Colorado		2,500	30,888	10,560	
Connecticut	600	19,864	15,880	2Q	
Delaware		720	13,800	14,490	
District of Columbia	1,950	12,051	16,068	2Q	
Florida		3,400	10,725	28,598	2Q
Georgia		1,404	9,864	28,496	2Q
Hawaii		130	9,646	9,646	2Q
Idaho		1,657	10,238	26,618	2Q
Illinois		1,600	17,069	15,431	2Q
Indiana		2,750	29,200	29,200	2Q
Iowa		1,230	7,956	21,294	2Q
Kansas		2,490	9,990	25,974	2Q
Kentucky		1,500	21,561	26,600	2Q
Louisiana		1,200	8,062	24,843	2Q
Maine		3,120	17,082	20,670	2Q
Maryland		864	10,080	10,444	2Q
Massachusetts	2,700	15,360	42,667		
Michigan		2,997	10,977	19,500	2Q
Minnesota		1,250	10,757	44,408	2Q
Mississippi	1,200	7,600	14,820	2Q	
Missouri		1,500	9,375	18,330	2Q
Montana		1,597	23,700	26,300	2Q
Nebraska		1,600	7,612	20,436	2Q
Nevada		600	11,287	23,478	2Q
New Hampshire	2,800	28,500	29,500	2Q	
New Jersey	2,060	15,833	20,583	2Q	

Source: U.S. Department of Labor, Bureau of Labor Statistics, 2007.

Table 4.3. continued

STATE		Minimum	Maximum	Total Max.	Quarters
New Mexico	1,716	8,255	11,570	2Q	
New York		2,400	14,235	15,795	2Q
North Carolina	3,586	14,625	25,116	2Q	
North Dakota	2,795	28,275	29,545	2Q	
Ohio		2,640	10,680	13,884	2Q
Oklahoma		1,500	10,039	17,128	2Q
Oregon		1,000	26,320	29,328	2Q
Pennsylvania	1,320	14,920	17,120	2Q	
Puerto Rico	280	5,320	5,320	2Q	
Rhode Island	2,060	12,900	28,672	2Q	
South Carolina	900	10,101	20,202	2Q	
South Dakota	1,288	10,764	18,252	2Q	
Tennessee		1,560	11,440	26,520	2Q
Texas		1,887	11,803	30,715	2Q
Utah		2,300	13,845	34,185	2Q
Vermont		1,723	12,375	13,410	2Q
Virginia		2,950	13,400	27,872	2Q
Virgin Islands	1,287	2,909	25,818	2Q	
Washington	2,200	22,050	39,690		
West Virginia	2,200	31,900	31,900	2Q	
Wisconsin		1,380	9,390	19,305	2Q
Wyoming		2,100	9,905	24,700	2Q

workers. However, states have a specified amount of money in their trust accounts with the Federal Government, and when the average length of time for Unemployment Insurance payments is less than anticipated, State trust funds grow, encouraging employers to seek to reduce their rates. When the average length of time for Unemployment Insurance payments is more than antici-pated, state trust funds shrink. When states run out of money, they may borrow from the Federal Government.

Benefit Duration

The length of time an unemployed worker can receive Unemployment Insur-ance benefits depends on a three-tiered time structure. First, a basic permanent program provides twenty six weeks of benefits. State trust funds provide funding for this basic program. Second, an Extended Benefit program may extend benefits for another thirteen weeks. The Extended Benefits program is available in states when unemployment in that state reaches a set per-centage of official unemployment, usually 6 percent. When this percentage is reached, the Extended Benefits program automatically becomes available to the states. Half of the funding for this Extended Benefits program comes from the Federal Government, and half comes from the state trust fund. Finally, Congress has approved Temporary Emergency Unemployment Benefits when unemployment remains high and unemployed workers are exhausting their basic benefits and their extended benefits. Temporary Emergency Unemployment Benefits usually extends the benefit period for unemployed workers for an additional 7–13 weeks. The Temporary Emergency Unemployment Benefits are created by Congress for short time periods, such as one or two years, and thus when they expire, they have to be re-created by Congress. The Federal Government fully funds Temporary Emergency Unemployment Benefits. See Table 4.4.

The original Social Security Act provided only for the basic twenty six weeks of coverage. Extended Benefits became a formal part of Title III Unemployment Insurance in 1970, and over the years, its elements have been changed numerous times. The Temporary Emergency Unemployment Benefits were first added in the 1970s and have been provided at various times by Congress over the past three decades. It is important to note that even though Unemployment

Table 4.4. Unemployment Benefits by State, 2001–2005

STATE	2001 Avg. Weekly Benefits	2002 Avg. Weekly Benefits	2003 Avg. Weekly Benefits	2004 Avg. Weekly Benefits	2005 Avg. Weekly Benefits
U.S. Average	$238	$257	$262	$263	$267
Alabama	**$164**	**$167**	**$176**	**$177**	**$182**
Alaska	$193	$193	$193	$194	$194
Arizona	$173	$176	$173	$177	$195
Arkansas	$220	$223	$229	$228	$230
California	$172	$217	$246	$260	$277
Colorado	$291	$313	$308	$298	$302
Connecticut	$277	$287	$286	$284	$295
Delaware	$221	$228	$235	$247	$247
District of Columbia	$262	$290	$258	$257	$267
Florida	$223	$225	$225	$223	$226
Georgia	$228	$239	$243	$242	$245
Hawaii	$297	$297	$312	$323	$337
Idaho	$223	$232	$232	$229	$235
Illinois	$269	$280	$281	$279	$285
Indiana	$244	$255	$263	$267	$278
Iowa	$250	$255	$260	$261	$271
Kansas	$261	$276	$276	$272	$278
Kentucky	$234	$246	$250	$257	$260
Louisiana	$194	$197	$195	$195	$192
Maine	$216	$224	$231	$235	$240
Maryland	$235	$241	$252	$254	$257
Massachusetts	**$335**	**$360**	**$357**	**$351**	**$357**
Michigan	$261	$276	$291	$289	$290

continued

Table 4.4. continued

STATE	2001 Avg. Weekly Benefits	2002 Avg. Weekly Benefits	2003 Avg. Weekly Benefits	2004 Avg. Weekly Benefits	2005 Avg. Weekly Benefits
Minnesota	$307	$318	$322	$318	$322
Mississippi	$163	$168	$173	$172	$186
Missouri	$200	$205	$206	$205	$206
Montana	$194	$187	$202	$197	$221
Nebraska	$205	$212	$216	$220	$225
Nevada	$228	$232	$236	$245	$258
New Hampshire	$241	$260	$259	$251	$252
New Jersey	$309	$331	$334	$331	$336
New Mexico	$193	$207	$211	$220	$218
New York	$269	$275	$272	$271	$276
North Carolina	$248	$259	$258	$256	$258
North Dakota	$218	$219	$222	$226	$238
Ohio	$248	$251	$252	$252	$261
Oklahoma	$228	$234	$229	$219	$221
Oregon	$256	$277	$258	$252	$261
Pennsylvania	$282	$291	$292	$294	$292
Rhode Island	$289	$304	$309	$324	$336
South Carolina	$206	$208	$210	$211	$217
South Dakota	$190	$198	$202	$205	$211
Tennessee	$198	$210	$210	$209	$212
Texas	$241	$259	$261	$259	$261
Utah	$253	$275	$269	$266	$263
Vermont	$233	$250	$255	$256	$267
Virginia	$235	$311	$276	$240	$246
Washington	$311	$329	$324	$310	$297
West Virginia	$202	$215	$220	$219	$225
Wisconsin	$242	$248	$252	$251	$253
Wyoming	$215	$232	$238	$238	$242

Source: U.S. Employment and Training Administration, 2007.

Insurance benefits may be available for as long as fifty two weeks, depending on the unemployment rates in a particular state, it does not follow that individual workers necessarily will receive fifty two weeks of benefits. Workers must be seeking jobs and willing to work in order to continue their eligibility for benefits.

The total maximum duration of benefits available will vary from state to state under the basic program. High unemployment in one state may "trigger" extended benefits in that state, but not in a neighboring state.

Since benefits are paid from trust funds, there is no way to know for certain what individual weekly benefits are likely to be in future years since unemployment may vary from one year to the next. Unemployment Insurance benefits are subject to federal income tax. Special rules also require states to reduce Unemployment Insurance benefits for the unemployed who receive government or private pension or retirement pay.

Program Issues Affecting Title III Unemployment Insurance

As mentioned above in 1935, unemployment seemed like a straightforward issue—persons were unemployed when they had no jobs. Today, however, the Unemployment Insurance program takes form from definitions of employment and unemployment. The Department of Labor, Bureau of Labor Statistics, officially defines those conditions that determine eligibility for Unemployment Insurance.[5] The most significant of these definitions are summarized in Box 4.1.

These definitions help explain the data provided in Table 4.1 that summarizes the major Unemployment Insurance program elements for the past thirty-five years. For example, in 2005, an average of approximately 2,662,000 persons were unemployed, representing 2.1 percent of the labor force, but only 35.7 percent of those unemployed were receiving unemployment benefits. The most reasonable explanation for this difference rests on the gap between the definition of unemployment and Unemployment Insurance eligibility. A person could have worked 1 hour in the reporting week and therefore not be considered unemployed. Or, a person could have worked full time, perhaps in sporadic work, but not have worked in enough quarters or earned enough to be eligible for Unemployment Insurance. Workers, too, may have exhausted their benefits, as 35.9 percent did in 2005. Workers may have also left their jobs on their own for various reasons; this accounted for an average of almost 900,000 unemployed in 2007.[6] These conditions placed on Unemployment Insurance account for the low ratio of Unemployment Insurance beneficiaries to the unemployed, and as a result, the ratio of unemployed to those receiving unemployment insurance has shown only a 10 percent fluctuation over the past thirty-five years.[h]

Thus, from a performance perspective, a large number of unemployed persons do not receive any compensation, and the levels of compensation are modest as reflected by the wide range of average weekly benefits paid to workers who do receive benefits. Table 4.4 shows that weekly benefit payments range from a low of $182 in Alabama to a high of $357 in Massachusetts. Thirty-four states make weekly payments at the national average or less. These state-by-state variations are clearly a product of the average wages paid in the states, but they are also a product of different formulas used by states to determine the amount of weekly benefits. High wage states like Alaska or New York do not necessarily pay higher weekly benefits than low wage states like Maryland that

---

[h] Working also affects Unemployment benefits in states that allow some work along with Unemployment Insurance, but then taxes the benefits at higher rates. Thus, some persons may be counted as working *and* at the same time may be receiving Unemployment Insurance.

may have high per-capita income but on average still pay low wages.[i] A weekly
benefit payment of $267.00 translates to about $6.68 per hour at a 40 hour
week. A $10.00 per hour part-time job of less than 30 hours would gener-
ate more than the average weekly unemployment insurance payment. Average
benefits have not kept pace with rising wages, generally. So low weekly benefits
would certainly contribute to the diminishing use of Unemployment Insurance among the unemployed. It is more profitable to work even at poverty
wage jobs.

A study authorized by the House of Representatives' Ways and Means Committee in the late 1980s found at least five reasons for the declining coverage
for unemployed workers: a decline in manufacturing jobs, worker mobility,
changes in federal policy (such as taxing Unemployment benefits), changes in
the way unemployment is measured, and finally changes in state programs.
These changes contributed between 22 and 39 percent of the decline in Unemployment Insurance coverage. As much as half of this decrease was due to
state-level changes attributed to state increases in the period of earnings for
eligibility for coverage in the state.[7]

Title III Unemployment Insurance Policy Issues

Funding, administrative responsibility assigned to the U.S. Department of
Labor, changing nature of unemployment, detachment from related Social
Security Act programs, separation from an entitlement philosophy character-
istic of the social insurances, changing labor markets, and economic globaliza-
tion are the most significant policy issues confronting Title III Unemployment
Insurance as it is provided today.

The program structure outlined earlier makes Title III Unemployment
Insurance unique among all the Social Security Act program titles. Title III
Unemployment Insurance is clearly a federal–state cooperative program, as
shown in Figure 1.2. Unemployment Insurance, however, has created a unique
form of joint responsibility of the Federal Government and the states. Fiscally, Unemployment Insurance depends on a complex hybrid of financing
mechanisms unlike other federal–state administered social welfare programs.
Title III authorizes federal grants to the states for administration of the State
Unemployment laws, Title IX authorizes the various components of the federal
Unemployment Trust Fund, and Title XII authorizes advances or loans to insolvent state Unemployment Programs. Unemployment Insurance also claims a
unique fiscal structure characterized by a tax offset rather than a direct grant-
in-aid or another method of direct federal and/or state financing. Program
implementation, however, rests with the Department of Labor.

---

[i] A distinction is made between earnings from wages and other forms of earnings.

Funding Unemployment Insurance

The tax offset, discussed above, is a unique form of social insurance funding, and liquidity of states' Unemployment Insurance accounts depends on each state's prior year's employers' unemployment experience ("experience ratings") sufficient in amount to cover the first twenty six weeks of unemployment insurance obligation. If the state moves to the Extended Benefit period, the Federal Government pays half of the cost of the state's Unemployment Insurance for the next thirteen weeks from its general revenue funds. This method of financing has produced unevenness in state trust fund reserves. For example, in periods of high unemployment state trust fund reserves may become exhausted, particularly if the experience of unemployment in the previous year was low and trust fund reserves were correspondingly low. States may borrow from the Federal Government, but since these borrowed funds have to be paid back in order to preserve the tax offset, states are likely to cut benefit payments to stretch the available funds cover more persons. States may have to extend benefits to all the officially unemployed, but states set the benefit amounts. Conversely, if unemployment in a state is low, state trust funds may become quite large, encouraging employers to request a reduction in their Unemployment Insurance tax liability.

Administration

As noted, the states administer Unemployment Insurance, but as part of a unique relationship with the Federal Government. Unemployment Insurance is the only title of the Social Security Act that is not administered under the broad authority of the U.S. Department of Health and Human Services. The U.S. Department of Labor administers Title III for the Federal Government, raising some question about a federal commitment to both the concept of social insurance and the commitment to income support. On the one hand, income maintenance reflects an overriding policy commitment of the Social Security Act, but labor force participation represents the policy commitment of the Department of Labor.

The United States Department of Labor evolved from the Bureau of Labor created in 1884 within the already established Department of the Interior. In 1903, the Department of Labor gained cabinet level status when Congress created the Department of Commerce and Labor. The independent Department of Labor was created by Congress in 1913, with an initial purpose to "to foster, promote and develop the welfare of working people, to improve their working conditions, and to advance their opportunities for profitable employment."

When the Social Security Act was created in 1935, Title III was kept under the Social Security Board that administered the whole of the Act at that time, while the administration of Title IX of the Social Security Act that spelled out the complex taxing provisions of the Title III program was turned over to the

Internal Revenue Service. During the 1940s, the administration of Unemployment Insurances was shifted from the Social Security Board to the Department of Labor. The Hoover Commission's numerous reorganization proposals for existing government agencies included reorganization proposals for both the Department of Health, Education, and Welfare and the Department of Labor, and President Truman advocated strongly with the Hoover Commission to obtain its recommendation to transfer Unemployment Insurance to the Department of Labor. Thus, Congress transferred responsibility both for Unemployment Insurance and the U.S. Employment Service (also then administered by the Social Security Board) to the Department of Labor, where both have remained since.

Today, the Department of Labor contains 12 bureaus and almost 20 sub-bureau departments; Unemployment Insurance is administered by a department in the Bureau of Employee Standards, one of the Labor Department's lower profile bureaus. The Department of Labor today focuses its activities on "macro" labor considerations such as those reflected in its twenty-first-century workforce agenda: getting more jobs, keeping workers safe, enforcing labor laws, improving training and education, and preparing the workforce for the future.[8] In 2008, Secretary of Labor Elaine Chao summed up the mission of the Department of Labor: "Getting people back to work is what this department does. Giving people hope for the future is our job." The emphasis that the Department of Labor places on programs other than Unemployment Insurance has allowed the development of a strong insurance program to drift over the years. Title III Unemployment Insurance program has become a lesser program for the Department of Labor.

The program context for Unemployment Insurance administration sets up a conflict of objectives. "Getting people back to work" is one objective. Providing income support for the unemployed is another objective. Usually administrated locally through state Departments of Employment Security, Unemployment Insurance is provided along with job counseling and placement at the point of client contact. State administrative agencies and legislatures are responsible for ensuring that the unemployment trust funds are adequate but are not a fiscal burden on employers. Thus, while unemployment compensation is extremely important to the unemployed individual, its program usefulness acts as a companion to getting workers back into the workforce. In this back-to-work environment, many of the Title III social insurance elements have been lost.

Changing Unemployment Concerns

Unemployment and employment are defined much differently today than they were in 1935. The definitions cited above from the Department of Labor establish a social microscopic view of unemployment that did not exist in 1935, raising important distinctions that have limited the scope of Title III. For examples, "structural unemployment" acknowledges that some portion of the labor force will always be unemployed, and these unemployed persons most likely are not eligible for Title III compensation today. Marginal workers, with employment spells, discouraged workers, workers holding more than one job are sub-definitions of unemployment that have an effect on Title III benefits. Title III Unemployment Insurance has done little to keep up with the economic problems faced by workers in these categories.

Detachment from Other Social Security Act Programs

Perhaps a product of its bifurcated program authority, and an inherent conflict between whether it provides income support or a vehicle to get people back to work, Unemployment Insurance lacks connectivity with other programs authorized under the Social Security Act. For example, employed workers may be eligible for Medicaid and the Child Health Insurance Program (see Chapter 8) or TANF financial support (see Chapter 6). But there is no administrative or legislative connectivity to these programs that would provide an unemployed worker automatic access to the benefits of these programs as is the case where children who receive TANF are automatically eligible for Medicaid. Many unemployed workers are eligible for Food Stamps (a program provided under the Agricultural Act, not the Social Security Act), but once again there is no administrative or legislative linkage between Food Stamps and Unemployment Insurance. In other words, Unemployment Insurance functions for the most part as a semi-autonomous form of social insurance with increasingly unclear social welfare objectives.

Detachment from an Entitlement Philosophy

While the Wisconsin labor economists sought a program that would confer unemployment compensation as an extension of employer obligations to their employees, omitting worker contributions, and the employer-driven method of financing have detracted from Title III entitlement. The burden of Title III financing rests with employers (or with the Federal Government). The Federal Government makes sure states have sufficient funds to meet their obligations. The obligation of employers and the Federal Government more likely resembles the obligatory nature of assistance programs rather than the entitlement philosophy underlying the Title II social insurance programs. The distinction between "pooled funds" and "deferred wages" as discussed above has vanished as Title III Unemployment Insurance has lost its connectivity between employers and employees envisioned by the Wisconsin School.

The creation of individual state accounts, funded by tax rates that differ by employer, has not made employers more sensitive to the long range needs of their employees. In fact, the tax-offset method and the need for federal supplemental funding relieve employers of most of the fiscal obligation for unemployment that the Wisconsin School sought to preserve. Title III Unemployment Insurance no longer depends on its original entitlement foundation that has been so important for the preservation and development of Title II Social Security.[j] Perhaps the rise of labor unions has promoted the voice of labor as a substitute for employers' commitments to their workers, but it may be more reasonable to suggest that the history of American capitalism makes the Wisconsin ideals seem like fantasy in today's world of labor economics. Individual workers know that Unemployment Insurance is available if they lose their jobs, but organized labor's focus on the individual worker today promotes work at decent wages: an important objective, but less in harmony with the plight of the worker who becomes unemployed.

Shifts in Employment Dynamics

Long-term stable employment, for example, where employees may stay with a single firm for most of their working lives has almost completely vanished. Workers today can expect between four and twelve major job changes during their working lives. This kind of employment dynamic has become a frequent product of the extensive corporate reorganization that has characterized the past fifteen years, business failures, and "economic globalization" that has resulted in both production shifts by major American corporations and job outsourcing. Not only have these labor force changes made the present Title III Unemployment Insurance even more obsolete, but these massive labor force changes have resulted in the loss of traditional job-related benefits for workers, such as pension protection (see Chapter 3) and medical insurance (see Chapter 7) in particular.

Globalization, Labor, and Title III Unemployment Insurance

The ability of Title III Unemployment Insurance to satisfy today's needs of unemployed persons is only magnified in the growing context of economic "globalization." In fact, the future adequacy of Unemployment Insurance could be even further eroded by massive global labor market changes. Production shifts by major American corporations have caused much more disruption for American labor than reported, according to a special study for the U.S.–China Economic and Security Review Commission authored by Professors Kate Bronfenbrenner of Cornell and Stephanie Luce of University of Massachusetts, Amherst. Their comprehensive study shows that in 2004, possibly over 400,000 jobs were shifted from the United States, doubling the number of job shifts that took place in 2001. Moreover, this study conflicts with reports of the U.S. Department of Labor that reported only 4,633 private sector workers lost their jobs in the first three months of 2004 due to global outsourcing.

---

[j] Unlike the employer's burden of Title II Social Security taxes, even though they are likely passed on to the public in the form of higher prices, the Title III program requires no similar private commitment to the program since employers receive credit for most of the taxes they pay.

Bronfenbrenner and Luce conclude that not only are global production shifts and outsourcing disrupting traditional American labor markets, but both features of globalization are having a profound effect on skilled and technical jobs; 70 percent of the production shifts were in communications and information technology, compared with 14 percent in manufacturing. These lost jobs, they conclude, are "likely to be good jobs, with full health care and pension plans, making the costs of these production shifts to workers and communities even higher."

> In combination, these data remind us that it is not a story of good jobs being stolen from US workers by low-wage workers in Latin America and Asia, especially China, with whom US workers can never hope to compete. Instead it is a story of the world's largest multinational corporations buying and selling companies and pieces of companies, opening and closing plants, downsizing and expanding operations, and shifting employment from one community to another, all around the world.[9]

Importing low-skilled replacement labor complicates this shift of American jobs to other countries. As noted above, low-skilled labor may not qualify for present-day Unemployment Insurance, even though this pool of labor is likely to have weak labor force attachment and likely to become unemployed. Thus, the consequences of economic globalization go well beyond a discussion of Title III Unemployment Insurance, but they do underline today's volatile American labor market and support calls for a much more robust approach to unemployment compensation than that provided under Title III.

A recent study by Robert E. Scott of the Economic Policy Institute found that workers with at most a high school education were particularly hard hit by growing trade deficits. They held 52 percent of jobs displaced, and they made up 43 percent of the American workforce. Scott also found that the North American Fair Trade Agreement (NAFTA) displaced 523,305 workers with a high school degree or less into lower-paying jobs. Retraining may be an option for these younger workers, but older workers will certainly need better benefits than those that Title III presently provides.[10]

The underdeveloped income maintenance element of Title III Unemployment Insurance is also obvious in the way America has responded to global economic shifts. In 1974, Congress included a program in the Trade Adjustment Act designed to assist American workers adjust to job losses brought about by foreign economic competition. The provisions of various forms of the Trade Adjustment Act were modified substantially by the NAFTA and again in 2002. The major provisions of this assistance allow eligible individuals who are age 50 and over and who obtain new employment at wages of less than $50,000 within 26 weeks of their separation to receive a wage subsidy of 50 percent of the difference between the old and new wages, up to $10,000 over a period of up to two years. They are also eligible for a tax credit covering 65 percent of qualified health insurance premium costs. In Fiscal Year 2006, USDOL received 2,440 new petitions and certified 1,426 persons at a cost of nearly $1.0 billion. Funding was appropriated from the Federal Unemployment Benefits and Allowances (FUBA) account. The use of Title III funds for worker retraining, rather than income maintenance, continues to reflect the emphasis of the Department of Labor to put work ahead of income maintenance.[k]

In addition to economic globalization, America has experienced legal and illegal immigration over the past decade that, except for immigration in the early 1900s, is unprecedented. Much of this immigrant labor fills low skilled, often seasonal or intermittent, jobs. But illegal immigrants have no access to Title III Unemployment Insurance, and legal immigrants are likely to lack adequate labor force attachment to achieve eligibility since the jobs they hold are not likely to qualify for benefit eligibility. There is no clear evidence against the supposition that unemployment, both sporadic or long term, is severe among this group of workers. Even though immigrant labor is filling necessary American jobs, their high risk of unemployment and low wages is not protected by Unemployment benefits.

Summary of Title III Policy Issues That Call for Attention

Less than 40 percent of the unemployed usually receive Title III unemployment compensation. Weekly unemployment benefits barely reach the levels of the minimum wage and fall below that in many states. Funding for Title III Unemployment Insurance falls almost exclusively on the Federal Government, eroding vestiges of social insurance from the program. The federal–state shared administrative structure for Title III diminishes its usefulness as an income maintenance program. These and other Title III program problems have been confounded by profound changes in labor markets, and the relationship of labor to its place of employment has become more distant than it was during the 1940s.

Title III Unemployment Insurance is a troubled program. It is troubled by its uncertainty as a social insurance program. It is troubled by its source of funding. It is troubled by the apparent lack of administrative authority for its implementation. It is troubled by new forms of unemployment. It is troubled by conflicting opinions over its influence on motivation to work. It is troubled by the wide variation of benefit eligibility, the low level of beneficiary

---

[k] Another alternate use for Title III funds was proposed on December 3, 1999, when the U.S. Department of Labor (DOL) issued a Notice of Proposed Rulemaking to create, by regulation, a voluntary experimental program that would give states the option of extending UC eligibility to parents who take time off from employment after the birth or placement for adoption of a child under the Family Medical Leave Act of 1993 (Public Law 103-3). The proposal immediately drew criticism from opponents who argued that such benefits would be contrary to the purpose of Unemployment Insurance benefits. On December 4, 2002, the Bush Administration concluded that the experiment was "poor policy" and a misapplication of federal UC law relating to the requirements that beneficiaries be able and available for work.

coverage, and the low level of benefit payments. It is troubled by the unanticipated, massive, unexpected changes in national and international labor markets. It is troubled by tepid political support. It is troubled by unresolved, tensions between labor, corporations, and the role of government. Title III Unemployment Insurance exemplifies the piecemeal, unplanned development of America's social welfare commitments. In sum, Title III Unemployment Insurance brings out the worst in the development of the Social Security Act.

Challenges Facing Unemployment Insurance for Future Consideration

Based on the present program structure and the policy issues raised by this structure, several issues deserve consideration as steps to making Unemployment Insurance a more effective social welfare program.

Entitlement Issues

Entitlement to social insurance, according to the discussion in Chapter 1, is based on an entitlement commitment spelled out in law, not a social obligation based on economic need. Social insurance constitutes a secured contractual entitlement to beneficiaries because beneficiaries have contributed some of their own assets, usually income from work, as a part of the contractual relationship. Since the contractual relationship to provide Title III lacks any contribution from beneficiaries, it creates entitlement ambiguity. Moreover, it is not clear whether employers or governments have the responsibility to provide compensation to unemployed workers. Title III entitlement ambiguity may account for the inability of the Unemployment Insurance program to break away from the form of unemployment characteristic of the 1930s or to respond more effectively to the problems of unemployment today.

Weak Funding Authority

The experience-rated unemployment tax was designed to assign the costs of unemployment compensation to individual firms, expecting that the resulting tax burden would encourage firms to stabilize employment and thus reduce unemployment. This financing choice, promoted by the Wisconsin school of labor economics, contained several problems that have become more clear as Title III Unemployment Insurance has developed. First, stabilizing employment took precedence over benefit adequacy, and this imbalance continues to exist today. Second, in reality the employer paid very little tax since the unemployment tax was offset by the Federal Government. Third, the offset employer's taxes only cover the first twenty-six weeks of unemployment and half of the additional thirteen weeks of Unemployment Insurance if it is needed. The rest of the unemployment burden falls on the Federal Government. In reality, therefore, the employers bear little obligation to reduce unemployment.

Administrative Ambiguity

A funding mechanism designed to encourage firms to stabilize employment may have had merit to address unemployment as it was understood in the 1930s. After all, encouraging firms to stabilize and expand employment was the major purpose behind President Herbert Hoover's failed Reconstruction Finance Corporation.[11] Title III followed in the tradition of an emphasis on employment over an emphasis on worker benefits. The assignment of Title III administration to the Department of Labor has reinforced an employment bias in program administration. In other words, the Department of Labor has less concern for issues associated with income maintenance, but more concern for establishing a stable labor force.

Unemployment in Today's Labor Environment

Concerns over the causes of unemployment and the effect of unemployment compensation on work motivation also trouble Title III. In spite of the fact that research has shown little influence of Unemployment Insurance on individuals' motivation to work, beliefs persist that people are motivated to leave work and refrain from finding work once they become unemployed because they can rely on unemployment compensation. The wide-ranging state eligibility criteria (Table 4.3) reflect the confusion over the amount of emphasis placed on work motivation. In spite of the fact that Unemployment Insurance requires people to seek and accept employment as a condition of eligibility and provides benefits only if the unemployment is caused by the employer, beliefs to the contrary exist. To be able and available for work in today's labor environment, changed as it is by globalization and large influxes of migrant labor, raises labor force issues well beyond Unemployment Insurance, or even the present efforts of the Department of Labor to make sure employees work.[12] Such issues do not find resolution in the present policy structure of Title III Unemployment Insurance.

Meager Benefits and Beneficiary Coverage

As discussed above, the small percentage of unemployed workers covered by Title III, the cash amount of benefits provided, the wide-ranging benefit payments from state to state, and the time limits on benefits, cause serious programs problems for Title III Unemployment Insurance. While these troubles may well be the result of a program that places the need for employment before the need for income support, the effect of these troubles has made Unemployment Insurance an ineffective income support program for persons who have worked and who have been a vital part of the American economy. Beneficiaries are not well linked to other Social Security Act programs where their income maintenance benefits might be enhanced.

Tepid Political Support

Title III's income maintenance characteristics have had little political support for nourishment or development. Employers find unemployment a burden to their enterprise, and organized labor has always shown a preference for stable, well paid employment over benefits for those who become unemployed. Historically, the Federal Government has supported the interests of business over the needs of unemployed labor.

Contemporary Labor Force Challenges

Changes in the American economy over the past decades have presented problems for labor that unemployment issues in the 1930s could never anticipate. These changes have been alluded to above, and it is important to recognize that the changes have brought new unemployment issues into sharp relief. The whole issue of American employment in the early decades of the twenty-first century must precede any efforts to formulate more appropriate ideas about unemployment in today's labor environment. At the same time, the changing American economy also requires further appreciation for the relationship between unemployment compensation and the income support necessary to sustain an unemployed worker financially and at the time support the worker's development and retraining to maximize their ability to participate in this new economic environment. As they were in the 1930s, labor force troubles today are a result of activities in the larger economy. Today, however, the American economy is not confined to America's physical geography.

Conclusion

When meeting a person for the first time, one of the first questions is, "What do you do?" In America, work is about more than money or income. Work defines the person; work has become a more important personal defining characteristic than religion, politics, or even place of residence. Thus, unemployment not only places persons in economically vulnerable situations, but it also strips them of their status and even their sense of self-worth. To be unemployed in America conveys a lack of personal and social character. Even menial work carries more status than unemployment.

In addition to lack of status, unemployment also results in loss of income. Even at the most generous average replacement rates discussed above, the loss of income from unemployment presents persons and their families with economic hardship. Bills cannot be paid on time, if paid at all. Planned expenditures—a new appliance, a gift, a vacation—have to be delayed; savings for retirement, children's education, or a home are often exhausted. Debts are accumulated that may take years to repay. Unemployment is not fun. Unemployment represents an economic crisis of lasting importance for those who suffer it.

However, unfortunately, Title III Unemployment Insurance has not shown much capacity to act as a counter-cyclical economic program. Although it has put some money into the pockets of the unemployed, there is no evidence that these funds have had any significant impact of ratcheting the American economy out of any economic slump. Nor has Title III Unemployment Insurance under the administration of the Department of Labor contributed any measurable achievements toward building a "full employment" economy as the Keynesians might have anticipated. Unemployment insurance provided a focal point for the social insurances developed under the original Social Security Act, but Title III's bland unemployment insurance initiative leaves a significant gap in America's social welfare enterprise.

Most important, Unemployment Insurance fails to address the personal consequences of unemployment. Its weekly benefits fall far short of maintaining enough income to allow individuals and their families to maintain their lifestyle without serious personal economic consequences. Its method of provision is personally demeaning, from the application process at the unemployment office to the pressure to find "suitable" employment. In spite of a potentially long and productive employment history, and in spite of the respectability that might have come from that employment, it is difficult for the unemployed person to assert a right to Unemployment Insurance. Regardless of any rewards employment might have conferred on a previously employed worker, they are all lost in unemployment. And, ironically enough, the conditions of eligibility for unemployment insurance require in part, that *unemployment is not the worker's fault!* It is little mystery that political and social support for more effective Unemployment Insurance is so limited.

Perhaps Unemployment Insurance was really never meant to be a social insurance program to begin with. Perhaps President Roosevelt should have left Unemployment Insurance to the Wagner–Lewis Bill rather than including it in the Social Security Act. Then, at least its pedigree as a labor force program would be clear. But today, we have a social insurance program under Title III of the Social Security Act that is noticeably out of harmony with both the needs of the unemployed and the expectations of social insurance. Of all the parts of the Social Security Act, perhaps Title III Unemployment Insurance is the best candidate for drastic revision. Unemployment Insurance needs a new policy direction and a new legislative framework relevant to today's unemployment problems. Yet, like other proposals for social welfare reform that will be explored in Chapter 10, change risks the loss of an important social welfare commitment. To do nothing to improve Title IIII Unemployment Insurance as it operates today, however, only insults the many who work yet risk unemployment *through no fault of their own.*

NOTES

1. U.S. Department of Labor, Bureau of Labor Statistics, *Monthly Labor Statistics*, September, 2007.
2. Edwin Witte, *The Development of the Social Security Act*. Madison Wi: University of Wisconsin Press, 1963, particularly pp 112–114.
3. *Florida v. Mellon, 273 U.S. 12.*
4. Edward Berkowitz, *America's Welfare State, From Roosevelt to Reagan* (Baltimore: Johns Hopkins Press, 1981), 34.
5. See http://www.bls.gov/bls/glossary.htm.
6. Bureau of Labor Statistics, 2007.
7. See http://waysandmeans.house.gov/media/pdf/greenbook2005/.
8. U.S. Department of Labor, Office of the Twenty First Century Workforce, Fall 2002.
9. *Rising Trade Deficits Lead to Significant Job Displacement and Declining Job Quality for the United States* (Washington, DC: Economic Policy Institute, 2007), 79.
10. Frank Brechling and Louise Laurence, *Permanent Job Loss and the U.S. System of Financing Unemployment Insurance* (Kalamazoo, MI: W.E. Upjohn Institute for Employment Research, 1995), particularly Chapter 1.
11. Andrew Dobelstein, *Moral Authority, Ideology and the Future of American Social Welfare* (Boulder, CO: Westview Press, 1999), 88.
12. See William Haber and Merrill Murray, *Unemployment Insurance in the American Economy* (Homewood, IL: Richard D. Irwin, Inc., 1966), particularly 265–272, for an early, yet comprehensive study of employability issues.

PART III

INTRODUCTION TO THE ASSISTANCE PROGRAMS

The assistance programs constitute one of the most contestable activities of American governance. This introduction provides a brief discussion of the characteristics of social welfare assistance and serves as background for discussing the specific assistance programs provided by the Social Security Act, Supplemental Security Income in Chapter 5 and Temporary Assistance to Needy Families (TANF) and other child welfare programs in Chapter 6. Chapter 1 framed important distinctions between social insurance and assistance programs. While social insurance programs are supported by statutory authority that grants a right to benefits based on contributions that meet statutory obligations, assistance programs in the American system confer no such statutory rights. Instead, assistance programs are a form of social welfare provision that places obligations on the society to provide benefits, rather than an exercise of beneficiary rights. In America's welfare idiom, assistance programs constitute residual social welfare responsibilities assumed by society when individuals find themselves in need and lack resources necessary to meet those needs. See Figure PIII.1.

Assistance programs in the United States, as a social obligation rather than any right, find support in the history of American social welfare development.[1] The early charitable efforts by religious groups and the Charity Organization Societies rested on forms of private philanthropy with meager public financial commitment. Although the social reformers' largely successful efforts to gain public financial support for assistance programs shifted much of the welfare obligation to government, the infusion of public funding failed to establish any welfare philosophy that differed from the old philosophy that welfare was a form of charity.[2] Thus, the Social Security Act reflected this residual tradition when it confronted the task of including welfare assistance as part of the nation's social welfare obligations.

The Legacy of the Social Security Act's Assistance Programs

Chapter 1 characterized assistance as America's oldest form of welfare, originally called relief or charity. This form of welfare requires highly discretionary decisions about those who seek relief and how much relief they need. The

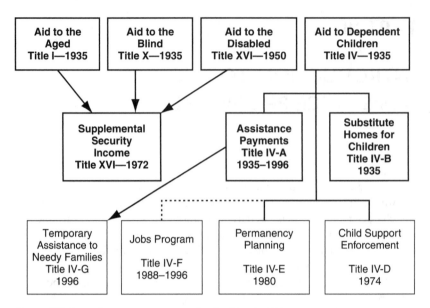

Figure PIII.1. Assistance Programs Authorized by the SSA, 1935–2008.
Source: Author.

early development of social work, begun by Mary Richmond, tried to make relief decisions less discretionary, more scientific, an activity known then as "scientific charity." But these early "scientific principles" did little to objectify welfare decisions. Choices still had to be made whether welfare applicants were "imposters" or "truly needy." One of the early distinctions used to establish true welfare need was whether an applicant was physically unable to work or just "work shy," and often an applicant for relief had to fail a "work test" that was supposed to prove he or she could not work in order to be granted welfare aid.

These highly discretionary decisions usually required a form of close scrutiny, or a form of "social investigation," that was only possible in a one-to-one exchange between an applicant and the person authorized to grant aid. Moreover, only the base minimum of welfare aid was provided once an applicant was approved. This meant that the applicant's resources had to be accounted for and a careful calculation of needs had to be made: how much money was needed for food, clothing, transportation, medical expense, and other needs. Obviously, the process was demeaning for the applicant and acted as a deterrent to asking for assistance.

When the Social Security Act accepted some responsibility for financing welfare assistance, it inherited earlier relief practices, and failed to change long-standing and deeply ingrained negative attitudes toward any kind of welfare. An American belief system anchored in personal responsibility and "rugged individualism" understood the need for welfare as a form of personal weakness. The historic scorn attached to those who needed welfare support was not lifted simply because the Federal Government included assistance programs in the Social Security Act. Although the widespread economic dependency caused by the Great Depression tempered the view of the self-sufficient American, the lesson that economic need was as much a system-wide economic failure as it was a personal one quickly was forgotten as the American economy improved. Thus, the painstaking work of establishing welfare eligibility, and carefully providing welfare assistance adequate for only life's basic necessities, continued to be based on a belief that the needy person would find a way to self-sufficiency only if the resources were meager and provided reluctantly. This welfare stigma has never left the assistance programs.

As pointed out in Chapter 1, the U.S. Constitution establishes an obligation to provide for the general welfare in both its Preamble and in Article I, Section 8. Similarly, state statutes and constitutions also contain statements that obligate them to provide social welfare. North Carolina's constitution provides a notable example. Written in 1865, it states:

> Beneficent provisions for the poor, the unfortunate, and orphans, being one of the first duties of a civilized and Christian state, the General Assembly shall at its first session appoint and define the duties of a board of public charities to whom shall be entrusted the supervision of all charitable and penal State institutions and who shall annually report to the governor upon their condition, with suggestions for their improvement.[3]

The word "duty" establishes a social obligation and clearly does not presume to confer any right to charity or assistance. In other words, "charity" is a duty of the state, not a right of an individual. Since the Federal Government has limited constitutional or statutory authority to provide welfare, and since the states had developed statutory authority to provide welfare assistance through an established network of state-administered programs, most of the authority to provide assistance rested in the states when the Social Security Act became law and continues to rest in the states today.

Welfare Assistance and the Social Obligation

The temperament of welfare assistance always sets a limit on the social obligation to provide it. Assistance was never an open-ended commitment, and it was provided only to the extent that recipients behaved in socially responsible ways. Pre-Social Security Act welfare was locally provided and often required recipients to work on farms in order to qualify for welfare support, and children were frequently apprenticed to tradepeople as welfare alternatives. African Americans were routinely denied assistance in order to keep them working, particularly in the Southern states. The original Social Security Act's Aid to Dependent Children program required that a "suitable home" be kept for children as a condition for providing assistance under this program. Unfortunately, these and other conditions have always been advanced as legitimate limits on the social obligation to provide welfare, and thus, assistance often has been used as a means to force individuals to conform to politically driven behavioral expectations.[a] Opponents of welfare assistance often argue that welfare tears down the character of those who receive it. This opposition to welfare has nothing to do with the substance level of the welfare, but with the conditions under which it is provided.

Thus, although welfare assistance constitutes a social obligation, there are considerable differences of opinion about the character of the obligation and how this obligation must be met. For example, social welfare obligations might be met either by government directly or by private interests and activities. Or, as discussed in Chapter 1, social welfare obligations may be met by providing money, in-kind products, or, in some cases, alternative living arrangements like homeless shelters. Even more ambiguity arises over the extent, or comprehensiveness, of the social welfare obligation. For example, does the social welfare obligation extend to persons who refuse to help themselves, either through work, or, historically, by refusing to ask for help from relatives and family? Thus, while an obligation to provide social welfare exists, the exact nature of that obligation lacks clarity. The definition of the social welfare obligation provided by the 1937 U.S. Supreme Court in its *Helvering v. Davis* decision (see Chapter 1) falls far short of answering nagging questions about a welfare obligation in the United States. Lacking clear guidance, the net result of social obligation ambiguities adds a highly discretionary dimension to assistance decisions. Thus, the assistance titles of the Social Security Act are constantly changing as Americans' views of their social obligation change.

The Social Obligation in the American System

Three elements of America's social welfare obligation, however, seem particularly important to the discussion of the assistance programs provided under the Social Security Act: economic need, lack of capacity for self-support and/or care, and living by the social rules.

Economic need constitutes the most critical factor defining America's social welfare obligation. As discussed at length in Chapter 1, American society, constitutionally, by statute, and by its moral foundations, accepts an obligation to provide assistance for those who need it. But defining who is needy, and determining how much of what kind of assistance is needed, becomes a very difficult undertaking. A considerable amount of energy has gone into untangling the many issues in assessing economic need without a satisfactory conclusion.[4] It is clear, however, that no set formula, no one-size-fits-all definition of economic need is satisfactory. Thus, a determination of economic need depends on the circumstances of the needy person, as well as on the perception of those circumstances by someone in authority capable of granting relief for that need. In other words, determining economic need is a highly discretionary activity.

---

[a] "Unfortunate" in the sense that the same rigorous expectation for personal behaviors do not apply as vigorously to persons who are not dependent on welfare assistance.

Economic need may not be readily apparent. For example, the U.S. has a poverty index (see the Introduction) that provides a benchmark for determining economic need, but the problems with this benchmark are extensive and well known.[5] With the possible exception of the State Child Health Insurance Program (see Chapter 8), none of the assistance programs provided under the Social Security Act use the poverty index as the definition of economic need, and all of the Social Security Act's cash assistance programs provide benefits below the levels of the poverty index. The fact that many more people in America are poor than the number that are receiving cash assistance raises the question as to whether America is meeting its social welfare obligations.

But if the poverty index indicates America's reluctance to meet its social welfare obligation, a more distressing indictment arises from the income discrepancy in America. Figure PIII.2 provides some perspective on the distribution of income in America. Figure PIII.2 shows that almost half of all the income in 2004 went to the top 20 percent of those who had income, while less than 5 percent of all income went to the bottom 20 percent of those with income. It is even more distressing that these shares of income have become even more unequal in the past fourteen years. For example, in 1990, the lowest

Distribution of income by income quintiles—1990

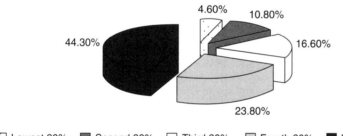

Distribution of income by income quintiles—2004

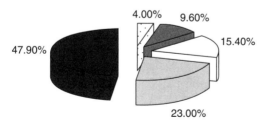

Figure PIII.2. Income Distribution in the United States: 1990 and 2004.
Source: Statistical Abstracts of the United States, 2007, Table 678.

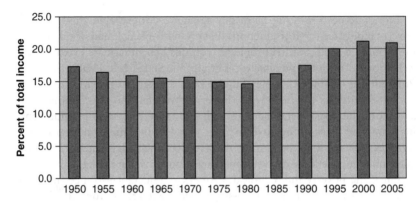

Figure PIII.3. Percentage of Income for the Top 5 percent of Population.
Source: Statistical Abstracts of the United States, 2007, Table 678.

20 percent of the families with income received 4.6 percent of the income, but in 2004, this percentage dropped to 4.0 percent. Thus, not only is income badly distributed in the United States, but unequal income distribution has persisted for the past fifty years and continues to worsen.

The income of America's top 5 percent of the population also reveals a sobering fact about America's disturbing income distribution. Five percent of Americans accounted for 20.9 percent of all of America's income in 2004. Figure PIII.3 shows the increasing concentration of income among America's very affluent. In America, the rich are very rich, and the poor are very poor relative to the rich. While no one would expect that income would be distributed equally, where each 20 percent of the population would receive 20 percent of the income, income distribution in America suggests a remarkably high level of economic need among the lowest 20 percent of Americans, and raises the question of whether even those who may have incomes above the poverty index might also be in economic need. At the very least, given the way income is distributed in America, America's social welfare obligation might be better understood as attaining a more equitable distribution of income.[b]

Beyond income, other factors complicate efforts to determine economic need. Some people may have resources that substitute for cash. Considerable social welfare discussion takes place over the cash value of in-kind welfare benefits (see Chapter 1). Food stamps, clothing, health care, housing assistance all contribute social welfare value when determining economic need. Assets, too,

---

[b] The Gini coefficient is used as a measure of wealth distribution. A low Gini coefficient indicates more equal wealth distribution, while a high Gini coefficient indicates more unequal distribution. Zero (0) corresponds to perfect equality (e.g., everyone has the same income) and 1 corresponds to perfect inequality (e.g., one person has all the income, while everyone else has zero income). While most developed European nations tend to have Gini coefficients between 0.24 and 0.36, the U.S. Gini coefficient is above 0.4, indicating that the United States has greater income inequality than European counterparts with similar economies.

complicate economic need. An elderly couple may have very low incomes, but they may have a house with considerable value. Some social welfare programs like Supplemental Security Income (SSI) (see Chapter 5) require evidence to make sure that assets are exhausted before persons are considered economically needy, even though the cash value of the assets is much less than the social and emotional value of the assets themselves. Although some assistance programs provide clear guidelines, determining the value of noncash resources also requires discretionary decisions.

A lack of capacity for self-support and/or care constitutes a second dimension of America's social welfare obligation. In addition to economic need, individuals must be unable to support themselves or otherwise care for themselves. This condition on the social obligation, like the determination of economic need, is more complicated than it appears. Some people are not expected to support themselves; with notable exceptions, a social welfare obligation is usually extended to children, the elderly, and the physically and mentally ill who are determined to be economically needy and unable to support themselves. But even this group of individuals is expected to show some willingness or ability for self-care even if it is insufficient for full self-support. While children are not expected to work, America has struggled with its obligation to support children financially, on the one hand, and with emphasizing the obligation of parents to support their children on the other hand. Title IV of the Social Security Act (see Chapter 6) has developed amidst the confusion of the American obligation to protect and care for children. Americans loathe economic dependency regardless of where it is found, even among children.

A quarrelsome relationship between work and welfare has always plagued the assistance programs. The pre-Social Security Act emphasis on work as an alternative to welfare was reflected in President Roosevelt's initiatives to move the nation out of the Great Depression. All Roosevelt's emergency relief programs required work in exchange for relief. Roosevelt disliked the "dole," as he called welfare, and as pointed out in Chapter 1, the Committee on Economic Security believed that federal money should be spent only to help people become employed, not to provide residual relief. Furthermore, eligibility for the social insurances under both Titles II and III was based on work. In justifying the social insurance programs, it made sense to argue that work would reduce the need for welfare, first because workers would not need assistance and second because workers would earn a right to social insurance. But the individual states were in a very difficult financial situation, in need of fiscal relief, and there was no work. Public relief was necessary and the states were the political structures most suited to provide it if the Federal Government would help.

The troublesome issue of work has compromised the development of assistance programs in the United States. Since work is the means to self-support, work has become a significant defining characteristic of assistance eligibility. If a person can work, and is expected to work, even if in economic need, assistance may be denied. Even if the ability to work is limited so that economic need persists, assistance may supplement work, but not replace it. There is little doubt that work defines a social and moral requirement of participation in the American community. But like economic need, the American work ethic requires careful scrutiny when it becomes a condition of the social welfare obligation. If work does not pay enough to allow people to take care of themselves and their family, then assistance becomes obligatory. But should the obligation to work take priority over the obligation to provide welfare? One of the most insidious injuries from a work obligation has been in the withholding of welfare to exploit workers by forcing them to work. For many years, states denied welfare benefits to African Americans long after they were "emancipated" from slavery, forcing them to continue to work for little or no wages. Some years ago, Richard Cloward and Francis Fox Piven argued that assistance payments were manipulated to make sure that the American economy had a plentiful supply of cheap labor.[6]

Perhaps a more fundamental issue concerning work is whether assistance should make up for inadequate wages. In other words, if work for wages is not sufficient to satisfy economic need, should assistance be substituted for insufficient wages? For example, if work does not pay enough to provide for self-support, does a social obligation to provide assistance exist? To argue that some jobs "just don't pay enough" avoids the issues of who should be responsible for adequate income from work: the public through government welfare or the employer?[c] The work obligation also raises questions over the ethic of forcing persons to work as a condition of providing assistance. In the early days of relief, Mary Richmond, the recognized founder of modern social work, encouraged a "work test" to determine whether relief applicants could or could not work and thus were truly economically needy. The 1996 welfare reform demands that people work as a condition of receiving welfare assistance under the Social Security Act, Title IV (see Chapter 6).

In the American view of welfare obligation, work has always been preferred to welfare, and the long-standing public aversion to welfare hardens when work is plentiful. But among many scholars and advocates for welfare reform, the work–welfare paradigm has never been simple. The many reasons why people do not work are compounded by bountiful evidence that many who do work remain in poverty, and whether welfare should be extended to persons who do not work, or who work and remain poor, continues to nag at the entire American social welfare enterprise.

---

[c] The Earned Income Tax Credit (EITC), discussed in more detail in Chapter 10, provides a clear policy issue with regard to work for adequate wages. Workers are granted an income tax rebate of an amount sufficient to make up the difference between what they earned through work and a certain prescribed minimum, a form of a negative income tax. While a very important income maintenance program for individual workers, the EITC raises the question as to whether the Federal Government should supplement low wage industries. The policy issue of the EITC is discussed in more detail in Chapter 10.

Playing by the rules also sets a boundary for America's welfare obligation. Work is a good example of playing by the rules. While work defines economic need it is also one of the social rules. In addition to work, other social rules set limits on the social obligation. For example, assistance provided under SSI does not extend to prisoners or fugitive felons. Citizenship or status as a legal alien is required for eligibility for most assistance programs. Thus, there are social rules, frequently vaguely understood, that define the extent of the social welfare obligation. Society may be obligated to provide welfare assistance to persons who play by all the rules, but society determines the rules as well.

For many economically needy persons, playing by the rules is a no-win situation. Playing by the rules, as a limiting condition on the welfare obligation, has led to considerable mischief in providing assistance to the needy. Sometimes the rules may be immoral, unjust, or sometimes the rules are simply private rules and pre-judgments that those who hold the resources seek to force on those who are economically vulnerable. Clearly, before the Federal Government assumed some responsibility for assistance with the Social Security Act, minorities, particularly African Americans, were denied assistance based solely on their race. And even after the Social Security Act provided assistance funds to the states, accompanied by clear nondiscriminatory language, African Americans were still denied assistance based on subtle racial factors, such as how they reared their children.

One of the most insidious efforts to use assistance to force compliance with highly idiosyncratic social rules has been repeated efforts to use assistance payments to assert control over the structure and function of American families in economic need. The assistance changes that created the SSI program in 1974 were motivated in part by a belief that a certain type of family form would reduce welfare dependency. The 1996 changes in Title IV assistance for children (TANF) contained several eligibility conditions that sought to create a particular family structure. Arguing that welfare families had limited social rights if they accepted assistance, TANF required that mothers with children work as a condition for receiving assistance for themselves and their children, restricted teenage female single parents from establishing their own independent households, rewarded states that raised the marriage rate among unmarried welfare mothers, and provided financial bonuses to states that reduced out-of-wedlock births.[7]

While parental responsibility laws in all the states make parents responsible for their children's well being, it may not follow that children should be denied assistance if their parents fail to meet obligations associated with family behavior advocated by those who seek to use welfare to establish selective family norms. Chapter 6 provides a full discussion of this issue, but it is important to note that the 1996 changes to Title IV of the Social Security Act modified an earlier welfare commitment to children "deprived of parental support and care" and established family specific criteria for welfare eligibility for their parents. Thus, there are serious issues inherent in a social welfare obligation limited by social rules of behavior. Such rules are unclear and thus require careful discretionary decisions.

America has never developed a clear philosophy that could provide guidance for meeting its social welfare obligations. The moral voice of welfare advocates has been drowned out by the clamor of a few remaining Social Darwinists who continue to excoriate the idea of welfare assistance and the persons who need it. In an environment where more generous and more flexible social welfare assistance is needed, it might be well to review John Locke's perspective of welfare that puts the social obligation to provide it in proper perspective. Arguably the intellectual fountainhead for the development of the American state, Locke put his ideas of charity into memorable prose.

> But we know God hath not left one man so to the mercy of another, that he may starve him if he please. . . . He has given his needy brother a right to the surplusage [sic] of his goods so that it cannot justly be denied him, when his pressing wants call for it . . . so charity gives every man a title to so much out of another's plenty as will keep him from extreme want, where he has no means to subsist otherwise, and a man can no more justly make use of another's necessity to force him to become his vassal by the withholding of that relief . . . than he that has more strength can seize upon a weaker . . . and . . . offer him death or slavery.[8]

Conclusion

Although the American obligation to provide welfare disavows any right to assistance, the limitations on that social obligation run the risk of violating the rights of those who receive assistance. Granting assistance does not deprive individuals of their constitutional and legal rights. Unfortunately, the conditions placed on America's social welfare obligations have frequently been abused and used to discriminate unfairly, and as such the rights of many individuals who have received assistance have been violated. There may be no "right" to assistance, but those who receive assistance cannot be denied their rights by accepting that assistance.

While on the one hand it may be impossible to achieve sufficient clarity of the conditions under which social welfare becomes an obligation, the ambiguity of the social obligation has resulted in the need for discretion in assistance administration. Training welfare administrators to separate "objective factors" contributing to welfare need and the social obligation from personal biases and prejudices continues to be an important requirement for implementing America's social welfare obligation. All too often the process of determining who is needy and under what circumstances creates thorny ethical dilemmas, since one person has legal authority over important life factors of another. No amount of statute law or administrative directives can eliminate the issues that arise with this kind of responsibility.

Each expansion of social insurance under the Social Security Act has uncovered another group of people in economic need who could not benefit from the social insurance expansion. For example, proposed social insurance expansion for the disabled uncovered persons who could not qualify for the existing assistance programs. Medicare uncovered persons who were not eligible for health insurance, and the health assistance program, Medicaid, was created. The parallel development of social insurance and assistance programs has created considerable confusion over America's social welfare objectives as set forth in the Social Security Act. The social insurances convey an earned right to benefits, but the assistance programs convey a social obligation to assist the poor, a social obligation weighted down by a long history of strong negative public attitudes. Those who benefit from social insurance overlap with those who are economically needy, and may still be economically needy in spite of their right to receive social insurance. The plight of the economically needy to obtain just treatment from the assistance programs rests on the benevolence of the Federal Government and the states. Not withstanding the value to the thousands who receive welfare benefits today, the social value of the assistance programs rests on poorly defined principles.

The Social Security Act now provides funding for two cash assistance programs and one medical assistance program. Title XVI, SSI, is discussed in Chapter 5, and Title IV, now known as TANF, is discussed in Chapter 6. Medical assistance, Title XIX, Medicaid, is discussed in Chapter 8 as part of the medical commitments authorized under the Social Security Act. As the details of the assistance programs become more clear in the next chapters, the social, economic, and political framework in which America's assistance programs must operate will provide a foundation for a final discussion of the legitimacy of assistance programs as an important element in America's social welfare enterprise in the concluding chapter.

NOTES

1. June Axinn and Mark J. Stern, *A History of the American Response to Need* (Boston: Allyn & Bacon, 2005). Blanche D. Coll, *Perspectives in Public Welfare. A History* (Washington, DC: Department of Health, Education, and Welfare, 1969).
2. Andrew Dobelstein, *Moral Authority, Ideology, and the Future of American Social Welfare* (Boulder, CO: Westview Press, 1999).
3. North Carolina Constitution, Article XI, Section 7 (1868). The provision was modified in 1970, when North Carolina created its Department of Human Services to replace its Department of Public Welfare.
4. Dobelstein, *Moral Authority*, chap. 3.
5. An annotated summary of research is found in Dobelstein, *Moral Authority*, 228–242.
6. Richard Cloward and Francis Fox Piven, *Regulating the Poor: The Functions of Public Welfare* (New York: Vintage Books, 1993).
7. Ron Haskins, *Work Over Welfare* (Washington, DC: The Brookings Institution, 2007).
8. John Locke, *Two Treatises on Government* (Cambridge: Cambridge University Press, 1960), Book 1, chap. 4, 42.

5

Title XVI: Supplemental Security Income

Supplemental Security Income (SSI) became Title XVI of the Social Security Act in 1972. SSI added another layer of complexity to America's assistance programs by combining two existing assistance programs that were created in the original Social Security Act—Aid to the Aged (Title I) and Aid to the Blind (Title X), and combined these two programs with a third program, Aid to the Disabled (Title XIV) created in 1950—into a single assistance program administered by the Federal Government and funded with federal general revenue funds. Today, two types of assistance programs exist side by side: Title IV, now called Temporary Assistance to Needy Families (TANF), the original form of federal–state assistance created by the Social Security Act in 1935, and Title XVI, the federally-administered form of assistance created by SSI. This chapter discusses SSI, and Chapter 6 discusses Title IV and its most recent reform, TANF.

Prologue

Supplemental Security Income (Title XVI) owes its heritage to two previous social welfare developments. First, SSI was created in the shadow of the fourth assistance program, Title XIV, Aid to the Totally and Permanently Disabled, which was created in 1950 in a determined effort to maintain America's two-tiered approach to social welfare: social insurance and welfare assistance. Second, SSI emerged from the failed effort to merge all of the assistance programs into a federal Guaranteed Annual Income program, promoted by President Richard Nixon's Domestic Affairs advisor Daniel Patrick Moynihan. Aid to the Totally and Permanently Disabled assistance program affirmed the traditional patterns of federal–state intergovernmental welfare program cooperation, while SSI sought to shift the entire burden of welfare assistance from the states to the Federal Government.

Aid to the Totally and Permanently Disabled (ATPD)

In spite of the continued expansion of Title II social insurance during its early years, the need for assistance in the states persisted. Many financially impoverished individuals who were unable to work did not meet the categorical requirements for Aid for the Aged (Title I), Aid for the Blind (Title X), or Aid to Dependent Children (Title IV). Additionally, the numbers of female household heads applying for Title IV assistance began a sharp increase after World War II, putting additional financial pressure on the states to meet financially obligatory assistance commitments. States were confronted with increasing numbers of financially needy individuals for whom there were no corresponding federal programs, and states began to pressure for a new federal–state general assistance program to help them fund general relief.

As part of its persistent effort to expand Title II social insurance, the 1948 Advisory Committee on Social Security recommended the expansion of Title II to include persons who were disabled and unable to work, but the Committee was not unanimous in its recommendations. At least two members of the Committee argued that protection against economic loss due to the risk of total disability should be provided by programs aided by federal grants to states and should not be included as part of the Title II federal contributory social insurance program. The preference for an assistance program for the disabled arose not only from the reluctance to expand Title II Social Security further, but also, according to Edward Berkowitz, from "the reality that public assistance paid higher benefits and reached more people than did Social Security between [the years] 1935 and 1950."[1] When Congress responded to the Advisory Committee's 1948 recommendations in 1950, it increased Social Security benefits substantially, but it failed to expand Title II Social Security to include a disability insurance beneficiary group.[2] Congress did, however, create a new federal–state administered assistance program, Title XIV, ATPD.

Title XIV, as an assistance program, served as a compromise to those who advocated for disability insurance as part of Title II Social Security in the face of rising assistance needs, and it also recognized congressional reluctance to accept the continued beneficiary expansion of Title II social insurances as a means to render the assistance programs obsolete as the designers of the Social Security Act had argued.[a] Although Title XIV thus satisfied some of the general assistance needs the states were facing, and delayed further expansion of Title II, pressure to expand Title II Social Security continued until Disability Insurance was finally established as part of Title II in 1956. As discussed in Chapter 3, the creation of Disability Insurance, however, differed from the previous pattern of Title II simply by expanding beneficiary coverage, and instead it created a separate subprogram under Title II with a separate trust fund but

---

[a] The integral argument discussed in Chapter 1 was used by early program administrators to expand the social insurance programs. As pointed out in Chapter 1, the administrators argued that the social insurance programs would replace the assistance programs, thus leading Congress to believe that the two types of programs were integrated.

remaining under the administrative authority of Title II. Title XIV and the subsequent development of Disability Insurance under Title II continued social welfare development under the "two-track" approach built into the original Social Security Act: social insurance administered by the Federal Government and welfare assistance administered by the states with grant-in-aid financial support.

The Guaranteed Annual Income

Supplemental Security Income emerged from one of the most confusing political, economic, and social environments ever facing social welfare development under the Social Security Act. Politically, an otherwise conservative Republican president supported and promoted what appeared to be a liberal Democratic program. Economic conservatives endorsed and promoted an expansion of assistance programs in the form of a guaranteed income. Constant dissatisfaction with the assistance programs became entangled in renewed debates over the relationship between welfare and family structure. Persistent proposals to reform welfare sought to eliminate social services as a part of providing assistance, and a highly recognized public official in the Johnson administration went to work for President Nixon, who, like his predecessors, also sought to reform welfare. On top of this complexity, Congress and federal Social Security administrators forsook a longstanding aversion to administering assistance programs and accepted federal responsibility for the first and only assistance program provided under the Social Security Act, funded and administered solely by the Federal Government, thus presumably dropping America's two-tiered welfare policy approach.

The socio-political environment and the Economic Opportunity Act: For social welfare policy development generally, and the Social Security Act in particular, the decade of the 1960s represented a concerted federal effort to reorganize America's social welfare commitments. Just as the original Social Security Act cannot be fully understood outside the political and economic context of the Great Depression of the 1930s, neither can the development of SSI be understood outside the political and economic context of the Kennedy–Johnson presidential years, the decade of the "New Frontier" in social welfare policy. This period realized some of the most far-reaching social legislation since the 1930s. The Civil Rights Act, the Voting Rights Act, the Fair Housing Act, Medicare, Medicaid, and the Economic Opportunity Act (EOA) established a new social and political foundation for American life. Medicare and Medicaid, discussed in Chapters 7 and 8, respectively, are direct products of the "Great Society" programs that fashioned a major change to the structure and social welfare commitment authorized under the Social Security Act. Although President Richard Nixon's welfare reform, SSI developed as a part of the legacy of the Economic Opportunity Act of 1964, President Johnson's "war on poverty."

Like many of his predecessors and successor alike, President Johnson pledged to eliminate poverty in America, and the EOA of 1964 became the centerpiece of Johnson's antipoverty efforts.[b] Two major characteristics defined the important EOA's programs that set it apart from other efforts to deal with poverty in America. First, the programs were created outside the authority of the Social Security Act, and they were administered under the authority of a new administrative structure, the Office of Economic Opportunity (OEO), rather than the Department of Health Education and Welfare. Second, as the name of Johnson's initiative illustrates, the programs themselves were focused toward providing economic opportunities for those in poverty largely through a service structure of self-help, vocational training, job placement, and better educational preparation to enter the workforce, rather than providing people with money.[c] The EOA initiative did not expand assistance programs, but rather relied on services, specifically "hard" job services, as the means to reduce and, in Johnson's rhetoric, eliminate, poverty. Thus, in a unique way Johnson's "war on poverty" emphasized what later was called a "service strategy," somewhat in contrast to an "income strategy," as a means to deal with the nation's problems of poverty. The juxtaposition of services and income approaches to dealing with poverty became an important policy issue not only in the creation of SSI, but also in the creation of Title XX, the social services amendment to the Social Security Act of 1974 (see Chapter 9). The services promoted under the EOA were not the self-improvement kinds of services, later called "soft services," that became an important issue in the development of Title XX, but services that would improve the capacity of individuals to become employed, so called "hard services" like education and skill training.

From early preliminary planning, the EOA avoided existing federal administrative agencies to administer its programs. The Department of Health, Education, and Welfare and the Department of Labor both lobbied heavily to become major program administrative agencies for the new War on Poverty programs as they were being debated in the early months of the Johnson presidency. Both agencies were rejected by the working group that established the legislative framework for the EOA. The Department of Labor had not demonstrated an ability to work effectively with the poor and Secretary of Labor Willard Wirtz wanted to create new jobs for the poor, while the president wanted to get the poor into existing jobs. The Department of Health, Education, and Welfare had become too "categorical" and the working group feared

---

[b] The activities that led to President Johnson's "War on Poverty" initiative were begun at the very beginning of John Kennedy's presidency.

[c] The Economic Opportunity Act created 11 new programs: Job Corps, Neighborhood Youth Corps, Work Study, Urban and Rural Community Action, Adult Basic Education, Voluntary Assistance for Needy Children, Loans to Rural Families, Assistance for Migrant Agricultural Employees, Employment and Investment Incentives, Work Experience and Training for AFDC mothers, and Volunteers in Service to America (VISTA). The Director of OEO was also responsible for coordinating antipoverty efforts in other administrative departments, such as the Department of Labor. Only one part of the EOA was assigned to the Department of Health Education and Welfare, Title V (EOA) Work Experience that established a work training program for Aid to Families with Dependent Children (Social Security Act Title IV) recipients.

that new initiatives would simply end up in old program categories. Wilbur Cohen, himself, seemed reluctant to take on new initiatives and reflected an institutional disdain for program innovation.

> [W]hen you've got some completely new ideas, they will go farther and faster in a new agency than in an old agency. . . . What you're doing is, you're being experimental and innovative—which requires a somewhat different mentality and experience than an old-line fellow who can take something and make it work in a methodical way.[3]

Johnson's "war on poverty" not only failed to eliminate poverty; it also stirred up considerable debate about the assistance programs and how they should be continued. Both Kennedy and Johnson disliked the assistance programs. The War on Poverty was an effort to circumvent assistance through opening economic opportunities so that the poor could become economically self-sufficient. But to achieve the goal of eliminating poverty through creating economic opportunities required a much greater commitment than Congress was willing to provide or President Johnson was bold enough to ask for. The War on Poverty, however, left assistance programs the worst of two worlds. It advocated replacement of assistance with a battery of innovative services programs designed to open opportunities for work for the poor, while hostile critics of government social welfare programs were quick to point out that neither assistance programs nor experience with Johnson's Great Society service-oriented programs showed a measurable reduction in poverty or the nation's social problems. The Great Society programs did not propose to eliminate assistance programs, allowing some to argue that the Great Society programs precipitated the wave of social racial unrest of the late 1960s by setting expectations for social change without expanding welfare assistance to those who continued to be in economic need.[4] In retrospect, however, the Great Society programs did raise public awareness of poverty and economic need, and the entire Great Society enterprise was severely compromised, economically and politically, by the war in Vietnam.

The economic environment: The failed Great Society, however, left one continuing legacy for the assistance programs. An income guarantee, not a service strategy or expanded assistance, emerged as the best way to address poverty. The idea of a Guaranteed Annual Income, or a negative income tax, or some form of income guarantee to replace assistance programs materialized from economists as an economic option to both expanded assistance and a service strategy. As early as 1946, Milton Friedman, the conservative economist at the University of Chicago, had proposed a negative income tax as a tool that would provide needed income to the poor while at the same time lower the profile of government in its efforts to manage the economy.[5] For Friedman and conservative economists, a negative income tax would also be more efficient than the existing system of state-administered assistance.[6] It was the idea of a negative income tax that appealed to Daniel Patrick Moynihan when he served as Director, Joint Center for Urban Studies, Massachusetts Institute of Technology and Harvard University, and Moynihan took these ideas with him when he became the director of President Nixon's Urban Affairs Council. The negative income tax became the centerpiece of the Nixon administration's welfare reform effort, called the Family Assistance Program (FAP).[d]

The 1966 Advisory Council on Public Assistance appointed by President Johnson to advise the Department of Health, Education, and Welfare on the future direction for the assistance programs had recommended that financial assistance be provided as a *right* to all who needed it and that states should establish a minimum income floor for the provision of all assistance programs. It called on the Federal Government to secure welfare rights to those who needed assistance.[7] This report and its recommended "right to assistance" were never implemented. Instead, in January 1968, President Johnson appointed The President's Commission on Income Maintenance, which concluded that cash grants were more important in fighting poverty than was generally appreciated, and called for "the creation of a universal income supplement program financed and administered by the Federal Government making cash payments to all members of the population with income need."[8] The recommendations of both these influential advisory groups were strongly influenced by the experiences with the OEO programs.

The Moynihan Enigma: Although the idea of the FAP had emerged as a result of the experiences and disappointments encountered with the "war on poverty" and its service strategy, FAP contained an important element that had not been part of earlier proposals for some form of federal effort to support a guaranteed income. FAP was a *Family* Assistance Program. In other words, FAP introduced the complexity of family policy into debates over income maintenance policy. For Daniel Patrick Moynihan, FAP provided the opportunity to use the welfare system to correct what he saw as the gradual deterioration of the American family that was responsible for the increase and continued need for assistance programs. Commenting that "the Great Depression made the proposition that the unemployed are somehow not looking for work seem absurd," Moynihan complained that in 1969, joblessness was portrayed as "nothing whatever to do with the character traits of the jobless." "American social reformers have grown increasingly offended by definitions of social problems which seem to locate the source of difficulty in the behavior of the individual in trouble rather than in some abstraction made up of persons not in trouble."[9] According to Moynihan,

> [welfare dependency] involves … the intellectual denial of a primary social reality, namely that family structure and functioning have consequences for children, and that by and large, families function best in

---

[d] In May, 1968, some of the leading economists meeting in Cambridge, Mass., signed a statement authored by Paul A. Samuelson, John Kenneth Galbraith, James Tobin, and Harold Watts calling for a Guaranteed Annual Income as a feasible and economically compatible means to end poverty in America.

traditional arrangements. . . . Just as significantly, among social activists the presumption was reinforced that family matters were not to become public questions.

[B]y mid-twentieth century American liberalism had come to associate the idea of family policy not just with political conservatism, but with catholic conservatism. . . . This brought to American public life a tentative assertion of Catholic social thought, in which the family is seen as the basic social unit, whose interests take priority, surely, over those of the marketplace; but also, in curious ways, over those of the state and the individual. . . . When in 1966 Americans for Democratic Action at length turned its attention to the subject of family policy there emerged a resolution calling for enlightened legislation facilitating abortion, birth control and divorce.[10]

In many ways, Moynihan's early life experiences help explain the many puzzles Moynihan created in his public life. Moynihan grew up in a single-parent, female-headed, Roman Catholic family in the "Hells Kitchen" section of New York City. His mother received welfare from time to time, and as a youngster, Moynihan worked odd jobs to provide additional family income, including work on the docks and tending bar at a tavern that eventually his mother owned. As he grew up, Moynihan saw similarities between the Irish who lived in the New York slums of the nineteenth century and the black ghettos of the twentieth century. In particular, he was impressed with the stability of the traditional two-parent Irish Catholic family compared with his own. His family was more like the black families that surrounded him, and he seemed to connect the cause of his poverty with his perceived cause of black poverty—family instability.[11]

Moynihan's early life seemed to pull him in two directions at the same time: a pattern of rambunctious living pulled him to wild parties and a frequent return home to tend bar, and a sophisticated lifestyle at prestigious universities provided socially and economically desirable opportunities by influential persons he met and impressed. Moynihan's wife, Liz, best represented Moynihan's sophisticated lifestyle, and she was extremely active in Kennedy's presidential campaign. She was responsible for introducing Moynihan into Democratic politics. When John F. Kennedy won the presidency, the new Secretary of Labor, Arthur Goldberg, hired Moynihan as an executive assistant on the recommendation of Assistant Secretary Willard Wirtz. By all accounts, Goldberg appreciated and promoted Moynihan's work in the Department. In 1963, Moynihan was appointed Assistant Secretary of Labor under Wirtz, who became Secretary when Arthur Goldberg was appointed to the U.S. Supreme Court. Moynihan joined Wirtz in objecting to the direction the EOA was taking, urging a de-emphasis of community action in preference for the creation of new jobs. But President Johnson rejected the Labor Department's proposal for creation of new jobs, and Secretary Wirtz blamed Moynihan for not pressing harder to have the position of the labor department included in the EOA.

Moynihan had been set back on two accounts: his emphasis on job creation was almost totally ignored [by President Johnson], and in working to develop the best possible program he had come into conflict with his boss, Willard Wirtz. Relations between the two men grew increasingly strained over the next year, and for Moynihan the department of labor became a difficult place to work.[12, e]

Moynihan's tenure in the Department of Labor shifted from dissatisfaction to controversial by his well-documented report on the plight of the Negro family in urban America.[13] The report marked the beginning of Moynihan's effort to develop a public policy on the American family. Moynihan's 1965 report concluded.

> At this point the tangle of pathology [the Negro family] is capable of perpetuating itself without assistance from the white world. The cycle can be broken only if these distortions are set right. In a word, a national effort towards the problem of the Negro Americans must be directed towards the question of family structure. The object should be to strengthen the Negro family so as to enable it to raise and support its members as do other families.[14]

The "Moynihan Report" became the substance of a major address prepared by Moynihan that President Johnson delivered on June 4, 1965, at Howard University. Johnson's address touched off a firestorm of protest from the African American community, which understood the speech as a criticism of the whole African American community. As the turmoil continued to boil, Johnson carefully backed away from the Moynihan Report under withering criticism that racism was the motivating factor for the report.[15] Moynihan, however, stood by his conclusions put forth in the report. Only by "strengthening" the dysfunctional Negro family could poverty be reduced. This thesis became the basis for his efforts to achieve a national family policy.

President Richard M. Nixon's Family Assistance Plan

Moynihan's disillusions with President Johnson and mainline Democrats seemed to add fuel to his fire for a family policy. The urban riots of 1967 also fueled Moynihan's thesis of family breakdown and the need for family policy. But while his message seemed to fall on Democratic deaf ears, Republicans listened intently, including the business leaders he addressed at an Arden House Conference arranged by New York Governor Nelson Rockefeller to consider new approaches to welfare. After Richard Nixon was elected president, Moynihan sent him a letter outlining his thoughts on welfare reform. Nixon

---

[e] "When Wirtz learned that Moynihan [was working for Senator Robert Kennedy in his presidential bid] he told Johnson, and Moynihan was forbidden to do any more work for Kennedy. Johnson never forgave Moynihan for working for Kennedy and never fully trusted him again. After the election, Wirtz decided to fire Moynihan." Schoen, 90.

brought Moynihan into his administration as his domestic policy advisor and secretary of his newly created Urban Affairs Council, in charge of all domestic policy formulation except economic policy.

By the time Richard Nixon assumed the presidency in 1969, the Great Society, its programs, and its president were in shambles. If America's social welfare commitments had reached a new high at the beginning of the decade of the 1960s, it had reached a new low by the decade's end. In this tumultuous environment, Moynihan proposed the FAP to President Nixon in 1969. FAP was a complicated form of (1) a guaranteed income for all families based on (2) the structure of a negative income tax. In its simplest form, FAP would ensure a guaranteed income by supplementing earned income so that no family received income below a prescribed minimum amount. As earned income rose, the amount of supplement would be reduced proportionally, but the reduction in supplement would be less than a dollar reduction in the supplement for each dollar earned, thus encouraging earnings from work. (See Box 5.1 below.) The prescribed minimum income amount would be set by the Federal Government and apply in all the states, thereby equalizing wide-ranging state-by-state assistance payment variation, and also eliminate a welfare bureaucracy that decided assistance eligibility. The Federal Government would administer and fund the entire cost of the program, removing the welfare burden from the states. The negative income tax would be the means to achieve the guaranteed income. People would be expected to work, and women receiving assistance under Title IV would be required to work. Eligibility for FAP would be based solely on economic need, and the baseline of economic need would be set by the Federal Government.[16]

Box 5.1 Managing Earnings under a Guaranteed Annual Income

Earnings create a structural problem for Guaranteed Annual Income proposals. If there are no reductions placed on the amount of earnings, generally referred to as "tax rates," then everyone would receive the income guarantee, regardless of how much other income the person might have from earnings or other sources. Guaranteeing a set amount of income to everyone, sometimes called a demogrant, would be economically prohibited. On the other hand, prohibiting individuals from keeping some of their income, particularly income from earnings would discourage them from working. Thus, the Guaranteed Annual Income struggled with the problem of deciding the percentage of income that should be disallowed while still granting a basic income guarantee.

Figure 5.1 illustrates the structural problem inherent in Guaranteed Annual Income proposals. Proposing a $10,000 Guaranteed Annual Income, for example, would extend an income guarantee to persons earning

continued

Box 5.1 continued

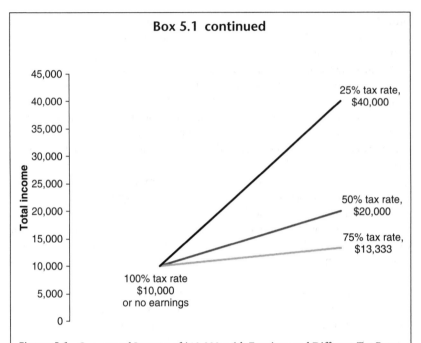

Figure 5.1. Guaranteed Income of $10,000, with Earnings and Different Tax Rates.

as much as $40,000 per year if $0.25 were reduced for each $1.00 in other income (25 percent tax rate), $20,000 if other income were reduced by $0.50, or $13,333 if other income were reduced by $0.75 for each other income $1.00. Extending the benefit level with a small tax rate expands the pool of persons eligible for the benefit. Choosing an "income reduction notch" that would encourage people to work, but at the same time is economically affordable is a major problem facing any Guaranteed Income proposal.

The complex political strands of Nixon's ideas about welfare reform are difficult to untangle from Moynihan's own unwavering support for the FAP. Nixon wanted a form of welfare reform that would repudiate the Kennedy–Johnson social welfare legacy. FAP represented a bold, new initiative that, in spite of extending the activities of the Federal Government deeper into welfare activities, confronted directly the "New Deal" and the "New Frontier" welfare thinking. There is no evidence to support the contention that Nixon expected FAP to improve social welfare for those who needed welfare assistance. None of Nixon's chief advisors, such as Casper Weinberger, known as "Cap the Knife," courted Congress for its welfare support. Instead, Moynihan carried the major liaison responsibility for FAP with Congress.

Moreover, it is difficult to separate Moynihan's disappointment with the previous Democratic administration from his motivation to champion an entirely new form of welfare assistance that would remove considerable welfare authority from the hands of entrenched social welfare bureaucracy. FAP was never proposed as an antiwelfare establishment welfare reform, but its repudiation of a social service strategy did not find support among social welfare advocates who had championed services as a way to help the poor escape poverty. But FAP did appeal to social welfare advocates who championed more adequate welfare payments and believed that the Federal Government was more likely to improve cash assistance payments than were the states. But when these welfare advocates found that the proposed federal FAP payments were every bit as minimal as those of the states, FAP lost the support of this group as well and turned Moynihan's Irish ire against them in all its fury.

Nixon's proposed FAP (H.R. 16311) was introduced in 1969. Not popular in Congress, it managed to pass the House of Representatives when Congressman Wilbur Mills finally agreed to support it in the Ways and Means Committee and sponsor it on the House floor. But it ran into insurmountable difficulty in the Senate. The level of income guarantee, the repudiation of social services, particularly rehabilitation services that had received emphasis under the Kennedy–Johnson years, and the work requirements included in FAP were among the problems Senator Russell B. Long and the Senate Finance Committee had with the bill. After two days of Senate hearings, Long requested that the administration withdraw the bill, which it did. But on June 10, 1970, President Nixon reintroduced what he called a "significantly altered" FAP. This version failed to improve the politically objectionable elements of FAP, such as work requirements, and the Senate Finance Committee dragged out the hearings until the 91st Congress adjourned. When the Congress reconvened in 1971, President Nixon introduced yet another revised version of FAP. H.R.1 was a 687-page rewrite of the previous FAP legislation, and the Senate was in no hurry to act on it either. By the time H.R.1 became law in September 1972, the six volumes of Senate Finance Committee transcripts and the 1,285-page Committee report constituted the most comprehensive review of the assistance programs since the Social Security Act was created in 1935.[17]

H.R. 1, extensively modified by Congress after its lengthy political journey, created Title XVI, Supplemental Security Income SSI in 1972, a new assistance program under the Social Security Act. The new program became effective in January 1974. Two major differences emerged in SSI that did not exist in the original FAP. First, the Aid to Dependent Children (AFDC Title IV) program was not included in the consolidation of the previous assistance programs. FAP was strictly a form of cash assistance without any funding for social services. But, second, limited funds for social services for persons receiving both SSI and AFDC were preserved over the strong objections of the president. AFDC was excluded from the consolidation because there was almost no agreement on whether the previous 1967 Work Incentive Program was effective (see Chapter 6), whether the income guarantee was too large or too small (see Box 5.1), whether the negative income tax would or would not stimulate a work effort among women who were expected to work, and whether it was possible to set a national minimum income level for children and their adult caretakers. The name "Family Assistance Plan" was dropped in favor of "Supplemental

Security Income" partly at the insistence of President Nixon, and partly at the insistence of the Senate. Thus, President Nixon obtained part of his welfare reform, but some of the more controversial elements of the original FAP were delayed until the next round of welfare reform proposals.

Prologue Summary

By insisting on a work element, the FAP created a structural problem over how to manage earnings under a guaranteed income. If earnings were reduced too much in determining eligibility for FAP, the income guarantee would discourage work. For example, if earnings were reduced dollar for dollar there would be no financial incentive to work. On the other hand, if earnings were treated too generously, larger numbers of people would have government assistance, and the government would be supplementing incomes well above the poverty line. Since the issue of work and earned income was a problem mostly for Title IV assistance recipients, and since there was strong support for parents of children on Title IV assistance to work toward financial independence, single mothers in particular, the guaranteed annual income solution for Title IV economically needy recipients did not present itself as a preferred solution. Thus, only economically dependent aged, blind, and disabled were included in SSI.

The political, social, and economic context for the development of the SSI program provides important insights into the ways SSI operates today. The decision to administer SSI as a federal assistance program was at first acclaimed by liberal welfare advocates as a step toward a national form of a guaranteed income for all Americans, and political support for SSI was fortified by the admirable record the Social Security Administration (SSA) had won in administering Title II Social Security. However, the matter of a service strategy or an income strategy for dealing with poverty was left undecided. Moreover, the creation of SSI put on hold any effort to establish a national family policy, such as that promoted by Daniel Moynihan, was also abandoned largely because family policy issues were insignificant among those who were supported by the SSI program. Yet conservative voices, including Moynihan's once he became Senator Moynihan (D, NY), in addition to a chorus of liberal voices, continued to press for a national family policy. The noted Gilbert Steiner of the Brookings Institution commented after a failed effort to achieve a family policy in the Carter administration that

> Even in the care of a more able administrative team . . . trouble was unavoidable, because diversity of family styles and traditionalism in family style peacefully coexist only so long as neither one gains actual or symbolic advantage over the other . . . Recognizing the pluralism of family life antagonizes those to whom that pluralism is an anathema.[18]

The controversy over social services and the use of assistance programs to achieve a family policy emerged again in the development of Title IV (see Chapter 6) and Title XX (see Chapter 9).

The Program Structure of Supplemental Security Income (SSI)

In creating SSI, Congress concluded, in part, "Building on the present Social Security Program, [Supplemental Security Income] would create a new Federal program administered by the Social Security Administration (SSA), designed to provide a positive assurance that the Nation's aged, blind, and disabled people would no longer have to subsist on below poverty-level incomes."[19] While this intent is straightforward, the program structure is considerably more complex.

Beneficiaries:[f] Persons are eligible for SSI if they are aged, disabled, or blind and meet the criteria for insufficient income and financial resources. **Aged** means a person aged 65 and older. **Blind** means an adult or a child with vision of 20/200 or less in the best eye, a serious limitation in the field of vision, or some other condition that may lead to disability. **Disabled** for an adult means a medically diagnosed condition that renders a person unable to work and can be expected to result in death or can be expected to last for at least twelve months. Disabled under age 18 means medically diagnosed severe functional limitations expected to result in death or last for at least twelve months. **Insufficient income** means limited income from employment (earned income), income from nonemployment sources such as pensions, including Title II Social Security (unearned income), and free food and housing. **Insufficient resources** means cash, cars, investments, insurance policies worth less than $1,500, and other resources that can be converted to cash with a value less than $2,000 per individual or $3,000 per couple. However, there are over 20 different kinds of resources that are not counted including burial funds worth less than $1,500, cars needed for work, household goods, personal effects, and others. The Social Security Administration exercises discretion in determining what items are not considered resources and their value.

In addition to the above, eligible persons must be a U.S. citizen, a qualified alien, certain types of refugees living in the United States and its territories, or a student temporarily studying in another country. Prisoners, fugitive felons, or persons absent from the United States for more than thirty consecutive days are ineligible to receive SSI benefits.

Benefits: The federal cash benefits for beneficiaries are adjusted each year based on changes in the cost of living index. Effective January 1, 2007, the federal benefit rate was $623 for an individual and $934 for a couple per month.[g] However, three important factors affect the actual cash benefit a beneficiary

---

[f] As with other social welfare programs under the Social Security Act, the SSI program characteristics can be quite detailed and change frequently. The most up-to-date program characteristics can be found at www.ssa.gov/ssi/text-understanding-ssi.htm.

[g] By contrast, poverty guidelines for a two-person family for 2007 was $13,690 per year. *Federal Register,* Vol. 72, No. 15, Wednesday, January 24, 2007. This put the SSI payment level at about 82 percent of the official poverty guidelines. Thus, SSI falls far short of keeping economically dependent persons out of poverty.

may receive: state maintenance of effort requirements, state supplementation, and reductions for income. **State maintenance of effort** has been required by states that were providing greater monthly benefits for persons eligible for Aid for the Aged, Aid for the Blind, and Aid to the Permanently and Totally Disabled before SSI was created. States whose payments were more than the established federal SSI payment were required to maintain the benefit level to those persons by supplementing the federal SSI payment with state funds. **State supplementation of SSI** is optional with other states, and today all but six states supplement the basic federal SSI payment. These supplements may be in the form of additional cash to the SSI beneficiary, in-kind support, such as custodial or in-home care, or some combination.

Reductions in the SSI payment from sources of income account for the greatest variation in the amount of SSI benefit a beneficiary may receive. Earned income, unearned income, in-kind income, and deemed income are all counted as income resources for determining the final SSI benefit payment. Generally, the first $65.00 and half of the remaining income is exempted from earned income and the first $20.00 is exempted from unearned income for computing the SSI payment to the beneficiary. If the total of these forms of income is less than the federal SSI payment, the beneficiary will receive a reduced SSI payment. If the total is more than the federal SSI benefit payment, the individual will not meet the low income eligibility standard. The overall income to the recipient from all the sources will not be less than the federal payment, but it is likely to be more than the basic SSI federal guarantee. Box 5.2 below provides an example of how the SSI benefit is computed taking into account different income sources.[h]

Supplemental Security Income payments may also be reduced through income deeming. Part of the income of a spouse or parent who is not a SSI recipient, but who shares a household with a SSI recipient, is deemed an income resource for computing the benefit for the person who is eligible for SSI. The SSA has detailed formulas for computing deemed resources, but generally the maximum amount of a deemed resource is approximately one-third of the SSI benefit guarantee.

Administration: Supplemental Security Income is administered by the SSA and is funded by general revenue funding of the Federal Government, rather than a form of trust fund. However, a considerable amount of SSI administration has been left to the states. Specifically, the states are responsible for certifying medical diagnoses that are required for disability eligibility, and states are responsible for administering any state supplementation they decide to provide to SSI beneficiaries. States that provide supplementation may either make the supplemental payments on their own or may ask the Federal Government to include the state supplement in the beneficiary's check. If the state chooses

---

[h] SSI settled on a fixed deductible and a 50 percent fixed reduction for earned income. (See Box 5.2.)

**Box 5.2 Hypothetical Example of SSI Federal Benefit, Social
Security Benefit, State Supplement, and Earned Income**

Social Security Benefit	$150
Basic Exemption	−$ 20
	= **$130** Countable Unearned Income
Gross Wages	$317
Not Counted	−$65
	= $252 divided by ½
	= **$126** Countable Earned Income
SSI Federal Benefit Rate	$623
	−$126 Countable Earned Income
	−$130 Countable Unearned Income
	= **$367** SSI Federal Benefit payment
SSI Federal Benefit Payment	$367
	(+15 State supplement payment for an individual living alone)
	= **$382** Total Federal and State SSI Benefit

---

to have the Federal Government provide the supplement, it must reimburse the
Federal Government for the amount of the supplement and pay an administrative fee for each federal transaction. Most of the 42 states that supplement SSI
do so at their own initiative.

Intersection with other social welfare programs: SSI overlaps Title II Social
Security, Medicare, Medicaid, TANF, Food Stamps, and vocational rehabilitation, in particular. As noted in Box 5.2, Title II Social Security is counted as
unearned income for determining the SSI benefit. In most states, SSI recipients are automatically eligible for Medic*aid*, although they may have to file a
Medic*aid* application. States pay the Medic*are* Part B premiums for people who
receive SSI benefits if they are also eligible for Medic*aid*, although details may
vary from state to state. The State Child Health Insurance Program is available for SSI child beneficiaries (see Chapter 8). SSI benefits are paid to the
blind or disabled adult or child, or aged 65 or older persons who are part
of TANF eligible households (see Chapter 6). The program structure of SSI
creates considerable opportunities for interaction with other social welfare programs, both those administered under the authority of the Social Security Act
and those administered under other federal and state authorities. Obviously,
changes to one or another of these programs usually affect thesis benefit, and
vice versa.

Summary of the program structure: Although the initial concept of an income guarantee that underlay the development of SSI appeared straightforward, the program structure to implement the concept has become quite complex. For example, in addition to the several categorical eligibility requirements discussed briefly above, rules for living arrangements, institutional living, HIV-infected persons, citizenship, drug and alcohol use, and homelessness are some of the more detailed criteria that further define categorical eligibility for SSI. The extensive eligibility rules have led to considerable program complexity. State supplementation along with rules for counting earned and unearned income, an emphasis on work, and interaction with other social welfare initiatives also have complicated SSI's program structure. Moreover, SSI's complex program structure has required frequent legislative and administrative changes in the program in an attempt to meet its original objectives. Instead of a program that provides a basic income guarantee to America's aged, blind, and the disabled, SSI has become a program highly dependent on the development of social welfare initiatives at the federal and state levels for its program integrity, and in fact, SSI has become a program of income support as a last resort. The reasons for this program drift can be found in the policy issues inherent in the creation and development of SSI, as discussed below.

The Policy Structure of Supplemental Security Income

By cobbling together three assistance programs into a single assistance program paid for and administered by the Federal Government, an assistance philosophy remained as the policy foundation for SSI. SSI was designed to provide income to the economically needy who were generally not expected to work. But SSI was also designed to provide a standard of economic support that would eliminate the wide state-by-state variation in assistance payments and state inconsistencies in the eligibility of persons who needed assistance. The assistance philosophy forced SSI to take into consideration both the reasons for economic dependency and the problem of not penalizing those who fit the category, still worked, but still remained economically dependent. The introduction to this discussion of Social Security Act's assistance programs pointed out that satisfying such assistance criteria required informed program discretion. But SSI proposed a bold attempt to eliminate discretion in deciding who is eligible for financial aid and how much aid they should be granted. Thus, the major policy issues raised by SSI develop from efforts to establish an income assistance program without exercising discretion in deciding who is eligible to receive assistance and how much assistance the beneficiary should be given. In other words, SSI attempted to graft social insurance principles on to an assistance program.

The SSI approach to providing assistance has led to an excessive number of rules that attempt to objectify beneficiary decisions, as the above discussion of

Table 5.1. Number of Recipients of Federally Administered Payments, by Eligibility Category and Age, December 1974–2005

Year	Total	Category			Age		
		Aged	Blind	Disabled	Under 18	18–64	65 or Older
1974	3,996,064	2,285,909	74,616	1,635,539	70,900	1,503,155	2,422,009
1980	4,142,017	1,807,776	78,401	2,255,840	190,394	1,730,847	2,220,776
1985	4,138,021	1,504,469	82,220	2,551,332	227,384	1,879,168	2,031,469
1990	4,817,127	1,454,041	83,686	3,279,400	308,589	2,449,897	2,058,641
1995	6,514,134	1,446,122	83,545	4,984,467	917,048	3,482,256	2,114,830
2000	6,601,686	1,289,339	78,511	5,233,836	846,784	3,744,022	2,010,880
2005	7,113,879	1,214,296	75,039	5,824,544	1,036,498	4,082,870	1,994,511

Source: Social Security Administration, Supplemental Security Record (Characteristic Extract Record format), 100 percent data. 2006 *Annual Statistical Supplement*, Social Security Administration, Table 7.A9.

the SSI program illustrates. Even so, major policy problems in the SSI program remain. In particular, first, SSI has failed to eliminate categorical variation in treatment of individuals as was so contentious in the state-administered programs that preceded SSI. SSI also failed to eliminate the wide variation in state-by-state beneficiary payments. Second, as alluded to above, SSI has raised serious question about the political and economic value of Title II Social Security for low-income earners. Finally, SSI has failed miserably to provide an income maintenance flow for eligible low-income individuals that comes anywhere near mitigating poverty among this group of economically needy Americans. SSI has come at the expense of a highly complex program with considerable discretionary authority still passed onto the states.

Table 5.1 provides a summary of the development of the SSI program during its twenty three-year history. Although the total number of SSI recipients increased by almost 48 percent from almost 4 million recipients to slightly over

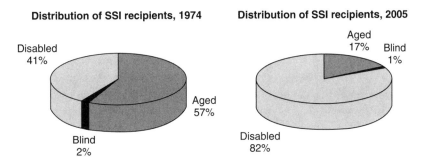

Figure 5.2. Changes in Distribution of SSI Recipients, 1974–2005.
Source: Social Security Administration, Supplement Security Income, Record (2006).

7 million, the number of SSI beneficiaries compared to the general population has remained rather constant at 2.4 percent or less since 1975.[20] Perhaps more striking than the increase of SSI recipients has been the change in their distribution. Recipients under age 18 increased by 93 percent since 1975, while the recipients age 65 and older decreased almost 18 percent during the same time period. Aged recipients, as a category, decreased almost 47 percent while the disabled as a category of recipients increased by almost 72 percent. Thus, the major changes in the distribution of SSI recipients have been due to increases in the younger and disabled recipients. The changes in the distribution of SSI recipients are illustrated in Figure 5.2.

Several factors have contributed to the demographic changes in the SSI population and as such have led to continued categorical SSI beneficiary treatment. An expansion of eligibility for disability to include mental impairments for children and adults following a period of Mental Health "deinstitutionalization" spiked SSI disability growth in the mid-1980s. In 1990, children on AFDC were made eligible for SSI benefits if they also met SSI

Table 5.2. Number and Percentage Distribution of Adult Individuals and Persons under Age 18 Receiving Federal SSI Payments, by Monthly Payment and Eligibility Category, December 2005

Monthly Payment (Dollars)	All Recipients	Adults			Blind and Disabled under Age 18
		Aged	Blind	Disabled	
Total					
Number	6,300,888	878,628	59,136	4,329,415	1,033,709
Percent	100.0	100.0	100.0	100.0	100.0
Less than 50 Dollars	8.1	13.4	8.6	8.4	2.0
$50–99 Month	5.7	10.3	5.8	5.9	0.8
$100–149 Month	4.9	9.5	5.0	4.9	1.1
$150–199 Month	4.1	7.9	4.2	4.0	1.3
$200–249 Month	3.5	5.6	3.8	3.6	1.5
$250–299 Month	3.4	4.9	4.3	3.5	1.9
$300–349 Month	2.8	3.9	2.9	2.7	2.3
$350–399 Month	7.4	11.2	8.9	6.7	6.9
$400–449 Month	2.2	2.1	2.1	1.8	3.9
$450–499 Month	2.2	1.4	1.7	1.5	5.6
$500–549 Month	2.0	0.9	1.3	1.4	5.9
$550–578 Month	1.1	0.4	0.8	0.8	3.1
$579[a] Month	52.7	28.6	50.7	54.9	63.8

Source: Social Security Administration, Supplemental Security Record (Characteristic Extract Record format), 100 percent data.
[a] Individuals living in their own household with no countable income were eligible for a federal SSI payment of $579 in calendar year 2005. No comparable table exists for years after 2005. While the payment amounts would be different, the distribution would remain similar.

eligibility criteria,[i] and more flexible diagnoses of disability among children contributed to the rise in the proportion of children receiving SSI according to the General Accountability Office.[21] During the 1980s, a new mental health policy that substituted "community based care" for institutional care left many of the mentally ill to seek SSI disability in order to have sufficient resources to live outside a hospital setting. Since SSI functions as an income maintenance program of last resort, any change in other social welfare programs will be reflected in SSI. For example, increases or decreases in Title II Social Security payments will be reflected in both the numbers of aged receiving SSI and the amount of SSI benefits the aged will receive. In other words, SSI is extremely sensitive to related social welfare program changes. Thus, SSI has been forced to continue a categorical approach to welfare assistance based on changes in other social welfare programs.

The distribution of benefit payments by eligibility groups is shown in Table 5.2. Whereas an average of 52.7 percent of all SSI recipients received the monthly maximum payment, only 28.6 percent of the aged receive the monthly maximum while 54.9 percent of the disabled, and 63.8 percent of the blind and disabled under age 18 receive the maximum payment. Without evidence to the contrary, it is possible to assume that both earned and unearned income, mostly in the form of Social Security, offsets more of the SSI benefit for the elderly than it does for the disabled and children (see Table 5.3). In other words, earned and unearned income for the aged reduces their SSI payment. More than one-third of the aged receive less than $150 SSI per month. Thus, SSI payments vary widely by category. (See Table 5.4.)

Table 5.5 below shows the wide variation of SSI benefits from state to state, a situation that is unavoidable in an assistance program. The average SSI payment for all states, all categories was $454.75 in 2006, but SSI payments ranged from a low of $173.49 for the aged in Arkansas to $644.49 for children in California. Thus, considering the income for determining the amount of SSI benefit and state SSI supplementation has undermined any effort to achieve SSI equality.

Title II Social Security Conundrum

The overlap between Title II Social Security and SSI has been discussed above and in Chapters 2 and 3. While some may suggest that Title II Social Security benefits should not be treated any differently than other cash resources, the fact remains that except for $20.00 per month, earned Title II Social Security benefits are lost for the low-income worker. The value of Title II Social Security to aged SSI recipients is reflected in Table 5.3. Fifty-seven percent of the aged availed Title II Social Security benefits, and another 18 percent had other forms

---

[i] In 1990, in the case of *Sullivan v. Zebley* (493 U.S. 1990) the U.S. Supreme Court held in part that children in AFDC households could be determined disabled for SSI purposes similar to the procedures used for adults. The number of children covered by SSI almost tripled after the ruling. The 1996 TANF welfare reform established stricter SSI eligibility rules for children. (See Chapter 6.)

Table 5.3. Persons Receiving Federally Administered SSI Payments and Other Income and Their Average Monthly Income, by Type of Income, Eligibility Category, and Age, December 2006

Type of Income	Total	Category			Age		
		Aged	Blind	Disabled	Under 18	18–64	65 or older[a]
Number	7,235,583	1,211,656	73,418	5,950,509	1,078,977	4,152,130	2,004,476
				Number			
With Unearned Income							
Social Security Benefits	2,528,975	692,332	26,913	1,809,730	77,401	1,309,629	1,141,945
Other	818,701	218,660	7,421	592,620	207,682	320,602	290,417
With Earned Income	275,252	18,236	4,319	252,697	3,024	244,228	28,000
				Percentage			
With Unearned Income							
Social Security Benefits	35.0	57.1	36.7	30.4	7.2	31.5	57.0
Other	11.3	18.0	10.1	10.0	19.2	7.7	14.5
With Earned Income	3.8	1.5	5.9	4.2	0.3	5.9	1.4
				Average Income (Dollars)			
With Unearned Income							
Social Security Benefits	462.49	457.69	478.15	464.11	206.47	482.78	456.70
Other	136.87	114.28	124.19	145.45	186.11	127.86	111.66
With Earned Income	300.34	360.77	478.57	292.86	335.76	301.36	287.81

Source: Social Security Administration, Supplemental Security Record (Characteristic Extract Record format), 100 percent data, 2007.
[a] Includes approximately 16,200 blind and 776,600 disabled persons aged 65 or older.

Table 5.4. SSI Recipients, by Type of Income, Eligibility Category, and Age, December 2006

Type of income	Total	Category			Age		
		Aged	Blind	Disabled	Under 18	18–64	65 or Older
All recipients[a]	7,235,583	1,211,656	73,418	5,950,509	1,078,977	4,152,130	2,004,476
No Other Income	4,011,553	427,225	39,102	3,545,226	801,905	2,471,026	738,622
Earned Income	275,252	18,236	4,319	252,697	3,024	244,228	28,000
Unearned Income							
Social Security Benefits	2,528,975	692,348	26,913	1,809,714	77,401	1,309,629	1,141,945
Veterans' Benefits	60,914	24,910	464	35,540	1,223	21,061	38,630
Income Based on Need	18,556	212	52	18,292	12,200	6,124	232
Workers' Compensation	4,963	398	17	4,548	12	3,989	962
Support from Absent Parents	141,036	1	872	140,163	137,274	3,761	1
Pensions	59,896	39,872	386	19,638	45	12,200	47,651
Support and Maintenance	306,491	88,290	2,568	215,633	49,999	147,659	108,833
Asset Income[b]	191,009	69,062	2,599	119,348	9,733	85,429	95,847
Other[c]	73,980	12,956	725	60,299	3,331	52,286	18,363

Source: Social Security Administration, Supplemental Security Record (Characteristic Extract Record format), 100 percent data.

[a] The sum of the entries may be greater than the total because some recipients may receive more than one type of unearned income or both earned and unearned income.
[b] Includes income received as rent, interest, dividends, and royalties.
[c] Does not include income deemed from a spouse or parent.

Table 5.5. SSI Payments by Beneficiary Category among the States

State or Area	Total	Category			Age		
		Aged	Blind	Disabled	Under 18	18–64	65 or older
All States	**454.75**	**373.05**	**488.42**	**471**	**541.85**	**470.64**	**375**
Alabama	403.24	189	381.25	427.62	534.74	423.81	229.78
Alaska	413.52	288.44	401.22	442.87	486.76	446.95	308.86
Arizona	433.79	311.97	434.11	453.05	531.86	448.63	323.64
Arkansas	395.90	173.49	371.92	420.67	532.03	410.99	207.43
California	581.12	522.47	641.04	604.61	644.49	615.33	530.67
Colorado	408.15	323.62	422.94	423.34	500.85	425.76	317.01
Connecticut	429.95	346.11	432.24	442.13	523.83	442.92	344.36
Delaware	423.68	277.72	414.2	438.68	513.06	426.59	291.10
District of Columbia	463.04	286.13	418.03	481.17	534.35	484.11	322.86
Florida	421.19	342.83	412.67	445.58	524.44	434.58	344.60
Georgia	401.76	232.67	417.98	427.15	525.81	429.03	252.07
Hawaii	459.79	384.54	452.01	489.65	501.84	495.46	398.71
Idaho	411.82	225.43	410.26	428.26	505.42	420.73	250.36
Illinois	454.04	360.66	447.04	466.58	538.4	464.03	361.77
Indiana	428.32	245.23	400.20	439.81	531.55	425.8	262.67
Iowa	397.90	225.62	382.28	413.77	509.66	407.43	245.45
Kansas	412.33	262.24	414.81	425.86	520.98	416.36	274.22
Kentucky	420.44	199.41	420.61	438.1	539.63	440.41	249.68
Louisiana	417.32	208.64	409.78	442.62	539.94	441.06	245.39
Maine	392.73	184.83	425.68	408.81	515.2	412.83	222.66
Maryland	437.1	342.79	419.01	455.19	515.05	457.67	342.48
Massachusetts	464.61	398.06	500.18	487.40	564.13	477.5	396.28
Michigan	452.32	316.71	442.89	463.33	541.14	460.11	326.02

Minnesota	430.77	350.63	434.47	443.46	518.73	435.16	360.53
Mississippi	398.64	181.44	369.14	427.2	535.38	425.74	227.31
Missouri	413.96	238.69	414.37	428.71	532.42	422.07	259.64
Montana	405.34	202.12	426.36	421.12	521.42	421.35	236.62
Nebraska	393.16	237.55	420.23	408.48	511.17	400.97	257.64
Nevada	423.98	335.79	486.04	453.60	511.52	439.65	334.8
New Hampshire	406.3	272.4	403.53	415	492.58	413.71	271.63
New Jersey	440.31	376.42	421.69	458.37	534.16	455.12	375.43
New Mexico	406.06	258.78	428	432.76	536.31	435.26	283.5
New York	484.2	396.47	462.31	508.01	559.81	514.73	415.64
North Carolina	390.07	203.67	391.95	415.72	514.7	409.77	240.78
North Dakota	365.92	224.78	410.33	384.71	486.25	386.27	241.17
Ohio	445.84	291.86	415.55	455.97	540.09	452.26	304.75
Oklahoma	412.98	221.12	410.66	433.11	529.49	430.02	245.84
Oregon	423.93	314.86	427.95	440.1	521.71	438.1	320.43
Pennsylvania	453.62	302.08	426.72	468.61	531.64	466.9	331.1
Rhode Island	455.9	331.79	427.47	474.44	581.48	469.24	347.3
South Carolina	397.35	204.77	395.46	421.91	520.15	420.32	243.68
South Dakota	382.4	213.83	404.68	407.29	499.36	405.74	247.46
Tennessee	404.51	202.11	424.65	426.75	529.72	429.97	243.84
Texas	394.66	264.32	418.6	429.13	525.41	423.09	272.09
Utah	419.11	345.86	422.08	427.25	490.71	420.41	340.11
Vermont	411.23	211.78	406.71	429.49	562.75	426.84	250.27
Virginia	405.57	293.39	405.89	425.18	510.48	423.56	295.56
Washington	449.06	392.36	441.75	457.41	518.16	457.13	388.3
West Virginia	428.57	194.9	421	441.44	529.96	448.36	260.97
Wisconsin	419.83	260.35	425.39	435.1	526.6	425.45	282.72
Wyoming	392.96	176.37	430.12	409.43	492.58	409.79	213.19

of unearned income. By comparison, 30.4 percent of the disabled had Social Security benefits and another 10 percent had other forms of unearned benefits. The average income of the aged with Title II Social Security benefits was $457.69 in 2006, but the average income for the disabled with Title II Social Security benefits was $464.11. In other words, the aged were not better off financially as a result of their Title II Social Security than the disabled. Or, put in other words, Title II Social Security is worth less to the aged than it is to the disabled since a higher Social Security benefit merely reduces the overall value of the SSI payment. Sources of unearned income are noted in Table 5.4.

Title II Social Security beneficiaries lose almost all their contribution to Social Security when they become eligible for SSI. In other words, SSI beneficiaries who have never worked are almost as well compensated as the SSI beneficiaries who have worked and have Title II Social Security earnings. While it is true that SSI guarantees a minimum income, or income floor, and it is reasonable to assume that the addition of earned and unearned income, including Title II Social Security income, reduces the amount of the SSI benefit, as shown above, there persists an equity issue in the overlap of these two programs. On the one hand, these people worked and built a social insurance benefit, yet they did not build enough in the Title II insurance program to realize that benefit. The policy nature of the assistance program requires that earned Social Security benefits be counted as income. The Title II Social Security/SSI problem provides a cogent lesson in America's effort to satisfy its social welfare obligations through its "two tiered" approach. At the very least, one might expect that SSI treat Title II Social Security as generously as it treats earned income from wages in determining the monthly benefit.

Supplemental Security Income and Poverty

While guaranteed income may have been promoted as a way to reduce poverty in America, SSI as it presently exists fails to achieve such an idealistic objective. Table 5.6 shows that in 2002, SSI payments alone accounted for only 75.8 percent of the poverty level for the average SSI beneficiary. This is a modest increase of only 5 percentage points in the SSI impact on poverty since its modest beginning in 1974. Even with the addition of Title II Social Security, SSI and Social Security together amount to only 78.6 percent of the poverty level. This meager 2.9 percent increase in the value of combined Social Security and SSI again suggests the limited added value of Title II Social Security for the low-income worker. The failure of SSI as an income maintenance program is further evident in the fact that in 1975, SSI with combined benefits provided 91.4 percent of the poverty level for beneficiaries. This percentage has slipped to 85.3 percent by 2002. Thus, SSI has failed to keep up with changing programs that also have an effect on reducing poverty. If SSI was designed to ensure that the poor do not live in poverty, even with combined benefits it has not achieved this goal.

Table 5.6. Comparison of SSI and Combined Benefits to Poverty Levels, Selected Years

Poverty Threshold and Benefits	1975	1980	1984	1992	1996	2000	2002
Poverty Threshold (Dollar)	2,572	3,941	4,950	6,729	7,309	8,259	8,628
Federal SSI Benefit:							
Dollars per Year	1,822	2,677	3,768	5,064	5,640	6,156	6,540
Percentage of Poverty	70.8	72.3	75.6	75.3	77.2	74.5	75.8
Federal SSI and Social Security:							
Dollars per Year	2,062	2,917	4,488	5,304	5,580	6,396	6,780
Percentage of Poverty	80.2	74.0	80.5	78.8	80.4	77.4	78.6
Federal SSI, Social Security, and Food Stamps:							
Dollars per Year	2,350	3,345	4,294	5,820	6,372	6,980	7,360
Percentage of Poverty	91.4	84.9	86.2	86.5	87.2	84.5	85.3

Source: United States Congress, Committee on Ways and Means, *The Green Book.* Washington, DC: Government Printing Office, 2006. Table 3.9. Data Source: Congressional Research Service.

Conclusion

"The Family Assistance Plan had been devised as first and foremost to provide a guaranteed income for children and for families with children. In the end the only persons left out were children and families with children."[22] Just as it was lost from *The Moynihan Report,* Moynihan's effort to create a family policy vanished from his FAP and SSI took its place. But Moynihan persisted to advocate for a government family policy as he railed against President Johnson's war on poverty. On the surface, Moynihan's pleas for a family policy appeared quite simple. "The object should be to strengthen the Negro family so as to enable it to raise and support its members as do other families. After that, how this group of Americans chooses to run its affairs . . . is none of the nation's business."[23]

> It would be enough for a national family policy to declare the American government sought to promote the stability and well-being of the American family; that the social programs of the federal government would be formulated and administered with this object in mind; and finally that the President or some person designated by him, would report to the Congress on the condition of the American family in all its many facets—not of *the* American family, for there is as yet no such thing, but rather of the great range of American family modes in terms of regions, national origins an economic status.[24]

The above quotes from Moynihan are as close as he comes to defining what would constitute a family policy and how welfare might be used as a means to achieve it. Moynihan's recognition that there is "yet no such thing" as *the* American family proved a stumbling block to realizing his Family Assistance Plan, and the vitriol stirred up by the *Moynihan Report* was replayed years later when President Carter, too, tried to establish a family policy, as discussed in the next chapter. Moynihan's withering attacks on "liberals" who argued that the social structure, not the family, bore major responsibility for America's continuing social problems and the forms of "family breakdown" contained a remarkable similarity to the views of those early social workers who, too, warned that continued welfare would weaken the family. The underlying idea that welfare policy could be manipulated to fix the family created a fundamental flaw in the FAP. Although Moynihan later observed that there is no single kind of American family, he failed to understand that there can be no family policy either.

Supplemental Security Income materialized from the flawed welfare reform efforts of the FAP largely *because* children and families with children were left out. Economically, SSI offered the opportunity to control rising welfare costs, which states seemed unable to do. Under SSI, the Federal Government would determine who was eligible for welfare assistance, and the amount of welfare assistance would be controlled by federal policy. As a federally funded and administered assistance program, SSI broke sharply with grant-in-aid funding that forced expansion of federal funding each time states liberalized their eligibility criteria or the level of their cash assistance grants. Politically, SSI allowed President Nixon to claim a major welfare reform victory, somewhat hollowed-out, however, without the financial work incentives that were supposed to reduce the need for welfare among financially dependent mothers and children.

The effort of President Nixon and his Domestic Affairs Advisor to "reform" welfare became tangled over policy debates outside the usual policy framework most familiar to assistance programs. A proposal for a guaranteed income implemented through a negative tax, both completely novel and untested social welfare ideas, raised economic debates over their implementation and ideological debates over their impact on work. In general, incrementalism supports social welfare policy development. From a legislative perspective, it is highly unlikely that an innovative, untested policy initiative will easily win approval, and as FAP and the eventual development of SSI clearly show, compromise characterizes most social welfare reform initiatives. The subtle family policy that lay at the roots of this welfare reform became more obvious when discussing welfare assistance provided for women and children under the authority or Title IV of the Social Security Act. Politically, a guaranteed income seemed inconsistent with previously failed mandatory work requirements for welfare mothers (the Work Incentive Program, WIN), but by leaving welfare families and their children out, SSI provided a politically harmless compromise for those who insisted that work, not a guaranteed income, provided the best way out of welfare for families and their children, since most SSI recipients were not expected to work. Finally, as an alternative to the failed social services strategy of President Johnson's War on Poverty, SSI's sharp reduction in social services also represented social welfare policies contrary to the political objectives of the work-oriented objectives of Title IV assistance. Cutting social services became a separate problem, as discussed in Chapter 9.

FAP and the resulting SSI foundered on its basic premise of providing a uniform baseline assistance amount to everyone in economic need and trying to do it with a social insurance policy. The subsequent experience of implementing SSI has demonstrated the variability of economic need, individually and regionally, the interaction of assistance with existing need-based social welfare programs, and the development of complex eligibility and benefit rules as an effort to replace discretionary decisions, and the development of SSI today, has undermined any previous argument for a guaranteed income as a replacement for assistance. Supplemental Security Income also departed from previous social welfare administrative practice. A belief that the Federal Government could manage the administration of assistance payments in an objective, nonprejudicial manner encouraged support for SSI among social welfare reformers. Much of the belief in federal administrative impartiality was due to the excellent record of social welfare administration won by the SSA. But, in reality, SSI was an assistance program, not social insurance. At the very least, a SSI benefit could not be established based on a formula, but was required to take economic need into consideration. Had SSI simply expanded Title II Social Security to include greater numbers of low-income aged and disabled, its social welfare administrative objectivity might have prevailed. But SSI was a different kind of social welfare commitment, and from the beginning, the states had to be included in its administration. As the states became more involved in supplementing SSI benefits, the ideal of superior federal objectivity gave way to the reality that states, too, had to use their discretion to implement programs fairly and impartially. SSI was forced to take a very narrow view of economic need, while states were forced to continue to assume responsibility for residual economic issues that SSI was unable to satisfy. Lacking clear constitutional authority, SSI has been forced to function as a program of last resort rather than one that would promote the general welfare of economically needy Americans.

While it would be unfair to conclude that SSI has failed to meet the social welfare objectives its advocates had promoted, the new era in social welfare assistance that SSI forecast has not materialized. SSI has not eliminated poverty, even the poverty of those dependent on it. It has not achieved uniformity of treatment among its beneficiaries. Perhaps most significantly, SSI has not achieved a comfortable fit into the architecture of the Social Security Act. Its overlap with Title II Social Security has diminished the value of the Title II Social Security contribution among low-income workers, and its inability to include economically dependent children in its modest level of income maintenance has weakened the economic value of Title IV assistance for children as Title IV has continued to develop its family policy elements. In many ways, SSI occupies an uncomfortable, compromised place in America's welfare enterprise as it is based on the Social Security Act.

Perhaps of greater concern for efforts to meet America's social welfare obligations, SSI seems to have stifled further consideration of income support initiatives, either federal or state, that would better meet the economic needs of the aged and disabled. Supplemental Security Income's political, ideological, and structural problems have left it far short of its original objectives, and render it an inadequate effort to realize America's social welfare obligation to provide adequate assistance for those in economic need. Perhaps most important of all, Americans' aversion to welfare has not been appeased in the aftermath of SSI administration, and its interaction with other social welfare efforts raise questions about its capacity to meet today's social welfare needs.

NOTES

1. Edward Berkowitz, *Disability Policy and History*. Statement before the Subcommittee on Social Security of the Committee on Ways and Means, July 13, 2000, 3.
2. H.R. 6000, P.L.
3. Quoted in Michael L. Gillette, *Launching the War on Poverty. An Oral History* (New York: Twayne Publishers, 1996), 343. See also statement by James L. Sundquist in Ibid., 23.

4. Charles A. Murray, *Losing Ground American Social Policy 1950–1980* (New York: Basic Books, 1994) and Charles A. Murray, *In Our Hands. A Plan to Replace the Welfare State* (Washington, DC: AEI Press, 1996). Daniel P. Moynihan, *Maximum Feasible Misunderstanding; Community Action in the War on Poverty* (New York: Free Press, 1969).

5. See Milton Friedman, *Essays in Positive Economics* (Chicago: University of Chicago Press, 1962) and Milton Friedman, *Capitalism and Freedom* (Chicago: University of Chicago Press, 1962). Friedman supported a guaranteed income as a way to reduce government by providing a grant of income without government intervention into a "free market system" that attempted to regulate the "marketplace" in order to improve the economic welfare of the poor.

6. See also Robert Theobald, *The Guaranteed Income* (New York: Doubleday and Company, Inc., 1965).

7. Advisory Council on Public Welfare, *Having the Power We Have the Duty* (Washington, DC: Government Printing Office, 1966), i–xviii .

8. See U.S. Congress, House of Representatives, Committee on Ways and Means, *The Social Security Amendments of 1971* (Washington, DC: U.S. Government Printing Office, 1971), 7. Because the Heineman Commission did not make its report until President Johnson left office, Daniel Moynihan argued that Johnson's efforts were disingenuous and amounted to an effort to leave a legacy for the Nixon administration that would be difficult for Nixon to fulfill. Still the Johnson Administration's Commission's recommendations were well known before President Nixon presented his welfare proposals in August, 1969. See Daniel Moynihan, *The Politics of a Guaranteed Income* (New York: Random House, 1973), 128–135. Moynihan's observations differs from the report of the Ways and Means Committee cited above. See 46–64.

9. Ibid., 24.

10. Ibid., 22–26.

11. Douglas Schoen, *Pat: A Biography of Daniel Patrick Moynihan* (New York: Harper and Row, 1979).

12. Ibid., 89.

13. U.S. Department of Labor, Office of Policy Planning and Research, *The Negro Family: The Case for National Action* (Washington, DC: Government Printing Office, 1965).

14. Ibid., 47–48.

15. See Lee Rainwater and William Yancy, *The Moynihan Report and the Politics of Controversy* (Cambridge: MIT Press, 1967).

16. Daniel Moynihan, *The Politics of a Guaranteed Income*, 138–140.

17. A detailed discussion of the development of H.R.1 is found in Andrew Dobelstein, *Politics Economics and Public Welfare* (Englewood Cliffs, NJ: Prentice Hall, 1980), 186–189. See also U.S. Congress, House of Representatives, Committee on Ways and Means and Senate Committee on Finance, *H.R. 1. Summary of Social Security Amendments of 1972 as Approved by the Conferees* (Washington, DC: Government Printing Office, 1972).

18. Gilbert Y. Steiner, *The Futility of Family Policy* (Washington, DC: The Brookings Institution, 1981), 45.

19. U.S. Senate, Committee on Finance, *Social Security Amendments of 1972* (Senate Report No. 92-1230) (Washington, DC: U.S. Government Printing Office, 1972, Sept. 26), 2.

20. U.S. Congress, Committee on Ways and Means, *The Green Book* (Washington, DC: Government Printing Office, 2006), Table 351. Data Source: Congressional Research Service.

21. See U.S. General Accounting Office, *Supplemental Security Income: Growth and Changes in the Recipient Population Call for Reexamining Program* (Washington, DC: Government Printing Office, 1995).

22. Daniel Patrick Moynihan, *Family and Nation* (New York: Harcourt, Brace, Jovanovich, 1986), 14.

23. U.S. Department of Labor, Office of Policy Planning and Research, *The Negro Family: The Case for National Action* (Washington, DC: U.S. Government Printing Office, 1965), 48.

24. Moynihan, *Family and Nation*, 11.

6

Who's Taking Care of the Children?
Title IV: Temporary Assistance to
Needy Families and Related
Programs for Children and Families

Introduction

The centerpiece of America's commitment to the welfare of children is Title IV of the Social Security Act—see Figure 1.1. In its original form in 1935, Title IV authorized a straightforward effort to provide financial assistance to children, by supporting them either in their own homes or in substitute homes, usually foster or adoptive homes, when their own homes were not considered suitable for rearing children. Originally called Aid to Dependent Children, Title IV constituted a companion assistance program to Title I, Aid to the Aged, and Title X, Aid to the Blind in the original Social Security Act. Title IV was created as an assistance program, and remains so today. The original, limited scope of Title IV in the original Act, however, has expanded well beyond providing economic protection for children, and the original Title IV now includes a number of social programs that have shifted the public commitment to children in a variety of new directions, blurring the principle of need-based assistance discussed in Chapter 1.[a]

Title IV survived the effort to convert all the assistance programs into a single federally funded and administered SSI program, and now it stands alone as the only federal–state administered and funded income maintenance assistance program. The historical policy concerns over providing cash assistance to economically dependent children have saddled the development of Title IV, provoking frequent efforts to add new programs to Title IV in attempts to confront contemporary social issues. Thus, the complex development of Title IV reflected in Figure 6.1 is compounded by frequent cycles to "reform" welfare.

---

[a] The development of programs to assist children in recent years has spilled over the line of providing services to children in financial need. While financial need remains the major economic eligibility criterion for the provision of Title IV services, the specific program exceptions to this general rule will be noted in the discussion below of the specific programs.

Through all of these efforts, the original Social Security Act's concern for the welfare of children seems to have been lost.

Present Context for Title IV Child Welfare

When most people think or talk about welfare, they are most likely talking about Title IV of the Social Security Act. Most "welfare reform" proposals, including the 1996 welfare reform realized by President Clinton, really have been about making incremental changes in a small part of Title IV, as outlined below. Most of the negative and pejorative comments about "welfare recipients" really are directed at a narrow element of Title IV adults. When policy makers in Congress discuss "welfare cheaters," they usually have in mind Title IV recipients, and it is sobering to hear legislators and their staffs discuss welfare and propose "welfare reform" with little perspective on the full welfare context of Title IV. Some of this misdirected conversation serves political objectives, but most if not all of this conversation reflects a glaring ignorance of Title IV assistance, particularly as it exists today.

As an assistance program, Title IV is the kind of social welfare that defines a social obligation, rather than guaranteeing benefits based on some contractual obligation to the beneficiaries. Title IV implies a social obligation to the nation's children. This form of welfare entitlement helps to explain the complexity and the many program changes that have taken place in Title IV since 1935. In other words, as the sense of social obligation for the welfare of children has changed over the years, the program components of Title IV have changed as well. See the Introduction to Part III. As Figures 1.1 and 6.1 below illustrate, Title IV has grown from two basic program categories to six, and the actual number of individual programs administered under Title IV's six subtitles has produced a complex network of child welfare and family policy initiatives.

For example, long-standing public concerns about child abuse and neglect came into political focus in 1974, and Congress passed the Child Abuse Prevention and Treatment Act (CAPTA, PL 93-247), a new program under Title IV. The provisions of the 1974 legislation amended Title IV-B of the Social Security Act (and later Title IV-E) and authorized funding to states to encourage them to expand efforts to identify child abuse and neglect cases that would normally be cause for placing children in foster or adoptive homes under Title IV-B. The Child Abuse Prevention and Treatment Act has been reauthorized at frequent intervals, as reported in Box 6.1 below, each time expanding the scope of the program. Each reauthorized CAPTA program modification sets in motion new program elements under Title IV-B eventually generating a large network of programs each with its own funding stream, administrative complexity, and political constituency. (See Box 6.1 below.)

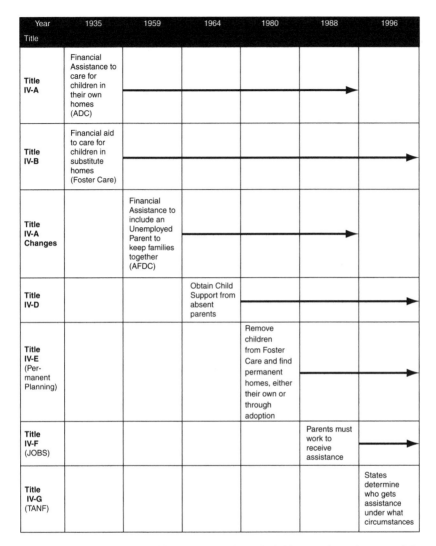

Year / Title	1935	1959	1964	1980	1988	1996
Title IV-A	Financial Assistance to care for children in their own homes (ADC)				→	
Title IV-B	Financial aid to care for children in substitute homes (Foster Care)					→
Title IV-A Changes			Financial Assistance to include an Unemployed Parent to keep families together (AFDC)		→	
Title IV-D			Obtain Child Support from absent parents			→
Title IV-E (Permanent Planning)				Remove children from Foster Care and find permanent homes, either their own or through adoption		→
Title IV-F (JOBS)					Parents must work to receive assistance	→
Title IV-G (TANF)						States determine who gets assistance under what circumstances

Figure 6.1. Modifications Affecting the Welfare of Children under Title IV-A of the Social Security Act.

Box 6.1 Summary of the Legislative History of Child Abuse and Treatment Under Title IV

The Child Abuse Prevention and Treatment Act (CAPTA) is one of the key pieces of legislation that guides child protection. CAPTA, in its original inception, was signed into law in 1974 (P.L. 93-247). It was reauthorized

continued

Box 6.1 continued

in 1978, 1984, 1988, 1992, and 1996, and with each reauthorization, amendments have been made to CAPTA that have expanded and refined the scope of the law.

CAPTA was most recently reauthorized on June 25, 2003, by the Keeping Children and Families Safe Act of 2003 (P.L. 108-36).

The Child Abuse Prevention and Treatment Act (CAPTA, P.L. 93-247) was originally enacted in 1974 and was later amended by the Child Abuse Prevention and Treatment and Adoption Reform Act of 1978 (P.L. 95-266). The law was completely rewritten in the Child Abuse Prevention, Adoption, and Family Services Act of 1988 (P.L. 100-294, 4/25/88). It was further amended by the Child Abuse Prevention Challenge Grants Reauthorization Act of 1989 (P.L. 101-126, 10/25/89) and the Drug Free School Amendments of 1989 (P.L. 101-226, 12/12/89).

The Community-Based Child Abuse and Neglect Prevention Grants program was originally authorized by (Title IV) Sections 402 through 409 of the Continuing Appropriations Act for FY 1985 (P.L. 98-473, 10/12/84). The Child Abuse Prevention Challenge Grants Reauthorization Act of 1989 (P.L. 101-126) transferred this program to the Child Abuse Prevention and Treatment Act, as amended.

A new Title III, Certain Preventive Services Regarding Children of Homeless Families or Families at Risk of Homelessness, was added to the Child Abuse and Neglect Prevention and Treatment Act by the Stewart B. McKinney Homeless Assistance Act Amendments of 1990 (P.L. 101-645, 11/29/90).

The Child Abuse Prevention and Treatment Act was amended and reauthorized by the Child Abuse, Domestic Violence, Adoption, and Family Services Act of 1992 (P.L. 102-295, 5/28/92) and amended by the Juvenile Justice and Delinquency Prevention Act Amendments of 1992 (P.L. 102-586, 11/4/92).

CAPTA was amended by the Older American Act Technical Amendments of 1993 (P.L. 103-171, 12/2/93) and the Human Services Amendments of 1994 (P.L. 103-252, 5/19/94).

CAPTA was further amended by the Child Abuse Prevention and Treatment Act Amendments of 1996 (P.L. 104-235, 10/3/96), which amended Title I, replaced the Title II Community-Based Family Resource Centers program with a new Community-Based Family Resource and Support Program and repealed Title III, Certain Preventive Services Regarding Children of Homeless Families or Families at Risk of Homelessness. In 2003, CAPTA was reauthorized and amended by the Keeping Children and Families Safe Act of 2003.

Source: Adapted from Administration of Children and Families, U.S. Department of Health and Human Services, 2005.

CAPTA's development, summarized in Box 6.1, demonstrates the byzantine program and policy environment that now characterizes Title IV. The incremental development of CAPTA provides a vivid example of Title IV, where policies and programs generally fail to find a concise policy direction. CAPTA's incremental development within the context of Title IV programs loses sight of any long-term policy objectives for children. Title IV's tortuous development also offers a sobering index of the social and demographic changes that have influenced American social welfare development. The changing role of women, from homemakers to active participants in the labor force, the transition of the form of the American family, a growing dissatisfaction with government financed public aid, and an increasing acknowledgement of children's rights are but a few of larger social and economic pressures that have forced changes in Title IV programs. The net result of these pressures on Title IV programs has fostered the series of disconnected social welfare initiatives that may well address the specific changed social condition, but lack solid connection with the Social Security Act's foundational child welfare objectives—the obligation to provide assistance for children in financial need.

The gradual shift away from Title IV income maintenance objectives presents a significant problem for America's child welfare commitments. Rather than an integrated set of initiatives with the objective of ensuring the well-being of children, today's Title IV programs lack a child-focused consistency, often fail to connect with one another, and in some instances, even serve to isolate children from related Title IV programs that could promote their overall welfare. The 1996 welfare reform, for example, places a greater emphasis on forcing parents to work and reduce the number of family welfare cases, than it places on efforts to ensure adequate well-being for children. Whereas the initial Title IV policy focus may have become too narrow for addressing the needs of children today, the development of Title IV programs without a committed vision for children has created a confusing patchwork of expensive and often intrusive government initiatives and policy problems as discussed below.

The Title IV programs also have been subject to change as America's social obligations to children have changed. The treatment of children in their pre-1935 social context stands in sharp contrast to expectations for the well-being of children in today's social context.[1] Although poverty remains at unacceptable levels among American children,[b] they are much better protected from socially abusive and neglectful practices through the development of child protective initiatives in the community, the workplace, and in the home.[2] But current child welfare policy also reflects a shift from public commitment to ensure the public welfare of children, to increased individual family responsibility for the welfare of children. This shift in emphasis, easily visible in the present-day program structure of Title IV, raises important public policy issues not only for the Social Security Act, but also for the direction of social welfare

---

[b] Poverty rates between 20 and 25 percent among children under the age of 5 years have remained constant for the past two decades.

policy initiatives that take place outside the Act. Title IV in its present program context has been the primary vehicle of government efforts that seek to shift its welfare obligation away from government responsibility for the welfare of children and to use the public social welfare obligation to influence the structure and function of the American family, as discussed in the previous chapter. The consequences of this subtle policy shift are discussed in the conclusion of this chapter.

Administrative Context of Title IV Child Welfare

As a set of assistance programs, all the Title IV commitments are funded by grants-in-aid to states, and all the Title IV programs are administered by the respective states under the supervision of the Federal Government. It is perhaps the Title IV programs that have been most abused by the grant-in-aid politics discussed in Chapter 1. As new child welfare concerns surface, advocacy groups have been successful in obtaining sufficient political support to modify one or another of the basic Title IV programs in order to address that particular concern. As child welfare concerns have shifted, program modifications have been added with the support of advocacy groups so that now a large network of social welfare programs subsequently is hung on the original Title IV subtitles. CAPTA is a good example of this kind of development through grant-in-aid financing bolstered by advocacy groups.

Title IV program development also provides an excellent example of how the grant-in-aid functions to develop a certain amount of national program consistency that if left to the complete discretion of the states would not be possible. Although there were some federal child welfare precursors to Title IV of the Social Security Act, it was the states that had child welfare laws in place before 1935. Even though state laws differed in their specific characteristics, all states provided some type of financial assistance to economically dependent children; all states had provisions to care for children who could not be cared for in their own homes; all states had statutes that required parental financial support of children. Essentially, the creation of the Title IV-A program in 1935 simply overlaid a federal grant of money to states to support their existing child welfare efforts, but, in return, the Federal Government required a measured amount of conformity of state programs in order to be eligible for the aid. The grant-in-aid provisions of Title IV brought the Federal Government into child welfare policy in such a way that in order for a state to be eligible to receive any child welfare monies, it had to reconfigure its child welfare statutes so as to conform with the terms of the federal grant-in-aid, thus creating some semblance of order to the wide-ranging pre-Social Security Act state child welfare programs.

The Federal Government continues to use its grant-in-aid power to implement its visions of child welfare to the point that any child welfare visions held by individual states have become lost in a warren of social programs designed to address wide-ranging, often disjointed, elements of child welfare. Often, those state innovations are combined by way of federal program changes and made mandatory on all the states, as shown by the 1996 welfare reform. Child day care, family preservation, enhancing child welfare by building strong families, promoting healthy marriages, promoting responsible fatherhood, assisting abandoned infants, assisting missing children and runaways, mentoring children of incarcerated parents, and a variety of special youth services are some of the child welfare programs that have been forged together under the major Title IV subtitles and through the grant-in-aid have been pushed on the states as state child welfare obligations. Some of these programs are time limited. Some are in the form of demonstration projects. Some are offered through private organizations, but all are offered through a federal–state administrative process, which leaves the major administrative burden with the states. Together, these expanded child welfare initiatives have created a labyrinth of child welfare programs, greatly complicating understanding and implementation of the basic purposes of Title IV.

Thus, whereas Title II Social Security expanded incrementally by changing eligibility criteria, staying within the philosophy of social insurance, Title IV has developed incrementally through frequent program expansions, often championed by narrowly focused child welfare advocacy groups; it has been modified by politically active constituents, creating new programs, changing existing programs, and appending new initiatives to established Title IV program elements even without a solid fit with the larger program contexts. As a result, the social welfare programs provided under the authority of Title IV today have become loosely connected to the original purposes sought for Title IV in the original 1935 Social Security Act. With the 1996 Title IV welfare reform that created Temporary Assistance to Needy Families (TANF), Title IV has become America's most confusing social welfare effort, and today it has become difficult to find the interests of the child in its policies and programs.

Program Structure of Title IV

Figures 1.1 and 6.1 summarize the basic program structure of Title IV social welfare. Both figures show the development of child welfare initiatives over the history of the Social Security Act.

Title IV-A provided financial assistance to needy children in their own homes when it was first created in 1935, and Title IV-A remained the primary source of financial support for children until the 1996 welfare reform (TANF). When first created, Title IV-A was called Aid to Dependent Children (ADC) because the financial welfare of children was the primary reason for creating this part of the Social Security Act. Since most children who were in financial need most likely lived in their own home an adult caretaker (usually a mother) could be included in the cash grant provided to support the children. The conditions for eligibility included "financial need," "continued absence from the home" of the adult "breadwinner," and a "suitable home" in which to rear a child. "Continued absence from the home" was usually due to the death of the "breadwinner" father.

As the structure of the American family began to change after World War II, and "continued absence from the home" was due more and more to separation and divorce, social welfare advocacy groups argued that the "continued absence from the home" eligibility criteria forced unemployed parents (usually a father) to "abandon" their families so that children could be eligible for financial support. In other words, early advocates for expanded child welfare financial assistance argued that the original Title IV-A was "anti-family" and contributed to "family breakup." Thus in 1959, Title IV-A was amended to allow an "unemployed parent" to remain in the household eligibility unit and become part of the financial assistance grant at the option of the states. Assistance payments under Title IV-A were then renamed Aid to Families with Dependent Children (AFDC). By the mid-1960s, all states had adopted these new child welfare assistance changes, which in the short range proposed a more stable environment for children, but in the long range began a shift in policy focus from the child to the family.

For all practical purposes, Title IV-A and most of its program elements were rendered obsolete when Congress passed major social welfare reform in 1996. This welfare reform, called TANF, now supersedes Title IV-A assistance by turning most responsibility for assistance to children and their families over to the discretion of the states, with some major limitations. This latest welfare reform created a new assistance environment as Title IV-G, which is discussed in detail below. However, it is difficult to understand the full significance of the 1996 welfare reform without acknowledging the original program context of financial assistance to children under Title IV-A.

Title IV-A was created as a program of financial assistance for children; such a program is usually called an entitlement, and as discussed in Chapter 1, the conditions of entitlement to assistance are different than entitlement to social insurance. In general, children and their parents were "entitled" to receive Title IV-A assistance only if they met the conditions for financial need, deprivation of parental support and care, and lived in suitable homes. But while the terms of the federal grant to the states for Title IV-A assistance set the broad terms for defining eligibility conditions, the details of determining these conditions were left to the states. States set the "standard of need" in the IV-A program. Likewise, states determined what constituted a "suitable home" in which Title IV-A assistance could be provided. Consequently, there existed a wide range of financial eligibility across the states, and even within states, leading not only to an uneven application of Title IV-A assistance, but provoking considerable tension between states, which sometimes set very high thresholds for verification of financial need, and the Federal Government, which often sought more generous eligibility thresholds in order to provide greater financial coverage to children and their families. Thus, differing opinions over both the conditions of financial eligibility and what constituted a suitable home often caused raucous conflicts between the states and the Federal Government.[3]

The administration and funding of Title IV programs provide an excellent example of "run-away" funding issues confronting the grant-in-aid discussed in Chapter 1. The idea of "entitlement" became associated with the Title IV-A program because children and the adults who cared for them were entitled to receive financial support if they met the eligibility conditions set by the states and overseen by the Federal Government. "Entitlement" to Title IV-A, therefore, was always discretionary, not contractual.[4] But once the applicants for IV-A assistance met the eligibility criteria, however, they were "entitled" to receive all the benefits the IV-A program offered. The Title IV program was often referred to as an "open ended" entitlement because once children were declared eligible for the program, the states had to provide the cash grants and the states and the Federal Government were required to provide the necessary funds to support the assistance payments. The financial commitments of the states and the Federal Government depended on the numbers of children who were declared eligible for the program. In other words, there was no limit set on the amount of funds that could be spent on this program.

The problem with this kind of welfare "entitlement"—that is, increases in both federal and state spending had to be provided—became evident during periods when the numbers of persons seeking Title IV-A assistance rose. Thus, if a state made its eligibility requirements more generous, then the Federal Government was forced to send more money to the state. In like measure, any liberalization in federal regulations required additional state spending. This kind of "entitlement" obligation led to Title IV-A spending that could only be addressed by changing either state or federal eligibility rules. This form of Title IV-A entitlement aggravated concerns over increases in welfare spending, and efforts to control grant-in-aid welfare spending were major factors in the development of both SSI and the 1996 welfare reform discussed below. The 1996 welfare reform did end entitlement to Title IV cash assistance by changing the terms of the federal grant from an open-ended grant-in-aid to a closed block grant. This change in Title IV funding, however, did not apply to the other program elements administered under the authority of Title IV. Even though AFDC has been replaced by TANF, the eligibility issues that defined the older Title IV-A program continue to raise problems for financial assistance for children under the present TANF program since eligibility determination for TANF continues to rest with the states, and even though most previous Title IV-A funding authority has been shifted to the TANF block grant, Title IV-A continues to provide limited funding authority to states for emergency and other child welfare needs. These and other policy problems are discussed below.

Title IV-B was also part of the original Social Security Act somewhat as a companion program to Title IV-A. Title IV-B was designed to provide financial assistance to take care of children in "substitute homes" when their own homes were not suitable to rear children. Originally, Title IV-B supported children in foster homes, orphanages, and later special treatment group homes. Title IV-B also provided funds to states for special services children might need as a result of being in substitute homes. Title IV-B was changed substantially when limited services for children originally funded under Title IV-C were placed under Title IV-B, and again in 1980, when Title IV-E was created.

Today, Title IV-B provides authorization for most of the services that are provided to children under the Social Security Act. Title IV-B contains two parts: **Subpart 1, Child and Family Services** includes continuing funding for **Children in Foster Care, Child Day Care,** and **Child Abuse and Neglect.** Most of the funding and authority for foster care services has been shifted to Title IV-E—see below. Funding for Child Day Care has been consolidated under the 1996 welfare reform, Title IV-G, TANF, although some funding is still available for child day care under Title IV-B—see below. Subpart 1 of Title IV-B also contains funding for **Family Preservation Services.** These are services designed to help risky families *prevent* neglect, abuse, or exploitation of children, which would cause children to be taken from their own home and placed in a "substitute home." Family Preservation also supports programs that make it possible for children to remain in or return from substitute homes to their risky families.

Table 6.1 summarizes the Foster Care program supported by both Title IV parts B and E. In 2005, approximately 513,000 children were in foster care supported by Title IV funds. More children come into the foster care system each year than leave it. Title IV-E was created to minimize the buildup of children in foster care by making sure that each child has a plan for exiting foster care. Both the buildup of children in foster care and the lengths of time children stay in foster care have decreased since Title IV-E was created. The largest percentage of children who leave foster care are reunited with their families.

Table 6.1. Characteristics of Children in Foster Care, 2005

Item	Amount	Percent
Children in Foster Care (rounded number)	513,000	
Children Entering Care	311,000	
Children Exiting Care	287,000	
In a Foster Home		46
In Other Foster Care Setting		54
Average Length of Placement	28.6 months	
Goals for Foster Child		
Return to Own Home		51
Adoption		20
Outcomes for Foster Child		
Return to Own Home		54
Adopted		18
Received a Subsidy		89

Source: U.S. Department of Health and Human Services, Administration for Children and Families, *Types of Maltreatment, 2005.* Washington, DC: 2007, Chapter 3.

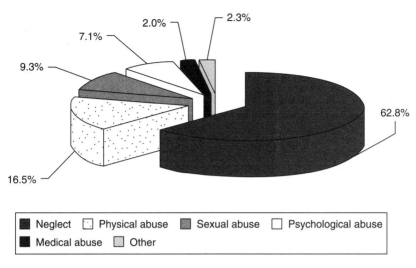

Figure 6.2. Types of Maltreatment/Abuse, 2005.

Title IV-B also provides the authority for CAPTA (see above), which provides grants-in-aid to states to develop programs that identify and take appropriate action on behalf of alleged abused and neglected children. States establish their own programs consistent with federal guidelines, and thus there is some variation in implementing and reporting on CAPTA. In 2005, approximately 3.6 million children were investigated as possible victims of abuse and/or neglect, and approximately 25 percent of these investigations were substantiated.[5] Neglect is the most common form of maltreatment or abuse.[c] See Figure 6.2 for data regarding the types of maltreatment/abuse for the year 2005. Title IV-B, along with Title IV-G (TANF), also provides authority for subsidized child day care. However, subsidized day care funds are provided to the states from several sources, and day care services and resources are discussed at the end of this section on Title IV's program structure.

Title IV-B, Subpart 2, Promoting Safe and Stable Families includes grants to states for **Family Support Services and Family Reunification Services.** Family Reunification Services are designed to facilitate the development of families sufficiently so that children who have been placed in substitute care can be returned to their families. Some of the services that can be funded under this part of Title IV-B include individual, group, and family counseling, inpatient, residential, or outpatient substance abuse treatment services, mental health services, assistance to address domestic violence, and services designed to provide temporary child care and therapeutic services for families, including crisis nurseries. (See Box 6.2 below.)

---

[c] Neglect includes both physical and emotional forms of neglect.

Box 6.2 The National Healthy Marriage Resource Center

The Office of Family Assistance has supported the Healthy Marriage Initiative by launching the National Healthy Marriage Resource Center (NHMRC) in September 2004. The NHMRC serves as a national repository and distribution center of information about healthy marriage programs and policy. The NHMRC serves a wide range of purposes including:

- To provide current information and resources for the public about what it takes to have a healthy marriage.
- To provide resources for practitioners and organizations wanting to implement healthy marriage programs and activities.
- To provide resources for organizational leaders interested in building community healthy marriage initiatives.
- To provide resources for individuals working to strengthen marriages through public policy.
- To provide research findings and reviews for individuals, couples, practitioners, organizational leaders, and researchers.

Source: U.S. Department of Health and Human Resources, Administration of Children and Families (au), *Child Maltreatment, 2005*. Washington, DC: Bureau of Children, Youth, and Family, 2007, Chapter 3.

Finally, Title IV-B, Subpart 2 provides grants to states to promote and support adoption of children when parental custody has been terminated. Table 6.1 above shows that 89 percent of the adoptions in 2005 were accompanied with a financial subsidy to the adopting family. Adoption subsidies were included with Title IV-E as an incentive for low-income families to adopt foster children. Title IV-B Subpart 2 funds, often combined with state and local government as well as private funds, support the parenting and healthy marriage classes that increase relationship skills within the family, the home-visiting services for young parents with first babies and other family-based services, respite care for caregivers of children with special needs, and numerous other unique and innovative programs and services that local communities rely on for risky families.[d] Some of the services under Title IV-B, such as child protective and adoption services, can be provided to children and families depending on a state's financial eligibility levels, even if the children are not considered to be in financial need.

Title IV-E was legislated in 1980 as a companion to Title IV-B. Originally called Permanency Planning, Title IV-E was developed to make sure that every child in the custody of a state had a permanent social plan for its development. In the late 1970s, concern for children focused on the uncertainty

---

[d] "Risky" families are those families that because of family structure or family problems are questionable for their ability to care adequately for their children.

that existed in the lives of children who lived in foster care. Foster care was originally visualized as a temporary solution for the care of children until they could be placed back in a permanent situation, usually via a plan to return to their own family or become a candidate for adoption into an otherwise "stable" family. Since prolonged care in a "substitute home" created an uncertain life for children, Title IV-E was amended to the Social Security Act in 1980 to remedy this problem. Title IV-E forced each state to review its entire child welfare caseload and create a permanent plan for each child supported by Title IV-B funding. Thus, Title IV-B and Title IV-E overlapped, and efforts to insure a permanent plan for Title IV-B children resulted in the gradual shift in the original Title IV-B programs to Title IV-E.

Title IV-E has three main program parts: (1) Financial Support for children in foster care, (2) Financial Assistance to support adoption, and (3) Financial Assistance for older children in foster care in order for children who are still wards of the state to receive educational and job-training services in order to facilitate their transition to adulthood after they reach age 18 and are no longer eligible for financial support. **Financial support to children in foster care** is available to children who meet Title IV-A eligibility requirements established before the 1996 welfare reform TANF, and children subjected to "aggravated circumstances" as defined in state law, and based on a judicial determination that continuation in the home from which the child was removed would be contrary to the welfare of the child. These latter provisions of Title IV-E cross the line of the usual definition of financial need characteristic of the original IV-A and B sections of the Social Security Act. The requirements for continued federal funding to the states under all elements of IV-E are dependent on a permanent plan for the child, and the requirements for meeting the conditions of a permanent plan for foster care or adoption are quite extensive.[6]

Financial support to states to facilitate adoption also crosses the line of usual understanding of financial need, as discussed in Chapter 1. Because many children in temporary foster care were "disadvantaged" because of race or physical or mental handicap, Title IV-E funds can be used to facilitate adoption of these children as well, regardless of their economic status. Amendments to this section of Title IV-E have made it easier for states to develop legislation to facilitate involuntary termination of parental rights in order to facilitate more timely adoptions. Title IV-E Adoption Assistance has become a rather large program and was funded at $1,797,000,000 for the fiscal year 2006.

Financial assistance for older children in foster care provides funding to the states to help children aging out of the foster care system receive appropriate education or job training in order that they can be financially independent. Provision of this form of assistance is contained in the child's permanent plan.

Squeezed between Titles IV-B and Title IV-E is **Title IV-D, Child Support Enforcement**. In 1974, Congress created Title IV-D of the Social Security Act largely as a response to growing evidence that absent parents were not paying child support as required by laws in all the states. Mandatory child support collections constituted only about 15 percent of what was owed by noncustodial parents and less than 75 percent of children living in single-parent households received any child support at all from an absent parent.[7] Thus, Title IV-D was created as an incentive to improve state child support collections in the belief that better financial support from absent parents would improve the well-being of children and reduce the costs of Title IV-A assistance.

In 2004, there were 15,803,921 active child support enforcement cases in the United States with 11,753,602 established support orders. The amount of child support due for 2004 was $28,979,678,335 in addition to $102,356,729,134 in child support owed in arrears, bringing the total amount of available child support to a staggering $130 billion! In contrast, only $20 billion was distributed to families, reflecting a serious discrepancy between the amount of child support owed and the amount available to children. (See Figure 6.3.)

The Title IV-D was also crafted as a grant-in-aid to states in order to provide maximum fiscal incentives to states to improve child support collections. The program had two parts: one for children who were receiving Title IV-A assistance and one for children who did not receive Title IV-A assistance payments. Title IV-D participation was required by everyone receiving Title IV-A assistance and continues to be required of everyone receiving TANF funds. In these cases, states are allowed to keep all of the money collected on behalf of children (with the exception of a $50.00 pass-through to the children), up to the amount equal to the Title IV TANF assistance grant. If collections exceed this amount, TANF grantees have the option of leaving the TANF program, but some stay on TANF support to maintain their Medicaid eligibility and other social welfare benefits.

As a requirement for continued TANF assistance, TANF requires that the custodial parent cooperate in locating the absent parent and establishing

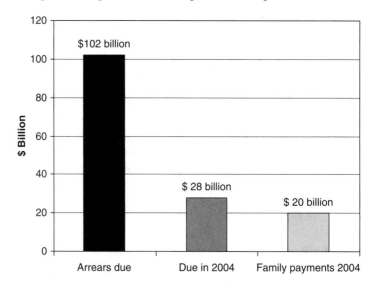

Figure 6.3. Child Support Enforcement, 2004 Values.

paternity, then signing a legal agreement that turns the child's right to child support over to the state. In addition to keeping all the collected funds for child support, the Federal Government reimburses states for 75 percent of their costs of administrating the program.

The second part of Title IV-D provides federal support to states that developed similar programs on behalf of children who were not receiving TANF assistance. In these cases, of course, any child support collected is kept by children and their custodial parents. States are also reimbursed for their costs of administering this program and are also permitted to charge a fee for providing services which would lead to child support from the absent parent.

Title IV-D has been amended over the years in order to improve child support collections for all children, not just those receiving TANF financial support. Two of the most significant changes require states to set uniform standards for determining the amount of court-ordered child support, and give the states and the Federal Government the ability to place a lien for any federal or state income tax return that might be due to a parent under a child support award ordered by the local court. Thus, the social welfare implications of Title IV-D have spread well beyond those efforts to provide assistance to children receiving Title IV-A/TANF benefits.

In 1988, Congress created yet another amendment to Title IV. **Title IV-F, Job Opportunities and Basic Skills (JOBS),** in many ways replicated the largely unsuccessful efforts to put custodial AFDC parents to work in 1967 and 1969 (The Work Incentive Program—WIN). It was the problems in WIN and AFDC work requirements that led to the compromise that omitted Title IV from the SSI program. JOBS sought to overcome the problems that plagued WIN and other Title IV work initiatives by allowing states to fund educational, job training, and job placement programs for custodial parents of children receiving Title IV-A assistance in order to get them into the work force and reduce AFDC assistance.

The JOBS program uncovered many problems inherent in requiring adult welfare recipients to work, including the costs of education and training, the costs of job creation, weak labor force attachment among adult welfare recipients due to physical problems, personal attitudes, and lack of supporting job services such as transportation and child care. By 1993, when discussions began about the next welfare reform (TANF), JOBS had produced little evidence that more welfare recipients were working, or that welfare recipients who were working were much better off financially. The lessons learned from JOBS became a centerpiece in the discussions during the 1996 welfare reform. Proponents of a work requirement argued that the JOBS program was not strict enough; TANF opponents argued that JOBS did not provide enough money to make it work successfully, and at best work participation would be minimal. JOBS was an optional program, but TANF required that Title IV recipients be made to work.[8]

Title IV-G, Temporary Assistance to Needy Families (TANF), is the most recent program created under Title IV of the Social Security Act. As stated above, TANF replaces most of the cash assistance program characteristics that existed under Title IV-A, and replaced all of the provisions included in Title IV-F, JOBS. As a block grant, TANF allows states wide discretion over deciding who is eligible for Title IV (TANF) financial assistance, how much assistance recipients will receive, and under what conditions recipients will be eligible for assistance, with three major exceptions: adults receiving financial assistance as a result of supporting financially eligible children must be working (with some important exceptions—see below), states may not use federal funds to provide financial support a family for more than five years, and states are required to maintain the same levels of state spending on TANF as they were spending on AFDC.

The decision to return wide-ranging discretionary welfare authority to the states, usually called devolution, was implemented with very generous federal funding in the form of a block grant. Originally authorized for five years, TANF was reauthorized in 2001 and 2006. Although Chapter 1 made a distinction between a grant-in-aid and the block grant, both funding mechanisms are essentially the same. Practically speaking, a grant-in-aid usually contains more specific conditions on the use of the funding, while the block grant has fewer restrictions on the use of the monies. Thus, TANF gives wide discretion to the states, but it still sets some conditions on the use of federal money.

Because states determine the specific conditions under which TANF assistance is provided, it is difficult to provide a clear summary of the kinds of individual state programs TANF supports. The variation in state TANF administration and implementation summarized in Box 6.3 provides some indication of the wide variation in state programs. As a result of state variations, much of the uniformity achieved in cash assistance as administered under Title IV-A has disappeared in the implementation of the TANF program. But even the information contained in Box 6.3 captures only a small portion of the TANF program in operation largely because the collection of state level information is uneven. The Nelson A. Rockefeller Institute of Government SUNY, Albany, has studied the implementation of TANF since its inception in 1996, and in its latest report, states that "[S]tate plans often tell little about what a state is actually implementing. In addition, state and local areas have little basic and timely information about low-income families and the new state systems are difficult to evaluate."[9]

Not only is it difficult to obtain adequate information of how the TANF program is implemented, but the outcomes of TANF are difficult to know as well. For example, the number of families receiving TANF today is about 46 percent of the number of families receiving AFDC before TANF was created. But it is difficult to know whether this reduction in welfare cases is due to former TANF recipients becoming employed, or whether they have left the TANF roles either due to some personal reasons or because they used up their limited eligibility time. And while the number of families receiving TANF has declined, the number of children being supported without support being extended to the adult ("child only cases") has almost doubled since 1996. In general, the outcome measures of TANF are much too equivocal to allow a comprehensive evaluation of the TANF program. A summary of some of TANF's program outcomes are presented in Table 6.2 below.

Box 6.3 Summary of State Variation in TANF Administration and Implementation

Form of Administration: State administered, locally administered, or some combination of both.

Benefit Levels: Average benefit $353.00 per month per family (2003) well below poverty guidelines.

Since 1995, 20 states increased benefits; three decreased family benefits.

Work Requirements: With children over age 6, these range from a requirement that recipients go to work immediately to within 24 months.

With a child under age 6, from no exemption to age of child 2 years old.

Work Requirement Wavers: Sixteen states have waivers from federal mandated work requirements.

Treatment of Earnings: Eighteen states disregard earnings, ranging from 100 percent exemption until earnings reach poverty level to exempting a flat 20 percent of earnings for determining financial eligibility.

Diversion Assistance: Twenty-eight states give a temporary grant before starting the TANF time limit.

Time Limits: Federal time limit is 60 months per family, cumulative total, but states can extend benefits past 60 months for 20 percent of the caseload.

Nine states have time limits less than 60 months.

Ten states have no time limits.

Family Cap: Twenty-three states allow an increase in financial assistance with the birth of another child.

The other states "cap" the payment level at family size at the time of initial payment.

Source: Abstracted from Department of Health and Human Services, Office of Family Assistance, *Temporary Assistance to Needy Families, Seventh Annual Report to Congress, 2006.* (based on 2003 data from state plans).

Table 6.2 shows the dramatic reduction in the number of welfare recipients between 1992, when welfare assistance to children and their families was still administered under Title IV-A, and 2003, the latest data available in the 2006 report on TANF presented to Congress. The total number of Welfare recipients has declined by almost 50 percent, but child-only cases have increased by 61 percent, suggesting that the TANF caseload decreases are mostly among the adults. The age of adult and child recipients seems to be constant during the reporting period.

Table 6.2. Trend in AFDC/TANF Recipient Characteristics, FY 1992–FY 2003

	FY 1992	FY 1994	FY 1996	FY 1998	FY 2000	FY 2001	FY 2002	FY 2003
Total	4,769,000	5,046,000	4,553,000	3,176,000	2,269,000	2,120,000	2,060,300	2,027,600
Child-Only Cases	707,000	869,000	978,000	743,000	742,000[1]	749,000[1]	753,300[1]	782,700[1]
Percent	14.8	17.2	21.5	23.4	32.7	35.3	36.6	38.6
Race (Percent of All Families)								
White	38.9	37.4	35.9	32.7	31.2	30.1	31.6	31.8
African American	37.2	36.4	36.9	39.0	38.6	39.0	38.3	38.0
Hispanic	17.8	19.9	20.8	22.2	25.0[2]	26.0[2]	24.9[2]	24.8[2]
Asian	2.8	2.9	3.0	3.4	2.2	2.1	2.2	2.0
Native American	1.4	1.3	1.4	1.5	1.6	1.3	1.4	1.5
Other	—	—	—	0.6	0.6	0.8	0.9	0.9
Unknown	2.0	2.1	2.0	0.7	0.8	0.7	0.7	1.0
Age Distribution (Percent of All Adults)								
Under 20	7.1	5.9	5.8	6.1	7.1	7.4	7.5	7.7
20–29	45.9	44.1	42.3	41.4	42.5	42.4	44.9	46.8
30–39	33.3	34.8	35.2	33.8	32.1	31.2	29.9	28.7
Over 39	13.6	15.2	16.5	18.6	18.3	19.0	17.7	16.8
Average Age	29.9	30.5	30.8	31.4	31.3	31.3	31.0	30.6
Employment Rate (Percent of All Adults)								
Employment Rate	6.6	8.3	11.3	22.8	26.4	26.7	25.3	22.9

Age of Youngest Child
(Percent of All Families)

Unborn	2.0	1.8	1.5	N/A	0.6	0.5	0.5
0–1	10.3	10.8	10.4	11.0	13.3	13.6	14.5
1–2	29.7	28.1	24.3	22.0	19.9	20.2	20.9
3–5	21.2	21.6	23.5	23.1	20.6	19.4	18.9
6–11	23.1	22.7	24.4	26.6	27.8	27.6	25.5
12–15	9.3	9.8	10.6	10.7	11.7	12.8	13.3
Age 16 and Older	3.5	3.5	3.8	4.7	5.1	5.0	5.4
Unknown	0.8	1.7	1.5	1.8	1.0	0.9	1.0

Race (Percent of All Children)

White	33.9	33.0	31.6	28.3	26.8	25.6	27.0
African American	38.5	37.9	38.4	40.2	40.1	40.8	39.1
Hispanic	18.7	21.2	22.4	23.4	26.8[2]	27.8[2]	27.5[2]
Asian	3.9	3.6	3.8	4.2	2.8	2.7	2.5
Native American	1.6	1.4	1.4	1.5	1.6	1.2	1.4
Other	—	—	—	0.7	0.6	0.5	0.6
Unknown	3.4	2.9	2.4	1.8	1.3	1.4	1.9

Source: TANF Data Report, ACF 3637.
[1] Excludes cases with a sanctioned parent.
[2] Can be of any race.
N/A Not Available.
Columns may not add to 100 percent due to rounding.

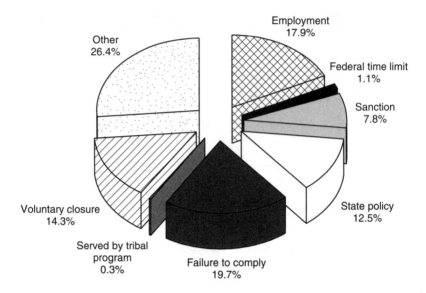

Figure 6.4. TANF Families by Reason for Closure, FY 2003.
Source: Office of Maternal and Child Health, Department of Health and Human Services, 2007.

Explanations for caseload reduction are not clear. Advocates for mandatory work argue that work for wages has substituted for welfare.[10] There is some evidence that welfare recipients have run out of their five-year eligibility window, or that they may be working at jobs that pay enough to make them ineligible for TANF, but not sufficient to bring them up to the poverty line or above.[11] The reasons behind the decreases in the Title IV welfare population remain unclear. (See Figure 6.4.)

Child Day Care: As noted above, Title IV-B was the original engine for child day care, but over the years, the demand for day care has expanded as women have entered the labor market in greater numbers. As a result, federal day care resources are pooled into a Child Care and Development Fund. Both Title IV-B monies and Funds from Title IV-G (TANF) are part of this fund, in addition to child day care money available under Title XX of the Social Security Act (see Chapter 9), the Head Start Program, and funds from the Department of Education. States have authority to set income eligibility for day care up to 85 percent of the state median income, but most states set program eligibility below 85 percent of the federal maximum in order to concentrate the funding on families with very low incomes. In FY 2003, approximately half of the day care funds went to families who were below 100 percent of the federal poverty level, another 29 percent had incomes between 100 percent and 150 percent of the federal poverty level, and 17 percent had incomes above 150 percent of the federal poverty level. In fiscal year 2003, 78 percent of families needed child day care due to employment, and another 12 percent needed day care due to some form of education and training. Six percent of the child day care was needed for protective services.[12] The program focus for child day care has shifted from

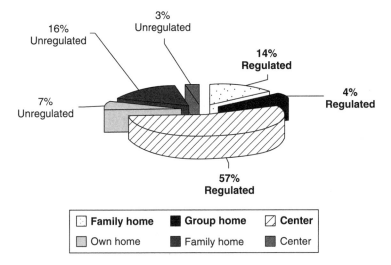

Figure 6.5. Percentage of Children in Day Care, by Setting.

a temporary option for children in trouble to providing a means to support working mothers.

Figure 6.5 provides a snapshot of the type of child day care that was used. Although most of the child day care was provided in a regulated day care facility, 26 percent was provided in an unregulated facility. It is quite possible that the percentage of unregulated day care is even higher due to "gray market" day care operations, mostly in individuals' homes, and usually unnoticed by state child day care organizations that track child day care. Nevertheless, 57 percent of all child day care is provided in regulated child care centers, and although regulations governing the operation of these centers vary widely from state to state, some measure of quality can be assumed to exist within these centers.

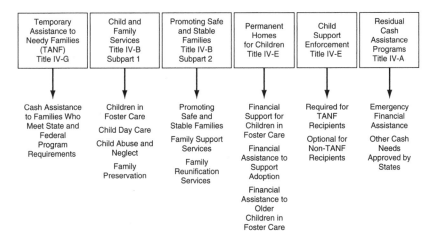

Figure 6.6. Summary of the Program Structure of Title IV, 2008.

Summary of Title IV Programs

The structure of the major social welfare programs provided under Title IV of the Social Security Act as presently implemented has been summarized in Figure 6.6.

The summary of the program structure of Title IV in the figure attests to the wide-ranging programs that have developed on behalf of America's children, who for the most part are living in some degree of economic need. Title IV's program structure reveals its movement away from economic assistance for needy children toward family-centered policies that may or may not reflect a social obligation to provide for the welfare needs of America's children. At the very best, the social welfare programs under Title IV have developed in an incremental manner without much regard for a focused child welfare policy. Title IV programs have expanded well beyond the usual view of assistance programs and well beyond the original commitment to children under the 1935 Social Security Act.

In spite of all these changes, with the exception of most of TANF, Title IV programs are funded by a grant-in-aid structure, with most of the funding coming from the Federal Government. Matching formulas range from 75 percent federal funds to 90 percent of federal funds, depending on the specific program under consideration. A major irony of Title IV program funding today is found in the fact that most of the funding comes from the Federal Government, but most of the program administrative elements are left to the states. One way to view this mismatch would be to suggest that the Federal Government gets the states to do things that the Federal Government is unable to do. Another way to view the mismatch would be to suggest that the Federal Government is paying for services that states have an obligation to provide. Politically, however, the Title IV form of intergovernmental social welfare funding and administration has proved beneficial to both the states and the Federal Government.

Policy Structure of Title IV of the Social Security Act

The complex program structure of Title IV befuddles the mind. Title IV's byzantine program structure not only reveals the results of welfare advocacy and the wide-ranging policy objectives that advocacy groups have sought in efforts to develop child welfare programs. Together, the programs and the policies they seek to serve raise serious questions: What is America trying to accomplish on behalf of the welfare of its children? What role should government play to advance a public policy agenda for children?

Child Welfare Policy foundation: One of the most dynamic times in the development of American social welfare policy came during the last part of the 1800s and the early 1900s. An unusual amount of social ferment was focused on efforts to improve the welfare of children. The "child saving" movement begun by Reverend Charles Brace led to the formation of the New York Children's Aid Society in 1853; the Society for the Prevention of Cruelty to Children was formed in 1870; institutional care for children in need sprang up across the country, and the "social reformers" led by Grace and Edith Abbott, Jane Addams, and others prevailed on the Federal Government to develop public policies and programs to promote the welfare of children, reaching a high point when President Theodore Roosevelt called the first White House Conference on Children in 1910, out of which was created the Children's Bureau in 1912. To these efforts were added, among others, federal child labor laws, systems to protect children in courts of law (juvenile courts), and the Maternal and Child Health program, legislated in 1921[13] and revived as Title V of the original Social Security Act.[14]

Although advocacy for child welfare policy and programs has continued, and remains strong to this day, by the time the Social Security Act became law many of these enthusiastic efforts to establish a framework for child welfare policy slowed in the face of declining public support. The work of the Children's Bureau was limited to collecting information and issuing reports, in spite of the leadership of some of the most effective social welfare advocates of that day, such as Julia Lathrop, Grace Abbott, and Katharine Lenroot. The 1921 Maternal and Child Health Act was narrowly reauthorized in 1926, and finally allowed to expire in 1929. The Great Depression, itself, deflected attention away from the welfare of children to the economic welfare of the nation. By all appearances, previous attention to children had little impact on Roosevelt's Economic Security Act, nor did his Chair of the Committee on Economic Security, Frances Perkins, herself a former advocate for the protection of children in the work place while Roosevelt was Governor of New York, advocate for children beyond the modest Title IV assistance provisions. Thus, somewhat by default, Title IV of the social Security Act became the focal point of American child welfare policy.[e]

The policy structure of today's Title IV programs has emerged from some of the most complex and ideologically driven issues of any of America's social welfare initiatives. When viewed in the context of the policy variety under the Social Security Act (see Figure 1.2, Chapter 1) Title IV policy variety portends its wide ranging program structure. First, all Title IV programs operate as grants to states and are administered by appropriate state agencies. Thus, they are likely to display unique program elements depending on the state in which they are provided. Second, most of the Title IV programs are provided based on financial need, and none of the Title IV programs contain elements that consist of entitlements based on law. All reflect a social obligation. Third, the kinds of social welfare products offered are both in the form of financial support and "in-kind" social services, and many of the social services are not

---

[e] This is not to deny the existence of a number of programs to assist children which exist outside the Social Security Act, such as Headstart, Child Nutrition programs, including School Lunch, Childhood immunizations, to mention a few of the most significant.

provided directly to the children, but are offered indirectly to their parents, their caretakers, or others who may become their caretakers. Thus, driven by child welfare advocates who often had very different political agendas, Title IV stands as one of America's most jumbled policy approaches on behalf of efforts to protect and improve the welfare of children.

Child welfare as America's social obligation: In the American idiom, child welfare policy, as distinct from other social welfare initiatives that include children, such as Title II Social Security, or as a unique field for policy development, emerged from a clear social obligation to protect and take care of children in financial need. The development of child welfare policy therefore arises from one of America's most deep-seated commitments, but empty of any contractual commitments America has to her children. A child's legal environment is poorly defined in either statute or case law, largely because of uncertainty over a child's autonomy. Thus, the idea of "children's rights" is a compelling notion for child welfare policy development, but children have no legal *standing*, legal protection, or claim to rights, such as afforded by the U.S. Constitution to adults. In other words, children have no *protectable interests* of their own.

In light of this conundrum, the whole of child welfare policy in America balances between two legal prerogatives: *parens patriae* and the doctrine of *parental liberty*, the right to bring up one's own child. *Parens patriae* is a common law doctrine originating in the seventeenth century when the King was "father of the country" and as such had the responsibility to protect those who could not protect themselves. The doctrine of *parental liberty* derives from a crucial American civil liberty and a corresponding civic responsibility that parents direct the child's education, health care, lifestyle, religious observance, discipline and social, economic, and personal development. *Parental liberty* was articulated by the U.S. Supreme Court in 1923 when it affirmed, under the Fourteenth Amendment, "the right of the individual ... to establish a home and bring up children ... according to the dictates of his own conscience."[15] Thus, children are dependent on their parents for their care and upbringing. But if their parents fail, the government assumes parental responsibility for children. The fundamental child welfare policy question in America, therefore, is who is responsible for the child: the parents or the state?

The delicate balance between *parens patriae* and *parental liberty* was well illustrated by the 1944 U.S. Supreme Court when it ruled that a minor child could be prohibited from selling religious magazines in public. Writing for the Court, Justice Rutledge stated

> It is cardinal with us that the custody, care and nurture of the child reside first in the parents, whose primary function and freedom include preparation for obligations the state can neither supply nor hinder. .... And it is in recognition of this that these decisions have respected the private realm of family life which the state cannot enter.

But the Court prohibited the child from selling the magazines not on religious grounds, nor as a violation of child labor laws, but on the grounds that the state had an obligation to protect the child from harm, even in an otherwise adequate family environment. "Parents are free to become martyrs themselves. But it does not follow that they are free, in identical circumstances, to make martyrs of their children before they have reached the age of full and legal discretion when they can make that choice for themselves."[16]

In the view of Gilbert Steiner, an astute critic of social welfare policy, the expansion of child welfare policy faced limitations as it moved toward the development of policies for all children. Steiner recognized the legitimate power of the state "to protect children against abuse and against the most dramatic and evident diseases" but questioned whether if "government should reach out to insure the maximum development of every child according to his own potential [it would] undermine some long cherished values relating to family life."[17]

The development of Title IV child welfare policy, therefore, rests on the legitimate obligation of government to ensure protection for children and all that protection for children entails in its social and economic ramifications, without violating the civic rights and responsibilities of the children's parents. With this policy focus in mind, it is possible to deconstruct the social welfare policy problems that have emerged as Title IV social welfare has developed over the years. Three considerations direct this discussion: (1) a policy shift from government's obligation to ensure the protection of children to placing greater expectations on the family to meet society's obligation to care for welfare of children, (2) the use of child welfare policy to achieve more far-reaching political goals than assistance to children, and (3) a proper role for government exercising its obligations under *parens patriae*. To the extent that Title IV is the foundation for America's social obligation to children, these questions are discussed in the context of Title IV programs as they exist today, even though the issues may have much broader social welfare policy implications.

(1) **A policy shift from a child-focused social welfare commitment to a family focus** under Title IV began as a benign effort with the 1959 amendments to Title IV-A to ensure a stable family environment for children by making sure that the child's financial well-being would not be compromised by the terms of the ADC program itself. Although the pre-Depression relief practices, too, attempted to increase family capacity to care for children, the 1959 policy acknowledgment of family significance took place in a larger social environment that extolled the traditionally idealized post–World War II family structure, on the one hand—two parents, a nonworking mother at home caring for two children, living in a single family home—but on the other hand, the reality of the changing traditional structure of the post–World War II family.[18] Studies that showed a changing family structure—increased separations and divorces, and more women working outside the home—led many social commentators to proclaim that the American family was "broken," thus holding

the family responsible for conditions that undermined the welfare of children, and warned that Title IV assistance was contributing to "family breakdown."

It was in this family-sensitive environment that Daniel Patrick Moynihan produced *The Negro Family: The Case for National Action* in 1965, which provided a vivid benchmark in the transition of child welfare policy. The substance of Moynihan's report and President Johnson's address at Howard University seemed simple and straightforward at the time, but the African American community was quick to see the dangers in developing a family policy. Among other individuals and groups, the Congress of Racial Equality (CORE) said the report assumed that white middle-class American values are the correct ones for everyone in America: "Just because Moynihan believes in middle class values doesn't mean that they are best for everyone in America." And Bayard Rustin commented acidly, "[W]hat may seem to be a disease to the white middle class may be a healthy adaptation to the Negro lower class. . . . It is amazing to me that Negro families exist at all."

While the 1959 policy changes to the Title IV-A program included language that Title IV-A changes were designed to "maintain and strengthen family life," the Moynihan Report went a step further. It proposed a deliberate government intrusion that would propose to create those stronger families. But the concerns raised by the African American community created two troubling questions: what was a "stable" and "successful" family, and should the resources of government be used to develop such "stable" and "successful" families? The second question, a potential assault on the doctrine of *parental liberty,* was set aside while political pundits attempted to answer the first question. As existing child welfare policies and programs were scrutinized for their impact on traditional family structures, the complexity of American families became clear.

An Object Lesson for Family Policy: The times of ferment for family policy did not end with the creation of SSI instead of Moynihan's FAP. To carry out a campaign promise, President Carter appointed his new Secretary of Health, Education, and Welfare (DHEW), Joseph Califano, to develop and implement a White House Conference on the Family. As planning for the Conference began to get off the ground, however, various groups sought access to the Conference planning process to ensure that their particular views of "family" would be recognized: a coalition of black organizations, a coalition of Catholic organizations, and finally a coalition of national organizations that had programs that helped families, including the YMCA and the Family Service Association of America, all offered to help plan the Conference, but to no avail. The Conference planners feared that any of these groups would lead the Conference away from their idea of a "neutral" family model. Thus, from the beginning, all parties involved saw the family in a form similar to their idealized view, rather than as family behavior, or how families cared for their children.

The final irony in this effort was that Carter chose the anticipated White House Conference on Children, which had met every ten years since its first meeting in 1909, as the forum for the Conference on the Family that he designated would be held in 1979. The feuding over the conference planning continued to the point that no national conference was held. After much debate within the Carter administration as well as in the country at large about what constituted a legitimate family, three regional conferences were convened in 1982.[19] Cultural moderates, feminists, gay rights activists, devout Catholics, and evangelical Protestants disagreed vehemently about policies ranging from legalized abortion to family leave. As a result of the inability to come to agreement about the nature of the American family, no White House Conference on Children, or of the family for that matter, has been held since this aborted 1979 effort.

The lessons of the Moynihan Report and the failed Conference on the Family demonstrate the impact on policy of the dynamic qualities of the American family. Today, the character of the American family is more diverse than it was thirty years ago. Not only is the structure of the American family more complex with respect to adults and their relationships to their children, but the range of how families rear their children defies any uniform categorization. One family may set "curfews" for their children; another may not. One family may have set meal times; another may not. One family may physically punish a child; another may not. And all families have become dependent on the school, church, and community to provide various activities that support and supplement the activities of families to the point that when such activities do not exist it appears that the family has failed. Thus, how to develop policy and programs to create "strong" and "supportive" families, the second question raised by the Moynihan Report, presents a grotesque visage: when is the family, however it is structured or functions today, appropriately raising its children, and when are children at risk so that government needs to step in and protect the interests of the child? In other words, who is caring for the children?

The TANF Retreat From Children: The development and implementation of the 1996 welfare reform (TANF) illustrate a monumental shift in child welfare policy. Perhaps the most disturbing element of child welfare policy development is a loss of vision. There have been over 400 books, articles, research reports, and technical studies analyzing how and why TANF developed, but few discuss the implication of TANF on the development of child welfare policy. In their enthusiasm for questionable political analysis of one small part of child welfare policy provided under Title IV TANF commentary has focused on the reduction in "welfare roles" and the ascendency of badly informed politically conservative thought that fails to illuminate the force of this latest welfare reform on America's obligation to her children. One such study has been produced by Ron Haskins. Presently a fellow at the Brookings Institution, Haskins previously held the position of chief staff member of the U.S. Congress, House Ways and Means Committee, subcommittee on Human Resources. Perhaps more than any other person, Haskins was responsible for the architecture of TANF. Haskins' detailed account of TANF's development makes clear several important features of this latest welfare reform.

First, the 1996 welfare reform was developed as a step in a politically partisan effort to remove the Federal Government from all of its social welfare commitments. Little thought was given to more comprehensive child welfare issues. Ron Haskins and some Congressional Republicans envisioned a welfare block grant as a major welfare shift that would go beyond devolution of Title IV cash assistance and include food stamps, school lunches, child care, and other federal welfare initiatives, thus becoming "a step on the road to a true federalist revolution."

> This movement of power and responsibility to the state level would then open the possibility that was (and still is) the most attractive of all to conservatives. . . . [I]f the federal responsibility for social programs were moved to the state level, why not also move the responsibility for raising the funds to pay for the programs to the state level? If this goal could be accomplished, federal income and corporate tax rates could be slashed and states would be responsible for raising the revenue to conduct social programs. Taken together these reforms would constitute a complete overthrow of the New Deal and the War on Poverty and return to a much smaller and less powerful meddlesome federal government.[20]

Second, although TANF came nowhere near achieving the above objectives, it did signal a change in the way legislation affecting the welfare of children is developed. Partisan politics, rather than a consideration for the welfare of children, provided the energy for the 1996 welfare reform. In Haskins' view, successful policy outcomes depend upon managing information to achieve political ends rather than airing all points of view.

> [P]oliticians use the products of social science to advance a political agenda. And whereas social scientists start with a question and follow strict rules to arrive at an answer, politicians usually start with the answer and use the results of social science—selectively if necessary—to support their predetermined answer. . . . But using facts correctly that do not provide the entire story is not regarded as particularly heinous in politics.[21]

The historically important child welfare policy issues were clearly abused in the development of TANF.

Finally, Haskins' account of the development of TANF provides vivid evidence of the changed character of the social obligation inherent in child welfare policy. An earlier obligation of the states and Federal Government to provide financial support for economically dependent children shifted to the requirement that parents work to support their children. Haskins calls work "the cannonball of the Republican welfare reform agenda." Time limits on receiving welfare, curbing "illegitimacy," and child care also became part of the Republican welfare reform agenda, but "work remained the central issue of debate," Haskins asserts. Republicans extolled the virtues of "work as the antidote to welfare dependency."[22] However, as the well-regarded political scientist and respected theorist of American Federalism Samuel H. Beer notes, "To refer to workfare as 'new,' however, can be misleading. The idea of governmental activity looking to work rather than the dole for relief of poverty has a long history. The ups and downs of which help explain the recent emergence of workfare in the pattern of policy."[23]

Inasmuch as children are no longer expected to work, the burden of "workfare" now falls on the parents. Thus, the shift in Title IV assistance is not as notable for its emphasis on work but is more important for its clear development of programs that place greater responsibility on the family to ensure the welfare of children, removing much of an earlier social welfare obligation for children from government.

The shift in the focus of child welfare policy to place greater expectations on the family enhances *parental liberty*, on the one hand, but at the same time magnifies the uncertainties of government responsibility on behalf of children who need protection for their well-being. Recent Title IV program developments such as family preservation, permanent family homes for children through adoption, preventing abuse and neglect, and family reunification all depend on a normative definition of family that finds sufficient social acceptance, but it is a normative view of the family that does not exist in contemporary American society. While it is essential that families meet their social responsibilities to their children, the boundaries of both *parental responsibility* and *parens patriae* have become more unclear as the character of American families have become more unclear, and the effort to balance the two has become an effort that requires means well beyond the present authority of Title IV of the Social Security Act.

An example of an intrusion into the family as a form of child welfare policy development that seriously weakens *parental liberty* occurred recently when the Department of Health and Human Resources (DHHS) required states to set standards for involuntary termination of parental rights when a child has been in foster care for 15 of the most recent 22 months as a condition for the state to receive funding under the Adoption and Safe Family Act discussed above.[24] Such a time table seems arbitrary and raises a question as to whether the Federal Government has statutory authority to enforce this requirement. It is the states that have the statutory authority to terminate parental rights, but states are forced to bring their child welfare statutes into harmony with this DHHS requirement as a condition for receiving grant-in-aid funding under this federal statute.[f] Whether the Federal Government is forcing the states to show greater respect for *parental liberty* or enhancing child welfare obligations under the *parens patriae* doctrine is unclear. A policy such as setting mandatory time limits for termination of parental rights may or may not be in the best interests

---

[f] The Department of Heath and Human Resources gives states flexibility in meeting this standard by providing a number of exceptions states may exercise in meeting the requirement.

of the child. But whether such a policy should be developed as an extension of Title IV administration is a serious policy question regarding the direction of child welfare policy.

It is difficult to conclude that family-focused initiatives act in the best interest of a child living in an economically impoverished environment. Moreover, to the extent that the present Title IV programs move to a focus on creating "stable" families for children rather than focusing on their economic needs, Title IV disconnects its child welfare initiatives from other welfare initiatives for children under the Social Security Act. Title IV social welfare programs in their totality have become incompatible with other efforts to secure the welfare of children that exist in other parts of the Social Security Act. For example, should Title II Social Security funds be provided to children living in neglectful families?

(2) **The use of child welfare policy to achieve more far-reaching social goals.** Efforts to "strengthen" and otherwise enhance the ability of families to rear children have not only weakened the nation's commitment to the welfare of children, but have also has provoked questionable governmental activities. The post-TANF Title IV policy shift to a focus on the family rather than on the welfare of the child has expanded the *parens partiae* powers of the state to set the conditions for what constitutes an adequate family. Title IV child welfare policy now uses its authority to achieve social goals for families that may or may not be in the best interests of children.

The Indian Child Welfare Act, P.L. 95-608, constitutes a clear example of the dangers inherent in attempts to set conditions for what determines an adequate family. This act was created as a response to removing of Indian children from their homes and placing them in non-Indian homes largely because the administrators of Title IV-B argued that many Indian homes were not suitable to raise children.[8] B.J. Jones reports that large numbers of Indian children[h] were removed from their homes and placed in non-Indian homes by state courts, welfare agencies, and private adoption agencies by non-Indian judges and social workers who failed to appreciate traditional Indian child-rearing practices. Observed day-to-day life in the children's Indian homes was deemed contrary to the children's best interests. Additionally, other children were removed from their Indian homes because of the overwhelming poverty their families were facing. Although, admittedly, poverty creates obstacles to child rearing, it was used by some state entities as evidence of neglect and, therefore, grounds for taking children from their homes.[25] The Indian Child Welfare Act essentially removes from the state courts the legal proceedings regarding foster placement, termination of parental rights and adoption decisions, and places these decisions in the hands of tribal courts. In addition, Indian parents have a series of legal protections under the law that prevent state

---

[8] Of course, similar activities have a long history in the experience of America's treatment of its Native Americans.

[h] The designation of "Indian" is preferred over "Native American" in most Indian tribes.

and tribal courts from removing Indian children from their families only if the cause for removal is inconsistent with Indian tribal traditions.[26]

As discussed above, the most nefarious legacy of the 1996 welfare reform can be found in the use of public policy to control individual behavior. Lawrence Meade, a strong supporter of controlling behavior through welfare, provided considerable intellectual energy for the 1996 welfare reform. Meade put the matter quite simply: "In policy terms, the leading issue is entitlement.... Should people be given aid on the basis of impersonal economic conditions such as income?" Meade asks. "Or should aid be conditioned in some way on good behavior?"[27] Meade's affirmative answer reflects this little discussed feature of Title IV assistance. Throughout its existence, Title IV welfare has been granted through discretionary decisions, usually applied informally at the state and local levels of welfare administration, thus allowing a form of behavior control in welfare administration.[28] Today, such generally frowned-upon practices have become part of formal policy, pushing the long-standing debates over child welfare policy to an overt level. A public policy that makes it possible to deprive children of basic necessities if their parents choose to have a child out of wedlock, or if welfare support is denied to a family and its children if a parent refuses to work, strikes at the heart of some of the most cherished American values, values that are not the exclusive domain of those who do not need welfare.

The present direction of Title IV assistance runs the risk of upsetting the delicate balance between "playing by the rules" on the one hand and abusing personal rights on the other. There has been little serious post-welfare reform debate over such issues,[29] and this kind of consideration was absent from the 1996 welfare reform debates. The overriding objective of the 1996 welfare reform was not a consideration of reforms that would improve the welfare of children, but rather a reduction in the AFDC caseloads through tough work requirements.[30] A review of the primary objectives of the advocates for the 1996 welfare reform debate was never permitted as part of the policy development process, according to Haskins' account.

(3) Finally, the shift in policy focus from the child to the family raises serious questions regarding **the proper role for government in exercising its obligations under *parens patrae*.** The problems identified above not only raise questions about who should decide when the state must intervene to protect the child, but also what kind of intervention is least intrusive for the child. The shift in Title IV policy from its original social obligation to ensure a level of financial support for children, either in their own homes or in their substitute homes, to policies that seek to establish suitable, permanent homes for children, either in their own homes or substitute homes, introduces government into the dynamics of family life and moves Title IV child welfare policy well beyond a concern for children with financial problems. While the Social Security Act establishes a solid policy framework for government to act on behalf of children when their financial well-being is threatened, extending this policy framework to support government intervention into the child-rearing affairs of

the family, or to attempt to make more families more competent, stretches Title IV authority beyond its modest purposes. The need to remove children from their own homes to protect their interests is not taken lightly, and termination of parental rights, voluntary or involuntary, temporary or permanent, represents a serious challenge to parental rights. However, the creation of a network of programs designed to promote a view of stable families as the base for Title IV welfare policy, from the Title IV-B programs through Title IV-G, raises serious question regarding sufficient statutory and ideological support for these policies.

Clearly, these are matters for states to determine under the present intergovernmental administrative structure of Title IV assistance. State courts have jurisdiction over such decisions, but they are burdened by inadequate resources to make such decisions under present Title IV funding. Courts are heavily dependent on social workers for the kind of information they need to make judicious decisions. But social workers may not have all the skills necessary to judge exactly what is best for a child, and they are usually burdened by large caseloads that limit the amount of time they can spend on assessing any one situation. Social workers in public agencies may not be in the best position to recommend actions that reflect the best interests of the child, but if not social workers, then who?

Conclusion

The child welfare policies promoted under Title IV of the Social Security Act have expanded considerably from initial protection of and financial concerns for children to policies aimed at creating strong and stable families for children. While such a development in policies and programs for children may seem logical and even consistent with efforts to enhance the social obligations of the family toward their children, this development takes Title IV child welfare policy away from its 1935 focus. The policy structure of Title IV has steadily moved away from a concern for the welfare of children to the establishment of family policy for low-income children, with a wide-ranging program structure driven by a labyrinth of policy options that have become difficult to realize. For example, there is no conclusive evidence to validate claims that restructured families are better able to advance the well-being of their children, nor is there any conclusive evidence to support claims that forced work will provide children with economically sufficient resources. The outstanding child support obligations alone attest to the basic failure of efforts to change parental behavior in ways that best meet the needs of children in financially dependent circumstances.

Table 6.3 presents a contemporary snapshot of American children. Over 25 percent of all persons in the United States today are children, age 18 and younger. Most children live in families, and over 70 percent live in two-parent (traditional) families. Almost 17 percent of children living in any type of family

Table 6.3. Children (Persons under Age 18 years) in Poverty, by Family Type

Total Population, United States, 2005[1]		296,410,404	Percent		
Children, Age 18, and Younger		81,739,249	27.57		
Children in Families		72,737,000	88.98		
Children in Other Settings		9,002,249	11.02		

Family Type	Percent All Children	Number This Type	Percent This Type	Number in Poverty	Percent in Poverty
All Family Types All Incomes	100	**72,737,000**	**100.00**		
Under Age 18 in Poverty				12,333,000	16.90
Under Age 5 in Poverty				1,149,000	
Married Couple Families All Incomes		51,379,000	70.64		
Under Age 18 in Poverty				4,185,000	8.10
Under Age 5 in Poverty				1,407,000	
Male Head, No Wife All Incomes		3,883,000	5.34		
Under Age 18 in Poverty				795,000	20.50
Under Age 5 in Poverty				287,000	
Female Head, No Husband All Incomes		17,475,000	24.02		
Under Age 18 in Poverty				7,353,000	42.10
Under Age 5 in Poverty				2,424,000	
All White Family Types All Incomes	79.10	**57,564,000**	**100.00**		
Under Age 18 in Poverty				7,934,000	13.80
Under Age 5 in Poverty				2,146,000	
White Married Families All Incomes		43,708,000	75.93		

continued

Table 6.3. continued

Family Type	Percent All Children	Number This Type	Percent This Type	Number in Poverty	Percent in Poverty
Under Age 18 in Poverty				3,289,000	7.50
Under Age 5 in Poverty				1,175,000	
White Male Head, No Wife All Incomes		2,991,000	5.20		
Under Age 18 in Poverty				555,000	18.50
Under Age 5 in Poverty				205,000	
White Female Head No Husband All Inc	10,865,000	18.87			
Under Age 18 in Poverty				4,099,000	37.70
Under Age 5 in Poverty				1,366,000	
All Black Family Types All Incomes	**16.80**	**12,228,000**	**100.00**		
Under Age 18 in Poverty				3,978,000	32.60
Under Age 5 in Poverty				1,333,000	
Black Married Families All Incomes		5,031,000	41.14		
Under Age 18 in Poverty				609,000	12.10
Under Age 5 in Poverty				184,000	
Black Male Head, No Wife All Incomes		747,000	6.11		
Under Age 18 in Poverty				189,000	25.20
Under Age 5 in Poverty				73,000	
Black Female Head, No Husband All Inc	6,450,000	52.75			
Under Age 18 in Poverty				3,189,000	49.40
Under Age 5 in Poverty				1,076,000	
All Other Family Types All Incomes	**4.10**	**2,945,000**			

Source: U.S. Census Bureau, Current Population Survey, 2007 *Annual Social and Economic Supplement.* Population Division, U.S. Census Bureau, Release Date: May 10, 2006. [b]Table 1: Annual Estimates of the Population by Sex and Five-Year Age Groups for the United States.

are living in poverty. African American married families account for only 41 percent of African American families with children, and the poverty rates for children in these families is only 12.1 percent, below the rate for all children in all types of families. But the poverty rate for children living in African American female-headed families is 49.4 percent. This is the kind of discrepancy that encouraged Moynihan to connect family structure with social problems. But any association between children in poverty and the type of family they live in is also likely due to the lack of money available to children living in these families.

While it is true that the greatest percentage of children living in poverty also live in female-headed single-parent families, both African American and White, there is no reliable evidence to support a contention that single-parent family structures are inherently less able to provide an adequate environment in which to rear their children. Moynihan is an excellent example of a successful product from a single-parent female-headed family. It would seem equally legitimate to conclude that fundamental economic disadvantages account for the number of single female-headed families in the first place, and those high rates of poor children in these families is an artifact of fundamental economic disadvantages. Whatever conclusion one might draw from the extent of children in poverty in America, it seems clear that regardless of the structural circumstances of their families, economic assistance to these children is still obligatory. Although with characteristic reluctance, Title IV was created to meet this obligation.[31]

The shift in Title IV policy focus raises a profound child welfare policy issue. If the foundation of child welfare policy emerges from the doctrine of *parens patriae*, then it would appear that protection of the child is paramount to protecting parental rights. In this case, removing children from their parental homes and providing some alternative form of child rearing becomes absolutely necessary in those situations where families are unable to do so. However, such a policy should apply equally to all families, not only to economically dependent families. Conversely, to level the family policy playing field, all families should be assured an adequate income before a decision is reached to remove children. Cost, of course, becomes a deterrent to implementing such a family policy. It may be more cost effective to fund efforts to try to fix families than paying for substitute care for children, and costs would deter ensuring that all families with children had sufficient income and a satisfactory social environment in which to rear their children. It would appear that the legal and administrative boundaries of the assistance framework of Title IV make Title IV the least likely place to develop and promote such a policy, even though Title IV has always been the vehicle to care for America's children. Until a better policy document is developed, Title IV might be best improved by returning to its original objectives of protecting children and providing cash assistance when they are economically needy.

NOTES

1. An important documentation of the shift in how children are viewed can be found in R. Takamishi, "Childhood as a Social Issue: Historical Roots of Contemporary Advocacy Movements," *Journal of Social Issues*, 35 (1978), 8–28.
2. June Axinn and Mark Stern, *Social Welfare: A History of the American Response to Need* (6e) (Boston: Allyn and Bacon, 2005), particularly 281–84.
3. *King v. Smith*, 392 U.S. 309 (1968) and Andrew Dobelstein, *Politics, Economics and Public Welfare* (Englewood Cliffs, NJ: Prentice Hall, 1980), 66. Gilbert Steiner notes, "The Flemming Rule, adopted administratively in 1961 and later written into the 1962 Public Welfare Amendments, provides that a state using a suitable home test could not deny assistance unless appropriate provisions were made otherwise to meet the needs of the child involved." *The State of Welfare*. (Washington, DC. The Brookings Institution, 1973), 179.
4. An important discussion on this issue is Alan Keith-Lucas, "The Political Theory Implicit in Social Casework Theory. *American Political Science Review*, 47, no. 4 (1953), p 1077, ff.
5. U.S. Department of Health and Human Resources, Administration of Children and Families, *Child Maltreatment, 2005* (Washington, DC: Bureau of Children, Youth, and Family, 2007), Chap. 3.
6. United States Code of Federal Regulations (CFR), 45, Subchapter g, 1356.10–1356.86.
7. Haskins, Ron, Brad Schwartz, John Akin and Andrew Dobelstein, "How Much Child Support can Absent Fathers Pay?" *Policy Studies Journal*, 6, no. 6 (December, 1985), 201–231.
8. Ron Haskins, *Work Over Welfare. The Inside Story of the 1996 Welfare Reform Law*. Washington, DC: Brookings Institution Press, 2006.
9. Rockefeller Institute of Government (2002). The variation in state welfare programs really began in 1993 when the Department of Health and Human Services began permitting flexibility to states to administer their AFDC programs. Between 1993 and 1996 when TANF became law, states had obtained over 100 different program waivers, including waivers to reduce benefits to mothers having additional children, welfare time limits, an increase in allowable financial resources limits, and requiring minor mothers to live with parents or supervising adults. See Andrew Dobelstein, *The 1996 Federal Welfare Reform in North Carolina. The Politics of Bureaucratic Behavior*. Lewiston, NY: Edwin Mellon Press, 2002, 33–34.
10. Haskins, *Work Over Welfare*, 27.
11. A small study by the author confirmed this observation. Andrew Dobelstein, *Leaving Work First: A Survey of Persons Who Left the Welfare Roles in Chatham County* (Chapel Hill, North Carolina: Conference on Poverty, Inc. 1999).
12. U.S. Department of Health, *Child Maltreatment, 2005*, 18.
13. Joseph Chepattis, "Federal Social Welfare Progressivism in the 1920's", *Social Service, Review*, 46, no. 2 (June, 1972), 213–239.
14. There are many important accounts of this period of social welfare history, with, arguably the most authoritative being Axinn and Stern, *Social Welfare*. See their Chapter 5.
15. *Meyer v. Nebraska*, 262 U.S. 390 (1923). A summary of U.S. Supreme Court decisions affecting parental rights and liberties can be found at www.liftingtheveil.org/supreme-court.htm
16. *Prince v. Massachusetts*, 321 U.S. 158, 166 (1944).

17. Gilbert Steiner, *The Children's Cause* (Washington, DC.: The Brookings Institution, 1976), 3.
18. See Robert Moroney, *Shared Responsibility: Families and Social Policy* (New York: Aldine Press) 1986.
19. Gilbert Steiner, *The Futility of Family Policy* (Washington, DC.: The Brookings Institution, 1981).
20. Haskins, *Work Over Welfare*, 85.
21. *Ibid.*, 49.
22. *Ibid.*, 10.
23. Beer, Samuel H, "Welfare Reform: Revolution or Retrenchment?" In Sanford F. Schram and Samuel H. Beer, eds. *Welfare Reform. A Race to the Bottom?* (Washington, DC.: Woodrow Wilson Center Press, 1999) 13.
24. U.S. Department of Health and Human Services, Administration for Children and Families. *Grounds for Involuntary Termination of Parental Rights*. Washington, DC., Children's Bureau, 2004.
25. B.F. Jones, "The Indian Child Welfare Act. The need for a separate Law." *Indian Law*, 12, no. 4, Fall, 1995.
26. See 25 U.S.C. 1901 et seq.
27. Meade, Lawrence M, "Introduction". In Lawrence M. Meade and Christopher Beem, eds. *Welfare Reform and Political Theory* (New York: Russell Sage Foundation, 2005), 12, and Meade, Lawrence M, *Beyond Entitlement. The Social Obligations of Citizenship.* (New York: Free Press, 1986).
28. Alan Keith-Lucas, *Decisions About People in Need. A Study of Administrative Responsiveness in Public Assistance* (Chapel Hill, North Carolina: University of North Carolina press, 1957).
29. See, for example, William Galston, "Conditional Citizenship". in Lawrence M. Meade and Christopher Been eds. *Welfare Reform and Political Theory*. New York: Russell Sage Foundation, pp. 110–126.
30. Haskins, *Work Over Welfare*, "[a]s Republicans viewed the world, the entitlement approach to welfare was precisely wrong, primarily because entitlement made it difficult to make benefits contingent on behavior." 27.
31. See Edwin Witte, *The Development of the Social Security Act* (Madison, WI: The University of Wisconsin Press, 1963), 162, ff.

PART IV

HEALTH: INSURANCE AND ASSISTANCE

Introduction

Health Care Under the Social Security Act

The Social Security Act has always acted as a policy document for the development of America's health programs. Originally, the Social Security Act authorized support for two health initiatives: Maternal and Child Health under Title V of the Social Security Act and Assistance to States for Public Health Work under Title VI (see Figure 1.1). Title V rescued the Maternal and Child Health program, which was legislated in 1921 and allowed to expire in 1929. Title V authorized the allocation of federal funds to states to provide services that would enhance the health of mothers and their young children. Title VI authorized grants-in-aid to states to help them set up public health services. Titles VIII and XIX were created in 1965, and later in the Act's history Title XXI was created in 2001.

In some ways, the inclusion of Title V and Title VI in the original Social Security Act satisfied some of the pressures for a more comprehensive medical insurance system as part of the original 1935 Act even though there was considerable pressure to include a form of health insurance in the original Act. Harry Hopkins, a member of the Committee on Economic Security and a close friend of the president, argued strongly that health insurance was the most urgently needed of all social insurance measures. At one time, Hopkins had been the New Orleans director of the Red Cross, and later he served as a director of the New York Tuberculosis and Health Association. However, Frances Perkins, Arthur Altmeyer, and Edwin Witte argued that under the existing economic circumstances, unemployment insurance should be given priority. Perkins, Altmeyer, and Witte all came from a labor background. They argued that labor would give only lukewarm support to any government health insurance program. If labor bargained with employers for health care and won, labor would gain more power; moreover, labor suspected government of siding with business and believed government supported health care would excuse employers from their responsibility. Perkins, Altmeyer, and Witte doubted that health insurance could be enacted over the vocal opposition of the medical profession, and they feared that the American Medical Association (AMA) would move against the entire Social Security Act if it included a form of medical insurance.

Roosevelt might also have been captive to advice from his White House physician and from the well-known Dr. Harvey Cushing, the father-in-law of his son, James. When a draft report of the Committee on Economic Security came out early in 1935, it contained a statement supporting the inclusion of health insurance in the Social Security Act package, and the AMA quickly began an intense lobbying effort in Congress against any health insurance proposal. Faced with mounting political pressures from the AMA, an Economic Security Committee that was sharply divided on the issue, Roosevelt's own uncertainties, and the growing concerns for the constitutionality of the various parts of the Act that would be sent to Congress, Roosevelt decided not to include a health insurance title in the Act. Instead, Roosevelt asked the Federal Security Agency to study proposals for a health insurance program that, presumably, could be implemented at a later time.[1]

Both Titles V and VI remain in the Social Security Act today, and both derive their funding authority from the Act. However, the administrative authority for both Maternal and Child Health and Public Health Work has been transferred to the Public Health Service (PHS), where they remain under the authority of the Assistant Secretary for Health in the Department of Health and Human Services, which oversees the Office of the Surgeon General. The original purpose of Title VI was to assist states "in establishing and maintaining adequate public-health services, including the training of personnel for State and local health work . . . ." The Surgeon General, the head of the PHS at that time, was given authority to distribute these funds to the states. John Parascandola reports,

> The Social Security Act of 1935 [Title VI] provided PHS with the funds and the authority to build a system of state and local health departments, an activity that it had already been doing to some extent on an informal basis. Under this legislation the Service provided grants to states to stimulate the development of health services, train public health workers, and undertake research on health problems. These programs were to be aided by the Federal Government but run at the state and local level, joining the various government units in a public health partnership.[2]

Parascandola observes that the development and passage of Medicare and Medicaid had little impact on PHS funded under Title VI and vice versa. Even though the PHS remained under the authority of the Federal Security Agency, first, and later under the Department of Health and Human Services, its administrative and program development initiatives remained separate from that of the various income maintenance elements of the Social Security Act.

Title V, Maternal and Child Health, followed a similar course of development. Title V provided grants to states to develop Maternal and Child Health programs as somewhat distinct from PHS. While public health covered the broad range of activities from providing some health services to concerns about safe drinking water, Maternal and Child Health programs were required to monitor and, through provision of specific services, enhance the health

---

Box PIV.1 Statutory Services Provided by MCH (Title V)

".... Improve the health of all mothers and children. . . .

.... Reduce infant mortality . . .

.... Increase the number of immunized children . . .

.... Provide health assessments for low-income children . . .

.... Promote health of mothers and children through prenatal, delivery, and postpartum care . . .

.... Provide preventative and primary care to promote the health $ of children

.... Provide rehabilitation services for children eligible for but not receiving services under Titles XVI and XIX . . .

.... Provide research, training, and assessment of serious childhood diseases, including Hemophilia, Cecile Cell, and Genetic diseases. . . ."

Source: Office of Maternal and Child Health, Department of Health and Human Services, 2007.

---

of mothers and newly born children. Both Titles V and VI were consolidated under the 1981 Health Services Block Grant. There are over 7,000 local, regional, and state public health programs in the United States funded with a mixture of federal, state and local funds. Maternal and Child Health programs are usually colocated with county health departments that receive Public Health funding. Maternal and Child Health programs receive about 80 percent of their funding from the Federal Government through the block grant. See Box PIV.1.

Interest in some form of health or hospital insurance continued, however, always in the face of strong opposition from the AMA. Between 1935 and 1965, perhaps as many as 20 legislative initiatives were considered by Congress and various presidents, including the more substantive National Health Bill, 1939 (Senator Robert Wagner), the Wagner–Murray–Dingell Bill, 1943, Wagner–Murray–Dingell, revised, 1945, the Forand Bill, 1959, Kerr–Mills, 1960, and finally King–Anderson, 1961, which, although defeated, provided some of the architecture for the 1965 amendments to the Social Security Act. All these and other less noteworthy bills were defeated or failed to come to a vote, except Kerr–Mills, which simply added health assistance for the aged as an addition to the 1950 amendments to the Social Security Act, providing financial support to states for medical services to the aged poor under the then existing Title I as Aid for the Aged.[3]

Perspective on Health Expenditures in America

Although Part IV of this book focuses on three titles of the Social Security Act—Titles XVIII, Medicare, Title XIX, Medicaid, and Title XXI, Child Health Insurance—it is important to note that the authority for almost all of the Federal Government's support of health care comes under the Social Security Act. Table PIV.1 shows that health spending constitutes almost $1.9

Table PIV.1. National Health Expenditures by Type, 1980–2004 [In billions of dollars (254.9 represents $254,900,000,000)]

Type of Expenditure	1980	Percent	1990	Percent	2000	Percent	2004	Percent
Total	$254.9		$717.3		$1,358.5		$1,877.6	
Annual percent change	15.2	—	11.8	—	6.9	—	7.9	—
Percent of gross domestic product	9.1	—	12.4	—	13.8	—	16.0	—
Private expenditures	147.6	**57.9**	427.3	**59.6**	756.3	55.7	1,030.3	54.9
Health services and supplies	137.0	53.7	400.9	55.9	705.3	51.9	964.2	51.4
Out of pocket payments	58.6	42.8	136.1	19.0	192.6	14.2	235.7	12.6
Insurance premiums	68.9	27.0	233.7	32.6	454.8	33.5	658.5	35.1
Other	9.5	3.7	31.1	4.3	57.9	4.3	70.0	3.7
Medical research	0.3	0.1	1.0	0.1	2.5	0.2	3.4	0.0
Medical facilities construction	10.3	4.0	25.4	3.5	48.5	3.6	62.7	3.3
Public expenditures	107.3	**42.1**	290.0	**40.4**	602.2	**44.3**	847.3	**45.1**
Percent federal of public	66.7	26.2	66.8	9.3	69.5	5.1	70.8	3.8
Health services and supplies	97.0	38.1	265.8	37.1	559.2	41.2	788.8	42.0
Medicare	37.2	14.6	109.5	15.3	225.2	16.6	309.0	16.5

Public assistance medical payments	27.9	10.9	78.7	11.0	207.5	15.3	303.7	16.2
Temporary disability insurance	0.1	0.0	0.1	0.0	0	0.0	0.1	0.0
Workers' compensation (medical)	5.6	2.2	17.4	2.4	24.9	1.8	33.5	1.8
Defense Department hospital, medical	4.0	1.6	10.4	1.4	13.7	1.0	24.4	1.3
Maternal, child health programs	0.9	0.4	1.7	0.2	2.7	0.2	2.7	0.1
Public health activities	6.4	2.5	20.0	2.8	43.4	3.2	56.1	3.0
Veterans' hospital, medical care	5.7	2.2	10.8	1.5	18.9	1.4	28.9	1.5
Medical vocational rehabilitation	0.2	0.1	0.3	0.0	0.4	0.0	0.5	0.0
State and local hospitals	6.6	2.6	13.2	1.8	13.6	1.0	18.4	1.0
Other	2.5	1.0	3.8	0.5	8.8	0.6	11.6	0.6
Medical research	5.1	2.0	11.7	1.6	23.1	1.7	35.6	1.9
Medical facilities construction	5.2	2.0	12.5	1.7	19.9	1.5	22.9	1.2

Source: U.S. Centers for Medicare and Medicaid Services, Office of the Actuary, Statistical Abstracts of the United States, 2007, Table 121.

trillion and consumes 16 percent of America's gross national product. The total national expenditures for health care have expanded ninefold in the past twenty-five years. Table PIV.1 also offers stark evidence that public and private expenditures for health care are almost equal, 45.1 percent in the public sector to 54.9 percent in the private sector in 2004. Approximately 73 percent of all public spending for health in 2004 (approximately $612.7 Billion) was provided under the authority of Titles XVIII, XIX, and XXI of the Social Security Act. In other words, over 32 percent of all public and private health spending in 2004 took place under the authority of the Social Security Act. Considering the fact that both Titles XVIII and XIX were added to the Social Security Act in 1965, thirty years after the Act was created, the present-day profile of the Social Security Act in the delivery of health care is stunning.

Table PIV.1 provides another important feature of how Americans spend their health care dollars. Thirty-five percent of all health care dollars are spent on private health insurance, constituting about 64 percent of all private health expenditures. Additionally, the majority of the additional 12.6 percent of private out-of-pocket health expenditures constitutes forms of co-payments and deductibles required under health insurance contracts. When the private health insurance expenditures are added to the public expenditures under Medicare, over half of all health expenditures take place through various forms of health insurance. To demonstrate the full importance of health insurance in providing health care at least part of the 16.2 percent of public spending for Medicaid should be added to the total of health insurance since most Medicaid dollars are used by the states to buy a form of health insurance for low-income persons. With the additional out-of-pocket expenditures of 12.6 percent, approximately 80 percent of all health dollars are spent through a form of health insurance.

Table PIV.1 provides opportunity for one final observation on how Americans spend their health care dollars. Public and private spending for medical research is less than 2 percent of all health spending, and spending for medical facilities is about 4.5 percent of all public and private health spending. This leaves about 14 percent of all health spending directly for health services, either in or out of a hospital, and less than 4 percent of all health expenditures are used for prevention: the material and child health programs (0.1 percent) and public health activities (3 percent).

Health Insurances as a Limitation on Health Care

The health expenditures reflected in Table PIV.1 suggest a paradigm of health care quite different from usual health care discussions. Clearly, health insurance has become the way Americans pay for their health needs. Health insurance may buy access into the health care system, but a person's health insurance does not buy a particular health care product. In other words, an individual does not go to a doctor or other medical provider and purchase a service as one might go to an automobile repair shop and buy a new battery. Instead, the individual receives a medical service and the provider or the individual is reimbursed for the cost of the service by an insurance company if the services are included in the person's insurance contract. Although the individual may pay some of the cost for the service, the amount of that payment is determined by the insurance company, rather than through some sort of agreement between the individual and the medical service provider. This distinctive feature of health care may be subtle, but it is very important to the development of health policy in America and the a growing dissatisfaction among Americans about how they receive their health care. At best, health insurance is an indirect way of receiving health care.

Second, since health insurance does not buy a health care product it acts to protect the insured against the cost of the product only if the insured needs the product and if the insurance covers the product. For example, if a person wants a hip x-ray, but has no medical need for an x-ray, the cost of the x-ray is not paid for by the insurance. Since the need for the health product most often arises when a person has a specific health problem, the focus of most health insurance is toward treating rather than preventing a health problem. In other words, one does not usually utilize ones health insurance when one is well, only when one is sick, since health insurance policies are selective in the kinds of medical services they cover. In this way, health insurance influences individuals to wait until they are sick before they seek health care. While health insurance has gradually allowed more payments for preventative health services, in general, health insurance has forced individuals to consider themselves healthy unless they are demonstrably sick. In this view, "health care" is more likely to be a form of "sick care."

Finally, since the great majority of health insurance is directed to seeking service when one is sick and thus treating a health problem, there is little health spending devoted to caring for persons who have medical problems that may not be cured. For example, most public and private health insurance programs limit the amount of time an individual can be cared for in a hospital or nursing home. Even long-term-care insurance policies limit the daily dollar amount that can be reimbursed for care in a long-term facility, or the length of time coverage is available, or both. The underlying assumption of health insurance coverage, therefore, reflects the attitude that individuals will get well, or be cured, or will have to pay for care on their own. Thus, the present system of health insurance places an emphasis on curing an illness rather than caring for it.

In some ways, health insurance is a two-headed hydra. Health insurance not only allows the recipient access to specific health services, but it also insures the health provider from loss of revenue as well.

In reality, finally, the American experience of health care depends on a form of insurance that provides access to a system of treatments when one becomes sick, suggesting that health in America is understood as the absence of disease.

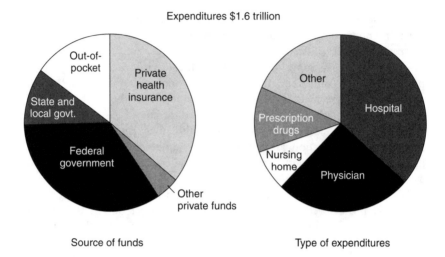

Figure PIV.1. Personal Health Care Expenditures, 2004.

Sources: Centers for Disease Control and Prevention, National Center for Health Statistics, Health, United States, 2006, Figure 9. Data from the Centers for Medicare & Medicaid Services.

In spite of the fact that America has undertaken several activities designed to promote health, such as the National Vaccination Program, the initiative to eradicate smoking, or mandatory safety measures, such as mandatory seat belt use, the idea of health for most Americans that goes beyond identifying health as the absence of disease has yet to command either private or public health dollars. Thus, the dominant paradigm of health care policy in America is a form of pre-payment for medical services when one becomes sick and thus needs a specific service. Figure PIV.1 reflects the dominant American health care paradigm. Both Titles XVIII and XIX have developed in this health care environment.

In both the public and private sector, insurance has become the mode for providing health care. In the public sector, Title XVIII, Medicare, corresponds to the typical private health insurance model—services which are and are not covered, co-payments for services, deductibles, and so forth—except Medicare is funded by the Federal Government and is available mostly to the aged and others who are eligible for Title II social security. Medicaid, Title XIX, is a program of federal assistance to help states pay the medical costs of low-income persons. But states do not usually use these federal funds to provide medical services directly either, through, for example, public health departments or state operated medical facilities, such as hospitals. Instead, for the most part, states contract with health insurance companies to administer their Medicaid programs. Even services that are provided to low-income people in public facilities are usually billed to the Medicaid insurance provider. Therefore, while Medicaid is an assistance program, and thus it meets the criteria for assistance programs as discussed in Chapter 1, it is administered as a medical insurance program. Finally, the State Child Health Insurance Program, Title XXI, is a medical assistance program that extends Medicaid or a Medicaid-like option to make it possible for every low-income child in every state to be covered by health insurance.

Conclusion

The medical amendments to the Social Security Act in 1965 were not only the result of a thirty-year history of attempts to build medical insurance into the architecture of American social welfare policy, but also, perhaps most significantly, the product of a unique period in American political history, not unlike 1935, when congressional leadership, the president, and the American people found agreement about a major expansion of social welfare policy. Next to the creation of the Social Security Act itself, the 1965 Amendments to the Social Security Act constitute a lasting social welfare landmark. But like other Titles of the Social Security Act, Titles VIII and XIX, and later Title XXI were forged from the fire of compromise, and as such they contained the seeds for many of the difficult health policy issues that continue to annoy, displease, and frustrate those who seek adequate health care today. The next two chapters examine Medicare (Title XVIII), Medicaid (Title XIX) and the State Child Health Insurance Program (Title XXI) to show how the programs these amendments have created do or do not satisfy the medical needs of the American people today. As the following two chapters unfold, Table PIV.1 provides a reminder of how the three health titles in the Social Security Act fit into the larger scheme of American health care policy.

NOTES

1. Arthur Altmeyer, *The Formative Years of Social Security*(Madison, WI: University of Wisconsin Press, 1966).
2. John L. Parascandola, "Public Health Service," in *A Historical Guide to the U.S. Government*, ed. George Thomas Kurian (New York: Oxford University Press, 1998), 487–493.
3. A summary of the build-up to titles XVIII and XIX is found in James L. Sundquist, *Politics and Policy* (Washington, DC: The Brookings Institution, 1968), chap. VII.

7

Title XVIII: Medicare Health
Insurance for the Aged

Medicare reflects perhaps one of the greatest ironies of social welfare policy development. The American Medical Association (AMA) and the American Hospital Association (AHA) opposed any form of medical insurance, even before medical insurance was proposed to President Roosevelt for inclusion in the original Social Security Act. AMA opposition persisted even as it appeared that some form of medical insurance would be created in 1965. But after medical insurance became law in 1965, and the Medicare program matured, physicians and hospitals found that they greatly benefited from its provisions. Today, although they often complain about Medicare reimbursement for medical services, doctors and hospital administrators have become some of Medicare's greatest beneficiaries.

The creation of Medicare took place in the distinctively American environment of social welfare policy development. Policy reforms that address human needs usually develop by directing public money into the private sector, and paying the private sector to respond to public problems. Most social welfare benefits for the economically needy result from private market expansion paid for by public funds. Thus, Medicare has benefited doctors and hospitals by expanding the health care marketplace rather than developing an alternative form of public health care.[a] This chapter discusses the Medicare program and its benefits, and puts Medicare in the context of the social insurances as discussed in Chapter 1, by illustrating the way that Medicare developed as a compromise to private medical practitioners and their insurers. The chapter also focuses the policy issues Medicare faces with particular emphasis on the role health insurances play as Medicare's implementing strategy and the subsequent ability of Medicare to meet the health care needs of America's elderly.

Medicare in Its Social Welfare Context

In 2006, 43.2 million people were covered by Medicare: 36.3 million aged 65 and older and 7.0 million disabled persons. Total benefits paid in 2006 were

---

[a] Any proposals to "privatize" Social Security (Title II) would force changes in Medicare as well.

$408.2 billion. Medicare income was $437 billion, expenditures were $408.3 billion, and assets held in U.S. Treasury securities grew to $339 billion. As Table PIV.1 attests, Medicare has become a major social program of federal responsibility.

The social, political, and economic environment that formed the context for the creation of Medicare helps explain the historic opposition to public health insurance by the AMA. Confusion and lack of clarity about expectations for public health care in the years preceding the creation of Medicare characterized public initiatives to formulate a clear health care agenda. In the wake of both the Great Depression and World War II, pressure mounted to improve American health care, but no clear picture emerged about what role, if any, the Federal Government would play to improve it. A proposal for government supported medical insurance was one of several federal health care initiatives promoted during these post–war years, and it took some time before public support for government financed health care became sufficient to neutralize the strong opposition exerted by the AMA. During most of his tenure as Chair of the powerful House Ways and Means Committee, Congressman Wilbur Mills opposed government-supported health care, particularly as form of medical insurance legislation until the political climate became more favorable in the 1960s (see Chapter 3). Economically, as with Social Security Title II, considerable funding concerns complicated the creation of any clear form of public medical care. Who should pay and how to pay for public medical care raised old questions about the fiscal soundness of all the social insurances.

Particularly in the development of Medicare, names are important. All too frequently advocates for and opponents of government intervention in provision of health benefits used different words and conveyed different expectations, as if desired outcomes for government intervention were the same. Health insurance, medical insurance, hospital insurance, for example, were often and still are used interchangeably as if they would result in the same kind of health intervention. Assuming that advocates and opponents were discussing the same principles was further confused by uncertainties about the nature of health care products sought by government intervention into a traditional pattern of doctor–patient fee-for-service pattern of health care. Thus, discussions over the larger issues of the nature of health care and how it could be enhanced failed to play a significant part in the development of Medicare. In other words, advocates for a form of government supported health care never clearly articulated the kind of health care products they sought, but instead fixed their attention on different approaches for achieving an elusive goal.

Lack of Clarity About Goals for Publicly Financed Health Care

One of the historic barriers to a form of national health care, generally, and health care for the aged specifically has been an uncertainty about what is being sought. During the thirty-year struggle that ended with the creation of Medicare, a wide range of different health initiatives was advanced by the Federal

Government. In 1938, the Technical Committee on Medical Care of the Inter-departmental Committee to Coordinate Health and Welfare Activities was created by President Roosevelt to attend to several residual issues that were not completely resolved by the Social Security Act. Medical insurance was one of those residual issues. In 1938, the Technical Committee report recommended expanding the original Social Security Act programs under Titles V and VI, recommended grants to states for hospital construction and medical care for needy persons, and recommended grants to states to help fund a general *medical care program*. Harry Hopkins endorsed these recommendations as first steps toward the development of a national *health insurance* program. But in presenting these recommendations to Congress as part of the National Health Bill in 1939, Senator Wagner spoke against "compulsory health insurance" and instead endorsed support to states to set up their own plans to provide medical care most consistent with the needs of the state.[1] Thus, medical care and health insurance were discussed as if they would achieve the same goals, even though they were not seen as similar initiatives at the time.

The Wagner–Murray–Dingell Bill, first introduced in 1943 and rewritten and reintroduced in different forms and by different sponsors in 1945, 1947, and 1949, proposed a national contributory health insurance program guaranteeing *everyone* thirty days of hospital care and unlimited doctor care. Inspired by the Beveridge report (1942) that led to the development of England's program of public health care, these legislative initiatives proposed "health insurance [that] covered virtually all kinds of care for virtually the whole work force and their dependents...."[2] Arthur Altmeyer arranged for Sir William Beveridge to visit the United States and discuss his ideas with influential congressmen as a means to rekindle an interest in health insurance, and perhaps more than any other event, the influential Beveridge Report rekindled the belief among Social Security administrators that "cradle to the grave" social insurance should include medical care, thereby initiating a dedicated effort to achieve medical *insurance*.[3]

But the Wagner–Murray–Dingell Bills, strongly supported by the Social Security administrators, with less enthusiastic support from President Roosevelt, never came to floor votes. Public support for an expanded federal presence in medical care was lacking particularly in the face of vociferous opposition from the organized medical community. The Forand Bill (Rep. Aime Forand, D, RI) introduced in 1957, constituted a renewed major effort on the part of the Social Security administrators supported by advocacy groups including Americans for Democratic Action, to achieve a federal program of medical insurance. The Forand Bill, written by Wilbur Cohen and other administrative staff members, proposed universal health insurance, including doctor visits and hospital care for the aged, which would all be financed by a health insurance tax. This proposal also died in committee. In the wake of increasing administrative pressure for medical insurance, the Kerr–Mills Bill, developed at the initiative of Wilbur Mills, proposed grants to states to provide medical aid for indigent elderly in the form of vendor payments for any state

approved medical services that low-income aged received.[b] Although Kerr–
Mills became law in 1960, ardent supporters of insurance inside the Social
Security Administration decried Kerr–Mills as inadequate and supported a new
administrative initiative, King–Anderson, that was introduced in Congress in
1961 and again in 1963. King–Anderson proposed a hospital insurance program for all the aged paid for by a Social Security tax. The substance of these
most important initiatives is discussed below.

Thus, by 1965, a confusing array of health initiatives had been introduced
and discussed. There were proposals to expand Maternal and Child Health and
Public Health programs under Titles V and VI (some of which were implemented); there were proposals to cover everyone and all health needs through a
form of public health insurance; there were proposals to provide only hospital
insurance to all the elderly; there were proposals to support states for medical care for medically indigent elderly; and there were proposals to encourage
the elderly to buy health insurance from private insurance providers. These
major and related minor health care initiatives provided little coherent focus
to define the kind of role the Federal Government might play in the development of health care. Whether health care, generally speaking, or hospital care,
specifically, was desirable, whether federal intervention should be restricted to
the economically indigent, and whether health problems should be left to the
private sector to figure out, with some support from the Federal Government,
all appeared to focus on the same issue, but, in reality, each focused on a different piece of the health care riddle. While there was strong sentiment that the
Federal Government should do something to improve health care, there was no
clear, consistent picture of what kind of involvement was most desirable.

Political Maneuvering

Beginning with original medical care proposals preceding the Social Security
Act, AMA presented a strong force opposing any encroachment on the private practice of medicine. The AMA viewed health care as a private matter
between a patient and a doctor, and felt that no one, particularly the government, should prescribe patient medical care. In spite of the fact that the 1920
Maternal and Child Health program, a health program that had won constitutional approval from the U.S. Supreme Court,[4] was revived by the original
Social Security Act, and continued to receive public funding under the Social
Security Act, and in spite of the fact that public health services were growing
in the states, efforts to expand these forms of public medical care failed to find
organizations that could advocate in their behalf. Unions provided only lukewarm support for public medical care; at first their attention focused on efforts
to include disabled workers under Title III of the Social Security Act and other
efforts to strengthen the Unemployment Insurance programs. Later, when the

---

[b] Supplemental Security Income under Title XVI had not yet been created. Economically needy
aged were still supported by the Aid to The Aged (Title I) assistance program. See Chapter 5.

U.S. Supreme Court affirmed the rights of unions to include health insurance in bargaining with management, public forms of health insurance became even less important to the union membership. The only constituency advocating for some form of public health care was comprised of the career administrators inside the Social Security Administration, led by the well-respected, knowledgeable career bureaucrat Wilbur Cohen.[c] Finally, Wilbur Mills had a tight hold on the reins on tax policy and Social Security legislation, and he offered little support for efforts to expand federal influence into health care.

But slowly the political environment began to change. First, Nelson Cruikshank, the AFL-CIO Social Security specialist, brought organized labor into a productive partnership with Cohen and career bureaucrats when the 1956 amendments to the Social Security Act creating Title II Disability Insurance were successfully maneuvered through Congress.[5] Cohen and Cruikshank became close colleagues in shaping the 1965 Social Security amendments (Medicare and Medicaid) bringing the administration and labor into a strong political counterpoint to the continuing opposition by the AMA. In 1956, Congress created a committee to study the problems of the aged, which evolved into the Special Committee on Aging. One of the major issues studied by the Committee was health care for the aged, a subject that gained national recognition at the White House Conference on Aging in 1960.[6] The elderly developed a strong political constituency supporting candidate Kennedy's political campaign and emerged as a strong advocacy force for health insurance. Finally, hospitals began to complain about increasing hospital costs for older people. Private hospital insurance coverage for older people was spotty and inadequate for most hospital stays. As a result, the AMA began to grow much less ardent in its opposition to some form of public medical insurance. In this changing political climate, health issues were shifting to a public concern from an earlier view that health was a private concern between doctors and their clients.

Several events in the 1956 session of Congress also strengthened the revival of the debate over health insurance under Social Security. First, Congress enacted a permanent program of government health protection for dependents of servicemen, then called "military Medicare." Second, Congress approved a plan to expand payments to medical vendors for the provision of health care to welfare clients eligible for benefits under the Social Security Act Title I (Old Age Assistance), Title X (Aid to the Blind), and Title IV-A (Aid to Dependent Children). Finally, Congress approved $30,000 to study the

---

[c] Wilbur Cohen left Health, Education, and Welfare in 1954 after President Eisenhower lowered Cohen's profile in the administration. Cohen returned as Undersecretary in the Kennedy administration and President Lyndon Johnson appointed him Secretary in 1969. During this interim, when he was a professor at University of Michigan, he continued to provide consultation to the department, including consultation on the various health bills. Eisenhower at first supported a form of health insurance to the consternation of the AMA, but he later took a "hands off" approach. See Theodore R. Marmor, *The Politics of Medicare*, 2e (New York: Aldine DeGruyer, 2000).

problems of the aged, noted above, out of which evolved a new Senate sub-committee charged with investigating the problems of the aged in depth. This subcommittee, later expanded into a full-fledged Special Committee on Aging, would ultimately become a forum for the health insurance debate, and finally became a permanent administrative agency within the Department of Health, Education, and Welfare. The camel's nose now was under the tent.

By far, the most significant renewal of the health insurance debate was the 1956 Social Security Act amendments, which added disability benefits to Title II Social Security, providing cash benefits for totally and permanently disabled persons aged 50 and over who had Social Security coverage. Because the disability amendments required determination of *medical* disability, physicians feared government interference with medical practice. To avoid this controversy, the amendments required such determinations to be made by physicians and placed medical disability determination under the authority of the states. Even so, the AMA conducted a vigorous campaign against the amendment. When labor joined the struggle for the amendment, a new political coalition developed, and when the amendment passed, medical insurance was given new life. Bolstered by its success in the fight for disability insurance, toward the end of the 1957 session of Congress, Representative Forand of Rhode Island introduced an administration-written revision of medical insurance. While the Forand Bill never made it out of committee, the Title II legislative successes in this session of Congress gave new political energy to government supported health care in some form.[7]

Economic Context of Federal Medical Insurance

Financing government medical insurance constituted a major concern. Some of the same issues around financing Social Security Title II arose over financing medical insurance. While financing Social Security retirement was based on the "contributory" principle (see Chapter 3), there was no president for funding a "contributory" national health insurance program. Furthermore, while Congress agreed to use general revenue funds to defray the costs of health care for assistance recipients, there was no support for the use of general revenues to fund medical insurance. The successful effort vastly to increase worker coverage under Social Security retirement in 1950, and the 1956 disability amendments, had pushed the "contributory" Social Security tax to what was seen as its limit at that time. Wilbur Mills insisted that Title II Social Security must remain "actuarially sound" and not be supplemented by general revenue funds. Mills feared that medical insurance would become so burdensome that general revenues would have to be used to support Title II Social Security if medical insurance became attached.

Mills also insisted that any federal support for medical insurance be kept separate from funds going into the Title II Social Security Trust Fund. Mills observed that the most politically important feature of Title II Social Security was the often disputed fact that workers were putting money away for future retirement benefits. Medical insurance tied to Title II Social Security would constitute using revenues of present workers to pay for present-day medical benefits that retirees had not earned, thus undermining Social Security's political credibility. Enacting health insurance, the AMA argued, "would impose an unfair burden on the Nation's wage earners and their employers to finance health care benefits for millions of older Americans who are [otherwise] self supporting."[8] Mills had become convinced that any medical insurance plan for low-income aged must be administered by the states and paid for by a grant-in-aid, not from designated social insurance funds.[9] Moreover, Mills wanted to keep any hospital insurance funding "earmarked" as a special tax in order to prevent mixing any medical insurance funding with Social Security revenue or general revenue funding.[10]

Mills' plan for medical aid to the low-income aged, introduced as the Kerr–Mills Bill in 1960, and signed into law, drew quick opposition from Wilbur Cohen and other Social Security administrators. The Kerr–Mills Bill was financed by the grant-in-aid to states and thus avoided complexities inherent in Social Security financing. The Kennedy administration, on the other hand, pressed on for a form of medical insurance funded as part of Social Security Title II, and it argued that Kerr–Mills Bill did not meet the nation's need. The administration prepared another medical insurance bill, the King–Anderson Bill introduced in 1961, and reintroduced in 1963. King–Anderson provided for sixty days of hospital care for the aged with benefits financed through a higher payroll tax and general revenues for those aged who were not receiving Social Security retirement or disability. A major problem with this bill was that it only covered hospital care, not doctors' fees, thus keeping doctors out of the debates. The AMA argued, however, that if King-Anderson were approved, those with hospital insurance would demand coverage of doctors' fees, greatly increasing the scope of the program. Instead, the AMA suggested a voluntary plan, "Eldercare," a hybrid of insurance and public assistance: Beneficiaries would pay part of the cost, and the federal government would pay the rest of the cost of hospital care and doctors' fees through general revenues.

But the form of payment for some kind of medical care was not the only economic consideration underlying the protracted debates over public medical insurance. Once again, tension developed between Keynesian economists who argued that higher taxes and accumulation of government trust funds would stifle economic growth. Mills was forced to consider the Keynesian argument that actuarial soundness in any program of social insurance came at the expense of economic growth. The Keynesians pushed for a general tax reduction to offset any reserves necessary to develop a fiscally sound medical insurance program, and in some respects Mills gave into Keynesian demands with the massive 1959 Social Security benefit increase that reduced Social Security trust fund reserves.[11]

The Health Insurance Compromise

When the showdown over health insurance came in the House of Representatives' Committee on Ways and Means in 1965, the debate over health insurance had narrowed to three competing ideas. One was the substance of the Administration Bill, based on King–Anderson. One was the AMA proposal (Eldercare) modified by Representative Byrnes. One was the Kerr–Mills grants to states for indigent aged medical care. According to Zelizer, in a move that took the entire committee by surprise, Mills suggested that all three initiatives be included as the 1965 Social Security Act amendments.

> Just moments into the session the Arkansas Democrat leaned back in his chair, turning to Wilbur Cohen, and said: 'Well, now let's see. Maybe it would be a good idea if we put all three of these bills together. You go back [Mr. Wilbur Cohen] and work this out overnight and see what there is to this.' . . . The announcement took participants by surprise. . . . Right then according to another participant, everyone in the room knew that it was all over.[12]

After the details were worked out, the administration's bill for hospital insurance became Part A of Medicare. Eldercare, promoted by the AMA and modified by Representative Byrnes, became Part B of Medicare, and the Kerr–Mills initiative of grants to states for medical services to the indigent became Part C of the House Bill and was ratified as Title XIX, Medicaid.

It would be remiss not to acknowledge the greater social, political, and economic context in which Medicare and Medicaid were created. The social climate that existed in America at the time was vigorously in favor of legislation to address longstanding social needs. Not since the Great Depression of 1929–1934 had the nation come together to attempt to develop the institutional structures necessary to address pent-up social problems. It seems proper that Titles XVIII and XIX of the Social Security Act, which were designed to improve health care in America, joined the Civil Rights Act, the Voting Rights Act, the Fair Housing Act, and other Great Society programs established by the Economic Opportunity Act, such as Headstart. Like the Social Security Act itself, Medicare emerged as a fulfillment of social commitments in a particular time in American history.

Medicare's Programs

With the exception of the Prescription Drug Benefit program added to Medicare in 2003, the essential elements of Medicare have remained unchanged since 1965: Medicare Part A provides hospitalization insurance for everyone who receives Title II Social Security. Medicare Part B provides optional supplemental medical insurance for Part A beneficiaries. Although the fundamental elements of both Part A and B remain unchanged, over the years, new hospital and medical service items have been included in these basic program parts,

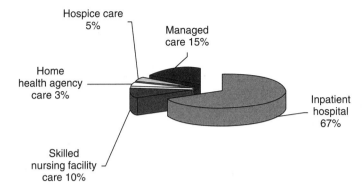

Figure 7.1. Distribution of Medicare Part A Funds.

greatly expanding the medical care provided by both, and requiring corresponding financing changes to implement the program changes. The major medical products provided under each part, the administration of each part, and the financing of each part are outlined and briefly discussed below.[d]

Medicare Part A provides hospital insurance for all Title II Social Security beneficiaries. Five types of hospital care services are covered (see Figure 7.1.):[13]

1. *Inpatient hospital care* covers costs of a semiprivate room, meals, regular nursing services, operating and recovery rooms, intensive care, inpatient prescription drugs, laboratory tests, x-rays, psychiatric hospitals, inpatient rehabilitation, and long-term care hospitalization when medically necessary, as well as all other medically necessary services and supplies provided in the hospital.

Limitations: A one-time deductible amount at the beginning of each benefit period ($992 in 2007) covers the beneficiary's part of the first sixty days of each spell of inpatient hospital care. If continued inpatient care is needed beyond the sixty days, additional coinsurance payments ($248 in 2007) are required through day 90 of a benefit period. Each Part A beneficiary also has a "lifetime reserve" of 60 additional hospital days that may be used when the covered days within a benefit period have been exhausted. Lifetime reserve days may be used only once, and coinsurance payments ($496 per day in 2007) are required.

2. *Skilled nursing facility care (SNF)* is covered by Part A only if it follows within thirty days (generally) of a hospitalization of three days or more and is certified as medically necessary. Covered services are similar to those for inpatient hospital care, but they also include rehabilitation services and appliances.

Limitations: The number of SNF days provided under Medicare is limited to hundred days per benefit period. Medicare fully covers the first twenty days of

---

[d] As with other social welfare programs, Medicare programs change frequently. To find the latest programs, check the *Federal Register*, CFR 4 (see Appendix A).

Source: Centers for Medicare and Medicaid Services, *Annual Report,* 2007.

care in a benefit period. But for days 21 through 100, a co-payment ($124 per day in 2007) is required from the beneficiary. After the hundred days of SNF care per benefit period, Medicare pays nothing. Part A does not cover nursing facility care if the patient does not require skilled nursing or skilled rehabilitation services.

3. *Home health agency care* is covered under both Part A and Part B. Part A covers the first 100 visits following a three-day hospital stay or a Skilled Nursing Facility stay; Part B covers any visits thereafter. Home Health Agency care, including care provided by a home health aide, may be furnished part time in the residence of a homebound beneficiary. Certain medical supplies and durable medical equipment may also be provided. A plan of treatment and periodical review by a physician is required.

Limitations: Home health care under Parts A and B has no co-payment and no deductible.

4. *Hospice care* is provided to terminally ill persons with life expectancies of six months or less who elect to forgo the standard Medicare benefits for treatment of their illness and receive only hospice care. Such care includes pain relief, supportive medical and social services, physical therapy, nursing services, and symptom management. If a hospice patient requires treatment for a condition that is not related to the terminal illness, Medicare will pay for all covered services necessary for that condition.

Limitations: The Medicare beneficiary pays no deductible for the hospice program but does pay small coinsurance for drugs and inpatient respite care.

5. *Managed Care.* See discussion under Medicare Part C below.

Financing Medicare Part A is provided almost entirely by the Hospital Insurance Social Security Tax. Congressman Wilbur Mills insisted that hospital insurance income be kept separate from Social Security retirement and disability receipts. Thus, an "earmarked" payroll deduction of 1.45 percent (2007) of earnings (2.90 percent for self-employed) is paid equally by employee and employer to the Hospital Insurance Trust Fund, which then reimburses hospitals for Medicare Part A expenses. There is no earning ceiling on the Hospital Insurance Tax, unlike the one on Social Security Title II. A very small portion of general revenue funds are used to supplement Medicare for persons who were unable to earn sufficient quarters of Social Security coverage to be eligible for the program.

Medicare Part B is a companion program to Part A. Everyone who is eligible for Part A has the option of joining Medicare Part B, and almost all eligible persons choose to do so. If people decide not to join Part B when they become eligible for Part A, there is a penalty of increased monthly premium for every year they do not join. Part B provides, in the words of the Social Security Administration, "protection against the costs of physician and other medical services." As a companion program to Medicare Part A, Part B insures against specified out-of-hospital doctor and other medical care costs while Part A insures against specified in-hospital costs. Part B covers a large number of specified out-patient medical services and supplies, including the following:

1. Physicians' and surgeons' services, including a very few specified services furnished by chiropractors, podiatrists, dentists, and optometrists; also covered are the services provided by these Medicare-approved practitioners who are not physicians: certified registered nurse anesthetists, clinical psychologists, clinical social workers, physician assistants, nurse practitioners, and clinical nurse specialists in collaboration with a physician.

   Limitations: Services provided by non-Medicare approved practitioners must be certified by approved Medicare practitioners.
2. Services in an emergency room, outpatient clinic, or ambulatory surgical centers, including same-day surgery.
3. Home health care not covered under Part A.
4. Laboratory tests, x-rays, and other diagnostic radiology services.
5. Certain preventive care services and screening tests.
6. Most physical and occupational therapy and speech pathology services.

In addition, Medicare Part B may cover the following:

1. Comprehensive outpatient rehabilitation facility services and mental health care in a partial hospitalization psychiatric program if a physician certifies that inpatient treatment would be required without it.
2. Radiation therapy; renal (kidney) dialysis and transplants; heart, lung, heart-lung, liver, pancreas, and bone marrow transplants; and, as of April 2001, intestinal transplants.
3. Approved medical equipment for home use, such as oxygen equipment, wheelchairs, prosthetic devices, and surgical dressings, splints, casts, and braces.
4. Drugs and biologicals that are not usually self-administered.
5. Certain services for diabetes.
6. Ambulance services, when other methods of transportation are contraindicated.
7. Rural health clinic and federally qualified health center services.

Limitations: All services must be either medically necessary or one of several prescribed preventive benefits. Part B services are generally subject to a deductible and coinsurance. Some medical services are subject to special payment rules such as blood or services performed in settings other than hospitals. Higher cost-sharing requirements (such as those for outpatient treatments for mental illness) may apply. The Social Security Administration warns. "The preceding description of Part B-covered services should be used only as a general guide, due to the wide range of services covered under Part B and the quite specific rules and regulations that apply." Regional Social Security offices are resources for answers to specific questions.

Financing Medicare Part B draws from a combination of public and private funds. General revenue funds from the U.S. Treasury comprise about 75 percent of the money used to support Part B. Premiums collected from individuals make up the other 25 percent of the funds used to support Part B. Premiums for participating individuals are generally set at a level that covers 25 percent of the average expenditures for aged beneficiaries. The standard Part B premium rate of $93.50 per beneficiary per month in 2007 will be adjusted based on income after 2007, with individuals earning $200,000 or more paying a monthly premium of $161.40 in subsequent years. Premium payments are altered for penalties assessed for late enrollment. Thus, Medicare Part B operates like private insurance programs, except that the costs for the program are heavily supplemented by the Federal Government from general revenues. It is important to note that no payroll taxes are used to support Medicare Part B.

Medicare Part C represents a confusing expansion in the development of Medicare that moves provision of Medicare benefits closer to the system of private health insurance. Medicare Part C actually began in 1972, when health maintenance organizations (HMOs) were growing in popularity as a means for both focusing health care on preventing illness ("health maintenance") and thus preventing costly medical treatment. The frameworks for HMOs were set by Henry Kaiser and were frequently known as Kaiser Medical Plans. Original HMOs were funded by individual payments based on the number of persons in the plan ("capitation") rather than based on a fee-for-service based on the number of services that the HMO provided. Medicare beneficiaries were permitted to assign their Part B benefits to approved HMOs. HMO members were able to use all the services the HMOs offered at no additional cost. Originally HMO services were focused toward prevention, but as individuals began to demand more services that the HMOs did not provide, and as private insurance companies met the health insurance demands for more services, HMOs were unable to compete with private insurers and gradually decreased in numbers. While today a number of insurance plans use the title of HMO, and while they provide financial support for preventative services, today's HMOs are quite different from their original prototypes. Today, Medicare provided by HMOs is also known as managed care.[14] A further discussion of HMOs can be found in Chapter 8.

In 1982, Medicare was amended to allow Medicare eligible persons assign their Medicare Part B benefits to certified HMOs, with the expectation that the full use of the HMO's services would reduce the overall costs of Part B expenditures for those persons.[e] In 1997, Medicare expanded the HMO concept to

---

[e] Federal statutes spell out the conditions that must be met before a medical organizations can be certified as a Health Maintenance Organization.

allow private insurance companies to contract directly with the Federal Government to provide both Part A and Part B benefits through their medical
insurance plans. Individuals who choose to assign their Medicare benefits to a
health insurance provider must be guaranteed the same benefit coverage specified under Medicare Parts A and B. The Medicare beneficiary may be covered
for other benefits as well, but may also be charged a copayment or a premium
for providing the added benefits. Called Medicare + Choice this change established an expanded set of options for the delivery of health care under Medicare
and was added to Title XVIII Medicare as Part C. While all Medicare + Choice
plans are required to provide the current Medicare Part B benefit package,
Part C offers an option for Medicare beneficiaries that allows participants to
establish a medical savings account after their deductibles have been met and
if they do not use all the services otherwise provided under standard Medicare
programs.

Part of the rationale for Medicare + Choice was not only to provide Medicare participants with options to exercise their Medicare benefits, but to begin
to shift the administration of Medicare away from the public sector to private
sector health care insurance options. The 2003 Medicare amendments renamed
Medicare + Choice Medicare Advantage, and expanded the kinds of medical
plans that could receive Medicare assignments to managed care plans, and to
private fee-for-service plans. At present, there is concern that financing Part C
is more costly than financing standard Medicare benefits.

Medicare Part D was created in 2003 by the Medicare Modernization Act.
Part D became effective in 2005, and provides subsidies for prescription drugs
through insurance providers. Essentially, Part D allows all Medicare beneficiaries to receive some type of prescription drug coverage from an established
insurance provider. The program is quite complex, but essentially, individuals
pay a monthly premium to an insurance company to receive needed drugs at
a reduced price for the beneficiary. The difference between this and what the
individual pays for drugs is made up by the insurance fee the individual pays
and funds from general revenues provided by the Federal Government. The
levels of drug coverage offered by insurance companies must be approved by
the Centers for Medicare and Medicaid Services before the insurance company
can offer its services to eligible individuals.

Participants must purchase their drug insurance from an approved insurance provider. The basic criteria for the plans require a maximum monthly
premium, after which the beneficiary pays 25 percent of the prescription drugs
covered by that insurer up to an initial coverage limit of $2,400. After the yearly
$2,400 is reached, the participant must then pay the full cost of the medicine.
When the beneficiary's payments reach $3850 for the year, the beneficiary
reaches the next level of coverage and pays $2.15 for a generic or preferred
drug and $5.35 for other drugs or 5 percent, whichever is greater. The lack of
coverage between $2,400 and $3,800 has been referred to as the "donut hole"
and has added considerable confusion about how Medicare Part D works in
practice.

Additional confusion over Part D coverage arises because different insurers offer different coverage on different drugs. While all plans have to offer the approved drugs, and not all prescription drugs are approved, insurance providers have latitude in offering different drugs in their plans. As a result, some plans may cost more than others. Thus, it is important for individuals to search through plans for those that best meet their prescription drug needs.

Financing Medicare

The specific funding for each part of Medicare is spelled out above. In general, however, all Medicare funds are "earmarked." Earmarked Medicare funding was created as part of the compromise extracted by Congressman Wilbur Mills. Thus, all the funds that support Medicare are placed in two funds: the Hospital Insurance Trust Fund and the Supplemental Medical Insurance Trust Fund. The 1.45 percent tax (2007) each on employee and employer go into the Hospital Insurance Trust Fund to reimburse expenses under Part A Medicare, and the premiums paid for Medicare Parts B and D, plus the general revenue funds are deposited into the Supplemental Medical Insurance Trust Fund. Earmarking general revenue funds protects those funds once they are committed to the trust fund, but that does not mean that the general revenue funds are guaranteed commitments to the trust fund.

Administration

Medicare is administered under the authority of the Department of Health and Human Services, the same cabinet-level organization with authority over Title II Social Security. While Title II is administered under the Social Security Administration, Medicare is administered specifically by the Center for Medicare and Medicaid Service. The Social Security Administration administers the whole of its programs, right down to the mailing of checks to Title II beneficiaries, but Medicare administration is much more complex. In the case of Medicare, the Federal Government contracts with nongovernment organizations to serve as fiscal agents between providers of medical services and the Federal Government. These intermediaries apply the Medicare coverage rules to determine the appropriateness of claims, and payments flow through the intermediaries to the providers. The intermediaries are established insurance companies, like Blue Cross, the most frequently used intermediary.

Because Medicare costs have risen sharply since its creation, cost containment has been an important consideration in Medicare administration, requiring elaborate protocols for reimbursing medical costs of providing Parts A and B services. Part A costs are reimbursed under an administrative procedure known as prospective payments in which each hospital stay is categorized into a diagnostically related group (DRG), and each DRG has a specific predetermined amount associated with it, which serves as the basis for payment after some adjustments for each hospital. Suppose, for example, that a Medicare eligible person enters the hospital with a heart attack. The specific elements of the heart attack are identified, and, for illustration purposes, suppose the hospital stay for this diagnostic group is three days at an overall cost of $5,000 in a particular hospital. The hospital will then be reimbursed $5,000 from the intermediary handling Medicare for this geographic area. In some cases, the payment the hospital receives is less than the hospital's actual cost for providing the Part A service for the stay; in other cases, it may be more. In either case, the hospital absorbs the loss or realizes a surplus. If the actual cost of this hypothetical event is $7,000, the hospital loses $2,000; if the cost of the event is $3,000, the hospital keeps the surplus.[f]

Special administrative protocols have also been established for reimbursing Part B services. At first, doctors were reimbursed for their services on the basis of reasonable charges. As fees began to rise, the reimbursement rates were changed to payments based on a fee schedule or the actual doctor fees if they were lower than the established fees. All medical provisions under Part B, including medical equipment, laboratory work, and other allowable medical products are reimbursed based on this fee schedule. If a doctor or supplier agrees to accept the Medicare-approved rate as payment in full ("takes assignment"), then payments provided must be considered as payments in full for that service. The provider may not request any added payments from the beneficiary or insurer. Since Medicare beneficiaries may select their doctors, if the provider does not take assignment, the beneficiary must pay the difference between what Medicare will pay and the cost the medical provider charges. This situation is the chief reason that beneficiaries buy additional private health insurance to cover costs that Medicare does not meet.

Administering Medicare requires collaboration between the Centers for Medicare and Medicaid Services and the Social Security Administration. The Social Security Administration must certify the income levels for Social Security Title II beneficiaries in order to determine the amount of Part B premium Medicare beneficiaries are required to pay. The Social Security Administration also determines low-income certification for Title II Social Security beneficiaries who will receive subsidized drug benefits under Part D. Additionally, the Social Security Administration must collect both Part A and Part B premiums paid through withholding deductions of Part A from payroll checks, and withholding Part B and Part D premiums from the monthly Social Security checks if premium payments are so made. The Social Security Administration must also certify that all funds from premiums and general revenues are placed in the appropriate trust funds.

Medicare Part D requires further collaboration between Centers for Medicare and Medicaid Services offered through state Medicaid programs. Prescription drugs that had been provided to low-income Social Security Title II beneficiaries by Medicaid will be provided, in most cases, by Medicare Part D.

---

[f] Reimbursement rates may also differ based on the services provided by the hospitals and their geographic location, among other factors.

Thus, Medicare will be more involved in the certification of state Medicaid plan approvals as a result of the Medicare Modernization Act.

Summary of the Medicare Program

The above detailed account of medical services covered by Medicare not only shows the complexity of the benefits that Medicare offers, but illustrates a gradual expansion of Medicare over the years, and movement toward private sector administration. Medicaid began in 1965, with two program components: Part A, hospital insurance, and Part B, supplemental medical insurance. A Part C was added to take advantage of the experiences of HMOs, and Part D, prescription drug benefit, was added in 2003, with the Medicare Modernization Act.

Medicare programs are framed by two structural considerations. First, although each of Medicare's program parts contains rich variety of medical products that are included for coverage, Medicaid covers only those products and services specifically stated under each of the program parts. In other words, Medicare does not provide insurance protection for all types of medical care, and while the medical products specified under the four parts include some preventative medical services, most of Medicare focuses on treatments. Second, Medicare is a social insurance program designed to facilitate the provision of health care to those over age 65 and disabled persons who are receiving Title II Social Security. Thus, Medicare is designed for older and disabled people. In other words, Medicare is a much more restrictive program of health insurance coverage than advocates for comprehensive health insurance might have desired. Thus, serious gaps in insurance coverage exist between those who are covered by Medicare and those who are covered by private health insurance programs. As a result, most Medicare beneficiaries also participate in private medical insurance plans that are designed to fill gaps in Medicare services.

Medicare has developed a complex program and administrative structure. The medical services covered by Medicare funding are wide ranging on the one hand, but on the other hand, each service has become quite specific in its provision as Medicare has struggled to contain program costs. Medicare's programs have also become more complex due to administration through intermediary organizations, mostly insurance companies. Sources of financing have also lent complexity to Medicare with funds coming from earmarked payroll taxes, premiums paid by beneficiaries, and general revenue funds. Finally, the use of insurance companies to administer Medicare under the policy directives set by the Centers for Medicare and Medicaid Services lends considerable confusion to final decisions concerning whether a Medicare beneficiary has or has not received a covered service. The Medicare program complexities present important policy issues, both with respect to the Medicare program and the part Medicare plays in the longstanding concern for improving medical care generally. Some of the most salient of these policy issues are discussed in the following section.

Medicare Policy Issues

Medicare Policy in Perspective

Table 7.1 provides a summary of Medicare programs since 1970, when they began to operate at full capacity. Presently, 43.2 million people are enrolled in Medicare, and almost all are enrolled in both Parts A and B at a cost of $408.3 billion. Almost all Title II beneficiaries are enrolled in Medicare. Today approximately 47 percent of all Medicare spending supports Hospital Insurance, Part A, compared with about 71 percent of medical spending for Hospital Insurance in 1970. In-patient hospital spending still commands the largest share of Hospital Insurance, although this percentage has decreased from a high of 97.9 percent in 1980 to 63.1 percent in 2006. However, Part A continues to spend 17.1 percent of hospital insurance through managed care alternatives, and thus if part of this amount for in-patient care could be factored into fee-for-service inpatient hospital costs, the percentage for in-hospital care would be higher. It is important to note the increased expenditures for skilled nursing and other forms of longer term care as part of the costs of Medicare Part A.

Whereas in 2006, Part B spending constituted about 53 percent of all Medicare spending, it accounted for only 29 percent of all Medicare spending in 1970. Interestingly, in spite of the large increases in Medicare spending over the last four decades, expenditures for physicians as a percent of fee-for-service have shown a slight decrease, but this decrease has to be balanced against the percentage of Part B that finances managed care organizations. The development of managed care under Medicare Part C has made it difficult to track the program expansion of either part A or B since the detailed program information for managed care operations is not available. Thus, it is difficult to determine whether managed care has provided better services, different, more preventative services, or provided the same services more economically. The decrease in administrative costs as a percentage of all Medicare expenditures does not take into consideration the hefty administrative costs of the managed care organizations.

If Medicare—health insurance for the aged—as presently implemented in all its iterations—provides any foundation for estimating the costs of health insurance for the nation, it appears that in 2006 the per-Medicare person payment was approximately $9,500 per year, not taking into account any co-payments or deductibles that Medicare eligibles would have paid (see Table 7.1).

Although Medicare provides a form of social insurance for aged Title II beneficiaries, it has become an administrative prototype for considering alternative ways to provide health care for Americans who are not Title II beneficiaries. Furthermore, Medicare's reliance on a medical insurance model that was developed in the private health care sector has influenced alternatives for providing health services in the private sector as well. The influence of the private sector on the present shape of Medicare, and the weight of Medicare on shaping private sector health care, make it difficult to discuss policy issues

Table 7.1. Medicare Enrollees and Expenditures by Program and Service Type

Medicare Program and Type of Service	1970	1980	1990	2000	2005	2006
Enrollees: Number in Millions						
Total Medicare	20.4	28.4	34.3	39.7	42.6	43.2
Hospital insurance	20.1	28.0	33.7	39.3	42.2	42.9
Supplementary medical insurance (SMI)	19.5	27.3	32.6	37.3	41.8	42.6
Expenditures: in $ Billions ($408.3=$408,300,000,000)						
Total Medicare	$7.5	$36.8	$111.0	$221.7	$336.4	$408.30
Total hospital insurance (HI)	5.3	25.6	67.0	131.0	182.9	191.9
Total Supplemental medical insurance (SMI)	2.2	11.2	44.0	90.7	153.4	216.4
Total Part B	2.2	11.2	44.0	90.7	152.4	169.0
Total Part D	—	—	—	—	1.0	47.4
Percent Distribution of Expenditures						
Total Hospital Insurance (HI Part A)	100.0	100.0	100.0	100.0	100.0	100.0
HI Managed Care Organizations	—	0.0	4.0	16.3	13.6	17.1
HI Fee-for-Services Utilization	97.0	97.9	94.6	80.2	84.6	81.1
Inpatient hospital	91.4	94.3	85.0	66.5	66.6	63.1
Skilled nursing facility	4.7	1.5	3.7	8.5	10.1	10.4
Home health agency	1.0	2.1	5.5	3.1	3.2	3.1
Hospice	—	—	0.5	2.2	4.7	4.6
Home health agency transfer	—	—	—	1.3	0.0	0.0
Administrative expenses	3.0	2.1	1.4	2.1	1.8	1.7
Total Part B and Part D	100.0	100.0	100.0	100.0	100.0	100.0
Managed Care Organizations	1.2	1.8	6.4	20.2	14.5	18.6
Fee-for-Service Utilization	88.1	92.8	90.1	79.6	82.7	79.3
Physician/supplies	80.9	72.8	67.3	—	—	—
Outpatient hospital	5.2	16.9	19.3	—	—	—
Independent laboratory	0.5	1.0	3.4	—	—	—
Physician fee schedule	—	—	—	40.8	37.9	34.6
Durable medical equipment	—	—	—	5.2	5.3	5.0
Laboratory	—	—	—	4.4	4.3	4.2
Other	—	—	—	15.0	18.0	17.3
Hospital	—	—	—	9.3	13.5	14.1
Home health agency	1.5	2.1	0.2	4.9	4.3	4.3
Home health agency transfer	—	—	—	−1.9	0.0	0.0
Administrative expenses	10.7	5.4	3.5	2.0	1.8	1.8
Total Part D	—	—	—	—	0.7	21.9

Source: Centers for Medicare & Medicaid Services, Office of the Actuary, Medicare Administrative Data, *Health, United States 2007*, Table 141.

affecting Medicare without reflecting on the bi-play between public sector health insurance for Title II beneficiaries and private health care in the larger American health care environment.

Medicare, as a part of America's larger health care arena, raises a number of instructive policy issues. Medicare faces sober questions in its administration, in its financing, and in its provision of health care for older Americans. Moreover, the policy issues raised by Medicare spill over into efforts to make health care more available and affordable to Americans in general. Not only has Medicare established an important public medical insurance program that draws its authority from the Social Security Act, but the policy structure of Medicare has also reaffirmed and further defined both how America funds medical needs and how Medicare's programs shape the provision of medical services in general.

The preceding discussion and description of the Medicare program prefigures today's Medicare policy problems. Three public policy issues, in particular, order the present Medicare program and suggest how health insurance is likely to evolve in the future. First, widespread confusion over a public understanding of "health care" persists among the public and among policy makers. The haphazard path to Medicare resulted from an uncertainty about what was sought as much as confusion over how to achieve it. Until public consensus develops over the kind of health care that government should support, regardless of how it will be financed, Medicare will continue to wobble toward its uncertain social welfare future. Second, as a social welfare commitment, Medicare administration is bizarre. Medicare administration is built on a health insurance model that may provide access to medical services, but one that also defines and limits the kind and amount of health services available to older people most likely need. Medicare's health insurance form is a product driven payment for prescribed medical services model. Medicare establishes limits based on available services rather than on the individual needs of the Medicare recipient. The health needs of the elderly range well beyond Medicare's prescribed medical services. Medicare has to contend with the deeply entrenched, very imperfect public support for health care as presently defined and insurance as the administrative tool for providing it. Third, Medicare policy development is challenged by its escalating costs and its present method of financing.

Health Care American Style: Treatment, Prevention, Care, Cure, or Confusion

One of the most pressing policy issues confronting Medicare emerges from disagreement about the kind of health care government ought to support. Obviously treatment, prevention, care, and cure are not dichotomous policy objectives for developing a national effort to provide health care for America's elders. But a policy priority has developed that closes debate about health care, a debate that could lead to a more effective, efficient, and cost conscious Medicare program. The preference for treatment over prevention and/or care in Medicare reimbursement policy has weakened somewhat over the past several years since Medicare began covering preventive services, first in 1981 with the pneumococcal (flu) vaccination, and later when Medicare began to reimburse providers for screening services, such as mammograms, designed to prevent costly treatments in both Medicare Parts A and B.[15] Moreover, Medicare Part A offers some reimbursement for forms of alternative hospital and nursing home care, such as in-home and hospice services, signaling greater emphasis on care, rather than cure. Unfortunately, older adults are not covered to receive all the preventive services they might need, beginning with more frequent visits to physician offices. Reasons for this vary, but the problem highlights the opportunity to improve preventive care for older adults.

Efforts to develop a coherent health policy that could be implemented under Medicare run up against unclear health care objectives. Certainly when one is sick, getting well is a clear health care objective, but individual and public health demand a broader consideration of health needs. Prevention, treatment, cure, and care are all necessary elements of any coherent health policy, and to a limited extent, Medicare attempts to satisfy these and other complex health care objectives, yet Medicare remains focused on treatment. A strong belief that the choice of health care is a personal choice further complicates any expansion of the discussion over health and health care objectives. One of the most bothersome features of "managed care" is that it takes the choice of health services away from the individual and puts it in the hands of the insurance provider.

While a balance between personal health goals and essential services needs to be struck, publically supported health care must focus on public rather than individual private health objectives. In analogous terms, when a car breaks we want it fixed. But we know preventative maintenance will deter breakdowns, and sometimes we have to manage with a car that will pass inspection, runs well, but is not in perfect condition. After all, cars are only new for a limited period of time. In like manner, some public health choices are already forced on individuals in the form of tobacco abstinence, seat belts, and mandatory state motorcycle helmet laws, for example. The question for Medicare policy revolves around which health services should receive government support. The health services paradigm in Figure 7.2 offers some perspective on this discussion.

In a statement by Peter R. Orszag, Director of the Congressional Budget Office (CBO), before the United States Senate on June 21, 2007, Orszag summed up the need to shift Medicare spending priorities.

> The current financial incentives facing both providers and patients tend to encourage or at least facilitate the adoption of expensive treatments and procedures, even if evidence about their effectiveness relative to existing therapies is limited. For doctors and hospitals, those incentives stem from fee-for-service reimbursement. Such payments can encourage health care providers to deliver a given service in an efficient manner but also provide an incentive to supply additional services—as long as the payment exceeds the costs of the services. For their part, insured individuals generally face only a portion of the costs of their care and, consequently, have only limited

financial incentives to seek a lower-cost treatment—a trade-off inherent in having insurance protection. Private health insurers have incentives to limit the use of ineffective care but are also constrained by a lack of information about what treatments work best for which patients.[16]

Prudence would dictate that a serious conversation about the health products that are essential to the good health of Americans take place before any efforts are undertaken to further redesign Medicare. Such a discussion is particularly important since Medicare Parts A and B provide public insurance coverage to almost all aged persons, and most of the money spent on the aged under Medicare is spent on prolonged hospital stays, or on treatments that have little chance of curing the major medical problems that face the aged. Conversely, Medicare does little to support ambulatory long-term out-of-hospital care or extended nursing home or intermediate forms of long-term care.

Medicare and the Health Insurance Conundrum

Medicare replicates most features of private health insurance, particularly in its reimbursement for services. The original prototype of private health insurance was developed by Justin Kimball in 1929 at Baylor University for school teachers in Dallas, Texas.[17] Because so many teachers had unpaid hospital bills, Kimball sought a way to help them with their hospital costs. After getting individuals to pay 50 cents a month, Kimball agreed to pay hospitals for twenty one days of in-patient care in a semi-private room. Kimball then negotiated with local hospitals for a reduced rate for anyone needing hospital care who

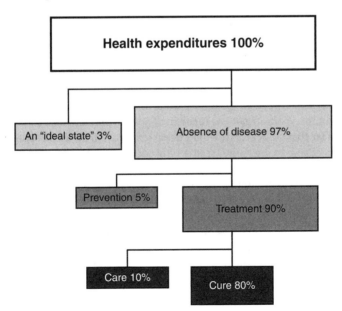

Figure 7.2. A Paradigm of American Health Care.

was covered by his plan, and hospitals were only too willing to provide reduced rates in exchange for guaranteed payments. Kimball's successful plan birthed the Blue Cross program. Ten years later, the California Medical Association established a similar program to cover payment of doctors' bills. The program was well received by doctors and patients, creating the Blue Shield insurance program. Blue Cross and Blue Shield were merged in 1984.

Blue Cross/Blue Shield plans grew in popularity as they were offered to employees on a group-to-group basis. Different groups had different monthly premium rates depending on the experiences of that group in the use of medical services. As these group plans grew, it became more obvious that retired people were left out as a significant group of people who needed health insurance. Thus in 1947, Dr. Ethel Percy Andrus, a retired high school principal, founded the National Retired Teachers Association (NRTA) to promote her philosophy of productive aging and to provide health insurance to retired teachers. In 1958, the American Association of Retired Persons (AARP) was created when Dr. Andrus opened NRTA to all Americans over age 50. AARP thus began by providing medical insurance for retired persons, and has become the largest member organization of the elderly population, and as such an important voice of advocacy for the interests of older Americans.

The Medicare program of today carries the legacy of the private insurance plans created by Justin Kimball, enlarged by Blue Cross/Blue Shield, and promoted as a major necessity by AARP. The widespread support for health insurance in Medicare's early years was fostered by assuring both the hospital and the doctor that they would receive payment for their services, if needed. And, as in the earlier and present insurance plans, what Medicare will pay for is carefully spelled out. Providing Medicare, a form of social insurance, through a private insurance model (an administrative model Title II Social Security fortunately avoided), has created an administrative structure for Title XVIII that has cast the Center for Medicare and Medicaid Services as a regulator, rather than as a direct administrator of Title XVIII benefits.

Perhaps it was inevitable, but the private health insurance model has eviscerated Medicare. While organized medicine opposed publicly supported medical care for fear that government would destroy a traditional doctor–patient relationship, organized medicine seems only too willing to allow the insurance industry to do exactly the same thing. Services delivered through a system of medical insurances as discussed above create a major public policy impediment for Medicare. Any efforts to modify or in some way to "re-form" Medicare and its program products must consider the problems raised by the insurance prototype. The salient features of medical insurance (or more popularly called "health insurance")—reimbursement for services by a third-party payee—lend important insights into the major problems facing today's Medicare program. Medicare's future direction is locked into the development of medical technology supported by a fee-for-service model. Medicare is caught in the web of health insurance that for policy purposes seems inescapable. In other words, it has become extremely difficult to talk about improved Medicare without accepting the limitations that medical (health) insurance has put around such discussions.

Today's form of Medicare administered as health insurance may provide access into the medical care system, but once inside the system, the provision of medical care takes on a byzantine character that reflects the patchwork of services for which insurances will pay. Medicare provides doctors and hospitals with a revenue stream to support the health services they offer their patients. In this way, Medicare protects doctors and hospitals from income losses. No doctor or hospital is likely to provide a medical service to the elderly if it is not a "covered" service, even if such a service is within the economic means of the older person to pay for it. In the process of administering Title XVIII, insurance companies reap tidy profits. In spite of rhetoric to the contrary, health insurance has little to say about the kind of health care people receive, or its quality. For example, if a patient receives poor quality service, neither the doctor, the hospital, nor the insurance company will refund the cost of the medical service.

Medicare as health insurance is rightly named a third party in providing health services. Health insurance acts as a reimbursement for services rendered by the medical community. Thus, in a peculiar way, health insurance is not about health, as such, nor is health insurance an insurance program as insurance is usually understood. Home, life, and automobile insurance, for example, indemnify, or protect, people against a known risk. In home and auto insurance, for example, a policy owner may be insured against a dollar loss due to fire, or in the case of auto insurance, the policy owner may be insured against a dollar loss in an accident. Health insurance does not protect or indemnify the policy holder against a known loss, but rather acts as a pre-payment for certain medical services, if needed or if approved (or covered) under the policy. Hospital insurance covers the costs of services rendered, rather than protecting against a knowable loss, since it cannot be known ahead of time who will use how many of the services that the insurance company agrees to pay for.

Moreover, Medicare as health insurance stands between the patient and the doctor in the provision of services. It does not integrate the interests and needs of patient and the doctor. As noted above, a patient or a doctor might want a particular medical service, but if that service is not reimbursable, the service may not be provided. The service could still be obtained, but at the full cost to the patient. Medicare also discourages competition among health service providers, as costs are reimbursed at standard rates and patients have no voice in setting the fees charged by service providers. Fees and reimbursement schedules are set by Medicare. The fact that consumers can choose to pay more to have services provided that best fit their personal preferences by stepping outside the Medicare system often forces them to buy supplemental health insurance from a private provider ("Medigap" policies).

Finally, Medicare as health insurance undermines a basic principle of social insurance. As discussed in Chapter 1, a statutory right to a social product distinguishes social insurance from assistance. The statutory right to social insurance derives in part from the beneficiary's "contributions" to the insurance program. Title XVIII beneficiaries do not contribute to their Medicare Part A, although they do contribute to Part B. The hospital insurance (Part A) payroll tax shared by employee and employer provides funds for current Part A expenditures. Workers do not build up a medical insurance entitlement the way they build up their Title II Social Security benefits. At best, Medicare confers a statutory right to medical insurance as a result of Title II Social Security coverage. In no way does Medicare provide a statutory right to health care. Moreover, the statutory limits on any Medicare right to medical insurance extend well beyond any form of a social commitment to health care or an implied obligation to provide it. Medicare, as presently administered, challenges the basic concept of social insurance so essential to the foundation of American social welfare policy, which supports the Social Security Act.

Financing Medicare Issues

By most accounts, Medicare, particularly Medicare Part A, is poorly financed, both in the way it is financed and in the amount of funds necessary to support Title XVIII program commitments.[18]

As noted above, the Hospital Insurance Trust fund receives monies collected as part of employee–employer Social Security taxes designated to fund Part A Medicare and the Supplemental Insurance Trust Fund receives funds from premiums charged to Part A beneficiaries to pay for Part B Medicare benefits. Neither fund is adequately funded according the 2007 Trustee Report. Under present income and cost assumptions, reserves in the Hospital Insurance Trust Fund Part A will continue to decline until the Hospital Insurance Trust Fund will be exhausted in 2019. At that time, the Hospital Insurance will be forced to run a deficit. The Supplemental Medical Insurance Trust Fund remains better funded because premium and general revenue income for Parts B and D are reset each year to match expected costs. However, Part B costs continue to increase at a rate of 11 percent annually, outstripping the 6.6 percent projected rate increase presently built into Part B premium rate structure. Thus, solvency of Part B will require continued increases in revenue either from beneficiaries or from general revenues as the costs continue to grow. Part D costs are expected to increase by 12.6 percent over the next decade. Since the Trustees estimate that the economy will increase only by 4.8 percent over the next decade, both Parts B and D will not be sustainable under present revenue projections.

Because projected Medicare income will not satisfy projected expenses, the Medicare Modernization Act of 2003 requires that the Trustees issue a formal warning of a projected shortfall, which in turn requires the president to propose to Congress a response to the projected shortfall within fifteen days after the release of the Fiscal Year 2009 Budget. The generally pessimistic report of the Hospital Insurance Trust Funds states that Medicare will "substantially increase the strain on the nation's workers," and that "the trust fund does not meet our test of long-range ... actuarial balance." The 2007 Trustee Report closes with the following admonition:

> These projections demonstrate the need for timely and effective action to address Medicare's financial challenges. Consideration of such reforms should occur in the relatively near future. The sooner the solutions are enacted, the more flexible and gradual they can be. Moreover, the early introduction of reforms increases the time available for affected individuals and organizations—including health care providers, beneficiaries, and taxpayers—to adjust their expectations. We believe that prompt, effective, and decisive action is necessary to address these challenges—both the exhaustion of the HI trust fund and the anticipated rapid growth in HI, SMI Part B, and SMI Part D expenditures.[19]

Medicare Part C represents a growing effort to "privatize" Medicare. The CBO reports that enrollment in Medicare Advantage health plans has increased to about 18 percent of all Medicare enrollment, due to changes in the 2003 Medicare Modernization Act. That increase reflects, among other factors, changes enacted in the Medicare Modernization Act that increased payment rates and added the prescription drug benefit to complement the medical benefits provided under Medicare Parts A and B. The CBO projects that Medicare Advantage enrollment could reach 26 percent of all Medicare beneficiaries by 2017.[20] The CBO reports that Medical Advantage plans funded under Medicare Part C are more expensive, not necessarily because they provide better services, but due to higher administrative costs. In 2007, CBO estimates, the average payment to Medical Advantage plans was 12 percent above traditional fee for service costs and the difference was even larger for private fee-for-service plans, averaging as much as 19 percent above traditional Medicare fee for service providers. The CBO argues that the higher administrative costs of Medical Advantage plans come at the expense of reducing the "intensity of utilization," limiting visits to specialists, hospital use, and tests and diagnostic procedures. As more persons take advantage of Medical Advantage plans, Medicare costs are likely to rise more quickly than forecast by the Trustees, and if the current trend is not addressed, medical services under Medicare Advantage are likely to deteriorate. If a concern over health care does not bring Medicare to the reform table, financing issues certainly will.

Obstacles to Reforming Medicare and Health Care

Medicare is the tip of the health care iceberg, and improvements and reforms in Medicare will take shape in the larger environment of American concerns over health care and national proposals to address those concerns. Clearly, America's deep commitment to health insurance as the venue for health care has frustrated efforts to create a national coherent health care policy. The most recent effort to reform America's health care system was initiated by President Bill Clinton in 1993. This highly publicized commitment to reform health care proved impossible. After campaigning for health care reform in 1992, President Clinton proposed a far-reaching health care reform policy, and in January, 1993, he appointed his wife, First Lady Hillary Clinton, to head a President's Task Force on National Health Reform. The Task Force began its meetings in private, but by May of 1993, conflicts over the propriety of the Task Force meetings lead to its dissolution. At the same time, partisan political pressure began to mount by Republican members of Congress, not only in opposition to health care reform, but in general to Clinton's social agenda. Neither Medicare nor Medicaid had resolved the problem of growing health care costs, and the problem of limited access to health care by uninsured persons had intensified during the two previous decades. It was in this environment that candidate Clinton pledged to address the growing health care crisis as president.

The President's initial health care reform proposal departed only slightly from policies in place at the time. The President proposed a form of universal health care based on a combination of mandatory health insurance coverage by employers and government insurance payments for those not covered by employers. The actual health care would be provided through HMOs, which would exercise a form of cost containment by limiting the range of services they provided: an early form of managed care. It all sounded so simple. President Clinton's first formal presentation of his plan to a joint session of Congress in September 1993 received a strongly favorable reaction from the public and members of Congress, but the intervening months from January to September allowed opposition to the proposal to develop. The insurance industry led the formal opposition through the Hospital Insurance Association of America, sounding themes similar to those that kept health care reform off the policy agenda for so many years—namely, that government controlled health care would limit the right of individuals to choose their own health care providers and decide on their own form of health care. In response to these criticisms, Mrs. Clinton attacked the "insurance industry," accusing it of greed and deliberately lying about the reform plan in order to protect its profits.

Since the original proposal was notably lacking in detail, controversy and misinformation over the proposal inevitably escalated. Small business owners joined those groups opposed to health reform, claiming that the costs of providing health insurance would be an excessive burden on them, and Republican opposition to the Clinton administration was able to seize on the growing discontent. Democratic and Republican Congresspersons offered alternate proposals, but by September, 1994, Senate majority leader George Mitchell announced that the plan was dead, at least for that session of Congress, and no similar health care reform has been proposed since, even though the struggles for health care reform continue. In 2008, both presidential candidates advertised national health insurance proposals, but implementation of these reform ideas will take a long time to materialize. Their plans, like most other national health care reforms, are based on the present Title XVIII model.

A shift in status among health insurance providers, from not-for-profit to for-profit organizations, raises another obstacle for any effort to reform Title XVIII or develop a national health care policy. Blue Cross/Blue Shield has become a formidable trade organization umbrella that links 40 Blue Cross/Blue Shield "sister" plans that operate in every state. Over 93 million people participate in Blue Cross/Blue Shield insurance plans. Begun largely as non-profit entities, the Consumers Union recently reported that by 2002, 37 state Blue Cross/Blue Shield programs had asked their respective states for a change in their corporate status, from not-for-profit status to for-profit status.[21] In addition to the Blue Cross/Blue Shield companies, the 2007 *Statistical Abstract of the United States* lists 4,200 private insurance companies that sell medical insurance, employing 458,000 persons with $24.1 billion annual payrolls.[22] Not only has the sale of private health insurance become staggering, but there is little consistency among these medical insurance plans regarding what benefits they pay. See Box 7.1.

Although the results may have turned out the same, it might have been more appropriate to propose Medicare reforms before trying to reform an entire health care delivery system. Theodore Marmor argues that the Clinton effort to reform health care left Medicare "subordinated to National health reform."

> [I]n the end of course, the Clinton administration's effort to enact "comprehensive" medical care reform ended in humiliating defeat. The plan's slow death in September 1994 prompted a furious continuing round of blaming, exculpatory rhetoric, and scholarly reconstruction. . . . It is worth noting, though, that even if the Clinton reform plan had succeeded, it would have failed to confront the most crucial problems Medicare faced . . . Acting within the constraints of what it regarded as politically feasible, the Clinton administration opted for a reform plan composed of managed competition and regional alliances, leaving Medicare largely alone.[23]

The experience of this disappointing effort to improve health care demonstrates the difficulty of Medicare reform that does not consider Medicare within the larger policy environment of health care, which goes beyond simply adjusting the practices of the health insurance industry. The fact remains that Medicare, although promoted as a social insurance program, is and has for some time been administered through a system of private health insurance organizations, setting up a potential conflict between private health insurance and Medicare. Efforts to "blend" one into the other have resulted in a confusion of purpose for both the private insurance and public support for health care. This unsuccessful "blending" is evident from the information provided in Table PIV.1, in the introduction to the discussion of Medicare. Present discussions to simplify and standardize health care services by making government the "single payer," similar to the way in which the Social Security Administration pays Title II Social Security benefits, have no future as long as larger health care objectives remain confusing, and as long as private health insurance plays such an important role in administering health care benefits.

Conclusions

Medicare, Title XVIII of the Social Security Act, along with Medicaid and State Child Health Insurance programs, Titles XIX and XXI, both discussed in the next chapter, provides one of the clearest examples of the how the Social Security Act attempts to integrate America's social welfare commitment into a unified whole. At the present time, the authority for almost all of America's public commitment to the health needs of its people rests in the three health titles of the Social Security Act: Title XVIII, Medicare, Title XIX, Medicaid, and Title XXI, State Child Health Insurance Program (SCHIP). The Social Security Act integrates health care for the aged, Medicare, with the social insurances provisions of Title II; the Social Security Act also provides the framework that integrates Medicaid and SCHIP with Title XVI, Title IV, and Title III. But while the Social Security Act provides the integrated framework for America's social welfare health initiatives, Medicare is a disturbing example of how specific health initiatives have become fragmented by endless incremental tinkering without clear policy objectives, and a slow drift to government support of private sector initiatives. Martha Derthick and others may criticize the development of Title II Social Security because it was driven by strongly held ideas among its administrators, but the development of Medicare has suffered due to the fact that it has taken place without clear health policy ideas (see Chapter 3).

Whereas Social Security Title II has been expanded by "backdoor" program changes that have major policy implications for Title II Social Security, Medicare was established as a distinct and separate element extending America's social welfare commitments to include health care for older Americans through a social insurance approach. For political legitimacy, Medicare narrowed its health care reach and clung to its association with Title II social insurance. But while Medicare is often promoted as an extension of America's basic social insurance principles, its unique policy structure sets it outside the same social insurance legitimacy that supports Title II Social Security. Medicare began as an effort to extend medical care to older persons through an extension benefits to Title II beneficiaries, but as America's desire to provide public support for health care expanded beyond health concerns of the elderly, Medicare became ensnarled in debates over larger issues of health care and health insurance. In its influence on health insurance, generally, Medicare has taken on a larger public profile than one of simply providing health care to Title II beneficiaries.

Box 7.1 Blue Cross Blue Shield Conversion Plans Reviewed*

The Blue Cross Blue Shield Association (BCBSA) changed their rules in 1994, allowing BCBS plans to become for-profit corporations. In 2003, there were 64 plans licensed by BCBSA: 38 nonprofit, 16 mutual, and 14 for-profit. As conversions go forward, consumer and community advocates are working hard to see that the health of community and the nonprofit charitable assets are well protected.

A "conversion" occurs when a nonprofit corporation transfers some or all of the control of its nonprofit assets to a nonprofit with a different mission, or to a for-profit corporation.

As of December 2003, the 38 nonprofit Blue Cross and Blue Shield plans across the country retained approximately $20 billion in surplus, an increase of 30 percent since 2002. For-profit Blues hold another $9 billion. Concerns about "excess surplus" in nonprofit Blues plans have arisen and advocates are seeking assistance in exposing excess surpluses and in determining how such excess surplus might be used, such as expanding coverage to the uninsured and reducing premiums of current policyholders. Beyond the issue of excess surplus, community advocates are seeking assistance in addressing broader issues of nonprofit health plan accountability to develop standards and strategies to ensure that their nonprofit health plans behave in a manner that satisfies "community benefit" requirements for nonprofits.

When a nonprofit health care organization becomes a for-profit company, its assets must continue to be used to fulfill its original purpose. In most cases, this is achieved by creating a new foundation dedicated to the health purposes of the former nonprofit.

Such foundations are known as "conversion foundations," and the sums of money involved are enormous. To date, more than 165 conversion foundations have been established and more than $16 billion have been preserved.

Blue Cross' North Carolina Conversion Effort**

Nonprofit health plans generally don't even like to use the word "profit" when they describe their earnings. So, it was awkward and complicated when Blue Cross and Blue Shield of North Carolina found itself recently making too much money while many people in the state were uninsured.

The North Carolina Blue Cross story began in 2003 when after a year and a half of battling the state insurance department over its desire to convert to for-profit status, Blue Cross abandoned the cause, after the insurer

continued

Box 7.1 continued

revealed that it made a record $196.3 million in net income for 2003—
a margin of more than 6 percent. Although CEO Bob Greczyn deemed
the year "exceptional, but not repeatable," the state insurance department
readied legislation that would boost regulatory control. Meanwhile, the
insurer furiously sought ways to show less profit—short of premium cuts or
rebates.

After the abandoned North Carolina conversion, the state took a hard
look at the insurer's finances and determined that Blue Cross premium
increases forced more small businesses to stop offering health insurance,
resulting in a greater number of uninsured. "You don't have to do much
to lower profits," an adviser to the North Carolina Insurance Commission
stated. "Simply showing proof of lower profits on the balance sheet is not
enough. Sure footing with regulators also depends on what the plan does
with its money."

Source: *Abstracted from © 1998–2005 Consumers Union. **Abstracted from Kara Olsen, *Health
Leaders News*, Jul 15, 2005.

Medicare was added to the Social Security Act after almost thirty years of
efforts to develop a foundation of public health care for Americans. Although
Social Security administrators persisted in expanding the Social Security Act
to include health care, the path to Medicare reflects a stumbling effort. From
the beginning, considerable lack of clarity persisted about the goals administrators were seeking. Some envisioned government-supported health care for
everyone, while the expectation of other advocates for government-supported
health care was that there should be payments for health services provided
by the medical community. As private medical care became locked into a system of health insurance, advocates for government-supported health care were
forced to rely on an insurance framework to achieve limited goals of health
care for the elderly. But the effort to extend the principles of social insurance
established through the original Title II retirement program never seemed to
satisfy the unique problems of health care. Medicare, therefore, emerged as
a compromise: hospital insurance for the aged supported by Social Security
taxes, health care insurance for the aged, supported by Federal Government
subsidies and premiums paid by the aged, and Federal Government assistance to the states for medical care for the financially indigent. This health
care troika represents the challenges to develop a base of health care for all
Americans.

Even when viewed in its narrow context of hospitalization and health care
insurance for the aged, Medicare still stretches the principles of social insurance. Medicare Part A, though funded from a payroll tax, is administered
through an insurance intermediary. Clearly, Blue Cross served as the administrative model for Medicare, and the role of the Center for Medicare and

Medicaid Services has been reduced to program oversight rather than program administration similar to Title II Social Security. Robert M. Ball, a key Social Security administrator at the time Medicare was being developed, recently recalled, "Government would be unobtrusive. Hospitals would be allowed to nominate an intermediary to do the actual bill payment.... The carrot was that hospital bills that had previously gone unpaid because many of the elderly had no money would now be paid."[24] Additionally, both Medicare Parts B and D operate in the form of health insurance plans, except that they are partially supported by federal funds from general revenues. As a form of health insurance rather than social insurance, Medicare sets strict limits on the kinds of medical services it will pay for, both for hospital stays and for out-patient medical services. In the words of Edward Berkowitz:

> In old-age insurance officials made an elaborate effort to create the illusion that a person saved for his retirement. In Medicare, this illusion could not be sustained. Instead, it was obvious that current workers paid the medical bills of current retirees. After all, plans called for paying Medicare benefits immediately rather than waiting to build up a trust fund. . . .
>
> Nor could the relationship between the money collected and the money spent be predicted with the same accuracy as in old-age insurance. In old-age insurance, it was demography, the number of older people in the population, that mattered most; and although one could not be certain about this number, one could at least make educated guesses. In health insurance, economics, the cost of medical services, mattered more than did the number of people eligible for services; . . . .[25]

Congressman Wilbur Mills envisioned the fragile nature of advancing government supported health care as social insurance when he insisted that Medicare Part A funds be part of the established Social Security tax principle, and that all funds collected on behalf of Medicare be placed in protected government trust funds. Mills' politically cautious protection of Title II Social Security came from a fear that general revenue funding for Medicare would weaken Title II Social Security (as well as weaken his political power in Congress), a fear that contributed further to the unsuccessful effort to weld Medicare on to social insurance. By separating what became Parts A and B, Mills was able to maintain a certain amount of political integrity for the Social Security earmarked tax. In the final analysis, Wilbur Cohen and the Social Security administrators who had advocated ambitious plans for government-supported health care were only too willing to accept Medicare and proclaim it as a major social welfare achievement. Robert Ball summed up the Medicare "triumph" most clearly. "As critics might say, our decisions were frequently the triumph of opportunism over principle."[26] Medicare may satisfy the social insurance principle of a statutory "right" to health insurance, but Medicare falls far short of any social insurance principle, or any statutory authority that guarantees a moral right to health care.

Today, Medicare has matured into a major commitment on the part of the Federal Government that shows little effect on the improvement of health care in America. According to Marilyn Moon and others,[27] Medicare has expanded from service to the elderly to service to the disabled and others such as persons with renal failure, and the inclusion of health promotion services after 1981 continued to expand the reach of Medicare. Beginning in 1984, the Medicare program now makes payments for graduate medical education to the approximately 1,200 U.S. teaching hospitals through two significant programs. The CBOs analysis of data from the Health Care Financing Administration concludes that for "average" hospitals an additional resident means that the hospital receives between $58,000 and $102,000 (in 1993 dollars) more in annual payments. Average stipends for residents range between about $30,000 and $38,000 per year depending on the resident's years of experience. Fringe benefits add an average of 18 percent to the stipend, resulting in an average range of compensation of between about $35,000 and $45,000.[28] The movement toward Medicare Advantage (Medicare Part C) moves more Medicare benefits toward the private sector, and the creation of Medicare Part D has pushed Medicare well beyond its modest 1965 beginnings. Caught in the tangled web of health insurance, a mismatch between the health needs of the elderly and the health services supported by Medicare continues to exist. While Medicare's beneficiary group now extends well beyond the elderly, it falls short of providing a model for the delivery of health care in America. Any serious proposals to improve Medicare will also have to contend with a multitude of historical and ongoing issues that face the development of health care policy in America. This task might prove too monumental for American government.

NOTES

1. Arthur Altmeyer, *The Formative Years of Social Security* (Milwaukee: University of Wisconsin Press, 1966), 95, 114.
2. Martha Derthick, *Policy Making for Social Security* (Washington, DC: Brookings Institution, 1979), 318.
3. Peter A. Corning, *The Evolution of Medicare: From Idea to Law.* Washington, DC: The Social Security Archives, nd.
4. *Massachusetts v. Mellon*, 262 US rr7 (1923) See Chapter 1.
5. See Derthick, 106.
6. See Andrew Dobelstein, *Serving Older Adults. Policy, Programs and Professional Activities* (Englewood Cliffs, NJ: Prentice Hall, 1985).
7. David Sundquist, *Politics and Policy.* Washington, DC: The Brookings Institution (1968), Chapter 7.
8. Julian E. Zelizer, *Taxing America. Wilbur D. Mills, Congress, and the State, 1945–1975* (Cambridge: University of Cambridge Press, 1998), 234–235.
9. Zelizer, *Taxing America*, 70–73.
10. Edward D Berkowitz, *Mr. Social Security. The Life of Wilbur J. Cohen* (Lawrence, KA: University of Kansas Press, 1995), 166–169.
11. Zelizer, *Taxing America*, 243–234.
12. Ibid., 241.

13. Abstracted from Social Security Administration, Office of Policy, *Annual Statistical Summary, 2006* (Washington, DC: Social Security Administration, 2007).

14. See Paul Starr, *The Social Transformation of American Medicine* (New York: Basic Books, 1982).

15. Today reimbursable preventative services include adult immunizations, colorectal cancer screening, screening mammography, screening Pap test and pelvic examination, prostate cancer screening, cardiovascular disease screening, diabetes screening, glaucoma screening, bone mass measurement, diabetes self-management, supplies, and services, medical nutrition therapy, and smoking cessation.

16. *Health Care and the Budget: Issues and Challenges for Reform.* Statement of Peter R. Orszag, Director, Congressional Budget Office before the Committee on the Budget United States Senate, June 21, 2007.

17. Odin Anderson, *Blue Cross Since 1929: Accountability and the Public Trust* (Cambridge, MA: Ballinger, 1974), chap. 4.

18. *The 2007 Annual Report of the Boards of Trustees of the Federal Hospital Insurance and Federal Supplementary Medical Insurance Trust Funds* (Washington, DC: Board of Trustees, 2007).

19. Ibid., 5.

20. Congressional Budget Office, *Medicare Advantage: Private Health Plans in Medicare* (Washington, DC: The Congressional Budget Office, June 2007).

21. www.Consumersunion.org/health/bcbs

22. *Statistical Abstracts of the United States,* 2008 (Insurance).

23. Theodore R. Marmor, *The Politics of Medicare,* 2e (New York: Aldine De Gruyter, 2000), 133–135.

24. Robert M. Ball, "Reflections on How Medicare Came About," in *Medicare. Preparing for the Challenges of the 21st Century,* eds. Robert Reischaur, Stuart Butler, and Judith Lave (Washington, DC: National Academy of Social Insurance, 1998), 31.

25. Edward D. Berkowitz, *America's Welfare State: From Roosevelt to Regan* (Baltimore: Johns Hopkins University Press, 1991), 167–168.

26. Ball, *Reflections on How Medicare Came About,* 27.

27. Marilyn Moon, *Medicare Now and in the Future.* (2e) (Washington, DC: Urban Institute Press, 1966).

28. CBO document. Financing of graduate medical education (GME)—the period of training after graduation from medical school—is provided predominantly through inpatient revenues (both hospital payments and faculty physician fees) and a mix of federal and state government funds. The Federal Government is the largest single financing source for GME through the Medicare program. Medicare recognizes the costs of GME under two mechanisms: direct medical education (direct GME) payments and an indirect medical education (IME) adjustment.

8

Titles XIX and XXI: Medicaid and the State Child Health Insurance Program

Introduction

Congressman Wilbur Mills' 1965 compromise created both a social insurance program and an assistance program. Medicare, the social (health) insurance program, became Title XVIII of the Social Security Act, and Medicaid, the health assistance program, became Title XIX. Thus, the 1965 amendments continued the tradition of creating two fundamentally different kinds of social welfare programs, social insurance and assistance, with the same purpose in mind: health care. Medicare stretched the definition of Title II social insurance, but by preserving the principles of a payroll tax collected along with Title II Social Security, using "earmarked" funding, and by creating a separate Hospital Insurance Trust Fund, Medicare has managed to preserve the structure of social insurance even though its social insurance philosophy has become compromised (see Chapter 7).

Medicaid, on the other hand, established health commitments under the Social Security Act as an assistance program. Medicaid provides grants to states for state-administered programs of medical care for poor people. Through one's personal contributions, statutes guarantee a right to Medicare for almost all retired persons receiving Title II Social Security.[a] Medicaid, however, confers no such statutory right. Medicare does require that prescribed medical services be provided, but only when applicants establish that their incomes make them financially needy can they receive Medicaid benefits. Medicaid statutes do set out the framework for economic need, in general terms, but individuals are required to prove that they meet those general eligibility conditions, and states have considerable discretion in determining individual eligibility status. Finally, while Medicare provides health insurance mostly for the elderly, Medicaid limits access to health care to those with low incomes who qualify regardless of age. The State Child Health Insurance Program (SCHIP), Title XXI, follows a pattern similar to Medicaid, as discussed in detail below.

---

[a] See footnote in Chapter 7 for specific eligibility conditions for Medicare Parts A and B.

The practice of developing parallel social welfare programs based on different entitlement criteria reflects, in part, America's deep social welfare ambivalence, and adds further confusion to a discussion over the direction of American social welfare policy (see Figure 1.2). If the cash assistance programs are understood as a process of incremental development that eventually grew from state-administered programs into a national, federal government–administered cash assistance program, as in the case of the development of Supplemental Security Income (Title XVI, see Chapter 5), Medicaid, a health assistance program made up of diverse state-administered health programs, may be the precursor to a national, federal government-administered program of health care. If the assistance programs fulfill limited efforts to expand America's social welfare obligations within the political and constitutional confines of American governance, through the use of grants-in-aid to states, then a Medicaid prototype may signal an alternative to health insurance as a way to obtain universal health care.

The notion that Medicaid might provide a foundation for a program of national health care may seem preposterous to some. After all, Medicaid as presently constituted provides health assistance; it is a program that helps the poor receive health care. But the Medicaid/SCHIP model of providing health care to those who cannot afford it may have more universal appeal than a model that involves helping persons buy health insurance. The development of SCHIP as Title XXI to the Social Security Act in 1997 seems to suggest a health care model that might lend itself to national consolidation into a single level health care program similar to the cash assistance transformation that created Supplemental Security Income.[b]

The Political and Economic Context for Medicaid/State Child Health Insurance Program (SCHIP)

The social, political, and economic context for the creation of Medicaid was discussed in the last chapter. Based on providing vendor payments to states for medical care for recipients of Old Age Assistance, the Kerr–Mills Bill formed the base for the 1965 compromise that created Medicaid. Perhaps it seemed wise at the time to create two separate programs—Medicare for the aged and Medicaid for the poor—or perhaps the Social Security administrators were just finally relieved to have a health insurance program after many years of wrangling with Congress. There is no evidence that those who were delighted with the Mills' compromise considered the problems that the dual programs of Medicare and Medicaid would create for one another. The earlier rhetoric that Social Security would eventually make assistance programs obsolete had certainly been abandoned by 1965 and administrative experience with Title II Social Security overlap among Old Age Assistance, Aid to the Blind, and Aid to

---

[b] This proposal is discussed further in Chapter 10.

Dependent Children signaled that assistance programs would not be easily absorbed into a larger framework of social insurance. Medicare and Medicaid were also bound to overlap and cause similar policy problems for the development of health care. Simply put, Medicare was created for the elderly; Medicaid was created for the poor. Large numbers of the elderly are poor, and since Medicare limits the amount of health coverage it provides, Medicaid has to assume the residual costs of medical care of the elderly who are, or who become, poor and who are no longer eligible for coverage under Medicare. Wilbur Cohen seemed well aware of this policy problem, even though it was not addressed as part of the Mills' compromise.[1]

The SCHIP is a different form of a Medicaid-type program for children. SCHIP was created in 1997 and added to the Social Security Act as Title XXI. Efforts to expand health care for children have had a long association with the Social Security Act, as noted in the introduction to Part III. After the creation of Medicaid, frequent incremental expansion of the scope of Medicaid coverage and services often focused on the needs of children. For example, the 1967 Medicaid amendments created the Early and Periodic Screening, Diagnostic, and Treatment (EPSDT) for persons under age 21 (see below) that established a baseline health care program for all low-income children. Medicaid coverage for all children in poverty and children living in families where family income was below 133 percent of the poverty level was included in the 1989 and 1990 federal budgets. States were also encouraged to take advantage of flexibility in Medicaid's program authority to expand their services since Medicaid was an "uncapped entitlement program."[c] By 1997, an estimated 21 million children were already enrolled in Medicaid largely through the optional expansion of state Medicaid plans.

President Clinton's advocacy for expanded health care for children is best seen in the context of his failed efforts to achieve a comprehensive health reform package (see Chapter 7). Clinton focused his attention on children who lived in families too wealthy to qualify for Medicaid (above 133 percent of the poverty level) but too poor to buy their own health insurance (below 200 percent of the poverty level) and who were not covered by employer health insurance plans. In spite of the failed Clinton health care initiative, Jeanne M. Lambrew, in a report for The Commonwealth Fund/Alliance for Health Reform, notes that Senators Orrin Hatch (R-UT) and Ted Kennedy (D-MA) collaborated to propose a large block grant for comprehensive coverage for children,

---

[c] If a person were determined medically eligible for Medicaid consistent with federal statutes, service had to be provided to that person. Thus, any expansion states undertook in their Medicaid programs required the Federal Government to match that expense. The provision of administrative "waivers" as a way to expand programs has been a characteristic means to develop new services without necessary legislation to support them. Such waivers also led to pre-TANF changes in Title IV (see Chapter 6). The Deficit Reduction Act of 2005 (P.L. 109-171) prohibits the approval of such Medicaid waivers in the future.

while Senators John Chafee (R-RI) and Jay Rockefeller (D-W. VA) proposed expanding Medicaid to provide health services for more children.[2] But in spite of bi-partisan support for some form of expanded health care for children, partisan differences over President Clinton's 1996 welfare reform proposals TANF threw Senate bi-partisan proposals to expand health care for children into the budget battle that caused a massive government shutdown (see Chapter 6).

The 1996 reform of Title IV that created TANF also led the way to the creation of the SCHIP in yet another way. By replacing Title IV-A assistance with the TANF block grant, many mothers and children who had been guaranteed Medicaid as Title IV-A recipients lost that coverage. As discussed in Chapter 6, the loss of welfare benefits for children was often raised as a problem in the debates over whether TANF would create unanticipated hardships for children. Some adjustments in Medicaid, therefore, were necessary to make sure that previously eligible Title IV recipients continued to have access to health care. The SCHIPs emerged from the budget battles of 1996–1997 in a final budget bill as a compromise health care program for children by expanding Medicaid's program structure and by creating a new program title to the Social Security Act, Title XXI.[d] Both Medicaid and SCHIPs are now available to states to provide medical care for low-income persons, SCHIPs mostly for children who live in families that are otherwise not eligible for Medicaid because their incomes are larger than the Medicaid income eligibility limits. The specific characteristics of these companion programs are discussed below.

The Context of Providing Medical Care

A brief review of the changing patterns for delivering medical care will help demonstrate Medicaid's significance in today's larger struggles to provide meaningful health care to low-income Americans.[3] Medical services were first provided in a simple fee-for-service relationship between an individual doctor and a patient. Because hospitals were largely resources for the terminally ill, most health care, even for desperately ill persons, was provided in the home by doctor visits. Medical care and medical practice became much more complex after World War II. New diagnostic methods, new therapies, and new drugs led to the development of medical specialties encouraging individual doctors to practice in groups of three or more. Group practices offered the advantage of access to colleagues with special knowledge and also allowed doctors to pool their resources to purchase or otherwise gain access to the new medical equipment and technologies that were rapidly developing in the 1950s.

Expanded medical technology brought hospitals into a new relationship with medical practice. Previously avoided, hospitals became centers of diagnostic

---

[d] Congress has developed an elusive way of settling social welfare program disagreements through the budget acts. Both Omnibus Budget Reconciliation Acts and Balanced Budget Bills have taken the place of separate statutes establishing social welfare programs. Chapter 10 discusses these developments in more detail.

and treatment modalities as the expansion of medical technology acceler-
ated and corresponding centers for medical education increased.[4] Responding to the rapid development of medical practice, the Federal Government
began to provide money to build hospitals (Hill Burton Hospital Construction Act, 1946) and to educate more primary care doctors (Comprehensive
Health Manpower Act, 1971 and the Health Professions Education Assistance
Act, 1976). Medical practice became more specialized as medical education
intensified. By 1978, the Chicago Medical Association identified over 75 different board-certified medical specialties, in addition to over 50 osteopathic
specialties.[5]

In the course of the development of group practices, industrialist Henry
Kaiser was influenced by a proposal from a doctor who offered to treat Kaiser's
employees for a fee-per-employee, a process later known as capitation. Regardless of what an employee needed, the fee-for-employees would remain the
same. Kaiser expanded the agreement to his other manufacturing sites, and
when the post–World War II construction boom expanded Kaiser's businesses,
Kaiser medical plans expanded to include the creation of hospital sites, all operating under a capitation agreement. Kaiser then opened his plan to the general
public. Kaiser Foundation Health Plans owned facilities such as clinics and
hospitals and employed doctors to provide medical care, all for a fixed fee-
per-person, rather than a fee-for-service, characteristic of Justin Kimball's plan
(see Chapter 7). The Kaiser plans also differed from health insurance because
the medical services they offered were managed by Kaiser. While most of the
Kaiser programs provided a full range of medical services, access to services
that Kaiser did not supply was not available under the Kaiser HMOs. Furthermore, Kaiser managed its health care in such a way so as to prevent the need
for costly medical services, providing them only when absolutely necessary and
sometimes not at all. In other words, Kaiser programs did not permit patients
to choose their own doctors, or in many cases to choose their form of medical
care. Instead, their care was managed by the Kaiser program they belonged to.
Thus, in the 1970s, there were two primary ways most people obtained their
health care: through the insurance based plan developed by Justin Kimball or
through the Kaiser-managed form of health care.

The developments in the provision of health care did not proceed in an
orderly systematic manner but rather came about haphazardly, often driven by
private market incentives instead of than concern for health. But several patterns of providing health care came together in 1972 when Congress created
the Health Maintenance Organization (HMO) Act as states and the Federal
Government struggled to control rapidly escalating medical costs that were
largely due to government spending for Medicare and Medicaid. This legislation allowed an organization to be designated as an HMO and thus receive
federal funding if it met three criteria: it provided comprehensive services
that included mandated Medicare and Medicaid services, it accepted payments
for services based on the number of persons served (capitation) rather than
on the cost of the services provided, and the health services the organization

provided were managed, and thus limited, to those services that would promote better health. Since 1973, HMOs have become quite complex in their
characteristics, spinning off many of their traditional activities to private practitioners and hospitals and recreating themselves under such organizations as
Preferred Provider Organizations, Point of Service Providers, Preferred Service Providers, and many others. Some HMO-related programs are owned
and operated for profit by large commercial enterprises; some are operated
by not-for-profit organizations, even governmental units; some are owned
and operated by the medical practitioners who provide the services. But
regardless of their legal and administrative status, HMOs and their prototypes have two features in common: their reimbursements are based on the
number of persons enrolled in the HMO, not on the basis of the services,
and the services they offer are managed, restricting a free choice of medical
services.

Because Medicare is a social insurance program and Medicaid is not, and
because states have considerable flexibility in how they spend their Medicaid
dollars, Medicaid offers a greater number of options for funding the way health
services are provided than does Medicare. Although states must ensure that
required and certain optional services are provided from their Medicaid dollars, states have a wide range of options available to them from whom to
buy those services. Thus, program delivery and the policy structure of Medicaid have developed within the context of diverse health care needs and the
many ways that health services can be provided in today's environment. In this
context, it is not surprising that states have moved toward HMO models of
service delivery that contain elements of both managed care and capitation
funding.

The Program Structure of Medicaid/State Child Health Insurance Program

The structure of both Medicaid and SCHIP follows the outlines of social assistance programs administered under grant-in-aid funding. Both Medicaid and
SCHIP require states to make available a basic set of programs, provide additional funding for certain "optional" programs that states may offer, and leave
states free to determine their own type of structure to administer the programs.
Neither Medicaid nor SCHIP are health insurance programs, nor do they constitute a health delivery system similar to the nation's public health clinics.
Medicaid and SCHIP help states buy health services in the private health care
sector, either through a form of insurance or through direct payments to service providers. Because states have wide discretion over how they spend their
Medicaid dollars, Medicaid is less a national program of providing health care
for low-income persons than it is a collection of 50 different programs. Moreover, because states differ in the amount of autonomy they allow to localities,
most states administer Medicaid in very different ways.

Medicaid/SCHIPs Services

Required Services: In spite of the complexity brought about by state-administered programs, Medicaid must provide the following services as a condition of receiving Medicaid grant-in-aid funding.[6]

Physician services
Inpatient and outpatient hospital services
Laboratory and x-ray services
Medical and dental surgery
Family planning[e]
Pediatric nurse practitioner services
Nurse midwife services
Nursing facility services for individuals age 21 and older
Home health care for persons eligible for nursing faculty services
Early and periodic screening, diagnostic, and treatment for persons
    under age 21

Optional Services: In addition to these services that must be provided with Medicaid dollars, states can choose all or some of the following twelve optional reimbursable services to offer to Medicaid eligibles.

Special clinic services
Dental and vision services and supplies
Prosthetic devices
Physical therapy and rehabilitation services
TB services
Primary care case management
Nursing facility services for individuals under age 21
Intermediate care facilities for mentally retarded persons
Home and community based care
Respiratory care
Personal care
Hospice care

Prescription drugs: Prescription drugs were previously covered under Medicaid optional services, but with the 2003 creation of Medicare, Part D states were able to shift this optional Medicaid service to Medicare. Children who receive EPSDT services are eligible to receive all the authorized medical

---

[e] Congressman Henry Hyde was successful attaching an amendment to Medicaid funding in 1976 that banned the use of federal money for abortions. Although many states continued to fund abortions for low-income women, they were forced to do so without federal matching funds. In 1980. the U.S. Supreme Court upheld the constitutionality of the Hyde Amendment (*McRae v. Mathews*), except in those instances where an abortion is necessary if pregnancy would endanger the mother's life. Later, Congress added exceptions to the Hyde Amendment in situations of rape and incest as well.

services, including any or all of the optional services offered by the state. Thus, EPSDT provides a comprehensive health care package for children that provides early intervention into children's problems and promotes healthy development.

Although states must provide the required and optional services they choose, they have discretion when it comes to deciding when such services are "medically necessary." States are also free to define the amount, scope, and intensity of the services provided, so they are able to place limits on doctor visits or hospital stays. Originally, states had to provide all services in all their administrative subdivisions—"state-wideness"—but in 2005, states were allowed to provide a "package" of services mostly for children, based on approved service "packages" offered by established commercial health care providers. These "packaged" programs are likely to be different in different parts of each state.

SCHIP services generally duplicate Medicaid services. Under SCHIP, states can create or expand their own separate child health programs, expand Medicaid, or combine both approaches. States can choose among commercial "benchmark" benefit packages, develop a benefit package that is actuarially equivalent to one of the benchmark plans, use the Medicaid benefit package, use existing comprehensive state-based coverage, or provide coverage approved by the Secretary of the U.S. Department of Health and Human Services. Thus, with the range of options given to states for the use of Medicaid/SCHIP dollars, it becomes impossible to discuss Medicaid/SCHIP as if they were uniform programs of providing medical care to low-income persons. Moreover, SCHIP has greatly complicated Medicaid programs and policy, and the provision of Medicaid programs now seriously overlaps Medicare, as discussed below.

Medicaid Eligibility

Eligibility for Medicaid is based on income, assets, and medical expenses. Categorically needy[f] are adults and children under age 6 and pregnant women whose family income is at or below 133 percent of the federal poverty level, children up to age 19 for all children born after September 30, 1983, in families with incomes at or below the federal poverty level. Once eligibility is established, pregnant women remain eligible for Medicaid for a period of time after delivery, regardless of any change in family income. Recipients of adoption assistance and foster care under Title IV-E of the Social Security Act are automatically eligible for Medicaid (see Chapter 6). States vary in their asset tests, but generally enrollees may not have assets of more than $2,000 for five

---

[f] "Categorical eligibility" for both Medicaid and SCHIP means that everyone who meets the income guidelines is considered in a category, even though the specific application of eligibility formulas may vary from state to state. Moreover, persons who are eligible because they are made eligible by other legislation, such as in the case of children who receive TANF, constitute another group of categorically eligible persons, and so forth.

years previous to application for Medicaid.[g] The medically needy are generally persons who have more income than the categorically needy but who have excessive medical expenses and are able to have those expenses subtracted from their income, thus making them medically needy.

SCHIP Eligibility

SCHIP provides access to health care for children who do not have health insurance. Eligibility for SCHIP also provides categorical eligibility up to 200 percent of the poverty level, with coverage available beyond the 200 percent level at state option. According to the Kaiser Family Foundation, in 1997, 20 states covered children in families with incomes up to 200 percent of the poverty level, and 23 states covered children with family incomes above 200 percent of poverty. Coverage of persons other than children is also allowed under federal waivers. According to the Kaiser Family Foundation, in 2007, 11 states used SCHIP funds to cover parents, four states covered childless adults, and 11 states used SCHIP funds to cover pregnant women through the option that defines a fetus as an unborn child. Legal immigrants in the country for less than five years are not covered under Medicaid or SCHIP even if they meet income eligibility requirements, and undocumented immigrants are eligible only for emergency Medicaid.[7] States are allowed to construct state plans to include co-payments for medical services provided under SCHIP (see Box 8.1) In some situations, a high level of co-payments has discouraged full participation by children and families who would otherwise be eligible to receive SCHIP services.

Eligibility to SCHIP only for uninsured children (and adults) has been a contentious issue. Thus, states must institute policies that discourage those who are otherwise eligible for SCHIP from dropping their private health insurance and applying for SCHIP instead. In most cases, states require a waiting period between termination of private health insurance and application for SCHIP. The reauthorization of SCHIP in 2007 stalled over the insurance controversy (see below). The 2005 Budget Reduction Act (see below) requires applicants for Medicaid to provide proof of citizenship to gain or continue eligibility, and while these requirements do not apply specifically to SCHIP beneficiaries, it will affect children in combined Medicaid/SCHIP programs.

Medicaid/SCHIP Administration

Both Medicaid and SCHIP are administered by state agencies that have responsibility for spending state and federal funds consistent with the law regarding Titles XIX and XXI. States may administer SCHIP as an extension of their Medicaid programs, as parallel combined programs with Medicaid, or as separate programs. The National Governors Association reported that

---

[g] This was one of the Medicare changes instituted by the 2005 Budget Reduction Act. (See *The Deficit Reduction Act of 2005*, this chapter.)

Box 8.1 SCHIP State Program Variations, Selected States

State	Requires Premiums or Enrollment Fees		Notes
	Yes	No	
Alabama	✓		$50 per child for families from 100–150% FPL $100 per child for families 151–200% FPL Maximum of 3 children per family pay premiums. No premiums for Native Americans.
California	✓		Based upon income. Premiums range from $4–$15 per month per child with a family maximum of $45 per month. 25% discount for those using Electronic funds transfer.
Illinois	✓		150% of FPL and above: $15 for one child, $25 for two. $30 for three; $35 for four; $40 for five or more children, per family per month.
Massachusetts	✓		Medicaid expansion: $12 per child per month with family maximum of $15 per month. Separate SCHIP above 150% FPL: $12 per month per child with family maximum of $36.
Nevada	✓		Based upon family size and income: 0–35% FPL: $0 36–150% FPL: $15 151–175% FPL: $35 176–200% FPL: $70 Native Americans are exempt from all premiums.
Tennessee		✓	
Texas	✓		Enrollment fee for each six months. 133–150% FPL: $25 per family 151–185% FPL: $35 per family 186–200% FPL: $50 per family
Utah	✓		101–150% FPL: $13 per quarter per family 151–200% FPL: $25 per quarter per family
Vermont	✓		$80 per month per family
Virginia		✓	

Source: Vernon Smith and Jason Cooke, Health Management Associates, and David Rosseau, Robin Rudowitz and Carlyn Marks, Kaiser Commission on Medicaid and the Uninsured. Kaiser Family Foundation, 2007.

when SCHIP first began, 19 states chose to expand their Medicaid programs, 11 states administered SCHIP as a parallel, combined program, and 10 states administered separate programs.[8] In 2006, 11 states administered SCHIP by expanding Medicaid, 21 states used the parallel, combined approach, and 18 states operated separate SCHIP programs.[9] Thus, SCHIP is a program that undergoes constant administrative change, reflecting different needs in the individual states.

States are granted wide discretion in how they allocate both Medicaid and SCHIP funds. Since both Titles XIX and XXI provide funds to states to pay for health services for low-income persons, states vary considerably in how these funds are spent. Initially most states simply contracted with insurance providers to reimburse those who provided the services. However, more recently, states are utilizing both commercial and not-for-profit managed care organizations based on the HMO model to provide services, and states reimburse these managed care organizations directly. Today, most Medicaid and SCHIP recipients are in some type of managed care plan. However, the Kaiser Foundation reports that "only 18 of the 224 reported Managed Care plans were public plans operated by counties; the rest are private firms like Blue Cross Blue Shield, WellPoint, United Health, Amerigroup, Centene, and Molina."[10]

Financing Medicaid and SCHIP

Both Medicaid and SCHIP are funded by federal general revenue funds distributed as grants to states and with required state matching funds. Medicaid is funded by an "open ended entitlement" grant, as discussed above. Medicaid, therefore, reflects the standard grant-in-aid financing mechanism discussed in Chapter 1. Medicaid requires the Federal Government to provide funds to states for all persons who meet the state eligibility requirements and become part of the states' Medicaid programs. As state Medicaid expenditures increase, federal funding increases as well (and conversely, if the Federal Government requires new services, states have to raise the funds to match federal spending).

SCHIP, on the other hand, is funded by a "capped block grant." Under SCHIP, therefore, the amount of the federal grant to the states is limited to a certain amount. Expanding SCHIP at the state level, then, does not result in additional federal spending obligations. SCHIP funding and Medicaid funding depend on different formulas and thus excite different political debates. Like the TANF block grant discussed in Chapter 6, SCHIP was granted federal funding for ten years, and because the funding for the grant is capped, the 2007 reauthorization of SCHIP proposed an increase in the amount of the SCHIP block grant. The reauthorization struggle between Congress and President George Bush in 2007 was over increasing the "cap" on the SCHIP block grant, as well as expanding eligibility for children beyond the present 133–200 percent of the poverty level.

Both the Medicaid open-ended grant and the SCHIP capped grant require state matching monies in order to obtain the federal funds. Federal reimbursement rates for Medicaid are based on a state's per-capita income.

Reimbursement rates, therefore, range from 50 percent to approximately 76 percent of federal funds, with states with lowest per-capita income receiving higher matching rates. SCHIP reimbursement rates are based on a combination of the number of children in the state, the number of uninsured children in the state, and the average health care costs in the state. SCHIP reimbursement rates range from 65 percent to 83 percent federal match. Administrative match for both programs averages about 50 percent.

The Deficit Reduction Act of 2005 (P.L 109-17)

P.L 109-17 required billions of dollars of spending reductions in a number of domestic programs, including Medicaid. The Act imposed new restrictions on Medicaid eligibility, particularly eligibility for long-term care. The most significant change affected effective time limits for transfers of assets the elderly might make to their heirs or donations to charity from three to five years, preceding Medicaid application.[h] The Act also makes more spousal income subject to the income test for long-term medical care, tightens the home equity assets provisions, sets a new schedule for Medicaid co-payments, tightens case management standards, and allows states to set up Health Opportunity Accounts similar to optional Health Savings Accounts, among other provisions. The Kaiser Foundation concludes:

> The [Deficit Reduction Act] both reduces federal and state Medicaid spending and also changes health care access and coverage for low-income beneficiaries. For the first time children could be subject to cost sharing under Medicaid, many adults could face a more limited set of Medicaid benefits than under current law, and the elderly could face delays in Medicaid coverage for nursing home services.[11]

Program Summary of Medicaid and SCHIP

Medicaid and the SCHIP, Titles XIX and XXI of the Social Security Act respectively, are social welfare assistance programs in the form of grants to states to provide medical care for low-income persons. Medicaid was originally created in 1965 as part of the compromise that created Title XVIII, health insurance for the aged. SCHIP was created in 1997 as an effort to extend medical care to more low-income children. Medicaid and SCHIP are partner assistance programs with Medicaid focusing on all low-income persons and SCHIP focusing mostly on low-income children. The overlap in the two programs is evident in the three distinct administrative approaches with which states have chosen to implement SCHIP.

Table 8.1 provides a summary of Title XIX, Medicaid. In 2004, there were 55.6 million Title XIX beneficiaries, almost half of whom were children under age 21. In contrast to the percentage of beneficiaries, almost half of the vendor

---

[h] The new "lookback" period became effective February 2006. Transfers after February 2006 will be subject to the five-year rule.

Table 8.1. Medicaid Recipients and Medical Vendor Payments, by Eligibility, Selected Years 1980–2004

Basis of Eligibility	1980	1985	1990	1995	2000	2004
Recipients			Number in Millions			
All Recipients	21.6	21.8	25.3	36.3	42.8	55.6
Basis of Eligibility:			Percent of Recipients			
Aged (65 Years and Over)	15.9	14.0	12.7	11.4	8.7	7.8
Blind and Disabled	13.5	13.8	14.7	16.1	16.1	14.6
Adults in Families with Dependent Children	22.6	25.3	23.8	21.0	20.5	22.2
Children Under Age 21	43.2	44.7	44.4	47.3	46.1	47.8
Other Title XIX	6.9	5.6	3.9	1.7	8.6	7.6
Vendor Payments			Amount in billions			
All Payments	$23.3	$37.5	$64.9	$120.1	$168.3	$257.7
			Percent Distribution			
Total	100.0	100.0	100.0	100.0	100.0	100.0

continued

Table 8.1. continued

Basis of Eligibility	1980	1985	1990	1995	2000	2004
Basis of Eligibility:						
Aged (65 Years and Over)	37.5	37.6	33.2	30.4	26.4	23.1
Blind and Disabled	32.7	35.9	37.6	41.1	43.2	43.3
Adults in Families with Dependent Children	13.9	12.7	13.2	11.2	10.6	11.8
Children Under Age 21	13.4	11.8	14.0	15.0	15.9	17.2
Other Title XIX	2.6	2.1	1.6	1.2	3.9	4.7
Vendor Payments per Recipient			Amount in Dollars			
All Recipients	$1,079	$1,719	$2,568	$3,311	$3,936	$4,639
Basis of Eligibility						
Aged (65 Years and Over)	2,540	4,605	6,717	8,868	11,929	13,687
Blind and Disabled	2,618	4,459	6,564	8,435	10,559	13,714
Adults in Families with Dependent Children	662	860	1,429	1,777	2,030	2,475
Children Under Age 21	335	452	811	1,047	1,358	1,664
Other Title XIX	398	657	1,062	2,380	1,778	2,867

Source: Health, United States, 2007, Table 144.

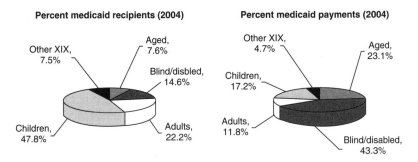

Percent medicaid recipients (2004)

Other XIX, 7.5%
Aged, 7.6%
Blind/disbled, 14.6%
Children, 47.8%
Adults, 22.2%

Percent medicaid payments (2004)

Other XIX, 4.7%
Aged, 23.1%
Children, 17.2%
Adults, 11.8%
Blind/disabled, 43.3%

Figure 8.1. Distribution of Medicaid Recipients and Payments (2004).
Source: Health, United States 2007.

payments for Title XIX services go to the blind and disabled. These comparisons are illustrated in Figure 8.1. Vendor payments per recipient for the aged, blind, and disabled (the three categories of Supplemental Security Income, Title XVI of the Social Security Act) averaged over $13,600 in 2004, in contrast to average payments for children that averaged over $1,600 per year.

Title XXI (SCHIP) data are not as well organized, but most reporting organizations agree that by 2005 approximately 4.4 million children were enrolled separately in SCHIP, and another 1.8 million were enrolled in integrated SCHIP/Medicaid programs, bringing the total SCHIP-enrolled children to approximately 6.2 million.[12] Added to the approximately 28 million, children covered under Title XIX (see Table 8.1) approximately 32.2 million children are provided some type of health care. Approximately, 700 thousand adults are also covered under the SCHIP program. Figure 8.2 shows SCHIP enrollment from 1998 to 2006.

The Medicaid/SCHIP trend to managed care, which combines with a decrease in the number of large scale commercial Medicaid service providers,

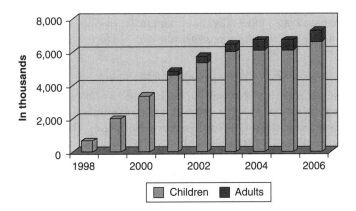

Figure 8.2. SCHIP Enrollment, 1998–2006.
Source: CBO 2007 Report to Congress.

appears to be consistent with the greater discretion that has always been given to states in Medicaid administration. States have broad guidelines for Medicaid program delivery, affording them flexibility to develop innovations for providing health care. As an open-ended entitlement, federal Medicaid financial matching is assured for new or expanded health care programs for low-income persons. The development of a full-service managed health care model seems to be growing in significance for Medicaid/SCHIP health assistance.

The Policy Structure of Medicaid and SCHIP

The program structure of Medicaid and SCHIP creates a policy framework for present and future federal efforts to provide a workable health care program for Americans who are limited in their ability to find health care either because they have no health insurance or because their limited economic resources prohibit any other access to health care. The development of Medicaid along with Medicare has put it in the center of debates over larger issues of health care reform in America. Thus, several Medicaid/SCHIP policy issues discussed below also have relevance for shaping health care policy on the national level.

(1) First, Medicaid has been changing from an insurance-dominated health care model to a managed care model of health care. (2) Second, Medicaid overlaps in service provision and spending with Medicare and has become more obvious particularly among the elderly who need forms of long-term care. (3) Third, financing health care under Medicaid has become much more flexible than financing health services under Medicare. Medicaid and SCHIP offer greater opportunities for increased health service flexibility. (4) Fourth, Medicaid and SCHIP create a complex policy and program structure for providing health assistance. The separate policy and program tracks of each add a layer of unnecessary complexity to efforts to provide health care for the economically needy. (5) Finally, the fact that Medicare has developed within a health insurance model while Medicaid and SCHIP seem to be moving toward an HMO/managed care model raises important policy distinctions between health care as a form of social insurance and health care as a form of welfare assistance.

Medicaid and SCHIP: A Different Model of Health Care

The assistance model of Medicaid and SCHIP devolves extensive discretionary program authority to the states, creating a large medical service tapestry filled with a cascading patchwork of medical service initiatives. Thus, while it is very difficult to make general statements about either Medicaid or SCHIP program development, it appears that states are moving their Medicaid/SCHIP spending to managed care organizations. In 2001, the Kaiser Foundation Commission on Medicaid and the Uninsured described Medicaid service structures based on data drawn from the Health Care Financing Administration (HCFA). The Kaiser Commission reported that enrollment of Medicaid recipients in "full risk" managed care was rising and constituted a "national phenomenon" likely to continue into the mid-2000s.[i] The Kaiser Commission noted that the percentage of all Medicaid recipients enrolled in full service, capitated, managed care health programs had grown to over 50 percent. Moreover, in its report, the Kaiser Commission noted that large-scale commercial managed care organizations were exiting the Medicaid market. "By June 1999, only 37 percent of plans that are large and affiliated with a national [managed care organization] firm participated in Medicaid, compared with 56 percent in 1996. Similarly, only 41 percent of Blue Cross Blue Shield plans participated compared with 59 percent in 1996."[13] Sixty nine percent of Medicaid managed care programs that left the Medicaid market in 12 high volume managed care states between 1998 and 2000 were commercial for profit companies.[14] The trend to managed care is also reflected in Tables 8.2 and 8.3, which show a gradual increase in recipients who receive their Medicaid services from capitated programs (54.2 percent in 2004) and the increase in vendor payments to capitated programs, amounting to 16.5 percent of all vendor payments in 2004, as shown in Table 8.3.

The managed care trend, combined with a decrease in the number of large-scale, commercial Medicaid service providers appears to be consistent with the greater discretion given to states in Medicaid/SCHIP administration. States have broad guidelines for Medicaid/SCHIP program delivery, giving them flexibility to develop innovations for providing health care. As an open-ended entitlement, federal Medicaid financial matching is assured for new or expanded health care programs that serve low-income persons. The development of a full-service managed health care model seems to be growing in significance for Medicaid health assistance. SCHIP is more limited in its funding options, but still retains considerable flexibility in its program development.

Medicaid Overlaps Medicare

Medicaid's policy structure as an assistance program creates a backup program to Medicare for older persons just as Supplemental Security Income backs-up Title II Social Security. About 16 percent of all Medicare beneficiaries are also covered by Medicaid reflecting the low-income status of many of Medicare's beneficiaries and the limitations on Medicare's benefits. Medicaid not only provides important services that Medicare limits or does not cover, especially the need for long-term care, but Medicaid also pays Medicare's premiums and cost sharing for low-income Medicare beneficiaries. Table 8.3 shows that 16.2 percent of the value of all Medicaid vendor payments goes to nursing facilities and another 13.5 percent goes to inpatient hospital care. Both skilled nursing and inhospital care are most heavily used by the elderly and the disabled and both services have limited Medicare benefits.

---

[i] No comparable current data are available, nor are data available specifically for the SCHIP program, but the trend identified by the Kaiser Commission is likely to have continued in SCHIP as well.

Table 8.2. Medicaid Recipients and Medical Vendor Payments, by Type of Service, Selected Years 1980–2004

Type of Service	1980	1985	1990	1995	2000	2001	2002	2004
Recipients					Number in Millions			
All Recipients (in Millions)	21.6	21.8	25.3	36.3	42.8	46.0	49.3	52.0
					Percent of Recipients			
Inpatient Hospital	17.0	15.7	18.2	15.3	11.5	10.6	10.2	9.9
Mental Health Facility	0.3	0.3	0.4	0.2	0.2	0.2	0.2	0.2
Mentally Retarded Intermediate Care Facility	0.6	0.7	0.6	0.4	0.3	0.3	0.2	0.2
Nursing Facility	—	—	—	4.6	4.0	3.7	3.6	3.1
Skilled	2.8	2.5	2.4	—	—	—	—	—
Intermediate Care	3.7	3.8	3.4	—	—	—	—	—
Physician	63.7	66.0	67.6	65.6	44.7	43.5	44.7	43.1
Dental	21.5	21.4	18.0	17.6	13.8	15.3	16.0	16.2
Other Practitioner	15.0	15.4	15.3	15.2	11.1	11.1	11.3	10.7
Outpatient Hospital	44.9	46.2	49.0	46.1	30.9	29.8	30.1	28.7
Clinic	7.1	9.7	11.1	14.7	17.9	18.4	19.2	20.0
Laboratory and Radiological	14.9	29.1	35.5	36.0	26.6	26.8	28.5	28.9
Home Health	1.8	2.5	2.8	4.5	2.3	2.2	2.2	2.1
Prescribed Drugs	63.4	63.8	68.5	65.4	48.0	47.6	49.4	50.3
Family Planning	5.2	7.5	6.9	6.9	—	—	—	—
Early and Periodic Screening	—	8.7	11.7	18.2	—	—	—	—
Rural Health Clinic	—	0.4	0.9	3.4	—	—	—	—
Capitated Payment Services	—	—	—	—	49.7	50.5	68.4	54.2
Primary Care Case Management	—	—	—	—	13.0	13.9	14.6	15.4
Personal Support	—	—	—	—	10.6	10.8	1.4	11.3
Other Care	11.9	15.5	20.3	31.5	21.4	21.5	37.2	22.9

Source: Centers for Disease Prevention and Control, *Health, United States, 2007*, Washington, DC: 2008, Table 145.

Table 8.3. Medicaid Recipients and Medical Vendor Payments, by Type of Service, 1980–2004

Type of Service	1980	1985	1990	1995	2000	2001	2002	2004
All Payments (Amount in $ Billion)	23.3	37.5	64.9	120.1	168.3	186.3	213.5	257.7
Vendor Payments Percent Distribution				Percent distribution				
Total	100.0	100.0	100.0	100.0	100.0	100.0	100.0	100.0
Inpatient Hospital	27.5	25.2	25.7	21.9	14.4	13.9	13.6	13.5
Mental Health Facility	3.3	3.2	2.6	2.1	1.1	1.1	1.0	0.9
Mentally Retarded Intermediate Care Facility	8.5	12.6	11.3	8.6	5.6	5.2	5.0	4.3
Nursing Facility	—	—	—	24.2	20.5	20.0	18.4	16.3
Skilled	15.8	13.5	12.4	—	—	—	—	—
Intermediate Care	18.0	17.4	14.9	—	—	—	—	—
Physician	8.0	6.3	6.2	6.1	4.0	4.0	3.9	4.0
Dental	2.0	1.2	0.9	0.8	0.8	1.0	1.1	1.1
Other Practitioner	0.8	0.7	0.6	0.8	0.4	0.4	0.4	0.4
Outpatient Hospital	4.7	4.8	5.1	5.5	4.2	4.0	4.0	4.0
Clinic	1.4	1.9	2.6	3.6	3.7	3.0	3.1	3.2
Laboratory and Radiological	0.5	0.9	1.1	1.0	0.8	0.9	1.0	1.0
Home Health	1.4	3.0	5.2	7.8	1.9	1.9	1.8	1.8
Prescribed Drugs	5.7	6.2	6.8	8.1	11.9	12.7	13.3	14.5
Family Planning	0.3	0.5	0.4	0.4	—	—	—	—
Early and Periodic Screening	—	0.2	0.3	1.0	—	—	—	—
Rural Health Clinic	—	0.0	0.1	0.2	—	—	—	—
Capitated Payment Services	—	—	—	—	14.5	15.7	15.8	16.5
Primary Care Case Management	—	—	—	—	0.1	0.1	0.1	0.2
Personal Support	—	—	—	—	6.9	7.0	2.8	7.2
Other Care	1.9	2.5	3.7	7.7	8.8	9.2	14.7	10.3

Source: Centers for Medicare & Medicaid Services, *Health, United States, 2007*, Table 145.

There is also a significant imbalance between the number of persons eligible for Medicare and the pattern of Medicaid expenditures. Of the 55.6 million persons eligible for Medicaid in 2004, 7.8 percent were age 65 and older and another 14.6 percent were blind/disabled, while 47.8 percent were children under age 21. But in 2004, payments for Medicaid services for the aged constituted 23.1 percent of all Medicaid vendor payments and another 43.3 percent of vendor payments went to support services for the blind/ disabled. By contrast, however, only 17.2 percent of payments were used to buy health care products for children under age 21.

Another way to view the mismatch between those eligible for Medicaid comes from the cost of service per recipient, also is shown in Table 8.1. In 2004, for example, the unit cost of service per aged recipient was $13,687 and $13,714 for the blind/disabled. But the unit cost for children under age 21 was $1,664, almost 8.5 percent of what was spent for older adults or the disabled. The ratio of Medicaid enrollees to Medicaid benefits is illustrated in Figure 8.1.

The Medicare/Medicaid overlap has developed from the policy structure of Medicare, a form of social insurance, and Medicaid, a form of assistance. The open-ended entitlement structure of Medicaid has inadvertently led to program expansion where the need for medical care for low-income persons has directed it, namely in the direction of highly institutional forms of expensive long-term care. The insurance features of Medicare set limits on payment for hospital and nursing care that cause Medicare recipients to exhaust their personal resources until they become economically needy enough to qualify for Medicaid. While it does not follow that Medicaid funds long-term care for the disabled and older people at the expense of funding the health needs of children, states might be able to expand services for children if the costs of long-term care could be somehow shifted. Even though the federal Medicaid grant to states is open-ended, states still have to allocate and spend state money in order to draw down federal dollars. States, however, are able to shift spending priorities without incurring additional state expense, but if the states extend their services they must allocate state funds for the expansions.

Another example of Medicare–Medicaid overlap became evident when the Medicare Modernization Act created Part D to Title XVIII. The cost of drugs for low-income individuals had been borne by Medicaid programs, but the 2003 Medicare Part D allowed the transfer of drug costs for low-income Medicaid to Medicare. While this feature of Medicare added yet another welfare-type element to Medicare, it relieved states of some of their costs associated with providing drugs for Medicaid-eligible persons.

Undoubtedly, the SCHIP will help Medicaid's structural issue of the mismatch between beneficiaries and benefits by providing more benefits for children, but SCHIP is funded by a capped block grant that limits its expansion. SCHIP is also limited by eligibility guidelines that discourage SCHIP from competing with private insurance. At the insistence of private insurance companies, SCHIP requires states to include in their eligibility criteria policies that discourage potential SCHIP beneficiaries from switching from private insurance to SCHIP.

Most of these disincentives are in the form of waiting periods or SCHIP co-payments. Thus, the policy framework of SCHIP does not easily lend itself to closing the gap between health spending for children and health spending for older people.

Financing: Medicaid/SCHIP Health Services

Service flexibility of both Medicaid and SCHIP has been enhanced by the method of financing them. Devolving health care program development to states and the generous use of program waivers has opened innovative ways to provide health care to low-income people. In this respect, states continue their traditional role as "laboratories" for social programs. States have been free to experiment with the most effective and efficient ways to use Medicaid/SCHIP monies to provide services not only to low-income individuals, but also to a growing number of persons well above the poverty line. The shift to capitated services noted above and the state variations in implementing their plans provide compelling evidence of the different approaches states are using to meet health needs of low-income persons. The flexibility of states was also evident in the transition of the low-income elderly who received their drugs as a state supported Medicaid benefit, to the new Medicare Part D program. When it became clear, for example, that low-income elderly were not receiving adequate drug coverage in this transition period, Martha Derthick reports, states provided wrap-around coverage until "dual eligibles" could be absorbed into the Medicare Part D program.[15] Medicaid/SCHIP service flexibility has allowed medical care for low-income persons to move outside the insurance model of providing health care, as discussed above, and embrace more comprehensive managed care delivery systems, and to move away from commercial to noncommercial providers of health care.

Medicaid and SCHIP have Created a Complex Program and Policy Structure

From a strictly policy viewpoint, there is no reason to have both Medicaid and SCHIP as two separate programs, with different rules for beneficiaries, benefits, and financing. Both are programs of medical assistance to persons who cannot buy health care in the private market. The health insurance conundrum sets the two programs apart. Medicaid provides benefits to persons who are not expected to have health insurance. SCHIP provides access to health care for children and a limited number of adults who may be expected to have health insurance but do not. Although most of those in SCHIP have limited resources and thus find health insurance too expensive for their budgets, the higher SCHIP income eligibility guidelines clearly make SCHIP a competitor with private insurance. Not only does it provide a motivation for individuals to drop private health insurance, but SCHIP also provides an incentive for employers to discontinue employer sponsored health insurance. In an important way, SCHIP was created as a health insurance alternative, but as a public alternative to private insurance. SCHIP has raised important political questions about the way to ensure that Americans have a minimum level of health care.

The health insurance conundrum was the reason behind the vitriolic political debate over reauthorizing SCHIP in 2007. Congress passed compromise legislation to reauthorize the SCHIP program, which expired on September 30, 2007. The President vetoed the Compromise Bill on October 3, 2007. The House Failed to override the President's veto. Then, a slightly revised version of the vetoed SCHIP reauthorization bill was introduced on the House floor on October 25. The revised bill proposed to set the top income limit of 300 percent of the federal poverty level for SCHIP eligibility, clarify that illegal immigrants are not eligibility for coverage, and phase out adult coverage, except for pregnant women. The House approved the revised SCHIP bill but fell short of a veto-proof majority. The Senate passed the bill on November 5, 2007. President Bush vetoed that bill on December 12, 2007. President Bush then signed legislation that would extend SCHIP funding, based on its existing policy framework on December 29 denying attempts to expand SCHIP because expansion would likely reduce motivation of individuals in the higher income brackets from seeking health insurance in the private sector. The extension of SCHIP should provide states with funds to cover those enrolled through March 2009, when reauthorization again will be necessary.

The Congressional Budget Office (CBO) concluded that a SCHIP private insurance substitution effect does exist, but to a limited degree.

> On the basis of a review of the available studies, CBO concludes that the reduction in private coverage among children is most probably between a quarter and a half of the increase in public coverage resulting from SCHIP. That is, for every 100 children who gain coverage as a result of SCHIP, there is a corresponding reduction in private coverage of between 25 and 50 children.[16]

SCHIP and Medicaid also disconnect on the topic of "wrap-around" insurance issues. Children must be uninsured to be eligible for SCHIP coverage, while children with other sources of health insurance are not barred from Medicaid. Under Medicaid, any other form of insurance pays first and Medicaid "wraps around" (supplements) that coverage.

> For example, Medicaid covers dental or vision care for children when these services aren't covered under the employer sponsored insurance. Some directors said it would be beneficial if states had the option under SCHIP to cover needed services that often are not covered by commercial insurance, and that it would be particularly important for children's dental, vision and behavioral health care services.[17]

The complex program and policy structure of Medicaid and SCHIP could be quickly eased by blending the two programs. The fact that many states use

Table 8.4. Medicaid Recipients and Medical Vendor Payments, by Type of Service, 1980–2004

Type of Service	1980	1985	1990	1995	2000	2001	2002	2004
Vendor Payments per Recipient				Amount				
Total Payment *per Recipient*	$1,079	$1,719	$2,568	$3,311	$3,936	$4,053	$4,328	$4,639
Inpatient Hospital	1,742	2,753	3,630	4,735	4,919	5,313	5,771	6,424
Mental Health Facility	11,742	19,867	18,548	29,847	17,800	21,482	21,350	19,928
Mentally Retarded Intermediate Care Facility	16,438	32,102	50,048	68,613	79,330	83,227	91,588	97,497
Nursing Facility	—	—	—	17,424	20,220	21,894	22,326	24,475
Skilled	6,081	9,274	13,356	—	—	—	—	—
Intermediate Care	5,326	7,882	11,236	—	—	—	—	—
Physician	136	163	235	309	356	371	378	426
Dental	99	98	130	160	238	270	293	318
Other Practitioner	61	75	96	178	139	149	151	160
Outpatient Hospital	113	178	269	397	533	546	571	639
Clinic	209	337	602	804	805	662	706	750
Laboratory and Radiological	38	53	80	90	113	131	154	168
Home Health	847	2,094	4,733	5,740	3,135	3,478	3,689	3,978
Prescribed Drugs	96	166	256	413	975	1,083	1,165	1,411
Family Planning	72	119	151	206	—	—	—	—
Early and Periodic Screening	—	45	67	177	—	—	—	—
Rural Health Clinic	—	81	154	174	—	—	—	—
Capitated Payment Services	—	—	—	—	1,148	1,257	997	1,415
Primary Care Case Management	—	—	—	—	30	29	28	58
Personal Support	—	—	—	—	2,543	2,639	8,290	2,946
Other Care	172	274	465	807	1,600	1,734	1,712	2,086

Source: Centers for Medicare & Medicaid Services, *Health, United States, 2007*, Table 145.

SCHIP to extend their basic Medicaid program of services suggests that the integration of the two programs would be a successful undertaking.

Finally, Medicare and Medicaid/SCHIP Implement Health Care from Two Different Policy Positions

Health insurance, in the case of Medicare, and a growing managed care model, in the case of Medicaid/SCHIP, provide two different models for the development of American health care policy. The Medicare approach derives from providing access to health care for all the elderly who are Title II Social Security beneficiaries. The Medicaid approach derives from providing medical care primarily to low-income persons. If America's health care goals are to provide access to health care for everyone, then perhaps the Medicare model of health insurances offers the most promising approach. However, if America's health care goals are to ensure that low-income persons have access to basic health care, then perhaps Medicaid/SCHIPs provides the best model. Health insurance for all would be extremely expensive, perhaps well over $9,500 person per year using the Medicare model (see Chapter 7). Table 8.4 shows the total Medicaid payment per person in 2004 was approximately $4,639. A form of universal health care would probably have to be adjusted for income, while Medicaid and SCHIP already include income guidelines. At any rate, health insurance (Medicare) and health assistance (Medicaid) have both demonstrated the strengths and weaknesses in addressing America's health care needs and provide important experiences for further health care policy discussions.

Conclusion

Medicaid and SCHIP have developed as federally funded state administrated health assistance programs to provide health care for low-income persons, with a particular emphasis on providing health care access for uninsured children. States have exercised their discretionary authority to create a wide-ranging collection of health care services and methods for providing the services that best seem to satisfy state-level health care needs. As health assistance programs, both Medicaid and SCHIP also provide back-up medical care primarily for low-income persons who are eligible for medical insurance under Medicare but exhaust their benefits. The 2007 struggle over SCHIP reauthorization highlights a fundamental tension between medical assistance and medical care secured in the private market by health insurance, an extremely important policy issue likely to affect all efforts to reform health care in America. The Medicaid utilization data in Tables 8.1, 8.2, and 8.3 show a shifting emphasis in the way health services are provided to the needy who lack other forms of access to health care.

Medicaid and SCHIP are state-administered health assistance programs, funded by adequate federal grants to states so that states can provide health care services to their low-income populations. Although certain services must be provided by the states in order for the states to receive Medicaid and SCHIP funding, the authority to develop and carry out health programs rests with the states. Neither Medicaid nor SCHIP offers any notion of a fundamental right to health care, even though both programs rest on a pre–Social Security Act obligation to provide health care for those persons, particularly children, who cannot afford to pay for it.

As social obligations, rather than as programs that satisfy personal rights, Medicaid and SCHIP confront the tension between the health care people want and what they need. In other words, assistance programs are not obligated to provide the resources people want, but they are obligated to provide the resources people need. Any balance between wants and needs requires discretionary decision making authority, and even though Medicaid and SCHIP require provision of specific services, neither program extends to beneficiaries the freedom to choose what services they will be given. Because populations and needs vary across the nation, states are in a better position to make decisions that balance wanted and needed medical care, in much the same way that localities are in a better position to balance these forces than states. In other words, discretionary decisions are best made as close to the provision of a service as possible. A national health program, such as Medicare, is a one-size-fits-all program. A state-based program such as Medicaid allows an adjustment between available resources, the health needs of the community, and the preferences of those who use the services.

Medicaid and SCHIP are programs that the Federal Government cannot administer directly, but which are appropriate for state administration. But social welfare program administration through the grant-in-aid is not without problems. The Federal Government, which grants the funds for Medicaid and SCHIP, and the states, which use the monies to implement programs, must work together in a complex series of exchanges often referred to as the American system of Intergovernmental Relations.[18] In 2005, grants to states accounted to 30.7 percent of all state government spending; the largest grant was Medicaid.[19] Medicaid is the nation's largest program of intergovernmental financing and administration, and as such Medicaid has become one of the most carefully guarded grants by the states. Medicaid's elaborate architecture is a product of both its cost and its importance to the states.

Liberal skeptics of state-administered programs often fear that states will be less generous in meeting social obligations than the Federal Government. Perhaps, a more balanced view of Medicaid and SCHIP suggests that neither the Federal Government, nor the states, nor even localities are by nature more or less generous in the ways they meet their social obligations. The obligation to provide health care to those who cannot afford it is a national obligation shared by the Federal Government, the states and localities. Medicaid/SCHIP attempts to meet this obligation through the provision of funds provided by the Federal Government, matched by the states, and programs developed and administered by the states are in the best position to balance wanted and needed health services. While it is true that a single program may be easier to monitor than a collection of many different programs, programs like Medicaid and SCHIP call upon the integrity of states to use their monies appropriately and without discrimination on the basis of race, nationality, gender, sexual orientation, or other factors that might contribute to prejudicial provision of health services.

The evolution of Medicaid and SCHIP toward forms of managed care offers the opportunity to evaluate the efficacy moving public support of health care away from personal health care preferences toward health products that satisfy community health needs. In this way, Medicaid and SCHIP might model future efforts to reform American health care.

Medicaid and SCHIP, like the other assistance programs funded under the Social Security Act, raise questions over how the social obligation to provide health care can be satisfied. Who should provide medical care to those unable to pay for it? What funds can be used to meet this obligation? These and other questions about providing medical care are not merely rhetorical debating points, but instead such questions define what kinds of programs will be created to meet America's social obligations. The constitutional constraints on the Federal Government were discussed in Chapter 1. The question for those who seek the development of social welfare policy in America has always been. "How can we do it?" Social Security, Title II, and Unemployment Compensation, Title III, have passed the test of constitutionality, and Medicare, which has been appended to Title II seems to have been inoculated against constitutional challenges. But a range of social welfare obligations that American welfare policy has tried to satisfy have had to rely on the ubiquitous grant-in-aid. Devolution of authority is characteristic of assistance programs not only because of the intergovernmental complexities of grant-in-aid funding, but also because decisions about who gets what require discretion. Any movement to develop better health care for Americans beyond the confines of the Social Security Act's Title XVIII, Title XIX, and Title XXI will have to deal with the policy issues that have emerged as Medicare, Medicaid, and SCHIP have matured. Chapter 10 provides some suggestions about how these policy issues might be addressed.

At least two conclusions can be drawn from the above discussion of Medicaid/SCHIP, however, and to a lesser extent from Medicare: First, while states are under federal scrutiny to provide Medicaid/SCHIP health services, health insurance provides no solution to the mounting problems in the development of health care for Americans. Health insurance may provide access to health care but it is poorly equipped to direct the character of health care itself or how health care is used. Second, while most discussions today center on the impending financial crisis confronting medical care, an obligation to provide necessary health care today has become a very significant ethical problem. Whether payments are made from private or public resources, the ethical considerations of what kind of health care will be provided, to which persons, under what circumstances are much more significant questions than any question of their cost or how they might be funded.

Those who seek to become president of the United States in the first decade of the twenty-first century propose various health insurance schemes to placate the American hunger for satisfactory and affordable health care. But these proposals amount to little more than a convenient way of delaying a confrontation with more fundamental issues that underpin today's health challenges. Providing health insurance for all may open the door to a variety of forms of health care, but health insurance as it has evolved will do little to address the challenge. In fact, proposals to universalize health insurance may be a subtle way of avoiding some of the more challenging issues of developing a coherent health care policy for Americans. Those proposals will simply allow the politically astute to shift the blame for a failed health care policy to the insurance providers.

Over twenty years ago, the noted medical sociologist David Mechanic wrote:

How is the public to be assured that their [health] needs will be met? How can access to entitlements, sensitive and responsive care, and a willingness to treat patients equitably be enforced? Only the naïve would assume that medical institutions and professionals under pressure would necessarily come to decisions in the public's interest, particularly when the public interest may be in opposition to their own. Yet we know from present experience how difficult it is to regulate relationships between medical institutions, processionals, and patients and what a costly burden these regulatory activities can be for all concerned.[20]

Mechanic continues,

We think of ethical dilemmas and choices as focused at the individual level, but health policy formulation is in one sense an enterprise in applied ethics. Our views of health and illness themselves, the range [among availability] of financing possibilities, the definition for what constitutes a medically relevant service, modes of payment, and the definition of providers eligible for [payment], all implicitly involve many social choices and value judgments that shape the delivery of services and scientifically impact the lives of patients and their families. Too often, what is defined solely as a financial or administrative judgment has enormous implication for who can be served, in what context and within what range of alternative options.[21]

The policy choices that lie ahead are much greater than a choice of insurance providers or the role of the Federal Government. In some ways, both Medicare and particularly Medicaid have opened a Pandora's box. America's health care commitments under Title XVIII, Title XIX, and Title XXI constitute bold steps that, in spite of the unfinished legacy they have left, prove inadequate on their own to bring about better health care for Americans.

NOTES

1. Edward D. Berkowitz, *Mr. Social Security. The Life of Wilbur J. Cohen* (Lawrence, KS: University Press of Kansas, 1995). See Chapter 10 in particular.
2. Jeanne M. Lambrew, *The State Children's Health Insurance Program: Past, Present, and Future* (George Washington University: Commonwealth Fund/Alliance for Health Reform, 2007), Bipartisan Congressional Health Policy Conference. January

2007. Senator Hatch's initiative in partnership with Senator Kennedy completely unnerved Senator Trent Lott, as described by James Carney (*Time* magazine, April 21, 1997): "No wonder Senate majority leader Trent Lott was so furious. Instead of working with his leadership to produce a Republican proposal, Hatch devised a bipartisan bill with Kennedy that Republicans will be hard pressed to oppose." Most people fail to realize that Senator Hatch and Senator Kennedy were close friends and often worked together in the Senate, where they were known as the "odd couple."

3. Marshall W. Raffle, *The U.S. Health System: Origins and Functions* (New York: John Wiley & Sons, 1980). See Chapter 3 in particular for the development of various models of medical practice in the United States.

4. William W. McLendon, *Bettering the Heaalth of the People. W. Reece Berryhill, the UNC School of Medicine and the North Carolina Good Health Movement* (Chapel Hill, NC: The University of North Carolina Library, 2007). See Part IV in particular.

5. Raffle, *The U.S. Health System*, 90–92.

6. Taken from Centers for Medicare and Medicaid Services. See Appendix I for updated required and optional services.

7. The Henry J. Kaiser Jr. Family Foundation, *SCHIP Reauthorization: Key Questions in the Current Debate.* (The Kaiser Commission on Medicaid and the Uninsured, CA, August 2007), 1.

8. Health Policy Studies Division, National Governors' Association, Center for Best Practices, *MCH Update: Early State Trends in Setting Eligibility Levels for Children and Pregnant Women.* September, 1998.

9. Congress of the United States, Congressional Budget Office, *The State Children's Health Insurance Program* (Washington, DC: Congress, May 2007). See also Cindy Mann, Diane Rouland, and Rachel Garfield, "Historical Overview of Children's Health Care Coverage," *Future of Children*, 13, no. 1 (2003), 38.

10. Kaiser, *SCHIP Reauthorization*, 2.

11. Kaiser Foundation, The Kaiser Commission on Medicaid and the Uninsured, *Deficit Reduction Act of 2005: Implications for Medicaid.* February 2006, 6.

12. Jeanne M. Lambrew, *The State Children's Health Insurance Program. Past, Present, and Future* (Washington, DC: The Commonwealth Fund, 2007) and Congressional Budget Office, *The State Children's Health Insurance Program* (Washington, DC: Congressional Budget Office, May 2007).

13. Suzanne Felt-Lisk, Rebecca Dodge and Megan McHugh, *Trends in Health Plans Serving Medicaid—2000 Data Update* (Washington, DC: The Kaiser Commission on Medicaid and the Unemployed, November, 2001), 6.

14. Ibid., Table 12, 20.

15. Martha Derthick, "Going Federal: The Launch of Medicare Part D Compared to SSI," *Publius* 37, no. 3 (Summer, 2007), 351–370.

16. Congressional Budget Office, *The State Children's*, 11, 12.

17. Vernon Smith, Jason Cooke, David Rousseau, Robin Rudowitz and Caryn Marks, *SCHIP Turns 10: An Update on Enrollment and the Outlook on Reauthorization from the Program's Directors.* (Kaiser Commission on the Uninsured, May 2007), 12.

18. For example, see Deil Wright, *Understanding Intergovernmental Relations* (3e) (Belmont, CA: Brooks Cole, 1988), particularly chap. 6.

19. *Statistical Abstracts of the United States*, 2007. Table 421.

20. David Mechanic, *From Advocacy to Allocation. The Evolving g American Health Care System* (New York, NY: The Free Press, 1986), 45.

21. Mechanic, *From Advocacy to Allocation*, 207.

PART V

TITLE XX: SOCIAL SERVICES AND THE SOCIAL SECURITY ACT

An Introduction to Title XX of the Social Security Act

With the addition of Title XX, the Social Security Act now contains four social welfare initiatives. Social insurances, assistance programs, and health programs were all part of the initiatives included in some form in the original Social Security Act. Title XX adds the social services (see Figure 1.2). It may seem strange to those who use the social insurances, depend on the welfare assistance programs, and/or benefit from the health programs authorized by the Social Security Act that no formal social services were discussed by the Committee on Economic Security, nor did social services become a formal part of the Social Security Act until 1975. Part of this omission, undoubtedly, was due to the emphasis on economic security as the purpose for the original Social Security Act. But part of this omission of social services from the original Social Security Act was also due to the long-standing tension between two social welfare constituencies: the social reformers and the social caseworkers.

Chapter 1 offered a glimpse of the role social reformers played in the development of America's social welfare enterprise. From the work of Dorothea Dix to the First White House Conference on Children (1910), this group of social welfare advocates sought commitments from the Federal Government and the states in order to establish a foundation upon which the Social Security Act, particularly its assistance titles, could be built. These social reformers sought structural changes in American society that would alter social and economic conditions that, in their view, gave rise to America's most pressing social problems. Clearly, many in President Roosevelt's administration were social reformers themselves or at least sensitive to the social reformers' agenda.

But there was another social welfare constituency, the social caseworkers, who perceived America's social problems differently. While not oblivious of America's depressing social problems, nor less concerned about social change than the social reformers, this group undertook to help America's disadvantaged lift themselves up in spite of the hardships they faced. As discussed in Chapter 9, the social caseworkers emerged from a lineage of social evangelists who became united under the leadership of Mary Richmond, who, arguably, was the founder of the Social Work profession.

The basic difference between the social reformers and the social caseworkers was not so much a different view of American society, but a difference over how to address America's social problems. According to Mary Richmond, the social reformers adopted a "wholesale" approach to social change, while she and the social caseworkers developed a "retail" method. The social reformers' "wholesale" method emphasized a single approach for all, while the social casework method sought an individual, one-at-a-time solution that would lead to true social reform. "Social case work does different things for and with different people—it specializes and differentiates; social reform generalizes and simplifies by discovering ways of doing the same thing for everybody," Richmond wrote.[1]

Based on the philosophical differences between the social reformers and the social caseworkers, it is easier to understand why the social caseworkers exerted little or no influence over the development of the Social Security Act, and why their views were largely ignored. In fact, the social caseworkers believed that providing cash assistance, without a careful assessment of how an individual might use that cash assistance, would undermine the character of the individual and contribute to further social disorganization. Thus, the negative attitude that Harry Hopkins and some others on the Committee on Economic Security held toward social caseworkers discussed in Chapter 9 is more understandable.

But the differences between the social reformers and the social caseworkers really go much deeper than their different approaches to social change. Philosophically, America's certainty regarding the "laws of science," which were transformed into a social theory by Herbert Spencer, challenged efforts of social reform, not because *laissez faire* government was ideologically preferred, but because the laws of nature were immutable—facts that governments could not change. The social caseworkers took comfort in Social Darwinism, while social reformers took umbrage from these views. This deep-seated difference not only prevailed in 1935, but still succeeds today in shaping ideology that blunts efforts to develop more effective social welfare policy.

The creation of Title XX of the Social Security Act represents an historic milestone in the development of American social welfare policy. The formal recognition of social services, integrated into an established social welfare policy document, challenges the historic ideological difference between social reform and individual development as methods to achieve social change. Title XX contrasts policy that does the same thing for everybody with policy that does different things for and with different people. As part of America's foundational social welfare document, the inclusion of Title XX raises a distinction between social welfare as a right and welfare assistance as a social obligation, between social insurance and welfare assistance, and more specifically between the goals of SSI and the goals of TANF. The provision of social services under Title XX might humanize the social insurances by articulating the individual characteristics of the beneficiaries. Title XX social services might also undermine efforts to bestow a form of welfare rights on the assistance programs, as an extended legacy of the 1996 welfare reform. The discussion of Title XX social services in Chapter 9 provides a framework for addressing these questions for American social welfare development.

NOTES

1. Mary Richmond, *The Long View* (New York: Russell Sage Foundation, 1930), 374.

9

Title XX: Social Services

Introduction

Title XX was added to the Social Security Act in 1975 after a long tussle over public funding for social services. The legislation that created Title XX contained two parts. The first part of Title XX finally established the legitimacy and funding for public social services (Part A); the second part (Part B) amended Title IV of the Social Security Act creating Title IV-D, the Child Support Enforcement program discussed in Chapter 6. The Child Support Enforcement Program was integrated into Title IV. Title XX, discussed in this chapter, is most frequently known simply as the social services title of the Social Security Act. Title XX was constructed to provide grants-in-aid to states and thus fit the policy framework of federal–state administered program, a program that provided in-kind products, and a program of entitlement based on need (see Figure 1.2). In 1981, the authority to provide social services under Title XX was combined with several other social service initiatives into a social services block grant, greatly expanding the original flexibility of Title XX social services so that all the federal funds from the Social Services Block Grant (SSBG) are used by states in just about any way states wish, with eligibility for services and specific services established by the states. Need-based criteria for social services were eliminated for all practical purposes by this 1981 consolidation, although need-based criteria still apply in some states and in some circumstances.

In many ways, the prolonged struggle to include social services as part of America's social welfare commitments highlights several of the major contextual issues that have also been characteristic of similar efforts to amend the Social Security Act discussed in the previous chapters. Formalizing social services with a specific title in the Social Security Act was an incremental process pushed along by social service advocacy groups. Advocacy support for social services developed as AFDC (Title IV-A) cases began an unprecedented increase during the mid-to-late 1950s. Leading advocates for social services argued that by applying social work counseling skills, the social pathologies that led to financial dependency could be reversed and that welfare recipients could be rehabilitated, but states and the Federal Government clashed over fiscal responsibility for social services. The development of Title XX, therefore, highlights social welfare debates over (1) opposing understandings about the best way to reduce welfare dependency, (2) political struggles between the states and the Federal Government, and (3) advocacy pressure on Congress that set in motion a contest over state versus Federal administrative social welfare authority. In addition to these general themes, the development of Title XX raised (4) confusion over the meaning and purpose of public social services themselves.

Context for Title XX Development

How Best to Reduce Welfare

The context for Title XX evolved out of different understandings about the best way to reduce welfare dependency, which were steeped in social welfare history. The use of social services as a tool to reduce welfare had created problems throughout the development of the Social Security Act. Harry Hopkins was scornful of social services as a way of dealing with economic need, as was reflected in an outspoken opinion given in a speech at the 1930 National Conference of Social Welfare.[1] Because charity workers of that day for the most part decried direct cash relief to the poor, as Roosevelt's Emergency Relief Administrator, Hopkins drew his immediate staff from trusted "social reformers" who advocated direct financial relief for persons in economic need rather than what were later called forms of "social rehabilitation."[2] The original Social Security Act contained no provisions that might provide any support for a form of social services. Even Title IV-B, which provided substitute homes for financially dependent children, was viewed as a program of financial support for children, rather than a social service, as it sometimes is viewed today. By 1945, however, social service proponents began to have a louder voice arguing that those who received financial assistance needed help using assistance to improve their lives. As a result of the experiences of providing assistance under Titles I, IV, X, and XIV (the four assistance titles that existed before 1962) a rudimentary form of social services crept into assistance administration, and these crude social services were paid for as a part of administrative costs.[a]

A legacy of social services as a means to reduce economic dependency reaches much deeper than American welfare politics. The legendary Saint Vincent de Paul (1576–1660) sought to help those in need by bringing the advice and council of the wealthy to the poor as the chief way to help them escape poverty. "To send money is good, but we have not really begun to serve the poor till we visit them," he preached.[3] The evangelical Scottish minister Thomas Chalmers (1780–1847) reorganized welfare relief in Glasgow, Scotland, by substituting church-based social services for provision of cash.

---

[a] See Charlotte Towle, *Common Human Needs* (New York: National Association of Social Workers, 1945). Towle's book evolved from research she engaged while a staff member of the Federal Security Agency. When the Federal Security Agency refused to make Towle's conclusions public, the National Association of Social Workers later published her research paper in book form. *Common Human Needs* is one of the first documents that argue successfully for the inclusion of social services as part of providing welfare assistance, and thus, according to the National Association of Social Workers, was sufficient reason for the Federal Security Agency not to publish it. Towle did not suggest replacing cash assistance with social services, only that both were necessary.

Arguing that Christian moral education "will make head against poverty in any other form than that of being fixed and legalized,"[4] Chalmers wrote, "[A poor family] gave way to this right moral suasion, and application for the stipulated quarterly sum was only made twice. ... Thus by a trifling expenditure, a sum of at least fifty-fold was save to the [public relief agency]."[5] Chalmers' method of substituting morally relevant social services for cash relief formed the basis for organizing welfare efforts in London and quickly spread to America through the creation of Charity Organization Societies beginning in 1877. It was through her participation in the effort to expand the effectiveness of the Charity Organization Societies in America that Mary Richmond sharpened her message of "a hand up, not a hand out,"[6] which later developed into the credo of the profession of social work.

The early social workers' fervor fanned their commitment to social services as a substitute for cash assistance and helps explains in part their resistance to the cash provisions in the original Social Security Act and Harry Hopkins' antagonism toward them. Up until the Great Depression, social welfare had been organized around the work of the Charity Organization Societies, which relied on private charitable giving and a parsimonious use of cash to augment social services that would lead the poor out of poverty. Early social workers accepted the assistance titles of the Social Security Act as necessary but not sufficient to help the poor. Determining eligibility for cash assistance, however, was not a straightforward activity, and it required a certain amount of skill, as discussed in the introduction to Part III. The early assistance workers therefore looked to the social workers as a source of knowledge about how to work with the poor, gradually integrating simple forms of social services into the act of providing assistance.

Thus, a form of rudimentary social services regularly became part of the standard activities of administering the assistance programs, and their importance was highlighted in a study conducted by the American Public Welfare Association published in 1952. Among its general findings that were favorable to social services, this study showed that those families that received social services along with their assistance depended on welfare for shorter periods of time than their counterparts who did not receive social services, and the children in families that received social services along with their assistance performed better in school.[7] The publication of the American Public Welfare Association (APWA) study, and a later follow-up study published in 1963,[8] brought continued pressure from those who provided assistance at the state level for a greater use of social services to assist welfare dependent adults.[b] As pointed out in Chapter 6, during the ten-year period between these two studies

---

[b] The APWA reports marked the beginning of a process, now quite familiar, of developing social studies designed to support particular social welfare policy goals, and used to support the position of advocacy groups in the push for social welfare development. Political advocacy turned scientific. As President of APWA, Dr. Ellen B. Winston shepherded the study. Winston later became DHEW Commissioner of Welfare in the Kennedy administration.

social service advocates joined with other welfare-friendly groups to support the 1959 amendments to Title IV that provided funds to states to support an unemployed parent in the Title IV assistance grant, and the change in the name of Title IV from Aid to Dependent Children (ADC) to Aid to Families with Dependent Children (AFDC).

President Kennedy's new Secretary of Health, Education, and Welfare (DHEW), Abraham Ribicoff, was sympathetic to the petitions of public welfare administrators for social services, and shortly after his appointment, he issued directives to various department heads supporting Social Rehabilitation Services (SRS) and a family-centered approach to reduce welfare dependency, leading to the creation of a new agency within the Department of Health, Education, and Welfare designed to coordinate all social services—Social and Rehabilitation Services (SRS).[9] At the same time, the Kennedy administration had shown considerable sympathy to America's poverty problems. The President's trip to Appalachia and Michael Harrington's galvanizing book *The Other America* drew early presidential commitments to improve the condition of the poor. Kennedy's re-creation of the Food Stamp program, and his ground work for what later became President Johnson's War on Poverty, raised congressional concerns about possible increases in public spending. The findings of the American Public Welfare Association fueled expectations that poverty could be addressed by providing social services rather than providing additional cash assistance to the poor. Thus, the Kennedy administration easily allied itself with social workers of the "old school," who advocated personal change as a new way of addressing poverty within the fiscal constraints of the assistance programs.

The pressure to fund social services, independent of other assistance administrative costs, was satisfied, in part, with the creation of the 1962 amendments to the Social Security Act. Under the pressure of the continued build-up of Title IV AFDC recipients, these amendments broke new ground in the provision of assistance by reorienting Title IV assistance from its traditional emphasis as a cash program to a program focused toward "rehabilitating" and "preventing" economic dependency. The 1962 statutory changes to Title IV provided funds specifically for social services and led to significant changes in the administration of Title IV assistance programs. In subsequent years, the DHEW required a separation of staffs in local welfare departments into two groups— those who determined eligibility for assistance and those who provided social services—and required the renaming of Departments of Public Welfare to Departments of Social Services. The 1962 amendments also provided generous funding to educate social workers who could provide social services in welfare departments.

But neither the 1962 amendments to the Social Security Act nor Ribicoff's commitment to social services as a form of social rehabilitation settled the conflicting views over the value of social services to the overall problems of reducing welfare dependency. Even though the case for social services was carried under a different banner as part of President Johnson's War on Poverty, social services failed to deliver reductions in welfare dependency.

Among the neoconservative critics of Johnson's "service strategy," such as Charles Murray,[10] perhaps none was more outspoken than Daniel Moynihan. Moynihan's disdain for social services, in general, and social workers, in particular, is well documented in his explanation of the creation of Supplemental Security Income (SSI), discussed in Chapter 5.[11]

President Nixon's welfare reform proposed a guaranteed income, the Family Assistance Plan independent of social services, but it also proposed continuing the mandatory work requirements for adults receiving AFDC, the Work Incentive Program (WIN) created as part of Title IV in 1967. Called WIN, the 1967 Title IV amendments were largely ineffective because, in the view of some, there were not sufficient social services available to help individuals transition from welfare to work, creating a somewhat paradoxical situation for Nixon's Family Assistance Plan. Daniel Moynihan and the Nixon administration inherited the Kennedy–Johnson social service legacy and wanted to move away from a service strategy. However, the expectation that Title IV recipients needed social services in order to transition to work forced the compromise that finally created Title XVI: Titles I, X, and XIV were consolidated into the new assistance program (SSI), without any funded social services, but Title IV was left to stand alone with its social service commitments in place.[c] In retrospect, funding for social services was left in Title IV largely because Congress accepted a strategy of social rehabilitation for Title IV adult assistance recipients, and it believed that social services were important in the process of moving persons from welfare to work.

Intergovernmental Struggles

Political struggles between states and the Federal Government, a frequent issue in the development of the assistance programs, became the center of a vitriolic confrontation over the matter of social services. The grant-in-aid financing structure allows a role for the Federal Government in social welfare policy development by defining the terms of federal spending, subsequently affecting state spending as well. The need for discretionary latitude for the administration of assistance programs at the state and local levels frequently conflicts with an ideal of program uniformity sought by the Federal Government. While such tensions are characteristic of American Federalism, they often escalate past tension and reach the level of conflict in matters of social welfare administration. Federal–state differences over program implementation shaped the context for developing Title XX, just as such difference had a major impact in the 1996 welfare reform of Title IV (see Chapter 6) and the 2001 State Child Health Insurance Program (see Chapter 8).

---

[c] Supplemental Security Income created a federal assistance program that was now sterile of even rudimentary social services, thus prompting the National Association of Social Workers to propose draft legislation to create state-focused social services as a companion to SSI in 1972. See Paul A. Mott, *Meeting Human Needs. The Social and Political History of Title XX* (Columbus, Ohio: National Conference on Social Welfare, 1976), 40.

Spending for social services grew rapidly with the buildup of social services that followed the 1962 amendments and the 1967 legislation sympathetic to social services in the Title IV program. The federal social service regulations promulgated in the 1967 legislation were formalized only months before President Nixon assumed the presidency. These regulations greatly expanded fundable social services to include persons or families that could qualify as potential, current or former welfare (Title IV) recipients. These expansive criteria for funding social services did not go unnoticed by the states. Since states were already providing financial support for a number of social services that had been independent of public assistance, it was convenient for states to argue that the mentally ill, persons in state correctional systems, and others, were potential, if not actual, welfare recipients, and thus the monies spent on these social services qualified for federal matching under the new welfare regulations. Lacking any clear social service definitions from the Federal Government, states quickly took advantage of the open-ended characteristic of social service funding to draw down large sums of federal monies to support their existing social services. The result of the states' liberal interpretation of federal regulations produced a fiscal nightmare for the Federal Government, particularly DHEW. State spending for matching federal social service funding increased sixfold in a three-year period.[12]

Political Advocacy

Chapter 1 discusses the politics of grant-in-aid funding. Advocacy groups develop cohesion and purpose when a specific grant-in-aid satisfies their interests. The groups, in turn, provide political support for political actors who supported the grant. Advocacy groups for social services, led mostly by the National Association of Social Workers and the American Public Welfare Association had a strong voice in social welfare administration during the Kennedy–Johnson presidencies. The career bureaucrats and the well-respected Wilbur Cohen in particular, who was appointed DHEW Secretary by President Johnson, had been and remained a strong ally of those seeking social services, and Cohen's support was clearly evident in the development of the 1967 regulations. Generally disliked among social welfare liberals, the Nixon administration provided an environment for other politically liberal groups to join in the social services fracas.

Although tension always existed between a service strategy and an income strategy for dealing with economically needy persons, the rapid expansion of social service spending contributed to the attractiveness of the income strategy promoted by Daniel Moynihan during the early days of the Nixon administration. But even before the Family Assistance Plan began to take shape, DHEW under the Nixon administration sought ways to restrict social service spending by seeking a "cap" on the social service appropriation. The eventual "cap" of $2.5 billion, however, resulted in a disproportionate distribution of limited federal funds. States like California and Illinois that had already expanded their programs drew down the bulk of the allocated funds, while states that were more cautious in shifting their social service spending to federally approved social services found that they were too late to benefit from the federal largess.[d]

Even though the 1972 SSI program had failed to include social services, the Nixon administration continued to insist that general social services had no place in welfare reform. In November and December 1972, DHEW issued guidelines to its regional offices that were designed to limit the scope of state social service spending and were to be used for approving state social service programs. In February 1973, DHEW issued proposed formal rules defining those social services that would be eligible for matching federal funding. These February regulations proposed to restrict federal matching funds for social services only for those services that were provided to potential welfare recipients whose incomes did not exceed 133.5 percent of the state's current financial assistance payment, restricted the purchase of social service from private social service agencies, and specified 17 social services that would qualify for federal matching funding.

Not only did these regulations propose limits on future social service development, but they also allowed the Federal Government to seek a return of federal funds from states that had previously offered unapproved social services. The outrage from the states was immediate and loud. The National Governors Association led the opposition to the February proposed rules aided by social welfare advocacy groups.[e] Meeting with members of Congress, the Governors sought to bring pressure on DHEW to liberalize its proposed social service regulations, and over 200,000 letters protesting the proposed regulations were received by DHEW. But when DHEW issued its final regulations in April, 1973, the restrictions placed on social services were largely unchanged. Between February 1973 and December 1974, a delegation of the National Governors Association met with representatives of DHEW at least four times, at the suggestion of Representative Al Ullman, a member of the House Ways and Means Committee who urged the Governors and DHEW to reach a consensus on their differences.[13]

Under increased pressure from the Governors and from social welfare advocacy groups, Senator Long opened hearings on the social service regulations. Not wanting to write detailed social service legislation, the Senate Finance Committee proposed and Congress passed legislation postponing all social service regulations until January 1975. But with time running out for Congress, the Senate Finance Committee proposed and Congress adopted legislation

---

[d] The 1972 legislation that "capped" social service spending at $2.5 million (part of "Revenue Sharing" under the Local Assistance Act of 1972) provided that state spending prior to the first quarter of fiscal 1973 would be reimbursed for expenditures that had taken place before the "cap" went into effect. See Andrew Dobelstein, *Politics, Economics and Public Welfare* (Englewood Cliffs, NJ: Prentice Hall, 1980), 191, for further discussion of this complex process.

[e] Mott, *Meeting Human Needs*, lists 33 national and state level advocacy groups that formed a coalition to pressure Congress to intervene with DHEW in the development of social service regulations.

on December 20, 1974, that specifically prohibited the Secretary of DHEW from denying payments to states "on the grounds that the payment is not an expenditure of the provision of a service." This legislation was signed into law by President Ford January 4, 1975, creating Title XX to the Social Security Act.

Background Summary

The Title XX social service context became unsettled as advocacy groups aggravated the antipathy of Congress over the discretionary authority of the Nixon administrative agencies. A robust amount of administrative discretion accompanies the implementation of any statute. After all, the administration of a grant-in-aid requires an administering agency to make legislation fit the circumstances that exist in a state if the legislation is to be implemented successfully. As early as 1970, when President Nixon resubmitted his Family Assistance Plan to Congress, Senator Long complained that DHEW failed to spell out how it would implement the legislation. To Senator Long, the Nixon administration was asking Congress for a blank check that would leave important details of the president's proposal in the hands of DHEW administrators. Senator Long complained,

> The question of administrative policy authority becomes even more important when it is noted that both Secretary Finch and Secretary of Labor Schultz who were the chief architects of the Family Assistance Plan have been replaced and no longer serve in those capacities. ... [W]e do not yet know how the new Secretar[ies] ... plan to administer this discretion ... nor do we know how long either of them will remain in office, or how their successors will apply the discretion they would assume under this bill.[14]

Somewhat ironically, the social services regulations proposed in February fueled the Senate's perception that now the Nixon administration was stepping beyond its traditional role of balancing federal expectations with state needs. Congress had passed the compromised Family Assistance Plan (SSI), an expansion of federal authority over an area of traditional state responsibility, eliminating social services for the aged, blind, and disabled, and instituting an entirely new way of dealing with welfare dependency, but now Congress was facing a Nixon administration initiative that would alter the framework of Title IV assistance by sharply restricting social services. Advocacy by the governors and well respected social welfare organizations spoke without any opposing coalition of groups advocating in support of efforts to restrict social services. The "hands off" approach Congress had taken toward social welfare had changed from the early days of the Social Security Act, when Congress respected the discretionary activities of the welfare administrators.

Social welfare became highly politicized over the February 1973 regulations. The welfare constituency that had supported the development of the Social Security Act and its programs in previous years had influence over the

Act's social welfare development through personal relationships between those sympathetic to social welfare development and high-ranking federal administrators who shared similar views, as pointed out in previous chapters. But the Nixon administration brought a group of people into welfare administration who were management oriented, rather than oriented toward social welfare issues. In retrospect, the Family Assistance Plan itself was an effort to shift the focus of assistance programs away from traditional social welfare concerns that required discretionary decisions to implement assistance programs, to forms of welfare that required no discretion in their administration. By eliminating social services, the Nixon Administration also eliminated the voice of advocates who were part of that Congress' political constituency and who had developed influence through grant-in-aid funding. The controversy over social services provided a golden opportunity for the Senate to exercise its authority over President Nixon and his administration, and with the help of the social welfare community, it did.

The Mystery Social Services

Finally, Title XX developed in the confusion over the meaning and purpose of social services. In spite of consistent pressure for a combination of services and cash payments in the assistance programs, there was little agreement among those in the social services community over the exact nature of social services. One of the first reports provided by the DHEW in 1967 defined social services as "those human services rendered to individuals and families under societal auspices," and Dr. Ellen Winston, Commissioner of Welfare in DHEW[f] at the time called social services "what a social worker does."[15] Thus, from the very beginning of their formal recognition, social services were poorly conceptualized by the welfare administrators, badly understood by the people who provided them, and strongly resisted by those who were forced to receive them.

The February 1973, DHEW regulations sought to resolve the ambiguity in social services by specifying 17 permissible services, a solution that was much too restrictive for social services advocates. Title XX addressed this dilemma in two ways. First, social services were separated into two types. "Hard" social services consisted of various forms of in-kind products, like day care, medical services, food, and clothing, for example. "Soft" services were forms of counseling that would be used to achieve goals of self-support and personal independence. Second, instead of providing a list of either hard or soft services that could be provided by Title XX funding, the legislation listed five goals that the services were proposed to meet, and whatever the state provided in the way

---

[f] Dr. Ellen Winston was intimately connected with the social service struggle. A graduate of the University of Chicago with a doctorate in sociology, Winston served as Director of Public Welfare in North Carolina for forty-two years. As president of APWA, she urged and oversaw the 1952 APWA study. Her able administrative skills were matched with her acute political sensibility. See Andrew Dobelstein, *Public Welfare in the American System: The North Carolina Experience* (a dissertation to fulfill academic requirements, Duke University, 1973).

of a service that in the view of the state met one or more of these five goals would thus constitute a legitimate social service.

An individual state plan proposing how federal money would be spent was always required for approval as a condition of grant-in-aid funding, whether for a categorical grant-in-aid program or for the use of block grant funds. Title XX, therefore also required that states submit a state plan for the use of Title XX funds, specifying the amount money that states proposed to spend, and the services states would provide with the funds. These proposed services would be required to meet one or more of the required goals. Then, prior to the next funding cycle, states were required to report the extent to which the services they provided were spent on the goals they specified in the state plan. The states did not have to document whether the substance of the goals were met, however. For example, states did not have to report the numbers of persons who became employed as a result of receiving counseling services under Title XX funding. Although this reporting approach was designed to provide accountability for the use of social service spending under Title XX, the idea was to determine the number and types of social services the money bought rather than accounting for social service spending by counting what social service spending actually produced. Thus, without clear definitions of social services, this form of reporting never generated any measurable outcomes from social service activities, provoking a social service mystery.

Background Conclusions

The social and political turmoil of the decade during which social services developed as a formal part of the Social Security Act contributed to a changed context for social welfare policy development under the Social Security Act. The Kennedy assassination, the war in Vietnam, the generally faulted overly optimistic War on Poverty, the urban riots, and the growing distrust of the Nixon administration leading to "Watergate" and Nixon's resignation all contributed to an environment of social and economic instability that affected social welfare development, and an accompanying distrust of government.

Arguably, however, the departure of Wilbur Cohen from the DHEW and Congressman Wilbur Mills' personal problems leading to his decision to retire from Congress provided a climax to these events for the social welfare community. After the "two Wilburs" left, government social welfare policy development under the Social Security Act experienced a shift to a decidedly partisan political character. The process of negotiation and accommodation between those who administered the Social Security Act, the various presidents, and the Congress, had clearly ended. The steady incremental development of both the insurance and assistance programs was replaced by a new political process wherein political differences resolved through negotiation were replaced by partisan political clashes. In other words, debates over social welfare development became a partisan political tool, not so much as a means to resolve ideological conflicts over welfare, but as a means to win a partisan political advantage. When contrasted with the 1962 amendments, in many ways the development of Title XX of the Social Security Act epitomized the change in the politics of welfare, where welfare debates served to achieve a political victory, rather than providing an opportunity to reach a compromise over a contestable difference in the direction of social welfare development.

The Program Structure of Title XX

Chapter 1 proposes a distinction between social welfare programs and the social welfare policies that underlie their development, cautioning that the distinction between social programs and their social policies may be difficult to make. The program and policy structure of Title XX represent a good example of how programs and policies are often fused together. Perhaps because Title XX emerged from a politically partisan struggle with the Nixon administration, Title XX policy, or even a general expectation for Title XX programs, was never clearly articulated. The five objectives set forth for Title XX social services, identified and discussed below, were stated in such nebulous terms that they proved inadequate for establishing a clear program of social services. For whatever reasons, however, the program structure of Title XX, both originally and throughout its development, continued to interact with changing understandings of social services policy, creating uncertainty about whether Title XX social services constituted a program, a policy, a combination of both, or neither.

The Omnibus Budget Reconciliation Act (OMBRA) of 1981 established a high water mark in the politics of social welfare budgeting.[8] Unhappy with the amount of federal spending allocated to domestic programs, President Reagan's budget director, David Stockman, proposed to the president that he, David Stockman, broker an agreement with congressional leaders to settle the differences between the president's budget and that proposed by Congress through a budget reconciliation process.[16] As a former Congressman, Stockman understood the congressional budget process, and he was confident he could convince Congress to accept some of the reductions President Reagan advocated, if Congress agreed to accept President Reagan's total budget figure in exchange for Reagon's deferral to Congress about where budget reductions would take place.[17] Congressional leaders assigned the president's proposed social welfare budget reductions to various congressional committees, and in order to avoid political pressure from social welfare advocates who would fight to preserve and perhaps even expand specific grant-in-aid programs, most committees took the programs under their jurisdiction, rolled them into a single block grant, reduced the amount of the total of the block grant, and passed

---

[8] The budget reconciliation process had been used before 1981 and many times since to resolve competing claims over the use of federal monies to support social welfare objectives. The budget reconciliation process was a major factor affecting the 1996 welfare reform discussed in Chapter 6.

the reduction of the total block grant to the states to let the states decide which programs to reduce. The SSBG was thus created by putting 12 existing social welfare grant-in-aid programs, including funding for Title XX, into one of the nine block grant programs created by the 1981 budget agreement, and the total expenditure for the new SSBG, which included Title XX funding, was capped at $1.7 billion.[18]

The Social Service Program under Title XX

On the one hand, social service advocates bewailed the reductions in social service spending, but on the other hand, the SSBG created an even larger environment for social service activity. The administrative authority for Title XX and the entire SSBG were given to the Office of Community Services, Administration for Children and Families, Department of Health and Human Services, as an administrative effort to coordinate social service spending and to make social services more effective. The program structure of social services under the SSBG, however, continued to depend on the creation of specific services that meet the five goals spelled out in the Title XX legislation and summarized in Box 9.1. Even though these five goals purport to govern spending decisions over all of the SSBG funds, the structure of the SSBG gives states unlimited flexibility to fund virtually any service they determine meets one of the goals. Not only are these five social service goals quite broad, but the words "as far as practicable

---

Box 9.1 Federal Criteria for Certifying SSBG Social Services

"Services funded by the SSBG as far as practicable under the conditions of that state are directed at one or more of these five goals:

- achieving or maintaining economic self-support to prevent, reduce or eliminate dependency
- achieving or maintaining self-sufficiency, including reduction or prevention of dependency
- preventing or remedying neglect, abuse or exploitation of children and adults unable to protect their own interest, or preserving, rehabilitating or reuniting families
- preventing or reducing inappropriate institutional care by providing for community-based care, home-based care or other forms of less intensive care
- securing referral or admission for institutional care when other forms of care are not appropriate or providing services to individuals in institutions"

Source: Office of Community Services, Administration for Children and Families, Department of Health and Human Resources, 2008.

under the conditions of that State" leave additional room for states to fund almost any activity with social service funds that the state wishes to fund. Furthermore, the goals for funding social services with Title XX now included as part of the SSBG funds overlap with monies available to fund services authorized under other programs. For example, "preventing or remedying neglect, abuse of exploitation of Children" overlaps with funding for children services under Title IV, CAPTA (see Chapter 6).

The ability of states to mix SSBG monies with social service monies that emerge from different sources of social welfare authority makes it almost impossible to determine a specific program structure for social services under SSBG funding. For example, when TANF was created in 1996 (Chapter 6), states were given permission to transfer a portion of their TANF funds to supplement their SSBG spending. Thus, monies allocated for Title IV services, such as day care, could be used for other social service purposes, even though TANF spending was restricted to persons whose incomes do not exceed 200 percent of the poverty level. While this provision enabled states to find a use for all their TANF funds, mixing different spending sources defies clear program expectations for social services, and while state discretion has great value, the uncertainty of state spending lacks accountability and weakens public support for social welfare in general.

To provide some structure for social service spending, the Federal Government provided a list of 29 "examples" of social services,[h] with language that defines each service (see Box 9.2). With the exception of the TANF funds, there is no federal income eligibility criteria that individuals must meet in order to be eligible for SSBG supported social services, although the five goals and the social service "examples" imply the use of funds for persons in some sort of economic need. Essentially, states are free to set levels of economic need if they so desire, but even if SSBG funds provide economically dependent persons with access to services they would be unable to secure on their own, focusing social service spending on the low income still does not limit cross-program spending. Furthermore, the list of "suggested services" provided by the Federal Government present a combination of both "hard" and "soft" social services. Thus, in the final analysis, there is no clear program structure to the provision of Title XX services under the SSBG.

---

[h] Adoption services, Case management, Congregate meals, Counseling services, Day care—adults, Day care—children, Education and training services, Employment services, Family planning services, Foster care services—adults, Foster care services—children, Health-related services, Home-based services, Home-delivered meals, Housing services, Independent/transitional living, Information and referral, Legal services, Other services, Pregnancy and parenting, Prevention and intervention, Protective services—adults, Protective services—children, Recreation services, Residential treatment, Special services—disabled, Special services—youth at risk, Substance abuse services, Transportation, and Other.

Box 9.2 Uniform Definitions of the Five Most Used SSBG Services

Day Care Services—Children

Day care services for children (including infants, preschoolers, and school age children) are services or activities provided in a setting that meets applicable standards of State and local law, in a center or in a home, for a portion of a 24-hour day. Component services or activities may include a comprehensive and coordinated set of appropriate developmental activities for children, recreation, meals and snacks, transportation, health support services, social service counseling for parents, plan development, and licensing and monitoring of child care homes and facilities.

Foster Care Services—Children

Foster care services for children are those services or activities associated with the provision of an alternative family life experience for abused, neglected, or dependent children, between birth and the age of majority, on the basis of a court commitment or a voluntary placement agreement signed by the parents or guardians. Services may be provided to children in foster family homes, foster homes of relatives, group homes, emergency shelters, residential facilities, child care institutions, pre-adoptive homes, or a supervised independent living situation. Component services or activities may include assessment of the child's needs; case planning and case management to assure that the child receives proper care in the placement; medical care as an integral but subordinate part of the service; counseling of the child, the child's parents, and the foster parents; referral and assistance in obtaining other necessary supportive services; periodic reviews to determine the continued appropriateness and need for placement; and recruitment and licensing of foster homes and child care institutions.

Home-Based Services

Home-based services are those in-home services or activities provided to individuals or families to assist with household or personal care activities that improve or maintain adequate family well-being. These services may be provided for reasons of illness, incapacity, frailty, absence of a caretaker relative, or to prevent abuse and neglect of a child or adult. Major service components include homemaker services, chore services, home maintenance services, and household management services. Component services or activities may include protective supervision of adults and/or children to help prevent abuse, temporary nonmedical personal care, house-cleaning, essential shopping, simple household repairs, yard maintenance, teaching of homemaking skills, training in self-help and self-care skills, assistance with meal planning and preparation, sanitation, budgeting, and general household management.

Protective Services—Children

Protective services for children are those services or activities designed to prevent or remedy abuse, neglect, or exploitation of children who may be harmed through physical or mental injury, sexual abuse or exploitation, and negligent treatment or maltreatment, including failure to be provided with adequate food, clothing, shelter, or medical care. Component services or activities may include immediate investigation and intervention; emergency medical services; emergency shelter; developing case plans; initiation of legal action (if needed); counseling for the child and the family; assessment/evaluation of family circumstances; arranging alternative living arrangements; preparing for foster placement, if needed; and case management and referral to service providers.

Special Services for Persons with Developmental or Physical Disabilities or Persons with Visual or Auditory Impairments

Special services for persons with developmental or physical disabilities, or persons with visual or auditory impairments, are services or activities to maximize the potential of persons with disabilities; to help alleviate the effects of physical, mental, or emotional disabilities; and to enable these persons to live in the least restrictive environment possible. Component services or activities may include personal and family counseling; respite care; family support; recreation; transportation; aid to assist with independent functioning in the community; and training in mobility, communication skills, the use of special aids and appliances, and self-sufficiency skills. Residential and medical services may be included as an integral but subordinate part of the services.

Source: As defined by the Office of Community Services, 2007.

Any evidence of a social service program structure must be gleaned from an examination of the services states are likely to fund with SSBG money. The wide-ranging state social service plans, however, provide only a very basic understanding of the program features of Title XX/SSBG social services. Even this effort is highly fragmentary, because not all states use Title XX/SSBG to fund all of the "suggested" social services, even though there is common knowledge that "suggested services" are being provided, but probably from a mixture of funding sources. For example, the single greatest SSBG block grant expenditure is for child foster care (14 percent of all funds), but only 38 states use SSBG monies to fund foster care. Most foster care funding is provided under Title IV of the Social Security Act, as discussed in Chapter 6, and thus SSBG funding for

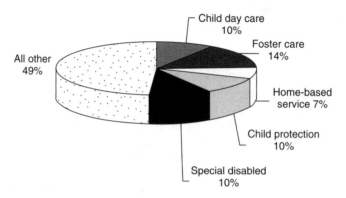

Figure 9.1. Distribution of SSBG Services.

foster care is most likely used to supplement other types of Title social service spending and vice versa.

Block grant funding for protective services for children is another of the top five SSBG spending categories (10 percent of all funds), but only 41 states use SSBG monies to help fund protective services for children. The rest of the funding for child protective services comes from Title IV-B and IV-E, also discussed in Chapter 6. Five services, such as child day care, foster care for children, protective services for children, home-based services, and special services for the disabled, therefore, constitute approximately 51 percent of all SSBG spending for the latest reported period of SSBG spending.[i] These spending patterns are summarized in Figure 9.1.

The age of the recipients of SSBG funding is another way to characterize SSBG social services. As might be expected, most of the social services are provided to children as seen in the age distribution in Figure 9.2 below. Children

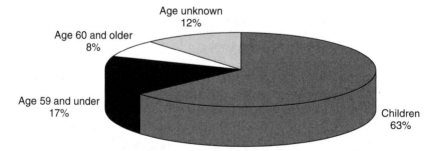

Figure 9.2. Age Distribution of SSBG Recipients.

---

[i] Annual Report of SSBG spending, 2005. Total SSBG spending included $1,700,000,000 Title XX funds, and $832,000,000 transfer funds from Title IV TANF for a total of $2,513,000,000 for federal FY 2005.

receive 63 percent of the Title XX/SSBG funded services, with only 8 percent of the services provided to persons over age 60. The cross-funding of social services with established Title IV obligations provides a more likely explanation for this spending mismatch than the likelihood that the elderly are less in need for social services than are children.

In conclusion, the program structure of the SSBG represents an uneven use of SSBG funds by the states, with states favoring the use of SSBG funds to provide services to children, especially for day care, foster care, and protective services. But even with an obvious preference for children's services, the actual use of SSBG monies among the states is much too diverse to summarize. Although the Office of Community Services requires and makes public each state's social services plan, a review of these plans fails to show any uniform use of social services. In fact, the funding aims of state social services programs are so unspecified that the SSBG acts more like a form of revenue sharing, the most flexible kind of federal grant-in-aid program.

Funding

As noted above, funding for Title XX/SSBG takes place through a capped block grant that allows maximum state program flexibility. SSBG funds are distributed on the basis of population only, with no provision for factors that would make the funds more redistributive, such as percentage of poverty in a state. Thus, states with the largest populations are likely to receive the largest share of the SSBG funds. No state matching is required in order to receive social service funds, but funds that are not spent by some states are available for distribution to other states, which can demonstrate the need for additional funding. Such open-ended funding criteria also contribute to questionable use of social services, particularly since there is a strong motivation on the part of the states to spend all their social service allocation with spending only a small amount of their own funds. Thus, as Figure 9.3 illustrates 45 percent of all SSBG spending takes place in three states: California (23 percent), Texas (12 percent) and Illinois (10 percent). The size of a state's population may have little to do with a state's need for social services.

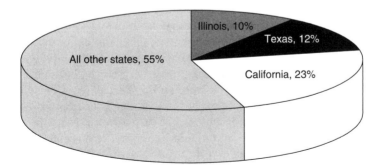

Figure 9.3. State SSBG Spending.

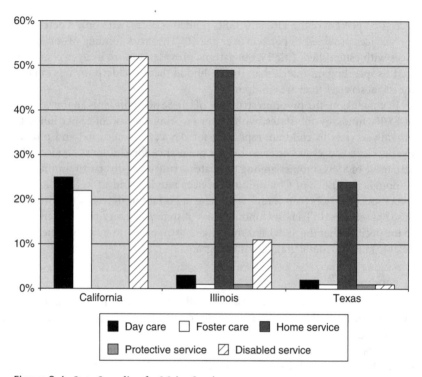

Figure 9.4. State Spending for Major Services.

The lack of a coherent use of Title XX/SSBG funds is also illustrated by Figure 9.4. A comparison of social service provided among the five greatest social service spending states suggests there is little or no pattern of social services, regardless of how states may define them. Thus, there is no framework that would provide accountability for social service spending. Comparing the five most used services with the states that receive the most funding for social services shows the variability that exists in social service spending in the states. California spends almost all of its social service monies on day care, foster care, and services to disabled. California spends none of its SSBG monies on either home-based services or protective services for children. Illinois, by comparison, spends only 3 percent of its SSBG monies on child day care, and only 1 percent each on foster care and child protective services, but it spends 49 percent of its SSBG funds on home-based service. Finally, Texas, the state that receives the third highest amount of SSBG funds, spends 2 percent of its social service funds on day care, 1 percent on child protective services, 1 percent of disabled services, and 24 percent on home services. The other 71 percent of Texas' SSBG spending is spread over the other program categories.

Funding for Title XX began with a $2.5 billion cap that was reduced to $1.7 billion when it was rolled into the SSBG in 1981, and the SSBG has remained at that funding level through 2007. In 2008, the funding will be reduced to

$1.2 billion, but as noted earlier, other monies can be rolled into social service spending by the states, and special federal appropriations to the SSBG also take place from time to time. In FY 2007, for example, $832 million was added to the SSBG as transfers from TANF (Title IV-G), and in 2005, $550 million was added to the SSBG for hurricane relief. Both the TANF and hurricane relief monies are restricted in their use. However, the definitions of the use of these funds allow the substitution of these funds for services that might have been funded under other program authorities. Any additional funding to the SSBG must follow the guidelines provided by the 29 "suggested" social service programs, but the generality of the guidelines provides no clarity for social service administration. Interestingly enough, the hurricane relief monies were allocated among all the states, although most of it went to Louisiana and Mississippi. Originally due to expire in 2006, states will be able to draw down hurricane relief funds until September 2008.

Title XX/SSBG Policy Structure

The unstructured program makeup of Title XX/SSBG points to a lack of its clear policy foundation. The formal recognition and funding for social services in 1962, provided no rationale for their usefulness to the assistance programs, nor clarity about their substance beyond the APWA 1952 study. While the 1962 amendments represented a major achievement for the profession of social work, which had for years promoted its helping methods in the assistance programs, the amendment was vague as to how social services would augment the assistance programs. At last, social services provided by qualified social workers gained the public status social work had sought for decades as it struggled to establish its professional identity. The test came in the midst of the rise in assistance caseloads of the late 1960s. As social workers claimed to have the skills necessary to confront the growing welfare dependency, the public looked to social services to address growing welfare concerns. "Social rehabilitation" became the general objective for social services. The WIN program, the substance of the 1967 amendments to Title IV promoted social rehabilitation as the goal, social services as the means, and social workers as the persons who could reduce welfare dependency. The results of this experience were modest at best.[19]

The 1962 amendments to the Social Security Act openly acknowledged and funded social services as important additions to the assistance programs, but the 1972 SSI program stripped social services from the process of providing assistance to the aged and disabled. The expectation for social services that continued to receive funding, therefore, drifted toward the Title IV programs where social services were still a relevant activity, and where states were free to determine their own social service programs. The continuing policy freedom of Title XX/SSBG has allowed states to develop social service programs that they believe are needed in their state and to use SSBG monies to augment social services that might also be funded under other program authority. Without clear policy goals to the contrary, social services have expanded as extensions of the social services that existed under the continuing assistance authority of Title IV, and most Title XX/SSBG funds continue to support Title IV-related programs.

"Free standing" or Specified Social Services

A fundamental policy issue developed over the value of social services to the goals of social welfare once they had independent authority. Decoupling social services and assistance following the 1962 amendments gave rise to an even higher social work vision: "freestanding," universal, publicly funded social services. As if "rehabilitation" was too limiting for the vision of social work, the questionable contribution of social services to the goals of the 1967 amendments and eliminating social services from SSI amplified the cry for more far-reaching, independent social services. Alfred Kahn, a well-known social work educator and social welfare policy expert, encouraged the movement to independent social services, arguing that existing social services were so closely tied into Title IV policy that they were ineffective and that pubic policy decisions that did not allow social services to "stand free could support a questionable [public] policy."[20]

At the height of the post-Title XX euphoria, Sheila B. Kamerman and Alfred Kahn provided a vision of social services that was enthusiastically endorsed by social workers. Noting that "the purview of social welfare has traditionally been limited to five fields: education, health, income maintenance, housing and unemployment," Kamerman and Kahn foresaw a sixth field, "the personal social service system" that "address[es] unique needs and institutional circumstances and have their separate, identifiable valued societal function." "An important characteristic of these services," Kamerman and Kahn continue, "is that they are not conceived as services for the poor alone."[21]

But Kamerman and Kahn's lengthy tome left the basic question over social services unanswered. The review of this enthusiastic polemic by the well-known Robert Morris of Brandeis University was more sanguine. Morris summed up the fundamental problem of social services: "There is little in the [Kamerman and Kahn] volume that clarifies what changes in human well-being are expected to result from our [social service] ministrations, although improved well-being is assumed."[22] Thus, in an all too characteristic American social welfare policy development, the incremental "tinkering" with social services has left them far short of the Kamerman and Kahn vision.

The irony of the social work effort to establish publicly financed support for its work arose in an environment that required a corresponding explanation of what social services could actually accomplish. In important ways, social work was promoting social services established on psychoanalytic principles that supported methods of helping persons examine their own psychological motivations. This was a historic form of social service introduced by Mary Richmond in the early 1900s, now infused by modified psychoanalytic theories that, like their historic antecedents, presumed that personal change would lead to changed behavior, and changed behavior would lead to an escape

from poverty. "Free standing" social services appealed to this method of helping. Social services tied to existing welfare programs with defined expectations
of what the services should accomplish did not. When tied to the assistance
titles, social services might at least promote their value as tools of social rehabilitation. But "stand alone" services had no defined social welfare social value.
To the extent that "free standing" social services promoted personal growth and
development, the whole effort to develop professional social services separated
the profession of social work from its traditional concerns for and support
of social welfare.[23] Assistance recipients found professional social work services unhelpful, and professional social workers found assistance recipients
unmotivated to accept help.[24]

Morris' conclusion defines the major policy problem with social services
as presently authorized under Title XX and funded through the SSBG. After
over thirty years of funding, there is nothing in the administration of public social services that clarifies the "changes in human well-being" that public
social services have achieved or seek to effect, and the subsequent movement of social work away from the poor in the face of its unsuccessful bid
for comprehensive social services has eroded the quality of the social services
presently offered under Title XX and the SSBG. Even social services specifically applied to serious problems, such as "Family Preservation" services,
fail to demonstrate their effectiveness. Daniel Moynihan, in his characteristic
disdain for social services, continued to raise serious doubts about their efficacy up to his last days in the U.S. Senate. In 1996, he complained that his
favorite ineffective program "was something called 'family preservation,' yet
another categorical aid program," concluding that evaluations have failed to
substantiate whether such programs are effective or not.[25] The policy structure of Title XX/SSBG social services is based on an enthusiastic but dubious
foundation.

Evaluating Social Services

The inability to evaluate social services raises a second serious policy issue. The
program structure of social services spreads them over numerous subject areas
all at the discretion of the states. There is no mechanism in place that could provide any reliable information about what the social services are doing, let alone
what they are accomplishing. This does not mean that the Federal Government
must be the evaluating authority. The authority to evaluate social services must
rest with the states under the present SSBG structure; yet states, too, have failed
to develop the intelligence necessary to use social services to achieve desirable social welfare objectives. At the very least, an acceptable state and federal
social welfare policy would require that the states assume the responsibility for
explaining the reasons they have spread their social service resources as they
have. Under the present circumstances, the responsibility for conceptualizing
social service takes place at the state level. The present reporting information
obtained by the Federal Government from pre- and post-social service plans

is useless for such an effort. Responsible social welfare policy requires a level of accountability for the use of public funds that is not present in the existing method of federal monitoring. Without prescribing how state social services should be conceptualized and evaluated, the Federal Government could simply require that states have such instruments in place as a condition for ongoing funding.

Quality Control

Issues of quality are an even more serious policy issue than either defining social services or evaluating their use. An effective social services policy would address two quality control issues: the quality of the services themselves and the quality of those providing the service. It might be useful to explore both these issues with an example. In the case of child day care, most states certify both that the service provided meets certain quality standards and that the provider has sufficient qualifications to provide the service. Granted that these quality standards are minimum, are not uniformly and rigidly enforced, and vary from state to state, elements of the facility are, at a minimum, evaluated for safety, cleanliness, and adequacy, while characteristics of the service providers are evaluated to make sure they have no criminal records or history of child abuse. Of course, one would hope for more rigorous standards of quality and a means to terminate the service if the standards of quality are not met and that these minimum standards are enforced.

The fact that most states have some standard that day care providers must meet attests to the need for quality control in all the social services provided with Title XX/SSBG funds. When one considers that many social services are often provided in inadequate facilities and without adequate supporting resources, and when one realizes that many of those who provide social services are poorly trained and marginally educated to do so and lack any certification as to their ability to provide the social service that they render, social services start to seem a nightmare. Considering that social service providers are intervening in the lives of other people, often as agents of government, such as removing children from homes or testifying as to a person's sanity, some obligation to protect the public must be enshrined in public policy. Although many individual social agencies have established quality standards for social service work, and many social service providers are highly qualified and certified to do their work, these efforts do not satisfy the overall issue of social service quality control. Notwithstanding the quality controls that do exist in specific instances of providing social services, without clear policy to ensure their quality, social services as now provided lack legitimate support for activities, that seriously intervene into others' lives. For example, the fulfillment of the obligation of government to protect the welfare of children under *parens patriae* demands a level of quality the social services have not been able to demonstrate (see Chapter 6).

The Value of Social Services to Social Welfare Goals

A final, less weighty consideration of the policy structure of social services concerns their relationship to the main policy objectives of the Social Security Act. If social services are important enough to claim a separate title in the Social Security Act, and are an important part of America's social welfare obligation, then they are also important enough to be monitored for their effectiveness in meeting those obligations. The social services that have been added to the Social Security Act both as amendments to Title IV and with the creation of Title XX offer one of the best examples of incremental development of the Act and its parts without a clear objective or purpose. As a consequence, the growing weight of social services has pushed the Social Security Act away from its primary mission of ensuring a modest level of income security for Americans. A more precise definition of social services might argue for their continued inclusion in the Social Security Act. But, incorporating "free standing" social services into the Social Security Act's social welfare commitments as they presently exist not only stretches the limited authority of the Federal Government, but social services now redirect the purpose of social welfare to activities that are less tangible and more difficult to monitor and evaluate activities. There may be many socially appropriate reasons to develop and support free-standing social services, but the purpose of these social services and the nature of their integration into the fabric of American social welfare policy have not been sufficiently accounted for.

Conclusion

The slow, steady development of social service activity that gradually integrated social services into the assistance programs came to an abrupt halt when the Nixon administration took office. First, the Family Assistance Plan, which looked innocent enough at its inception, stripped social services from the assistance programs after the 1962 amendments had given previous social services their legislative authority. But SSI failed to include Title IV in its reorganization of the assistance programs, encouraging social service advocates to seek expanded services under Title IV and to urge the further development of social services completely independent of assistance programs. For its part, the Nixon administration persisted in its efforts to restrict social services by defining fundable social services and limiting their funding, and social services became a battleground between social service advocates and the Nixon administration. Thus, the political struggle for social services was not about their importance to America's social welfare commitments, since this relationship had never been made clear, but rather a contest among political adversaries. Without a Wilbur Cohen to direct a negotiated settlement among political adversaries and with Congress unhappy with the president, independent social services emerged from this contest, not because social services established their effectiveness, but because they won the political struggle.

Social services were the source of yet another irony in the Nixon Administration's effort to reform welfare through the Family Assistance Plan. Nixon gained office in part by challenging the social service strategy of Johnson's Great Society. But he also argued that the social services provided largely to African Americans and were not available to the whole "silent majority." The development of Title XX was as complicated by a confusion of sometimes conflicting policy objectives as was the development of Title XVI. In many ways, the development of the political contest over the 1996 welfare reform that created TANF began with the tangential changes in social welfare policy direction that began during the Nixon administration.

In her analysis of the development of social services, Martha Derthick concluded that the administrative bureaucracy within the DHEW lost control of the social services that had developed parallel to the assistance programs. "[T]he disintegration of specialized, professional control removed an important counterweight at the federal level to the influence of politicians" and "disintegration of professional control at the federal level increased the influence of politicians at the state level."[26] Derthick argues that the 1967 DHEW reorganization that created the SRS, and the later Nixon effort to set fiscal controls on all domestic spending, including social spending, deprived the professional social welfare specialists in the Bureau of Family Services from setting standards for social services.

> Had services grants remained under the jurisdiction of the BFS [Bureau of Family Services], and had that bureau been permitted to perpetuate itself, services would have taken a highly predictable course: lower case loads for workers, lower supervisory ratios for casework supervisors, more professional training for workers, more elaborate individual services plans for clients, and a slow steady reaching out for more clients.... Professional administration turned out to have had the virtues of its defects.[27]

Ten years earlier, in her seminal work on Title II Social Security, Derthick concluded, "The executive leaders of Social Security believed their program to be a special case that merits insulation from partisan politics and standard processes of budget preparation.... In that sense, they designed Title II Social Security to be uncontrollable."[28] Title II, Derthick argues, was made uncontrollable because administrators isolated program development from political discussion. But Derthick argues that better professional control of social service development leading to Title XX could have *prevented* it from becoming uncontrollable. Derthick's somewhat different critique on the role of professional administrators in social welfare development raises an important issue. In the case of Title II Social Security, the professional administrators certainly guided its development throughout most of its history, often without political input. But Derthick points to the lack of professional control of social services, which undermined the orderly development of welfare relevant social services. When should welfare policy development be left to the fortunes of political discourse, and when do professional administrators know best?

Social Services: The Comfort Food of Social Welfare

Social services do not deserve the vitriol of Daniel Moynihan or others who believe that social services have no place in the repertoire of social welfare policy. Nonetheless, the social welfare value of social services has never been clearly justified. In 1965, Henry J. Meyer published the results of a study he and his colleagues conducted on the effect of social services in helping adolescent girls improve their lives. Meyer and his colleagues found that the social services the girls received had no measurable effects on their behaviors.[29] Meyer and his colleagues, including the highly esteemed Edgar Borgatta, who developed the Borgatta Scale, a well-known statistical instrument, were summarily attacked as heretics by the social work community that had inherent faith in, but little substantive evidence about, the value of social services. On a grander scale, there is little evidence that the massive effort to develop public social services in the aftermath of the 1962 amendments contributed anything to the overall economic improvement among welfare recipients and others in poverty. One noted social work educator, George Hoshino, called the contribution of social services to the welfare of economically dependent persons "dismal."[30]

On the other hand, a reassuring voice when a child is in trouble, or a thoughtful reflection with a helping person when facing a major personal crisis, or a serious conversation with a knowledgeable person for those who need help sorting out problems in their lives and seeing how they might do things differently, all are necessary and comforting activities. Whether individuals should be denied such comforts just because they cannot afford to pay for them is clearly a social welfare policy issue.

Wilbur Cohen was a member of the energetic group that helped shape the original Social Security Act into its present form, and his influence extended to some of the most significant developments in both the insurance and assistance programs. Likewise, Wilbur Mills, arguably one of the most astute tax experts in the history of Congress, also oversaw and, in the final analysis, promoted some of the most far-reaching additions to the Social Security Act. And it may be that the character of social welfare political discord can be traced to the end of the partnership between Wilbur Mills and Wilbur Cohn. After an entire career in what was then the DHEW, Wilbur Cohen, who became DHEW Secretary in the spring of 1968, resigned shortly after President Nixon assumed office. Wilbur Mills lost control of the House Ways and Means Committee after a sex scandal in 1974, and he declined to run for Congress in 1976. As Derthick points out, Cohen could have counseled the disputing parties about how to settle the social service controversies, had anyone asked him, and Mills could have found a political solution. The politics of welfare moved in a different direction beginning in the 1970s, and Title XX social services was the flagship.

NOTES

1. Robert E. Sherwood, *Roosevelt and Hopkins* (New York: Harper, 1948), 45–47.
2. Andrew Dobelstein, *Moral Authority, Ideology, and the Future of American Social Welfare* (Boulder, CO: Westview Press, 1999), 77–78.
3. Quoted in Frank Watson, *The Charity Organization in the United States* (New York: Macmillan, 1922), 19.
4. Thomas Chalmers, *On Political Economy in Connection with the Moral State and Moral Prospects of Society.* (New York: D. Appleton, 1832), 12.
5. Quoted in Carl DeSchweinitz, *England's Road to Social Security* (Philadelphia: University of Pennsylvania Press, 1943), 111.
6. Mary Richmond, *Friendly Visiting Among the Poor* (New York: Macmillan, 1899).
7. Gordon Blackwell and Byron Gould, *Future Citizens All* (Chicago: American Public Welfare Association, 1955).
8. Elaine M. Burghess, *An American Dependency Challenge* (Chicago: American Public Welfare Association, 1963).
9. See Andrew Dobelstein, *Politics, Economics, and Public Welfare* (Englewood Cliffs, NJ: Prentice Hall, 1980), 22–23. Established: In the Department of Health, Education, and Welfare (HEW) by HEW Secretary's reorganization, August 15, 1967.
10. Charles Murray, *Losing Ground* (New York: Basic Books, 1994).
11. See also, Daniel P. Moynihan, *The Politics of a Guaranteed Income* (New York: Vintage Books, 1973). In particular, see pages 306–315.
12. Paul E. Mott, *The Social and Political History of Title XX* (Columbus, Ohio: National Conference on Social Welfare, 1976). See page 22 in particular. The lack of social services provided by public agencies did not slow the growth of social service spending since public agencies simply purchased services from private agencies.
13. Mott, *The Social and Political History of Title XX*, 40–41.
14. U.S. Congress, Senate Committee on Finance, *H.R.16311, The Family Assistance Act of 1970, Revised and Resubmitted,* 51.
15. Mott, *The Social and Political History of Title XX*, 46.
16. See John Palmer and Elizabeth Sawhill, *The Reagan Record* (Cambridge, MA: Ballinger, 1984).
17. For a beginning understanding of this complex process, see Robert Keithy and Bill Heniff, *The Budget Reconciliation Process* (New York: Nova Science, 2006).
18. See U.S. General Accounting Office, *Block Grants: Overview of Experiences to Date* (Washington, DC: U.S. Government Printing Office, 1985).
19. Leonard Goodwin, *Do the Poor Want to Work?* (Washington, DC: The Brookings Institution, 1972).
20. Alfred Kahn, *Social Policy and Social Services* (New York: Random House, 1973).
21. Sheila B. Kamerman and Alfred J. Kahn, *Social Services in the United States. Policies and Programs* (Philadelphia: Temple University Press, 1976), 3, 4.
22. Robert Morris, "Social Services in the United States: Policies and Programs," *Social Service Review* 60, no. 3 (1969): 373.
23. Andrew Dobelstein, "The Bifurcation of Social Work and Social Welfare: The Political Development of Social Services," *Urban and Social Change Review*, 18, no. 1 (Winter, 1985).
24. Harry Specht and Mark Courtney, *Unfaithful Angels. How Social Work has Abandoned its Mission* (New York: The Free Press, 1994).

25. Daniel Patrick Moynihan, *Miles to Go: A Personal History of Social Policy* (Cambridge: Harvard University Press, 1996), 147 and 48.

26. Martha Derthick, *Uncontrollable Spending for Social Service Grants* (Washington, DC: The Brookings Institution, 1975), 112.

27. Derthick, *Uncontrollable Spending for Social Service Grants*, 111.

28. Martha Derthick, *Policymaking for Social Security* (Washington, DC: The Brookings Instituton, 1970), 416–417.

29. Henry J. Meyer, Edgar F. Borgatta and Wyatt C. Jones, *Girls at Vocational High: An Experiment in Social Work Intervention* (New York: Russell Sage Foundation, 1965).

30. George Hoshino, "Money and Morality: Income Security and Personal Social Services," *Social Work* 60, no. 3 (April 1971): 20.

10

The Social Security Act for America's Twenty-First Century

Introduction

Between the lines of the Social Security Act is a story about the historic shift in America's welfare commitments seventy-five years ago, which ushered in the full partnership of the Federal Government. It is the story of how America created comprehensive social insurance programs for retired and disabled workers and their families, providing them with cash income and health insurance. It is a story about how America has used its unique intergovernmental structures to overcome limitations in the U.S. Constitution in order to provide financial and medical support to people in economic need. While perhaps not as comprehensive in its social welfare provisions nor as generous in its benefits as the systems in other economically advanced nations, the Social Security Act represents a significant achievement as America forges ahead into the twenty-first century. For all of its limitations, the Social Security Act offers tangible evidence of our nation's commitment to provide for the general welfare of all Americans.

The previous chapters provide the details of the Social Security Act's story. These chapters tell why and how the various parts of the Act developed; they report the programs' different parts and explain how and to whom the programs are provided; they examine the policies, or the objectives, of existing programs, raising challenges for better harmonizing the social policies and programs. The previous chapters depict the incremental development of the Social Security Act, sometimes with small steps, other times by large jumps, creating the present wide array of policies and programs authorized under the Act. Some of this incremental development was driven by clear goals; some of the development was driven by pointed social concerns that needed an expedient response, and some of the Social Security Act's incremental development has been driven by narrow partisan political objectives. The previous chapters point to the changes the Social Security Act must tackle in order to respond to America's twenty-first social welfare challenges.

If the 1996 welfare reform debates accurately indicated the direction of America's social welfare future, the Social Security Act and its programs will certainly fail to satisfy America's social welfare obligations. Expedient program development within a growing partisan political climate has fostered a contemporary policy environment of social welfare discourse that is largely devoid of substantive concern for the welfare of economically disadvantaged Americans. Beyond the present political controversies directed at some of its fundamental elements, the legacy of and the expectations for the Social Security Act continue to represent the way America cares for its economically disadvantaged; the Social Security Act is the manifestation of some of America's highest ideals as they are expressed in the Declaration of Independence, affirmed in its Constitution, and inscribed on the magnificent statue dedicated to liberty that stands at the historic point of entry into this country. The future development of the Social Security Act as simply a political document, devoid of its fundamental concern for the welfare of Americans, undermines liberty for the economically depressed and freedom for those who are forced to work for their welfare benefits. If it is to continue as America's foundational social welfare commitment in the twenty-first century, the Social Security Act must continue to give voice and substance to some of the most important ideals America lives by today.

The Social Security Act contrasts with earlier and present-day Federal Government social welfare ventures. The Federal Government provided pensions for *Union* Civil War disabled soldiers in 1890, later extending benefits to *Union* Civil War veterans and their wives. The Federal Government did establish the Freedmen's Bureau after the Civil War to help resettle newly emancipated African Americans, a program administered by the Union army, which was short on both cash and empathy for the newly "freed" men. The Federal Government did provide free land to those who sought to settle the West under the Homestead Act (1862), at the expense of many Native Americans who had already claimed those lands. The Federal Government did give states land to establish institutions of higher learning, the Land Grant Colleges, in 1862, but these grants had as much to do with providing military training as they did with preparing men to be better farmers.[a] Today, the Social Security Act is buttressed by the Housing Act, which provides access to housing while protecting housing investments, the Earned Income Tax Credit (EITC), which mitigates low-paying employment, and other public commitments, described below, but these and other Federal Government efforts, often driven by larger political purposes, pale in comparison with the social welfare commitments made by the Social Security Act.

America's lofty ideals find their most meaningful expression through the institutions of American governance, but clearly these institutions have given precedence to national economic development in ways that continue to frustrate social welfare development. American governance is negative governance in its most general understanding. America's governing structures were established to restrain government and to check the expansion of government power. The national government was given specific powers that defined what

---

[a] The initial Morrill Act stated in part, "... without excluding other scientific and classical studies and including military tactic, to teach such branches of learning as are related to agriculture and the mechanic arts ... in order to promote the liberal and practical education of the industrial classes in the several pursuits and professions in life ..." (7 U.S.C. § 304) See Chapter 1 for further discussion.

it could do. These powers were specified, limited, and divided among different functional units, or branches, so that no single part of the Federal Government could exercise all of the specified power, and those powers not specified in the Constitution of the United States were left to the individual states and to the people. Creating and sustaining the Social Security Act in this type of governmental structure is a major achievement and a challenge for twenty-first-century America.

America's twenty-first-century social welfare challenge, however, is further burdened by the limitations of American governance, which has favored the development of free economic enterprise over the development of welfare. The Federal Government reserved to itself the power to regulate commerce between the states, establish a common currency and set its value; it set up a National Bank to protect economic development in ways that private banks could not; it intervened in private enterprise only when one enterprise monopolized the free economic expression of another. By contrast, the Federal Government reserved no welfare powers to itself; its commitment to promote the general welfare was unaccompanied by any specific authority to do so. The development of any form of public welfare policy languished in such economically friendly but laissez faire social welfare environment. Until the Great Depression of 1929–1934, America encouraged economic development with less than modest government concern for the welfare of individuals. The Great Depression and its economic consequences for individual Americans forced the Federal Government to take steps to "promote the general welfare," even in the face of economic advice to continue its laissez faire course. The vision of those who created the Social Security Act and their commitment to American ideals, rather than America's governmental framework or its economic philosophy, account for the crucial place the Social Security Act holds today as the foundation document of American social welfare policy. Thus, the Social Security Act needs continued public nourishment and sustained enlightened leadership if it is to grow effectively into the twenty-first century.

The Social Security Act in Today's Environment

This chapter summarizes modifications that the Social Security Act must consider making today because of the significant changes that have come over the national landscape, perhaps even drastic changes, since the Act was created in 1935. Demographically, America has not only grown in size, but the character of the American population has become different. At the beginning of the twenty-first century, America is facing the largest heterogeneous influx of foreign-born people since the Western Europe immigration in the early 1900s. Today, arrivals from Pacific Rim nations have changed the character of America's Western states, while migrants from Mexico and other South and Central American states, many of them illegal immigrants, have flooded the Southwest and Southeast, bringing cultural preferences that have challenged American's usual respect for some degree of difference. African Americans are on the cusp of achieving fully functional citizenship, and the rights of Native Americans are gradually being restored. Today's large-scale social and demographic changes have not only stretched traditional American cultural patterns, but they have had a profound impact on America's social welfare commitments and the capacity of the Social Security Act to respond to them.

The culture shock brought about by the changing nature of the American family has been difficult to assimilate. Beginning with the changing economic and social roles of American women, taking them from being homemakers to important economic players in individual families as well as in the nation at large, to the growing acceptance of radically changed forms of marriage, which now have legal sanction in a number of states, child-rearing environments that are common today were unthinkable forms of legitimate family life seventy years ago. Social and cultural changes, such as the idea that same-sex partners can legally adopt a child, or that female partners can conceive and rear a child without the assistance of a male, or that unions of same-sex couples can be recognized as legitimate marriage, or that out-of-wedlock childbirth is no longer socially taboo, or that divorce is an acceptable way to deal with un-reconciled marital problems, or that once unacceptable sexual mores are now commonplace, have placed enormous pressures on all of America's social institutions, and provisions in the Social Security Act must find ways to integrate these new patterns into our commitments to children.

Economically, a "global economy" has produced permanent shifts within America's labor markets. Outsourcing of both parts and finished products in the manufacturing sector has re-focused the nature of American jobs from manufacturing to services. Today, all jobs are subject to change, and there are no longer sanctuaries of lifetime employment. On the one hand, America has been exporting low-skilled jobs, but on the other hand, America is also importing low-skilled, poorly educated laborers, creating a mismatch between American workers and American jobs. While official unemployment remains within economically tolerable limits (as presently measured), there is reason to believe that long-term, hard core unemployment persists, particularly among inner-city youth who have dropped out of the labor force. Poverty rates in America have remained relatively unchanged over the past decades in spite of unprecedented American economic growth. New labor demands simply have not kept up with domestic labor resources.

Changes in the character of the American economy have also challenged the ability of elderly Americans to live out their retirement years in relative economic security. Volatility in preretirement investments has devastated retirement plans for many of the elderly. The collapse of large employers has left many workers without their retirement packages, including health care benefits, and uncertainties in the housing market, one of the traditionally safest forms of retirement savings, has left many elderly without adequate resources in spite of their well-developed financial plans. America's future is in the hands of its children, but the elderly are America's heritage, the architects of a great nation.

Politically, support for social welfare, particularly government-supported social welfare, declined gradually after the Kennedy–Johnson efforts to reenergize America's social welfare commitments. President George W. Bush's determined efforts to turn Title II Social Security into a private retirement system showed both the distaste for a government commitment to its elderly and an ignorance about Social Security's significance, while the 1996 welfare reform evidenced a conservative political repudiation of America's social obligation to children. While political decisions have always determined the framework for America's social welfare commitments, recent welfare politics have taken advantage of legitimate differences over the nature of America's welfare obligations to further partisan causes, rather than as a spur to resolve conflicting claims over the use of scarce public resources to assist economically dependent Americans. As social welfare decisions have become polluted by partisan politics, public conviction to provide help for needy Americans has diminished correspondingly.

Finally, the outlook of Americans in the 1930s was very different from how they view their lives today. The economic panic that gave rise to the Social Security Act has been replaced by a growing economic malaise that is characterized by lower wages, rising personal debt, rising health care costs in the face of diminished health services, and persistent poverty, crime, and deterioration in our urban centers while corporate salaries reach all-time highs. The 1930s attitude that government could fix the problems gave way in the 1980s to the attitude that government is the problem. And while this view may have abated somewhat in recent years, there is still a large measure of antipathy toward government that is endemic to American political culture and discussions of its social welfare obligations. Unlike the environment of the 1930s, American government's grudging response to today's economic disquiet blankets our nation in a peaceful state of economic depression.

The Social Security Act stands amidst a host of challenges to America in the twenty-first-century. Anchored in history, the Social Security Act and its commitments to social welfare are challenged by an America that is very different in many ways from how it was in that history. How the Social Security Act responds to these changes in American life will determine whether American social welfare policy will continue to give voice and substance to the lofty ideas today's Americans have inherited from their ancestors, or whether today's Americans will repudiate those goals in favor of more self-serving ones. Social welfare in America is at yet another social welfare crossroad, with the Social Security Act as its guidepost.

The Theory of Social Welfare Imbedded in the Social Security Act

While battered by contemporary social, economic, and political challenges, an underlying theory of social welfare in the American system provides support for the Social Security Act and the program changes these challenges demand.

First, the Social Security Act provides a structure for America's commitment to ensuring income maintenance to Americans through a form of social insurance for the retired and the unemployed and by assisting states in providing welfare assistance to others, notably the disabled and children. Second, the Social Security Act has also established a foundation for ensuring access to health care for the aged and disabled social insurance beneficiaries, and for "medically indigent" persons. Third, the Social Security Act provides a foundation for the development of far-ranging forms of social service, which states provide to their residents. Finally, the Social Security Act acts as an instrument of social welfare linkage with contemporary public policy undertakings that hold social welfare relevance, but that were developed outside its authority.

The social welfare architecture that is in place finds underpinning from its theory of welfare; a welfare architecture does not have to be created anew in the face of today's challenges, nor is a new theory of welfare necessary. In other words, the structure of the Social Security Act is compatible with a theory of social welfare in the American system that still holds today, at least in part. Although the original Committee on Economic Security crafted its proposals pragmatically from the hard datum of the early 1930s, their efforts were not empty of a theory of welfare in the American experience. Thus, the Act's fundamental division between insurance and assistance, the former a federal obligation and the latter the responsibility of the states, the former based on a contractual "right" and the latter based on economic need, not only reflected long-standing welfare practices, but also legitimated America's theoretical framework for meeting its social welfare obligations. Furthermore, although highly idealistic, the expectation that a gradually expanding base of social insurance would eliminate the need for most, if not all, assistance programs explained a seeming inconsistency between the two kinds of welfare activity. Although evidence of a strained relationship between insurance and assistance remains today—assistance satisfies residual social insurance limitations—the social insurances provide the overarching structure to American social welfare; remove them and America's social welfare enterprise unravels into chaos.

The development of health initiatives under the Social Security Act also remains consistent with this theory. A form of health insurance was proposed for the original act, and although two titles of the original act were devoted to providing a residual form of health care, it was the intense pressure from the medical community that thwarted further development of independent health policy and programs under the Social Security Act for thirty years. Theoretically Medicare, Title XVIII, and Medicaid, Title XIX, followed the established two-track social welfare division between insurance and assistance. Both titles were created as companion programs that would mediate between different ideological approaches to America's welfare obligation to ensure access to health care. Clearly, the Social Security Act was the appropriate public instrument upon which to rest these new initiatives. Both Medicare and Medicaid were integrated with existing commitments under the Act. Medicare functioned as an extension of benefits for Title II recipients. Medicaid extended the commitment of the Federal Government and the states to provide medical assistance to the needy. Although both titles dealt with health, they were, in fact, forms of social welfare since they were designed to protect individuals from the costs of medical care rather than as efforts to create different forms of providing health services. Recognition of the social welfare characteristics of Medicare and Medicaid is important for considering present day efforts to reform health delivery systems in the face of the unprecedented role that private insurance has come to play in providing access to the health care system.

Splitting assistance for needy children from assistance for the needy aged and disabled, implemented through the Supplemental Security Income (SSI) program (Title XVI), fractured the Social Security Act's underlying welfare theoretical framework. SSI grafted a basic assistance program on to the social insurance programs, causing policy and program problems for both. At the same time, a fascination with the potential for developing family policy as a base for assisting needy children led to an expansion and extensive modifications of Title IV assistance programs and set assistance for children on an independent welfare course.[b] In light of the experiences with SSI and the subsequent changes to Title IV assistance, SSI has failed to standardize assistance, as reformers had hoped, and while Title IV changes have reduced Title IV assistance cases, they have not done so by putting people to work, or creating stable families that are more responsible for their children. Fortunately for the welfare of children, the other titles of the Social Security Act continue to provide both direct and indirect social welfare benefits to children under Title II, Title III, Title IV, Title XVIII, Title XIX, Title XX, and Title XXI. Thus, the dramatic changes in Title IV assistance have left child welfare policy much more dependent on other titles of the Social Security Act to meet children's social welfare needs. The 1972 welfare reform that created SSI also contributed to unraveling the Act's theoretical framework, as proposals for the Family Assistance Plan were promoted as if welfare assistance could be addressed through "objective" decisions rather than the discretionary decisions of traditional American welfare practices.

The welfare theory underlying the Social Security Act provides the rationale for linking different welfare activities under the authority of the various Social Security Act titles; in addition, the welfare theory supporting the Act does not restrict its programmatic activities to those activities spelled out in its titles. Instead, the Social Security Act integrates its commitments with social welfare initiatives created outside the Act for different social objectives, but with social welfare implications. For example, the Food Stamp program, ERISA, and the EITC have become important forms of income maintenance that are outside the authority of the Social Security Act but still closely linked with the Act's main commitments. The present-day Food Stamp program grew out of a

---

[b] It is interesting to note that post-colonial state welfare laws that required adult children to support their dependent parents had been eliminated decades before efforts were made to enforce the obligations of parents to support their children.

practice of distributing surplus farm goods to low-income persons in 1961, when President Kennedy authorized a previously unused statute to provide vouchers to low-income persons allowing them to purchase surplus farm goods. Food stamps were made permanent on the recommendation of President Johnson in 1964. Although efforts to integrate the Food Stamp program into the structure of the Social Security Act have been unsuccessful, and while Food Stamps have remained part of the U.S. Department of Agriculture, Food, and Nutrition Service, the Social Security Act has facilitated the compatibility of Food Stamp eligibility with most Social Security Act programs, particularly Titles III, IV and XVI, and Food Stamps provide an important form of benefit extension in cases where the Social Security Act's programs are insufficient to meet the full range of economic need. The overlap between Food Stamps and other forms of income maintenance may present administrative complexities, but in the present environment, income maintenance programs and Food Stamps complement one another for households that need them. In 2007, Food Stamps provided an average of $95.64 per month to 26,466,000 households at a total federal cost of $30.4 billion.[1]

Another example of a public policy instrument with social welfare implications might be found in the 1974 Employment Retirement Income Security Act (ERISA) and its accompanying Pension Benefit Guarantee Corporation (PBGC), designed to promote defined benefit retirement plans and protect the value of all types of private retirement instruments for the beneficiaries (see Chapter 2). ERISA and PBGC insure private, employer-based pensions, protecting most of their value for retired workers when employers default on their retirement commitments. The idea, attributed to President Roosevelt, that Title II Social Security, personal savings, and private pensions would make up the retirement income package, has been made more secure by ERISA. Once again, it is important to note that Title II Social Security was never intended to provide all the income resources the elderly would need in retirement. ERISA acts to preserve the 1935 limited expectation built into Title II Social Security. Title II Social Security and SSI burdens would be overwhelming without ERISA and PBGC, and the decrease in private defined benefit plans raises concerns over the future development of Title II Social Security, as discussed below.

Finally, the EITC, created by Congress in 1975, has become an important source of income maintenance for low-income workers. Revised and expanded a number of times since 1975, including a doubling of the program in 1993, and presently indexed with the cost of living, the EITC provides a "negative income tax" for low-income workers. The Internal Revenue Service (IRS) estimates that 21,000,000 families received approximately $36 billion from the IRS in 2004, with the average payment of $1,784 for each qualified tax payer.[2] EITC is an economic instrument that integrates income maintenance with active employment, something structurally difficult for the Social Security Act to do. EITC requires employment with maximum wages not exceeding $36,384 per year per taxpayer with three or more children (2007). Most significantly, EITC meets an important social welfare function, as Steve Holt of the Brookings Institution reports:

> The EITC has proved remarkably successful in reducing poverty. In 2003 the EITC lifted 4.4 million people in low-income, working families out of poverty, more than one-half of them children. Today the EITC lifts more children out of poverty than any other social program or category of programs. Without it the poverty rate among children would be 25 percent higher.[3]

Although the EITC raises the policy question of whether public funds should support low wage employment, or whether this burden should rest with employers, EITC represents another effective income maintenance program tightly connected with the social welfare objectives and existing programs of the Social Security Act. For example, EITC fills the gap between unemployed persons who receive Title III benefits and workers with meager wages. A recent report by the Congressional Budget Office on the effects of the EITC concludes that increasing EITC by 25 percent would result in an additional $1.4 billion going to persons working but earning less than poverty-level wages.[4]

Food Stamps and EITC are among a number of public policy instruments, such as low-income housing under Title II of the Housing Act, that address some of social welfare issues brought about by the changes in American social, economic, and political life. In many ways, these new instruments address social welfare obligations that the Social Security Act failed to address, even though the Social Security Act remains America's core welfare organizing document. The welfare theory supporting the Social Security Act makes it possible to bring what might otherwise be excessively diverse public programs into a form of harmony with larger social welfare goals.

Expanding Welfare Theory through the Social Security Act

The incremental changes in the Social Security Act, along with the development of new instruments that also address America's social welfare obligations, prompt several important observations about the social welfare theoretical framework underlying the Social Security Act and America's social welfare enterprise. The following considerations inform an expanded welfare theory appropriate to America's social welfare obligations in the twenty-first century.

First, America's social welfare obligation is inescapably linked with work. Work is the portal through which all welfare obligations pass. From the social insurances to the assistance programs, and extending to some of the new social welfare instruments, work is the fundamental factor that determines welfare eligibility. Social welfare obligations are extended to those who do work and provided grudgingly for those who cannot work. In American social welfare development, no welfare obligation exists to the exclusion of these two groups. The social insurances are closely integrated with work, and the assistance programs are designed to provide income to the economically needy who cannot work. America's "work ethic" has always been the defining force in social welfare policy development and remains so in twenty-first-century America.

But a major unresolved policy issue arises when work does not pay enough to prevent economic dependency. The transformation of America's labor force has refocused public policy attention on the inability of low-income workers to earn enough to escape poverty, and the increased social welfare obligations exacerbated by low wage employment have shifted social welfare policy development to providing welfare benefits to those who work but still have economic need, and to a modification of Title II Social Security that loosens the link between earnings and benefits. The social services funded under the Social Security Act's Title XX, EITC, and expanded access to medical care for children (Title XXI), for example, command special attention for reshaping the Social Security Act. Where does the responsibility rest when it comes to taking care of those who work but do not earn enough to pay for child care or health care? Once the work obligation is met, then a welfare obligation begins. Both EITC and Title II Social Security provide a prototype for expanding a basic element of America's social welfare principles.

Second, America's social welfare obligation is also inescapably linked with the American economic system. America certainly does not lack the economic resources to provide a higher level of social welfare, as suggested in Chapter 1. America, however, is limited in its structural ability (and perhaps its commitment) to translate those economic resources into useful social welfare products. While structural limitations facing the Social Security Act are discussed in Chapter 1, the development of new public policy instruments provides evidence that less familiar sources of federal authority also offer promising opportunities for social welfare development. America's tax structure, as part of its macro-economic policy, offers greater opportunity for social welfare development than has been exercised. One such opportunity may exist in the tightening of tax laws.

The Federal Government exempts selected items from tax liability. Table 10.1 shows that tax expenditures, as these exemptions are called, equal almost 25 percent of the amount that the Federal Government collects in taxes, and states are likely to grant similar tax exemptions. In other words, if there were no tax expenditures, and if the Federal Government collected all of its taxes allowable under present law, it would have about 25 percent more revenues. Thus, while present federal (and state) spending for social welfare may be close to publicly supportable limits, additional public resources may be available by closing some of the present tax "loopholes" or using tax expenditures more effectively to support social welfare objectives. By redirecting tax expenditures to social welfare objectives, America's economic resources might

Table 10.1. Tax Expenditure Estimates Relating to Individual and Corporate Income Taxes, by Selected Function

Function and Provision	Sub-Total	2007	Sub-Total	2008
National Defense:		3,100		3,200
International Affairs:		21,300		21,020
General Science, Space, and Technology:		16,000		10,240
Energy:		6,910		6,940
Natural Resources and Environment:		1,970		2,080
Agriculture:		1,420		1,460
Commerce and Housing:		370,770		230,315
Financial Institutions and Insurance:	23,230		25,165	
Housing:	191,270		205,150	
Commerce:	156,270		170,2	
Transportation:		3,750		3,975
Community and Regional Development:		3,830		4,050
Education, Training, Employment, and Social Services:		99,126		103,721
Education:	19,150		19,410	
Training, Employment, and Social Services:	79,976		84,311	
Health:		160,240		181,270
Exclusion of Employer-Provided Medical Insurance	141,270		160,190	
Income Security: Exclusion of Employee Benefits:		127,990		12,209
Net Exclusion of Pension (employees) Contributions and Earnings:	6,750		6,869	
Net Exclusion of Pension (employees) Contributions and Earnings:	115,880			
Earned Income Tax Credit	5,360		5,340	
Social Security:		26,560		27,950
Veterans' Benefits and Services:		5,840		4,390
General Purpose Fiscal Assistance:		60,850		55,050
Interest:				
Deferral of Interest on U.S. Savings Bonds		1,330		1,340
Addendum: Aid to State and local governments:		86,360		80,090
TOTAL TAX EXPENDITURES (in Millions of Dollars)		$948,066		$705,820
($705,820 = $705,820,000,000)				

Source: U.S. Office of Management and Budget, Budget of the United States Government, Analytical Perspectives, http://www.whitehouse.gov/omb/budget/fy2008/

be realigned to make the Social Security Act programs more effective for those they serve.[c]

An interesting fact emerges from an examination of Table 10.1. Corporations, as such, are not the largest beneficiaries of favorable tax treatment; individual taxpayers are. Housing, Health, and Income Security tax expenditures provide over half (50.56 percent) of all the "tax breaks," most of which go to individual taxpayers: Housing, $191.2 billion ($89.6 billion in mortgage and real estate tax credits), $160.2 billion for health ($141.3 billion for non-taxable employer funded health care), and $128 billion for income security ($121.2 billion in lost taxes for individual contributions to retirement instruments, such as IRAs). A recent report by the Government Accountability Office concluded, "All federal spending and tax policy tools, including tax expenditures, should be reexamined to ensure that they are achieving their intended purposes and designed in the most efficient and effective manner."[5] The extent to which these and other tax expenditures meet social welfare obligations once again calls attention to opportunities for adjusting the Social Security Act to the twenty-first century.

An important paradox also emerges when social welfare policy is examined from an economic perspective. The Keynesian economic dogma that still underlies American macro-economic policy argues that economic growth depends on aggregate spending either by individuals or by government. Economic recession looms when consumer spending begins to lag and in this environment consumers are encouraged to spend by extending credit at low interest rates or by reducing taxes giving consumers more "spending power." Americans are not encouraged to save except when their lack of saving threatens to become a social welfare problem. Saving enough money for retirement tomorrow reduces spending for economic growth today. This paradox appears in the behavior of individuals as well as that of the national government. Improved social welfare development would achieve a better balance between spending and saving if it were carefully to consider and harmonize the purposes for both without departing from underlying Keynesian economic theories (see Chapter 3).

Third, Americans' authentic compassion for and generosity toward other Americans in personal crisis presents another startling paradox for the development of social welfare policy in America. On the one hand, Americans are willing and eager to help the disadvantaged, but on the other hand they want to help in a way that best suites their own interests. This mixed match of motivations contains more energy than simply a distrust of government. The willingness to help Hurricane Katrina victims, for example, or to extend generosity to persons in distressed nations, somehow falls short of equal

---

[c] "Tax expenditures are revenue losses—the amount of revenue the government forgoes—resulting from Federal tax provisions that grant special tax relief for certain kinds of behavior for taxpayers in special circumstances." United States Congress, Government Accountability Office, "Tax Expenditures Represent a Substantial Federal Commitment and Need to be Examined." Washington, DC: USGAO, September, 2005, 12.

enthusiasm to help America's long-term poor, who are likely to be blamed for their own poverty. The historic difference of opinion over the best way to help people in need persists as an undercurrent in most social welfare policy debates. In an important way, therefore, a welfare paradox develops; to help, but to help in a personally chosen manner reflects a legitimate difference over an expression of American liberalism: Where does individual responsibility end and social obligation begin? It is difficult to anticipate the development of more effective social welfare as long as advocates for individual responsibility and advocates for social obligation fail to define a common aegis under which social welfare policy can be developed.

Private charitable efforts to assist the poor never have been adequate to make a serious dent in economic dependency and related social problems. Based on reports from the IRS, the U.S. Census Bureau estimates that philanthropic giving in 2004 totaled $248.5 billion with about 75 percent of the total donated by individuals. However, over 35 percent of the total private giving was allocated to religion, and another 22 percent was allocated to health and educational purposes. Less than 8 percent of the total charitable funds, approximately $19.2 billion, were allocated for human service purposes (see Table 10.2).[6] The Center on Philanthropy at Indiana University estimated that less than one-third of the money individuals gave to nonprofits in 2005 was focused on the needs of the economically disadvantaged, and only 8 percent of individuals' donated dollars were provided to meet basic needs of food, shelter, or other necessities.[7] Thus, while the charitable spirit is strong in America, it needs a public effort

Table 10.2. Private Philanthropy, by Source and Allocation of Funds, 2004

In $ Billion		
Source	**Amount**	**Percent (%)**
Total	**248.5**	**100.00**
Individuals	187.9	75.61
Foundations	28.8	11.59
Corporations	12	4.83
Bequests	19.8	7.97
Allocation	**248.5**	**100.00**
Religion	88.3	35.53
Health	22	8.85
Education	33.8	13.60
Human Service	19.2	7.73
Art and Culture	14	5.62
Public Benefit	13	5.23
Environment	7.6	3.06
International	5.3	2.12
Foundations	24	9.65
Unallocated	21.4	8.61

Source: *Statistical Abstracts of the U.S.*, 2007, Table 567.

to legitimize it.[d] Charitable giving is a clear example of American generosity compromised by the expectations and motivations of the donors.

The above caveats contextualize the fundamental American theory of welfare reflected in the Social Security Act, as discussed above. Unquestionably, the American theory of social welfare contains serious limitations for developing more effective and efficient social welfare programs required by the demands of the twenty-first century. However, one does not just go out and create a new theory to fit new expectations. New expectations must be fit into America's theoretical welfare framework, and as new demands push the limitations of America's approach to meeting its social welfare obligations, America's welfare theory will be reformed as the program changes suggested below are implemented.

Reforming the Social Security Act

Remodeling the Social Security Act provides the best option for protecting and advancing America's social welfare commitments. The previous chapters point out the strengths and weaknesses in the programs generated by the Act's 21 titles and numerous programs those titles authorize. Apart from this critique, however, any effort to recommend large-scale changes in the Act is beyond a discussion of the individual titles presented in the previous chapters. Therefore, with an informed recognition of the limited usefulness of commissions, task forces, and study groups, such opportunities for collective thinking still remain the best means for providing the intelligence necessary for reshaping American social welfare commitments and reaching recommendations for revitalizing the Social Security Act. To the extent that the preceding discussion of the many parts of the Social Security Act and its programs has some usefulness, and in recognition of the above observations of the theoretical context for social welfare policy development in America, the following guidelines might shape a collective discussion about remaking the Social Security Act. Obviously, the guidelines offered below need careful consideration by the country as a whole before they could be converted into useful proposals.

Further Incremental Adjustments to the Social Insurances

Title II, Social Insurance

The wisdom of those who created the original Social Security Act, and the wisdom of their successors, should not be repudiated by the present-day concerns

---

[d] In recent years, private human service organizations have been able to use small amounts of private money as a match usually at the 10 percent level, in order to qualify for an allocation of public dollars, usually 90 percent, to support the provision of services from their private organizations. See Andrew Dobelstein, in *Encyclopedia of Social Work*, 20th ed. Mizrahi, T., & Davis, L.E., Eds. (New York: Oxford University Press, 2008).

raised about the social insurance programs. Title II Social Security has constitutional affirmation.[e] Its political legitimacy is protected by its contributive provisions. Its economic foundation is secured by its trust fund, and its social welfare value to millions of Americans has been well documented. Unfortunately, the incremental expansion of Title II Social Security by creating new beneficiary categories has fragmented the administration of its programs, even though Title II expansion has put in place a relatively stable, comprehensive social welfare foundation of benefit entitlements based on law.

With considerable caution for opening the program as it presently stands to political mischief, the present Title II beneficiaries and benefits would profit from an unlocked review. Even though Title II Social Security is, and must, by its present structure, remain a defined benefit program, where individual benefits are calculated on the relationship between contributors and respective retirement benefits, it is possible to collapse the expansive list of beneficiary categories into perhaps three or four, without losing the important relationship between contributions and benefits; benefits for retired workers and spouses, benefits for covered workers' families, and benefits for disabled workers might be three such categories. Such a consolidation would provide more transparency and political support for Title II Social Security. Railroad retirement, for example, needs to be fully rolled into Title II.

Benefits should also be adjusted to provide greater equity among the beneficiary groups, based on the contributory history of the primary wage earner, and the benefit base for all beneficiary categories should be increased to the point that no beneficiary would receive benefits that fall below an established relationship to the poverty guidelines. Since Title II benefits are subject to federal (and in some cases state) income taxes, benefit increases for persons with higher incomes could be adjusted through the tax system. Once the beneficiary base was increased, the annual Cost of Living Adjustments (COLAs) would be sufficient to keep benefits adequate. While insuring more adequate benefits would introduce a greater distributive element into Title II Social Security, such a policy trade-off seems consistent with its history and appropriate to the overall development of Title II as a foundational social insurance program.

The Social Security Trust Funds constitute the greatest economic and political assets to the future success of the Title II Social Security program. Most of the discussions about the adequacy of the trust fund(s) are spurious, although

---

[e] From time to time the constitutional authority for the social insurance programs has been debated, particularly after the U.S. Supreme Court's 1960 ruling in *Flemming v. Nestor* (U.S. 603). The *Nestor* case appears to be a narrow opinion regarding the deniability of Social Security benefits to a deportable alien "not a citizen of the United States and [living] outside the state." The 6 to 3 decision found that benefits based on earnings, not on taxes paid, do not constitute an accrued property right, even as the Court reserved to Congress the right to make changes in the Social Security Act. Justice Black in dissent argued that Social Security benefits are not government gratuities but constitute a contractual obligation, even though they may not constitute property rights.

the arguments are likely to continue. The fiscal arguments that have prevailed have resulted in a reasonable balance between the size of the trust fund(s) and future beneficiary needs. Regardless of the limitations, the trust fund(s) is more than an accounting artifact, and in the minds of the public, the trust fund(s) represent an earned government guaranteed benefit. The adequacy of the trust fund(s) is protected by the tax system and can be preserved by raising more revenue. In the short range, removing the income cap would protect present reserves, and in the longer term the Title II (FICA) tax rates could be made more progressive. At the very least, the public would benefit enormously from a better understanding about how Title II trust funds operate, and a better public understanding could silence the political rhetoric. The most serious problem exists for the Health Insurance Trust Fund that supports Title XVIII, as discussed below.

Table 10.1 shows that one of the largest tax expenditures excludes certain amounts of income used for the development of private pension instruments and selected other employee benefits. A prudent examination of the effectiveness of these tax expenditures might reveal that they contribute less to the development of such instruments than they are worth in loss of taxes. If elimination, or reduction, or redirection of this tax expenditure is appropriate, the additional revenues might be directed toward PBGC funding in order to provide better pension protection. Low wage workers, those with intermittent wage histories, and workers in uncovered employment continue to present issues that detract from Title II comprehensiveness. People forced to work for their welfare (Title IV) benefits, or people who have exhausted their eligibility for Title IV benefits, are likely to fall into uncovered, or marginally covered, categories. Whether Title II can respond to the needs of these people is worth further exploration.

Title III, Unemployment Insurance

Two issues might be considered when discussing how Unemployment Insurance should be revised to make it more effective. First, the unemployment insurance scheme that created the Title III fiscal foundation may have been constitutionally appealing to its creators, but in practice it has failed to reduce unemployment in high risk employment sectors; it has contributed to uneven treatment of both employees and employers; it fails to protect adequately the worker against income losses due to unemployment; and as it turns out, the costs of Unemployment Insurance are borne almost exclusively by the Federal Government. Labor market changes have produced patterns of unemployment today that make the present form of Unemployment Insurance quite inadequate. A worker–employer contributory program with a federal trust fund administered by the Federal Government, perhaps by a special unit in the Social Security Administration, to replace the present individual state accounts would allow more uniform treatment of all employees. The present system was designed to discourage worker mobility, but in today's labor market, worker mobility becomes essential, and a national unemployment insurance system would promote worker mobility through benefit portability.

Second, job training, counseling, and placement, which are currently responsibilities of states, could remain so and continue under the direction of the Department of Labor. Perhaps special efforts could be provided to chronic and long term unemployed who have been underserved by labor development efforts because for the most part these persons are not considered to be part of the labor force. Title III offers the opportunity for social welfare policy to respond positively to the rapidly changing employment issues discussed above, somewhat in contrast to the punitive approaches reflected in Title IV TANF. For the most part, previous job training activities have not enhanced employment potential for unemployed workers. Most of the effective job training and worker skill development takes place on-site, financed by the employer. A national worker retraining program has been discussed from time to time as part of manpower development legislation, but such an initiative has never been fully and consistently implemented. If the Labor Department were free from Title III benefit administration, it might have the opportunity to look more seriously at American workforce needs as the "global economy" continues to place new expectations on America's labor force. That such an important social insurance commitment of the Social Security Act, Title III, which should become so ineffective and out of touch with the other social insurance efforts, particularly in today's dynamic labor market, attests to the need seriously to consider efforts to improve it for the integrity of the entire Act.

Adjustments to the Assistance Programs

Title XVI: Supplemental Security Income

As suggested in Chapter 5, SSI has not worked out as many of its supporters had anticipated. Discretionary decisions characterize assistance programs, and SSI does not constitute an exception. While a federal income standard for eligibility determination and benefit payment has been established, some states were required to supplement benefits at the beginning of the program, and all states were free to supplement benefit payments, which they do in widely different ways. Thus, from a practical perspective, there is little difference between the SSI program and the grant-in-aid assistance programs it replaced. Considerable discretion characterizes state-level provision of very necessary SSI supplements, and although there is a core of uniformity in federal rules governing SSI benefits, the state variation in administering these rules quickly erodes most of the program benefit uniformity SSI proposed to establish.

SSI has also created a policy problem because of its overlap with Title II Social Security. Even though Title II benefits were counted as assets in determining eligibility for Titles I, X, and XIV, which preceded the creation of SSI, putting the two programs together draws particular attention to counting Social Security benefits as unearned income. Social Security benefits have been earned, and at the very least, they should be treated as such rather than valued, as they are in reality, at $20.00. The loss of Title II benefits is an insult to low-income workers.

While it would be an enormous and difficult task, the Social Security Act would benefit from completely restructuring SSI. One approach would provide present SSI recipients with Title II benefits equal to at least the present SSI guarantee or a higher level if the basic Title II benefits were adjusted to higher levels, as suggested above. Aged or disabled persons who needed additional benefits would become the responsibility of the states, similar to the practice of state supplementation that exists at the present time. A capped block grant could then be provided to states to defray some of the costs of present state levels of supplementation, with the understanding that Title II Social Security could not be counted as assets for determining eligibility for state supplementation.

This solution to the problems generated by SSI would strengthen the value of Title II Social Security, honestly recognize the need to supplement SSI beneficiaries, and provide funding to states to help them meet the social welfare obligations to the aged and disabled economically needy. The changes would recast benefits to low-income aged and disabled as an assistance program, which it is, rather than an income guarantee, which it is not.

Title IV: Temporary Assistance to Needy Families (TANF) and Related Title IV programs

The Title IV programs have become inexorably entangled in the issues that plague social welfare development under the Social Security Act. An insistence on "work first," the name often given to the 1996 welfare reform, those federal structural limitations that make the states the best source of providing financial assistance to children, and ingrained negative attitudes toward children and their parents who need financial assistance, all have contributed to the chaotic development of Title IV as it exists today. But Title IV is the foundation for America's child welfare policy, just as Title II has been the social welfare foundation for the elderly. Title IV clearly needs repair.

Repairing Title IV must recognize and refocus Title IV social welfare on its fundamental purpose: the economic well-being of financially dependent children. In spite of the persistent, weakly supported views that strong families make strong children and that children's economic welfare is best promoted by their parents' employment, Title IV operates best as a means to help states support poor children. From earliest colonial days, poor children have been stigmatized, and aid to their mothers for their support has been inadequate. Historically, the poor children were forced into apprenticeships or rounded up and sent to live with others. Today, they must find shelter with friends and extended family. Over the years, the social reforms that humanized the treatment of children, unfortunately, did little to dispel America's deep-seated antipathy toward poor children, simply replacing an insensitivity to their needs by blaming their parents.[f]

In America, there is little doubt that the civic right to rear children is a private matter, but this right does not necessarily trump the social obligation to protect children, and while economic need never should be a reason for taking children from their families, the social obligation to children makes paramount the provision of adequate income to them. The summarized discussion of TANF in Chapter 6 should be sufficient to confirm that the reduction in TANF caseloads has not been accompanied by an improvement in the welfare of children. Nor have efforts to stabilize families arrested any decline in the number or percentage of poor children. The repair of Title IV might begin most productively with a revision of TANF. A TANF revision would ensure that every family with children, regardless of its family structure, had an income base compatible with or equal to the poverty level. The income base could include all sources of income, from child support to earnings, and the TANF block grant to states should satisfy this purpose first before transferring funds to various services.

Such a revision in TANF would require a change in welfare philosophy toward poor children and their families. Instead of welfare policy designed to effect changes in the family, a different philosophy would accept family limitations, and make sure that all families had adequate financial resources in order to provide for their children. If changes in family behavior also resulted from providing more adequate income, then the benefits would be enhanced. A similar change in attitude toward work would also be necessary. The real value from work accrues to the individual not through the value of earnings, important though earnings are, but in the value of work itself. Good work, at any income level, is satisfying work. Low-income mothers who raise children should not be denied the opportunity for satisfying employment, nor should they be forced to sacrifice the option of full time responsibility for child rearing if they choose this form of rewarding work. Of course, this outlook is extremely idealistic, but it represents a different philosophy of welfare that should at least be discussed and taken into serious consideration in any discussions to change Title IV policy.

Returning the economic welfare of children to the center of Title IV policies and programs will require reorientation of other existing Title IV programs. The policy and programs that have been developed under Title IV-E, for example, will need to focus less on stabilizing families in order to reduce foster care, and instead focus on what plans best satisfy the economic and emotional needs of the child. In other words, without diminishing the value of a family for the benefit of a child, the alternative forms of family that exist in America

---

[f] While some might argue for some sort of social insurance for children, it is important to recall that Title II Social Security does function as a social insurance to children, although limited to children whose parents have a Social Security benefit. An expansion of provision of benefits under Title II might be given further study.

today provide ample alternatives to the traditional nineteenth-century idealized family form for rearing children. Poor children can and ought to have "soccer moms" even if they are not their biological moms. Greater economic stability is much more likely to bring poor children into the mainstream of twenty-first-century America than the family type in which they are raised. These changed Title IV objectives would greatly strengthen related programs for children under other titles of the Social Security Act.

Adjustments to the Health Programs

America's approach to health care requires a fresh face before the Social Security's health titles can be properly evaluated and modified. To give it such a makeover, it is important to separate the idea of health care from the idea of access to health care. These are two separate issues that have become completely mixed in the public's mind. It has also become clear that the historic private practitioner-centered model of health care is no longer going to be most people's principal form of providing health care. Specialization, driven by new medical technologies, has forced the development of new medical care set-ups like group practice and multi-functional clinic forms of medical services. Even in situations where there is an individual practitioner, access to necessary diagnostic equipment requires specialized technicians. Outpatient hospital-based treatments have expanded and substitute for an increasing number of in-hospital and practitioner in-office treatments.

Even limited access to this expanded health care system is complicated by insurance programs that may grant access to one part of the service by reimbursing for that service, but not provide access to the whole service because they then deny reimbursement to related services. Moreover, insurance financed health care usually only pays a portion of the specific health care costs, depending on the terms of the insurance policy. The service recipient pays copayments and deductibles that may require large up-front costs before insurance begins to pay health care costs. In most cases, health insurance reimburses health providers for the diagnosis and treatment of health problems, rather than placing an emphasis on individual practices that may help persons stay healthy.

In order to understand the proposals for reshaping Titles XVIII, XIX, and XXI, a new model of health care, summarized below, proposes a parallel addition to the existing model of care and access. This new model proposes a nation-wide system of health care centers administered by or administered under contract with the Federal Government. These centers would provide basic services, specifically those presently provided under Medicare and Medicaid, and would be funded by existing federal health spending and optional buy-ins by persons not presently covered under the health titles of the Social Security Act. Such a new model of health care would allow changes to the Social Security Act proposed in the following discussion.

Title XVIII: Medicare

The development of health policy within an insurance context accounts in large measure for the surreal expansion of the cost of health care. Over 65 percent of private medical spending is channeled through health insurance plans, and over 68 percent of public medical spending takes place under the Social Security Act, also allocated mostly through an insurance framework (Table IV.1). The Title XVIII Medical Insurance Trust Fund continues to be the most vulnerable of all of the Social Security trust funds. In addition, Table 10.1 shows that the largest tax expenditure for individuals is the exclusion from income for employer provided health insurance benefits. Adjusting the costs of health services with the way they are funded constitutes a priority for any effort to reform health care, particularly the tax expenditures for employer provided health benefits that support Medicare Part A.

The most serious fiscal problem concerns Medicare, Part A. Part A funding is not able to keep up with the expansion of additional covered services, and the Medicare Insurance tax has risen to 1.45 percent of payroll placing a greater burden on the payroll tax. The solvency of the Medical Insurance Trust Fund remains a critical public policy issue. Financing Medicare Part B is less troublesome since its costs are partly covered by premiums paid by Medicare beneficiaries, and recently the premium cost per Medicare beneficiary rises proportionally with taxable income. The monthly premium for Part B benefits, however, constitutes a heavy financial burden for many Medicare recipients.

One way to begin to address the frightening costs of public spending for medical care would be to modify both Medicare Parts A and B. Attempts to justify the social insurance features of the payroll tax to support Medicare Part A have always been controversial inasmuch as this element of the Social Security Act does not contribute to a future benefit for the tax payer in the same way that the tax for Title II Social Security retirement and disability does. Thus, it would be prudent to supplement the Medical Insurance tax with general revenues, as is done with Medicare Part B, in order to preserve the solvency of the Part A Medical Insurance Trust Fund.

Since Medicare Part B was part of the compromise that was struck to create Title XVIII, it would not be unreasonable to reform Part B into the nation-wide system health care centers discussed above. These centers would be available primarily to Medicare Part B participants, and would expand the health maintenance organization alternative presently available under one of the Medicare options, except they would be operated under the authority of the Federal Government, either directly, or under contract. These centers would provide those presently allowable Part B services and would be the only source of medical care authorized for Medicare Part B recipients. In other words, there would be no reimbursement for medical services provided to Part B recipients from private sources under various health insurance instruments. Since Medicare is the primary service provider for Part B beneficiaries, along with supplemental medical insurance many Part B beneficiaries also carry, they could choose to keep their secondary forms of coverage for services not provided by the health centers in order to receive those services from private practitioner sources.

The proposed nationwide health centers would be funded with the present Part B premiums, and could also be opened to anyone else who would be willing to pay the equivalent of the Medicare Part B premium. The difference between the cost of services provided by the nationwide health centers and the Part B private income would come from eliminating the $160 billion health tax expenditure. The proposed nationwide system of health centers could be developed in established public health programs that exist in almost every county in the United States or they could be colocated with existing federal or state public health service centers. While the proposed nationwide health centers concept departs radically from insurance-driven access to health care, this advanced form of providing health and medical services would not preclude individuals from purchasing health insurance that could provide access to services not offered at the nationwide health centers, or for services offered through private providers.

Obviously, efforts to create such a modified health care system would face exceptionally stiff political opposition from private insurance providers. This does not mean that they should not be explored.

Title XIX and Title XXI: Medicaid and the State Child Health Insurance Program

The Medicaid program provides federal funds to states to assist their efforts to supply needed medical and health services to medically (economically) needy persons. States must offer federally required services or provide access to these services either through insurance instruments or through other instruments that offer medical and health services states might choose. As pointed out in Chapter 8, in addition to the required services, states already make available a wider array of services that they deem necessary under Medicaid authority, and states offer these services through a number of health-related instruments.

The proposed nationwide federal health centers would provide an effective and efficient way for states to meet their Medicaid commitments. If states choose to use these proposed centers as the source for delivering Medicaid services, state Medicaid dollars would provide yet another source of funding for this advanced form of medical service delivery. The State Child Health Insurance Program, Title XXI, as an extension of Medicaid, would, indeed, be able to guarantee minimum health care for all children from the nation-wide federal health centers.

Summary: Improving the Social Security Act's Health Care Commitments

The Social Security Act presently contains all the necessary Federal Government's authority for providing publicly financed health care for Americans.

Considering that health expenditures constitute about 25 percent of all Federal Government spending, unscrambling this public commitment to health care is crucial to the future status of the Social Security Act. While it may seem prudent to establish a separate social welfare instrument independent of the Social Security Act to address the many concerns involved in providing health care for Americans, there are several major problems associated with such an alternative. First, and most important, health care, and the provisions that exist under the Social Security Act to provide it, touch every aspect of social welfare policy and programs under the Act. Even though the Act contains three separate titles that authorize health care spending, these separate titles are linked with others; Medicare is linked with Title II Social Security; Medicaid is linked with Title XVI and Title IV assistance, and the State Child Health Insurance Program is closely linked with Titles IV and XIX. Separate the public commitment to health care from the Social Security Act and both health care and the other social welfare initiatives under the Act will suffer. Since the Social Security Act already possesses all the authority necessary to develop a different means to assure health care for all Americans, a considerable amount of health care would come under the direct supervision of the Federal Government. In conclusion, without a new model, the national clamor for better health care will not likely be met by simply modifying the present system of insurances as the method to access, fund, and supervise health services.

The Social Services: Title XX and the Social Services Block Grant (SSBG)

The social services provided under the Social Security Act present a special social welfare conundrum. First, social services are provided both under the extensive Title IV programs and under the authority of the Social Services Block Grant. While the present SSBG authority allows an interchange of funds to promote a flexible use of these monies, there is limited intelligence to inform program administrators what these funds are buying and allow an evaluation of the best use of SSBG funds. Second, an inability to define social services, and to specify necessary social services, has led to an array of eclectic activities that may or may not serve important social obligations. Finally, the elusive content of the social services themselves defies efforts to control their quality. Interventions in individual lives, even on superficial levels, is an activity that requires a level of competence that social services as presently funded has not been able to guarantee.

Given these problems, the social service commitments authorized under the Social Security Act might be improved by separating those services essential to the economic welfare of children under Title IV from other Title IV services that are not essential to the economic welfare of children and those services offered under the authority of Title XX. This process would require defining Title IV services in specific terms and then ensuring that those services are provided by qualified persons. This is a task that federal Title IV agencies like the Administration for Children and Families must do in order to lend legitimacy to the provision of these services. While such efforts in the past have been met by objections from state agencies that fear the development of federal standards that cannot be met, it is still possible to set the standards and deal with issues of noncompliance as they arise. Those social services that do not meet the basic purpose of Title IV policy, and those social services that cannot be defined could continue to receive funding under Title XX and the SSBG, appropriately capped to prevent their expansion.

Concluding Thoughts

In many ways, the Social Security Act is dated, and its effectiveness has been sapped by the incremental changes made to it over the past seventy years. However, to abandon the Social Security Act in the face of the large-scale changes in American political, social, and economic life would be a foolhardy, catastrophic retreat into the past. Policy makers also cannot continue to tinker with the Social Security Act, adding new parts and changing existing parts as new social concerns surface and as old concerns seem less significant, represents a haphazard effort to deal with America's social and economic challenges and burdens the foundations of the basic social welfare commitments made explicit under the Social Security Act. This form of incrementalism lacks consistent policy themes; it suggests an instability in American social welfare commitments, namely that efforts created today are likely to change tomorrow depending politically expedient goals, as experienced in the 1996 welfare reform.

The Social Security Act never created a policy framework capable of addressing fully the many social problems of the late 1930s. A revolutionary document for its day, the Social Security Act by today's standards set out narrow limits for its social welfare objectives—establishing a foundation of economic security for aged retirees and providing a permanent commitment to help states pay their welfare costs. Over the years, presidents proposed and Congresses supported efforts to expand the scope of these limited social welfare commitments. The expanded insurance programs, particularly the Title II programs, satisfied the ideals of their original developers, within the boundaries of defined benefit insurance programs. The expanded assistance programs developed within the context of the dynamic interplay of American Federalism and its resulting intergovernmental relationships. The health programs found their authority in a compromise with the established social insurance principles and the federal–state relationships of the mid-1960s. In its development, therefore, the Social Security Act has remained relatively confined within its original limited policy boundaries and true to an historic American theory of social welfare.

Critics of America's social welfare commitments may lament the limited ability of the present Social Security Act to address contemporary social welfare problems, but further expanding the social welfare commitments, piece by piece, under the Social Security Act may continue to unravel the effectiveness of this fundamental document, and permit further erosion of public support for social welfare. Instead, a more reasoned approach to meeting today's social welfare challenges may rest in efforts to make the Social Security Act more effective in the objectives already assumed under its authority, and to preserve its capacity to link new social welfare relevant instruments into a coherent social welfare agenda.

There is little evidence to suggest that increased social welfare spending alone will either prevent or resolve existing social problems. For the most part, addressing larger social problems will require structural changes in America's political and economic institutions. A cogent case can be made that political and economic structural changes would do more to alleviate economic dependency than income maintenance efforts, and there is sufficient empirical evidence to support such contentions. *Brown v. Board of Education*, Civil Rights and Fair Housing acts, Title VII of the Higher Education Act, numerous administrative rulings and court cases establishing fair employment practices, as examples, all have contributed significantly to the economic improvement of women, minorities, and economically disadvantaged populations. While there is an important social welfare spillover from these important changes in American life, the Social Security Act does not have the authority to address such necessary social changes, and attempts to use the Social Security Act to effect structural changes indirectly have been unproductive and have contributed to weakening the Act's authority.

Reasonable goals for uplifting the Social Security Act by strengthening its basic programs, however, offer the opportunity to move America's social welfare commitments to new levels. Just as it can become the framework for a more comprehensive, equitable, and inclusive health care system, the Social Security Act can become the document that ensures that no American will live in poverty conditions. Such an approach to social welfare development is neither a minimalist approach to social welfare reform nor an apology for the Social Security Act. Those on the left believe the Social Security Act is an inadequate social welfare document; those on the right believe that welfare concerns are individual concerns, and that the Social Security Act undermines basic American values; many of those in the middle want to pick a fight with government in general, and social welfare is a convenient subject. The Social Security Act stands above these quarrels as a monumental policy benchmark for meeting America's social welfare obligations.

When President George W. Bush proposed to substitute a form of private pensions for basic Title II social insurance, he provided a good example of the dangers inherent in confronting the challenges that face the Social Security Act. Sounding the frequent alarm that the Social Security program is running out of money, President Bush argued that present and further expansions of Title II would exhaust its funding, and that the increase of private, government-backed, alternatives for creating retirement income provided better retirement benefits than Title II Social Security. The partial truths in the Bush proposal, stripped of its political hyperbole, raised a serious but an uninformed public debate about the capacity of Title II Social Security to meet its present obligations or to take on new ones. In a similar manner, the weight of continued social welfare commitments added to the basic Title IV program has led to the misinformed debate over the purpose for this assistance program and shifted a public obligation to provide necessary assistance to financially dependent children, first from government to the family, and then from family to the individual, thus forming the basis for the 1996 welfare reform that emphasized work over welfare and sharply curtailed federal welfare benefits for children.

These and other examples discussed in the preceding chapters expose the dearth of public understanding about the nation's social welfare obligations and how the Social Security Act provides a framework for satisfying these obligations. The deficiency of public understanding begins with a general public disinterest, spreads to inadequate educational preparation, and ends up with those in policy-making positions who, either out of ignorance or out of ideologically driven motivation, pass misinformation back to the public, perpetuating a myth that social welfare policy and the programs of the Social Security Act are too difficult to understand and too uncontrollable to reform. An open, honest, reasoned debate by all parties stands above any other recommendation for uplifting and restructuring the Social Security Act. Not until all the voices are heard and all the information is openly shared will the Social Security Act be redesigned as the foundational document that will meet America's social welfare obligations of the twenty-first century.

NOTES

1. U.S. Department of Agriculture, Food and Nutrition Service, *Fact Sheet* (Washington, DC, 2008).
2. U.S. Department of the Treasury, Internal Revenue Service, *Earned Income Tax Credit Tax Fact Sheet,* 2008.
3. Steve Holt, *The Earned Income Tax Credit at Age 30. What We Know* (Washington, DC: The Brookings Institution, February 2006), 13.
4. www.cbo.gov/doc7221, 2.
5. U.S. Congress, Government Accountability Office, "Tax Expenditures Represent a Substantial Federal Commitment and Need to be Examined." Washington, DC: U.S.GAO, September 2005, 1.
6. U.S. Bureau of the Census, *Statistical Abstracts of the United States, 2007*, Table 567.
7. The Giving Institute Center on Philanthropy, *Giving USA* (Bloomington, IN: Indiana University, 2007), 8.

Index